King Alfred School and the Progressive Movement, 1898–1998

King Alfred School
and the Progressive Movement,
1898–1998

Ron Brooks

UNIVERSITY OF WALES PRESS 1998
CARDIFF

British Library Cataloguing-in-Publication Data.
A catalogue record for this book is available from the British Library.

ISBN 0–7083–1453–8

Book design by Neil James Angove
Typeset at University of Wales Press
Printed in Great Britain by Bookcraft, Midsomer Norton, Avon

To Jean
in celebration of a forty-year partnership

Contents

Foreword

School histories are usually written for past pupils and centenary histories to record their glorious deeds. This book is neither a simple trip down memory lane nor a canter along a golden highway. I am grateful to the council of King Alfred School, and in particular to its archives committee, for encouraging me from the outset to place the school in its broader historical and educational context, and to point to the school's shortcomings as well as to its successes. Unrestricted access to the full range of documentary and other materials, carefully preserved by the school archivist, Brian Rance, and the unstinting assistance of Areta Hautman, particularly in distributing questionnaires to every generation of KAS pupil and council, and in arranging interviews, have been of immense help in writing more than a chalk-face history. To the many ex-Alfredians who completed the questionnaires and allowed me to interview them, I owe a great debt. While I cannot name individually everyone who helped me because of their number, I should like to thank parents, staff, the present headteacher, Francis Moran, and chair of council, Kara Conti, and two past headteachers, Nikki Archer and Alan Humphries, for their advice and encouragement.

For particular assistance with the reproduction of photographs and for the provision of many of the originals I would like to thank Dan Robinson.

Ron Brooks
Bangor,
April 1998

Acknowledgements

The author and publishers wish to thank the following for kind permission to reproduce the following photographs in this volume:

British Architectural Library, RIBA, London (no. 2)

Tessa and Jenepher Horton (nos. 78, 79, 80, 83, 84, 85, 86)

The Hulton Getty Picture Collection for two photographs from *Picture Post* (nos. 96 and 103) and one by the Keystone Press Agency (no. 110)

Diana Shelley for the photograph by Gene Shelley (no. 109)

BBC Picture Archives (no. 113)

Cecil Lush (nos. 126, 129, 135, 136)

Adam Kossoff (nos. 125 and 132)

Sacha Lehrfreund (nos. 154, 159, 169)

van Heyningen and Haward (no. 161)

The King Alfred School Society for most of the other photographs.

Every effort has been made to trace the copyright holders of photographs in this volume. In the case of any queries, please contact the publishers.

Introduction

'People used to ask me if all the teachers were stoned and did we all sit up trees barefoot in lessons,' recalled one former student when asked what other people in North London thought of King Alfred School. 'The zoo on the hill,' replied another. Such comments indicate that in the history of King Alfred School as in that of other progressive schools myth is often more potent than fact, and would suggest that whether its 'free love and communism' or a libertarians' charter, in the public mind all of the independent progressive schools share similar characteristics. The purpose of this book is to show how distinctive King Alfred School was and is, even within the ranks of such schools and to demonstrate its unique position within the broader history of education which stems from its origins.

It was by intent rather than coincidence that King Alfred School was born amid the growing political and educational controversies of late Victorian Britain. This basic fact distinguished it from its progressive predecessors, Abbotsholme and Bedales, and gave it a relevance to contemporary educational debate then and since which neither can match. In the view of the founders of King Alfred School, single-sex and boarding education, no matter how liberal in spirit, could scarcely serve as a paradigm for the new, day secondary schools which were emerging in Wales and were soon to appear in England under Balfour's Education Act of 1902. The North London Fabians intended to set up an independent coeducational day school in the capital, where much of the debate was being conducted by one of the Fabian Society's leaders, Sidney Webb. Fee-charging, and thus freed from dependence upon the state, it could offer itself as a 'demonstration school', unlike the earlier generation of independent, progressive schools with their boarding 'cuckooism'. However, the fact that the founders failed to persuade parents in other parts of London and elsewhere to set up similar schools is an indication of the limitations of its impact.

King Alfred School thus remained the only one run by the society set up to found such schools. Nevertheless it never forsook its missionary role both educationally and constitutionally. In the case of the former it aimed to show the value of coeducation, and the compatibility of success in public examinations with a form of organization which gave pupils a great deal of responsibility for their curricular decisions and which put great value on informal, non-authoritarian, staff–student relationships. In the case of the latter the fact that throughout its history control has resided ultimately in the hands of parents and not with headmaster-legislators makes its constitutional arrangements of great interest to educators today.

Chapter 1

Shedding Shackles:
The Rationalist Experiment,
1898–1901

King Alfred School (KAS) in Hampstead, north London, was founded in 1898, in an age of educational experiment and innovation. Whereas many educational ventures of the time set up by small groups of idealists soon foundered or lost their crusading zeal within a few years, King Alfred School has developed over the last century with its original ideals largely unchanged and its enthusiasm for its distinctive form of education undiminished. That it not only survived but prospered was not simply a matter of good fortune. Without the determination and perspicacity of its founders and the dedication of several generations of its staff, the path was more likely to lead downhill and to oblivion, rather than uphill and to the broad educational community which exists today. The success of the Hampstead venture was by no means certain. A similar experiment at Letchworth Garden City devised by J. J. Findlay, who gave KAS its model curriculum, and by John Russell, the school's second headmaster, quickly ran into the sand.

The historian who wishes to explain the longevity of the King Alfred School ideal is doubly fortunate; first of all, in having to hand a comparable and contemporaneous experiment, which though sharing some things in common with the Hampstead venture had such a spectacularly different outcome; second, in having access to the carefully preserved records of four generations of Alfredians,[1] and especially those which cover the critical early years of the school's existence.

King Alfred School is usually listed among the independent progressive schools but such a classification, as with most general classifications, tends to disguise significant differences between the various members of the genus. Certainly, the small group of Hampstead radicals who founded the school would have preferred the more specific epithet 'rational' to the more bland adjective 'progressive'. The historian would not disagree. While King Alfred School shared some concerns with its two 'progressive' predecessors, Abbotsholme, founded by Dr Cecil Reddie in 1889 and Bedales, founded by J. H. Badley in 1893, especially the desire to foster individual abilities and talents, in its origins, organization and in several aspects of its educational philosophy and enterprise there were many important differences. In its approach to the problems of the late nineteenth century, it had more in common with one of the other principal movements of the age, the garden city movement, than with the other progressive schools. It was not a mere coincidence that the first garden suburb was created in Hampstead, six years after the founding of King Alfred School, or that the King Alfred curriculum was thought suitable for implementation by the municipal authorities at Letchworth, the first of the garden cities. Both emphasized the need to combat the worst excesses of Victorian industrialism, whether they were in narrowly utilitarian education or in the broader sphere of social deprivation, by scientific study, appraisal and planning. The move towards the new order in education as in urban society was to be achieved through the strict application of scientific principle, no matter what traditions were thrown into question in the process. There were to be no 'no-go' areas in education; the British veneration for religion, a value-for-money utilitarianism, examinations or indeed the hallmark of independent schooling, single-sex boarding facilities: none was to remain immune from critical scrutiny. The basic curricular building blocks were to be the latest scientific discoveries about child development, just as in the case of the garden city movement, the corner stone was to be the careful application of scientific principle in population and urban planning. Whilst Badley at Bedales could boast, 'I had no definite plan. My ideas grew as the school grew,'[2] King Alfred's founders had a definite but not immutable scheme and a vigorous, rational approach to curriculum planning.

Many histories of independent schools fit easily into the 'great headmasters' genre; King Alfred School does not, for in its first few years the main moving force behind the school was not its headmaster but a group of distinguished Hampstead residents who had set up the King Alfred School Society (KASS) in 1897. Their intention made their educational venture singularly different from many which had gone before. The society's object, recorded by its assiduous chairman, F. W. Miall, was 'the furtherance, *in every possible way, of true educational methods*' (my italics) as understood by the members.[3] Even before the society was officially founded it was the intention of its original advocates that the society should be more than a single school, that more than one school should be founded and that the creation of schools was not to be seen as the only way of propagating their educational philosophy. The educational problems of the age could not be overcome through the founding of a single institution on the lines of Abbotsholme or Bedales, no matter how excellent it might be. The 'preliminary circular' of July 1897 which first floated the idea of a society indicated that the thoughts of the founders were on a very different plane from those of the creators of the earlier progressive schools. Theirs was not to be a token protest against contemporary education practice through the setting up of a single school which, by boarding its pupils, would be both physically and ideologically isolated from the rest of society. The society intended to set up coeducational day schools in urban areas, in regular contact with the local community through an open-door policy, and with the broader educational community through the dissemination of the reformist ideas and through a programme of public lectures.

The small group who responded to the 'preliminary circular' in October 1897 were radicals in the strict sense of the term; that is, they wanted the root-and-branch reform of much current educational practice in the state and independent sectors of education. Its composition is perhaps indicative of their radical approach to the politics and practice of educational reform. The moving spirits and inspiration behind the circular were two women, Isobel White Wallis and Alice Mullins. In a way they represented the twin pillars of the society, scientific method and the free cultivation of individuality. Isobel White Wallis shared the interests of her husband, E. White Wallis, a well-known scientist and Alice Mullins was involved in the work of the sculptor, Roscoe Mullins. Mrs White Wallis ably undertook a whole range of duties from that of diligent scribe or secretary, to the organizing of meetings, but her main achievement was to ensure from the outset that the King Alfred School Society was more an educational movement than an educational body. She was one of its chief propagandists in the press, encouraging the discussion of a wide range of views and questioning many contemporary values and practices. In this she was assisted by Alice Mullins, in whose studio the meeting which drafted the initial circular of July 1897 was held. Even from these preliminary observations it can be seen that King Alfred School differed from earlier progressive schools in that it owed its origins to a society which thought in much larger terms than that of simply creating schools and much of the initial inspiration came from women and not just men. Interestingly, the society's Hampstead school was officially opened in 1898 by Millicent Garrett Fawcett, leader of the suffrage movement, and many of its pupils came from Hampstead Garden Suburb, the brainchild of Henrietta Barnett, wife of Canon Barnett of Toynbee Hall.

The ideology of 'the founders'

The July meeting called by Mrs White Wallis with the hospitality provided by Mrs Roscoe Mullins was attended by five other Hampstead residents. They included F. W. Miall who, beside acting as a very efficient chairman, had, as a journalist, an extensive range of press contacts in and around London, which served well the propagandist aims of the society. Miall's brother, Professor L. C. Miall, Professor of Biology at Leeds University, was also drawn into the movement in 1898 and, with an intense interest in educational reform, served as the society's first president from 1899 to 1908. Two other people well able to put their professional expertise and other skills at the immediate disposal of the July meeting were Gerald C. Maberly, barrister at law, whose meticulous eye for detail led him beyond his legal sphere to that of honorary treasurer, and Godfrey Hickson, who acted as the society's first honorary solicitor. The ideological needs of the new reform group were served by Cecil Sharp, Principal of the Hampstead Conservatoire of Music, and Sir Hamo Thornycroft, sculptor, who created the statue of King Alfred at Winchester. Their common concern that education should be directed towards the development of individuality was later articulated at length by Charles F. Voysey, in his book *Individuality*.[4] His children were among the first generation of KAS pupils.

While at this early stage the group, whom one is almost inclined to call 'the magnificent seven', had no definite curricular model in mind, they had a fairly clear idea of the direction in which educational reform should proceed. Their thinking was greatly affected by what they

1. The Voyseys: early school patrons and advisers (from Stuart Durant, *C. F. A. Voysey* (Architectural Monographs, 19), 128)

perceived to be two grave threats to the spiritual health of late Victorian England, the first of which was rampant materialism. Charles Voysey, who at this time was entering his most productive years as an architect, expressed this concern when he wrote, 'Spiritual culture can not be tested by competitive examination like mathematical knowledge, and so, in a materialistic world, little counts that is not marketable.'[5] This led to the narrowing of educational goals so that education for the privileged few was seen largely in terms of access to increased wealth and power, and for the masses in the form of a brief, utilitarian education in the three Rs to promote national economic efficiency without overeducating the nation's children so that they questioned the values on which elementary education was based. Socialists, such as the Rugby-educated R. H. Tawney, would have agreed with Voysey's fundamental point that, when education is regarded as a means to the accumulation of wealth and power, when we say things should be learned because they are useful, we are forgetting that the cultivation of character is far more important than any worldly success. Where Tawney would have disagreed with the founders was in their view that encroaching collectivism constituted the second serious flaw in Victorian society. Whereas Tawney, on the radical left, looked to the state to redistribute wealth to enable all to have the basic necessities, only after which a liberal education for all was truly possible, Voysey on the radical right argued that 'when it becomes necessary to fix a standard when large numbers have to be marshalled for any purpose, it must result in the neglect of individual qualities'.[6] What happens, he and the founding group argued, was that rules and regulations predominate and education is reduced to 'the teaching of modes and manners' with the emphasis upon strict discipline and utilitarian goals. They thus favoured the creation of small, independent schools under the control of a body which would be ever watchful of any drift away from individualism and toward formalism.

However, it would be wrong to assume, because those who attended the July meeting were interested in what they termed 'rational' education, that they were a small circle of armchair theorists, or what their critics termed 'a clique of enthusiastic faddists' devising Utopian solutions to philosophical problems. Idealists they were, which in education is no bad thing, but what provoked their discussion of fundamental principles was their disquiet at particular developments and practices within state and independent education in the closing years of the nineteenth century. Theirs was a response to pressing issues of the 1890s. The fact that these issues were generic issues, inherent and recurrent in the British education system, and their answers to them generic answers, as appropriate in the late twentieth century as they were in the late nineteenth century, should not blind us to the peculiar historical circumstances which gave rise to their concern. The minutes of the meetings of the council of the society and the matters raised in the press by the founding members show that they believed that there was a deep malaise in contemporary education in its

2. Voysey's KASS logo and his explanation (RIBA Library (449))

various forms. In a press interview in February 1898 Mrs White Wallis drew attention to the current situation where 'by means of examinations and other aids, children are ground in a mill where individuality is repressed and where humanity is minted into pieces as like each other as the coinage'.[7] The group were particularly concerned about 'the great juggernaut of modern education, the examination craze' with the over-pressure on children caused by the 'medieval method of cramming with juiceless facts, names and dates'.

They were not tilting at imaginary windmills. Across the country, elementary education had been dominated since 1862 by the system of payment by results (the Revised Code) whereby a teacher's salary was geared in part to examination results in the three Rs, and teaching had been reduced to mass, mechanical instruction, with large classes. Though this system was substantially modified nation-wide in 1890, and the system of annual examinations reduced in severity, in London the opposite was the case. Sidney Webb, with a concern for national efficiency of which the authors of the Revised Code would have been proud, instituted his 'capacity catching system' in London whereby children were pushed through the selective examination sieve so that the meritorious few could be separated from the unworthy many.

The July group questioned the whole ideology which underlay late Victorian education. They stood against the intensely competitive spirit found in state and independent schools and declined to set up any system of prizes and scholarships in the schools run by the society. What they questioned was any practice which hindered the development of natural relationships between teacher and pupil and teacher and parent, and the pupil's all-round development including the training of the senses and powers of observation. Examinations discouraged healthy relationships resulting in overpressure on pupils, an overemphasis on books and rote learning and over-reliance on cramming and homework. In the case of public schools, and the newly established progressive schools, this artificial and unnatural world was propped up still further by the boarding of pupils often in single-sex institutions. This practice was denounced as 'cuckooism' by a leading member of the society[8] for it destroyed the development of natural and harmonious relationships between pupil and parent and parent and school. Religion which was often taught in state and public schools to instill awe, reverence and discipline (what the founding members termed 'servility') was also denounced as standing in the way of a sound education which should encourage confidence and the development of mutual respect.

It was not simply their alternative ideology which distinguished the founding members from most other education groups and movements of the period. They were, in the main, parents not professional educationists, 'who were casting about to find means for the better education of their boys and girls'.[9] The King Alfred School Society began as a parent-led movement, unlike the Letchworth garden city education movement which lacked both a coherent ideology and full parental support, and which was led in the main by non-local, professional educators. The July meeting knew the direction in which it was headed and the lion in its path. Existing schools, they argued in their preliminary circular on the proposed rational school, were out of touch with 'the broader and healthier views of the training of children that science and the scientific study of child-nature have roused'. What they were seeking to do was to set up a permanent school in which 'this rational spirit could find expression'. The lion in the path was the state which was about to strengthen its control over education through the creation of a Board of Education. The history of state involvement in education from the first state grant to education in 1833 to the drafting of the Revised Code in 1862 and its subsequent implementation gave no grounds for hoping that the Board, whose creation had been under serious discussion since the Bryce Report of 1895, would have a broad and sympathetic view of the goals of 'rational' education. The preliminary circular made it clear that their scheme could only proceed if sufficient parental support was given to it. Income from fees would enable the school to be independent of the Board. This was a wise decision for, as the Letchworth Garden City Education Committee soon discovered when attempting to implement a scheme similar to that of the King Alfred School Society, the Board would not meet the additional costs necessitated by such innovations as smaller classes, regular medical inspection and outdoor studies. The Letchworth scheme fell apart because ultimately it was forced to turn to the Board for help; the King Alfred School Society, despite its grave early financial difficulties, was determined to maintain a strict independence in order not to subvert its founding principles.

The Findlays and the King Alfred School Society

There were, however, restrictions on what a small group of enthusiastic lay people who were not experts in educational planning or methodology could achieve. The preliminary circular and the Memorandum of Association which developed from it represented the limits as well as the substance of their early achievement. It laid down the broad principles upon which schools run by the King Alfred Society should operate and set the target date of Easter 1898 for the opening of its first school. What gave the initial committee the confidence to move ahead so quickly was the acceptance by Joseph John Findlay and his wife of its invitation to take part in the next stages of planning. In the summer of 1897 under the firm guidance of Mrs White Wallis it drew up a preliminary circular for interested parents to sign, planned a general meeting to give further publicity to their ideas and drew the Findlays into their deliberations. Their efforts bore fruit when the general meeting of 18 October gave support to the scheme. A week later a small committee including Mrs White Wallis, Mrs Roscoe Mullins, Miall and the Findlays met to elaborate the plans for the twin ventures.

The formation of the society took precedence, with agreement being quickly reached on registering the King Alfred School Society as a limited company, and on the Memorandum of Association to facilitate registration under the Companies Acts. The Memorandum, signed by the founding members, enunciated the broad aims of the society. Its twin pillars were to be the promotion of 'Educational Science' and the founding of schools 'to give practical expression to the best theories of Education extant, and particularly to the theories enunciated by Educational reformers, such as Pestalozzi, Herbart, Herbert Spencer, Louis Compton Miall, and others working on similar lines'. The problem of how a curriculum based upon the ideas of such a disparate group of educational reformers could be made to appear coherent and non-contradictory was left to the Findlays to resolve. For the moment, the committee was more concerned to indicate general directions than to draw up practical schemes. Maberly and Hickson, barrister at law and solicitor respectively, were more anxious in their legal submission to provide the machinery whereby these ideals could be realized and to secure independence for the society than they were to debate the minutiae of educational principle and practice. The latter could be left to the professional expertise of those best qualified to deal with curricular issues. The Memorandum of Incorporation gave the Society powers to invest funds and gifts, and to purchase and dispose of property. It also reiterated the importance of gearing any curriculum to what was known about child development and not to the requirements of examination bodies, although it recognized the need for independent inspection of its schools by people who were 'in sympathy with the aims and principles of the Society'. This instrument thus protected the independence of the society and its schools, although there was an explicit recognition that the society could co-operate with other bodies to achieve its ends.

It was at this stage that the Findlays were invited to plan the first school and its curriculum. They were eminently suited for both tasks. Mrs Findlay had trained students in Froebelian teaching techniques at

Sheffield, and Joseph Findlay, in 1897, was a lecturer in the College of Preceptors in London, a body for training teachers which had been founded fifty years earlier with the principal aims of 'promoting sound learning and advancing the interests of Education'. Its first professor, Joseph Payne, established the tradition of disseminating information on the ideas and experiments of Continental reformers, a tradition which Findlay continued in his lectures and research in the 1890s. From 1891 to 1893 he was a student of education in Germany where at Jena and Leipzig he had become particularly interested in the ideas of the German philosopher, Herbart. But it was not only their professional interests which attracted the Findlays to the venture; it fitted in well with their personal plans. In a letter which he wrote to the committee a week after the general launch of the Hampstead venture he outlined his plan for the first school.

> My duty to the College of Preceptors requires me to make it clear that I cannot undertake any responsible post in your new school. I may serve on a committee or give advice or offer an occasional lecture: but any position of responsibility would be beyond my range, . . . My wife and I think it time to commence the plan which we have had in our mind ever since we came to London . . . to start a small school for little children teaching others alone with our own 2 little ones. She wishes to carry on their education till they are 8 or 9 years of age and with that she would train a few students as she formerly did in Sheffield. Our plan was to share this little school in our own house . . . it has seemed to me feasible for us to move into St John's Wood for the next 3 years because I am now certain that I can remain in St John's Wood for that time: – later than that I cannot say. If then the 2 plans were combined you would start with 3 classes:
> A Kindergarten 2 Transition – up to 6 or 7
> A First Form – up to 8 or 9 years
> A Second Form – up to 10 or 12 years
> And the staff would consist of Mrs Findlay, aided by a trained mistress and a few students, teaching principally in the Kindergarten and the 1st form and a master teaching principally in the 2nd form.[10]

Why Findlay was willing to play a carefully circumscribed role in the new school but not become its first headmaster is not an easy question to answer, although probably it was because the Hampstead venture was on a small scale. A few months later he gave up his lectureship at the College of Preceptors to engage in a much larger educational enterprise in Cardiff, as headmaster of the city's first intermediate school. It was the first venture by the state into secondary education, and the forerunner of secondary schools which were set up in England after the Education Act of 1902. Findlay's commitment to the King Alfred School Society and its Hampstead school was different from that of the original members. His was more professional than personal in that it offered him the opportunity for involvement in an educational venture outside mainstream education. He was interested in the school as a scientific or 'rational' experiment akin to the two demonstration schools which, as Sarah Fielden Professor of Education, he launched in Manchester from 1903 onward. He described the purpose of such schools in *The Demonstration Schools Record* (1908):

> Just as the medical student requires his Anatomy and Physiology before he turns his attention directly to Medicine, so the student of Education should know something of the subject of Education, the child, before being set to teach and to train him. True, he already possesses popular knowledge of what school children are like, but his knowledge is of no greater value for scientific purposes than the popular knowledge of the laity about the human body compared with the more exact knowledge required from the medical student. Hence the first course of study is not concerned at all with school problems as such, but with the Mental and Physical Life of School Children. It is intended to be, and on the whole is, treated as a piece of elementary scientific work.

The society was fortunate in having a dispassionate critic and director whose outlook was so very different from that of its other members. As the son of a Wesleyan minister and former headmaster of two Wesleyan Proprietory Schools (Queen's College, Taunton and Wesley College, Sheffield) and compiler of a school hymn book, he was called upon to advise on a school in which religious instruction was banned; as former master at Rugby and author of the eulogy *Arnold of Rugby* (1896) he was asked to set up a school whose vowed intention was to free independent education from the cramping customs of nineteenth-century public schools. In addition, all his advice on the King Alfred Society's radical, alternative form of education was being offered when, at the same time, as headmaster of Cardiff High School he was basing the new state secondary education on the traditional public school model and ensuring that religion played a central role in education as was befitting of a leading school in the principal city of Wales! As a member of the Bryce Commission he had backed the idea of a new unified central authority, the Board of Education, from whose inspectors the King Alfred School Society wished to maintain a strict independence. These essential differences in outlook and experience made him a more, rather than less, valuable adviser to a group who could otherwise have been labelled a body of eccentrics with esoteric ideas.

The principal achievement of the Findlays was to turn a series of broad educational goals into a malleable curricular model within a little over a month, from late October to early December 1897, when a proof copy of the school's preliminary prospectus was available for discussion by the council. So swiftly did the Findlays undertake the task that it was completed before the council had decided upon a name for the new school. Since it was due to open the following Easter, their priorities were understandable. The nature and urgency of the project, together with the speed with which it was accomplished, help to explain some of the curious features of the preliminary prospectus. The impressive list of five Continental and British reformers who, in the Memorandum of Association, were said to inspire the new movement, was reduced, in the preliminary prospectus, to just two, Froebel and Herbart. 'The scheme of Teaching', it declared, 'will be devised largely on the principles due to Herbart and Froebel.' This was a rather unusual shortlist in that the only thing that the authoritarian Herbart and the democratic Froebel had in common was their Germanic origin. Findlay had studied their ideas when he was a student of education in Germany from 1891 to 1893 and was able to mould what were apparently contradictory theories and approaches to education into a coherent programme of reformed education. Froebel's presence on the list is explained by Mrs Findlay's professional interest in Froebelian teaching techniques. Froebel's emphasis upon spontaneity and on the need to combine close observation with 'self activity' was well in keeping with the ideas of the founders. The principal function of the school was to encourage natural development, what Froebel had termed 'kindergarten'. Mrs Findlay's professional expertise in 'kindergarten' teaching techniques ensured that it remained the guiding concept in the education of young children. Pestalozzi was not mentioned possibly because Froebel, as one of his disciples, incorporated many of the Swiss reformer's views in his own theories, although Froebel found Pestalozzi's greater emphasis on receptivity rather than upon creative self-expression unacceptable.

Findlay's pragmatic and eclectic approach to curriculum design is reflected in the priority which he gave to Herbart whose teacher-centred and formal approach to education scarcely seemed to meet the ideals of the founders. However, Findlay ignored that for which Herbart was best known, the mechanical, five-step approach to lesson delivery (aim and preparation, presentation, association, formulation and application) and accepted instead the Herbartian concept of the correlation and concentration of studies. Findlay constantly referred to his programme as 'the concentrated curriculum'. 'Severe intellectual study' would be confined to the mornings, with older children only returning in the afternoon for lighter occupations such as drawing, manual training, gardening and educational walks. He believed that 'the formation of character' would be greatly assisted by such concentration of the curriculum in that, when teachers and pupils were freed 'from the stricter restraint of school lessons' in the hours of 'recreation and other occasions', there would be full opportunity to develop 'a tone of natural good order and sympathy'. Classes would be small and the mutually beneficial influence of teacher and pupil on each other would be assisted by adopting the public school practice of 'consulting tutors'. Findlay's essential point was that the individual needs of children would 'not be sacrificed to any theoretical scheme', no matter how eminent its author.

The religious controversy which so bedevilled (and I choose that word carefully) state education at the turn of the century was one which could have wrecked the society's plan for a new school. The judicious handling of this issue in the preliminary prospectus and in the curricular statement meant that dissension over religion was avoided and the curriculum was not subverted for sectarian ends. The lasting formula which was adopted was contained in two brief sentences.

> The education will be conducted in a religious spirit, with a due respect to the religious convictions of parents but free from connection with any religious or political organisation. No inquiry will be made into the religious beliefs or practices of either parents, teachers or children.

There was to be no religious instruction per se although the Bible could be used as a source of stories. Rational education challenged the cherished Victorian belief that the moral education of children was to be achieved solely through Bible teaching. In an age when the popular heroes were religious men – Livingstone, the African explorer and missionary, General Gordon, the soldier and philanthropist – it was almost instinctive for state education to be equated with religious instruction. The Committee of the Privy Council on Education which controlled state provision from 1839 to 1899 laid down the rule that 'Religion ought to be combined with the whole matter of instruction and to regulate the entire system of discipline'. The concept of religious teaching as a means of imposing discipline was clearly at odds with the underlying principles of the King Alfred School Society. The society was part of a small but growing movement that presented moral ideals and standards upon a rational as distinct from an authoritarian basis. This movement was particularly strong in London. A number of ethical societies had come into existence in the 1880s, which formed themselves into The Ethical Union in 1895. Lecturers from the Froebelian Education Institute took part in a course from October 1896 to March 1897 designed to help teachers give more efficient moral teaching. One of them was Miss Alice Woods of Maria Grey Training College, who joined the provisional committee of the King Alfred School in December 1897 and was a member of the first council which was set up early the following year. The Moral Instruction League was also set up in 1897 'to substitute systematic non-theological moral instruction for the present religious teaching'. Though its concern was education in state schools in general, and school board education in London in particular, it shared with the King Alfred School Society a strong opposition to establishment ideas on religious instruction in schools. Dr Michael Sadler, who produced a *Report on an International Inquiry into Moral Instruction and Training in School*, was an early sympathizer with the ideals of the King Alfred movement.

The careful handling of these critical issues represents only part, and not necessarily the major part, of Findlay's achievement. His main contribution to the success of the venture lay in the advanced design of the curriculum of the new school, which differed in concept from the state bureaucratic model and in clarity from those of earlier progressive schools. The dominant curricular model of the late nineteenth and early twentieth century was the single-subject model, where the curriculum was designed in terms of a number of subjects each allocated a number of hours per week according to the importance which was attached to that subject area. This arrangement, formalized in the Board's regulations for secondary schools (1904), made the curriculum the servant of examinations, led to compartmentalization, to the over-crowding of the curriculum and to overpressure on pupils as new subjects were added, and to the exposure of pupils to a series of random and disjointed experiences. When Isobel White Wallis denounced examinations as the great 'juggernaut' of the age she was condemning the whole system of curricular arrangements which gave support to examinations in the elementary schools, and which was shortly to be extended even more rigidly to state secondary schools under the 1904 regulations. That the society was alert to the danger of the latter is clear from the following note appended to the 1899 prospectus: 'In view of Secondary Education soon coming further under State organisation, The King Alfred School Society is anxious to have many of its Schools established to demonstrate the great advantages of reform.' What Mrs White Wallis and the society turned to Findlay for was a different curricular model which matched better their educational ideology. What he came up with was a radical alternative, better suited to the more liberal goal of the all-round development of personality. This was the areas-of-experience model. Whereas other progressive schools of the 1890s were working generally towards such a paradigm, Findlay spelt it out in considerable detail, as can be seen from the extract from the preliminary prospectus in Table 1. This provided the substructure or foundation upon which the King Alfred School's superstructure was raised. The table shows his starting point, the identification of the six areas of beneficial experience to which pupils would be exposed through a variety of means. This identification gave balance and coherence to the curriculum and ensured that no area was neglected or downgraded. Hence those subject areas which were pushed to the periphery of the state curriculum because they were not regarded as important or because they were not easy to examine cheaply *en masse*, such as the arts of expression in speech and music or the manual arts, were given equal status in the King Alfred School curriculum with the more 'prestigious' subject areas. Recreation, which in the elementary school was frowned on as allowing the devil to make work for idle hands, was seen in the 'rational' schools as making a positive contribution to education.

His next step was to detail the principal means by which the six areas of experience (the humanities, nature knowledge, arts of expression in speech and in music, arts of representation and other manual arts, abstract sciences and recreation) could be presented to pupils of different ages. Here his wife's kindergarten experience and his own experience in teaching older pupils, especially in modern languages at Bath College, proved invaluable. The latter explains the prominence of French and French studies.

What was important was the framework and the principles upon which it was based, not the detail. The latter could be varied in accordance with the resources and the particular interests and areas of expertise of the teachers. State education had struggled into existence as an exercise in remediation, that is with the vowed intention of correcting what were perceived to be working-class weaknesses: insobriety, brutish behaviour, indiscipline and ignorance of the Bible and basic skills. By the end of the nineteenth century state education was slowly throwing off this yoke. The King Alfred School Society intended from the outset not to take on such constraints, to view education not in remedial terms but as a means of assisting natural growth and development. The scientific study of child development was intended by Findlay to help realize this goal.

Table 1 **The Findlay curriculum**

	Junior School		Commencement of Senior School
	Early childhood (kindergarten): ages 4–6	Later childhood: ages 7–9	Early boyhood or girlhood: ages 10–12
Group A: The Humanities (story, history, literature)	Fables, simple stories not limited by time, space, or other sense experience. (Varying with the seasons and months of the year)	Stories (from simple but classic literature) leading from Legends to authentic history, e.g., The story of The Patriarchs, Ulysses, Norse Sagas, Robinson Crusoe; finally, The Settlement of England, St. Augustine, Alfred, Canute and Harold. The Story of the Exodus	Great English Heroes and Kings from 1066 to 1700 and ending with the connections between French and English History. (Compare Groups **B, C, D**, below.) The Kings of Judah and Israel.
Group B: Nature, knowledge (including geography)	Collection and observation of all kinds of simple objects, related, week by week, to the story in Group **A**.	Geography of England, beginning with that of the neighbourhood. Study of familiar animals and plants (associated partly with the life of our forefathers in the woods and fields of old England. See Group **A**.) All examined at first hand from Nature, and classified in an elementary way.	Geography of France and S.W. Europe. Beginnings of Physiography and simple experiments in Physics (compare Columbus, Bacon, etc., connected with Group **A**)
Group C: Arts of expression in speech and in music	Songs and Speech chiefly connected with the stories in Group A and the Nature Knowledge in Group **B**.	Reading and Writing and Tonic-Sol-fa singing commenced. The subject matter sought from Groups **A** and **B** chiefly. Simple Composition: oral and written.	English Reading, Writing, Composition, continued. French commenced and made very prominent in the last year. The subject matter sought from Groups **A** and **B** chiefly. Singing.
Group D: Arts of representation and other manual arts	The Kindergarten Gifts and Occupations:- representing, in a variety of forms, objects from Groups **A** and **B** and other interests of the child.	The Kindergarten Gifts and Occupations continued and developed .Drawing from nature, etc. Subject matter from Group **A** and **B**. Gardening connected with the botany lessons.	Drawing, Modelling, & c., Gardening, Cardboard work, or Carpentry. Beginnings of Geometrical Drawing, Maps, Diagrams: All connected with Groups **A** and **B**. Drawing from nature and from Norman and Early English decoration, to be found in the neighbourhood.
Group E: Abstract sciences, number, form, language	Beginnings of Number – up to 10. Recognition of simple Geometrical Forms (according to Frœbel's doctrine) — all in the concrete from Group **B**.	Beginnings of Arithmetic. Number up to 100 or beyond. Geometrical ideas further developed —- all in the concrete from Group **B**. First ideas of Theory of Music.	Number beyond 100. Ideas of time from History, of space from Geography. Definitions of Geometry. First ideas of Grammar, in French and English. Music continued.
Group F: Recreation	Physical and Musical Drill. Kindergarten Games. Short walks. Free play between lessons.	Physical and Musical Drill. Continuation of Kindergarten games. *Short* excursions and walks (see Group **B**). Free play between lessons.	Physical and Musical Drill. School Games. *Short* excursions and walks (connected with Groups **A** and **B**). Free play between lessons.

Note: After 12 years of age a large number of hours per week will be given to Latin, if boys are entered with a view to proceeding to a Public School. The previous thorough pursuit of French will make the approach to a second foreign language far more easy. The French teaching will be planned so as to conduct the lessons *wholly in French*, as soon as possible.

However, the limitations of the 'scientific' or 'rational' approach were clear. Education is inseparable from judgements of value and commits educators to morally legitimate procedures and goals. What constituted the King Alfred Society's educational values had been laid down by the founding members. Findlay devised an appropriate curricular model for realizing their aims. Its details were never intended to remain unaltered. In their first meeting on 25 October 1897, to consider in detail how they should implement their scheme for a rational school, the founders agreed 'that the object of such society should be the furtherance, in every possible way of true educational methods as understood by the members and specified by them in the Memorandum of Association'; but it was deemed advisable to state matters of detail as the 'intention of the founders rather than to attempt to make them binding on the future of any schools to be conducted by the Society'. It was its values not its particular objectives or curriculum which were to remain the guiding spirit of the society and its schools.

The King Alfred curriculum was as much a challenge to the traditional preparatory and public school curriculum as it was to the state curriculum. This was not simply in its being a coeducational day school providing education only up to the age of twelve. It was different in concept, especially in the attention which it gave to practical skills. Educational historians such as Correlli Barnett[11] and Martin Wiener[12] have shown how traditional preparatory and public school education scorned technical skills. The aim of the traditional preparatory and public school was to produce the scholar and gentleman, to develop an élitist culture based on classical literature, which regarded technical skill as inferior. It is hardly surprising that the King Alfred School Society, partly under the influence of two eminent sculptors, Roscoe Mullins and Hamo Thornycroft, should have emphasized the importance of technical and practical skill in the all-round development of character. This is perhaps something which previous progressive schools had not fully appreciated.

There is no better example of the repressive conventions which KAS aimed to avoid than Findlay's own school in Cardiff. The curriculum which Findlay introduced into the school of which he became headmaster in September 1898, Cardiff Boys' Intermediate School, contrasted sharply with King Alfred's. It was remarkably conventional. Having gained the headship in the face of stiff competition from a strong local candidate, two headmasters and a professor, he proceeded to impose the traditional public school curriculum on this new experiment in Welsh secondary education. His was very much a subject-based model, with religious instruction heading the list. Graduates from Oxford and Cambridge were employed to teach most subjects, except the manual arts which were taken by the school caretaker! He was severely criticized by Sir Philip Magnus who condemned the curriculum for being 'somewhat bookish in character' and for overburdening pupils: 'The pupils work at too high pressure; the attention of the masters is distracted from the true aims of school teaching by the necessity of preparing pupils for so many different tests.' His school entered pupils for the examinations of the Central Welsh Board, the matriculation examinations of the University of Wales and London, the scholarship examination of most universities and the various qualifying examinations of a host of professional bodies. Findlay created a special 'examination department' under a carefully appointed teacher. The Welsh intermediate, or secondary, school revolution was remarkably conservative in comparison with that in Hampstead. That it was so is explained by his educational philosophy which rested not on intrinsic goals, as in the case of the King Alfred School Society, but on the external factors of social class and future employment. Writing to *The Times* in May 1900 Findlay commented,

> The School Boards have now a unique opportunity of serving the country in a way that has hitherto been impossible. Surely they will accept this chance, instead of directing all their attention to ambitious flights up imaginary educational ladders. This opportunity consists in the possibility of providing schemes of study expressly adapted to the needs of that immense class of boys and girls who leave school at 14 and 15 years of age to enter retail trades, junior clerkships and technical artisan employments . . . the future career of the pupil is the leading thought to guide us in determining the duty of a school.[13]

Findlay's curriculum in Cardiff was not directed to natural child development but 'with a view to callings in life (as solicitors, bank managers, accountants, doctors, teachers etc).' While he wanted an education ladder available to all with the ability to climb it, he nevertheless argued strongly in favour of a differentiated curriculum not on the basis of individual needs but on the basis of future occupation. On leaving Cardiff in July 1903 for a professorship at Manchester, he changed his position, favouring the King Alfred School curriculum in his submission to the Letchworth Garden City Association in September 1903.

Findlay was thus involved in several reform movements of the period, in Hampstead, in Cardiff and to a lesser extent in Letchworth. His constant concern was that each should operate within carefully defined parameters. His parting message to the society before he left for Cardiff in 1898 was that it should avoid 'overambition'.

In accepting the post of Director, I must adhere strictly to the policy of not engaging to do more than we can really hope to perform. Our zeal for reform makes us liable to commit the Society to obligations which are beyond our powers . . . I trust that my zeal for reform is genuine but I have witnessed many efforts at reform which have failed because the reformers have been too ambitious.[14]

His Cardiff headship left very little time for him to devote to the affairs of the society and its Hampstead school in the years to 1903. However, on becoming Professor of Education at Owen's College, Manchester (later Manchester University), in the autumn of 1903 he joined the council of the society and he remained an active member until the 1930s. In 1922 he became the society's third president.

The headship of Charles E. Rice, 1898–1901

The democratic processes adopted by the founders and the provisional committee, which extended even to the choice of name for the society, meant that even the idea of opening a school at Easter 1898 seemed overambitious. Each step in the setting up of the society and its first school was discussed initially by a founding committee, or the provisional committee as it became after 23 November 1897, before being put to a general meeting. By mid-December 1897 only a few preliminary details had been approved. After much discussion it was finally agreed that the society should be called the 'King Alfred School Society' in preference to the 'New Century Society'. The latter was indefinite in its relationship with education whereas the approaching millennial celebration of the death of King Alfred (849–99), whose scholastic achievements and education programmes were enshrined in legend, gave the former not only Findlay's support but that of a majority of those present at the general meeting on 16 December 1897. Miall had been empowered to open a bank account; the matter of incorporation, although under way, had to wait another six months before it was effected; the rights and privileges of donors to the experiment were still being defined. By the beginning of January 1898 these extended to life-membership of the society to those contributing £20 and over, and the right of those donating £100 to 'nominate one child to the school in four years at half fees'. The appointment of the society's first council of eleven members was left in the hands of the provisional committee. Thus at the beginning of the new year much had still to be done if the school was to be opened by Easter.

The matter of school premises was one of the first to be discussed in January 1898, and resulted from Findlay's imminent London accommodation problem. His advice to council was initially to restrict the school to 'no more than two classes, a Kindergarten and First Form under 10 years of age'. With his plans for the future being uncertain he suggested that the society consider taking on a shared house on a six months' trial, paying Mrs Findlay 'whatever salary you can afford during that time'. The Findlays would share the house with the school; this modest beginning, he believed, was 'the only possible way of starting at Easter', especially if they also appointed the daughter of A. R. Wallace, 'a most competent and suitable teacher', at '£100 a year or £70 and residence'. Findlay's proposals were accepted and the opening date of Easter unanimously agreed. The rest of the house was guaranteed by Mrs White Wallis and two others and negotiations went ahead for a tenancy of Peterborough Lodge. However, the problem of school premises was finally resolved when Mrs Mullins reported to the council meeting in February 1898 that '24 Ellerdale Road had been selected as a suitable house in which to open the first school of the Society'. The matter was not entirely straightforward. The length of the lease (one, seven, fourteen or twenty-one years) had to be decided, and the risk of an injunction being taken out against the school by neighbours had to be considered.

Staffing the first school was the next issue facing the council. Findlay was appointed Director of Education without teaching duties for twelve months, in return for which he received 'residence for himself and family and education for his two daughters'. Mrs Findlay became principal of the Kindergarten, and was given charge of the society's house and its maintenance in return for a salary 'of not less than £100'. She was also to provide lunch for children and residence for assistant teachers, if required. Miss Wallace was offered the position of first-form mistress and an assistant mistress, working part-time for the school and part-time as a clerk for the society, was to be appointed at £20 per annum. Findlay had a Miss Mabel Williams in mind for this post. An assistant master, without salary, was also to be appointed, a certain Mr Austin having apparently drawn this short straw. This complement of staff would make the first venture 'nothing more than a junior school for children under 10' and in Findlay's view this was how the school should remain after September 1898 'unless we gain much more support'. He was against a more ambitious arrangement including the engaging of 'a master (for £150 or £200 a year), finding playing fields etc' without such support. Even these minimal arrangements remained fluid, for Miss Williams and Mr Austin were unable to give as much time to school duties as was first expected, and the opening date for the school was postponed until September 1898; even a September launch was subject to 'the Society raising further funds', although at the general meeting of the society at the end of March, Alice Mullins kept the Easter date to the forefront of discussion.

What perhaps is surprising is that in all of the discussions about staffing there was no reference to a headmaster. The first mention in the council minutes occurs on 23 March after the matter had been decided rather than discussed: 'The position of Headmaster was offered to Mr Rice and accepted by him, and the general conditions of the appointment were agreed upon.' Findlay's appointment to the Cardiff headship certainly made it more necessary to have a headmaster at Hampstead to take charge of the day-to-day implementation of the scheme and to undertake some of the duties hitherto allotted to Mrs Findlay. Rice's appointment and the speedy revision and publication of the school prospectus helped to make an Easter start, or slightly later, more likely.

It was perhaps natural for the King Alfred School Society (about to found the third independent progressive school) to look to the second, Bedales, for its headmaster. Rice had been one of two assistant masters who had been at Bedales since it was founded by Badley in 1893. Had the society asked Grant Watson, a thirteen-year-old scholar at Bedales, for a reference they might have thought twice about inviting him to occupy the headship of its Hampstead school.

'Mr Rice, who taught science [at Bedales] was a relaxation', commented E. L. Grant Watson later.

> He was easy-going and a bad disciplinarian. We all liked him, and showed our appreciation by making his classes as difficult as possible. His red, jovial face seldom showed anything but a smile, and his slow apprehension was usually too late to prevent the tricks we played him.

Rice introduced exploratory and experimental methods in his science teaching at Bedales so it could have been that in hindsight his freer discipline was mistaken for 'bad' discipline in an authoritarian age. He also taught woodwork, metalwork, English and mathematics, which made him the kind of versatile headteacher which a society dedicated to raising the status of handwork, whilst maintaining the central importance of the basic subjects, wanted. His original aim had been to train as a doctor, and in 1897 he left Bedales to go to the Royal College of Science but was persuaded to take the King Alfred headship.[15] In the words of Badley, Rice's brother-in-law, he thus 'was the first of a dozen members of our staff who have gone from their experience at Bedales to become Heads of Schools of their own and thus helped to diffuse more widely the new educational ideal'. However, 'the new educational ideal' of the independent progressive school movement was capable of a wide variety of interpretations. The liberal Christian ideal of Bedales, devised and sustained by the headmaster-legislator, Badley, differed significantly

3. The first pupils, 1898

from the rationalist ideology carefully constructed and maintained by the council of the King Alfred School Society. In short, simply translating the Bedales model to Hampstead would have been disastrous, a fact which Rice and the society recognized. They were as much in an experiential-learning situation as were the pupils of the King Alfred Society School, yet one cannot help but feel in the first few years that the pupils learnt more readily and effectively on occasions than did the society and its first headmaster. The directness of dialogue and informal interaction between teacher and pupil which characterized effective learning in the classroom was not paralleled in the council chamber. The list of 'ladies and gentlemen who might be considered suitable as members of Council or honorary fellows' which was drawn up a few weeks before the Hampstead school opened on 2 May 1898 did not include Rice's name. Communication between the council and headmaster was to be by letter or 'visitor', which not only emphasized the hierarchical nature of relationships but denied the opportunity for informal discussion from which a new and growing educational venture could benefit. It was not that the society was unwilling to reconsider its constitutional arrangements and procedures. For example, in order to promote efficiency it amalgamated the school committee and the society committee to form the general purposes committee later in the year. However, the headmaster was neither a member of council nor of its committees in the first few years of the school's existence, nor was the issue of his membership even under 'reserved-item terms' ever openly discussed.

It should not be thought, however, that the council was engaged in some kind of conspiracy to deprive Rice of any part in the decision-making process. Though his position was markedly different from that of Badley at Bedales, he was given a large measure of freedom in the day-to-day running of the school. This extended not merely to the purchase of essential pieces of furniture and apparatus such as desks, clocks and science equipment but to matters which in some ways cut across basic principles of the Society, including compromising the principle of day schooling through taking boarders. The two boarders he accepted helped to augment the number of pupils, which when the school was officially opened by Mrs Fawcett on 24 June 1898 stood at seven (five boys and two girls in the age seven to nine group) and which had expanded to twenty (seven of whom were aged ten or more) during the autumn term. The latter group enabled Rice to organize a senior as well as a junior school. With a bank balance of £70. 18s. and liabilities of £187. 7s. at the time of the *de facto* opening in May, every additional pupil was critical to the future financial health of the Hampstead venture. Council made membership of the society and school more attractive by operating a discount scheme for parents with several children at school and to parents who were life members of the society. The society also vigorously pursued its vital publicity work through conferences, the first of which was addressed by Dr Boulting, a council member, on the subject of the moral training of children and the second by Frances Warner on 'Child culture and mental training'. Ever alert to current developments in education which connected with vital matters of society principle, the council also organized a conference on 'The relation of examination to inspection under the new Education Act' which Professor Heath was to introduce. The founding members, especially Sharp, Miall, Mullins and White, kept steadfastly to their original brief as laid down in the preliminary prospectus and Articles of Association.

Rice also exercised a large measure of control over the curriculum. Part of his achievement was to translate the ambitious Findlay curriculum into a more modest workable scheme. While respecting the broad principles upon which it was based, his task was to mould to the Findlay scheme the needs of a small school with all the restrictions which that implied. In his report to the first annual general meeting of the society in October 1898 he referred to the progress made in achieving a truly coeducational curriculum, and in introducing the principle of the co-ordination of studies. 'At present on the science side', he declared 'carpentry lent itself readily to geometry, mechanics etc., and upon the arts side where history, geography and literature were being already co-related and made to fit the personal experience of children.' The emphasis which Findlay had placed upon the idea of concentration was also respected by Rice.

At the centre of the concentrated curriculum was the child itself. In Rice's view, all theory should be drawn from practice or personal experience, while at the same time every new theory should be put to further practice, 'so that the abstract and the real were made to act and re-act upon one another'. He concluded by saying that, when first invited to take charge of the school, he doubted whether such a venture were needed; the objects of the society seemed so simple that he felt all schools must be doing such rational work. However, his six months' sojourn in the neighbourhood had convinced him that the ideas of the society were needed in Hampstead and he was hopeful of the practical use of the first school.

While Findlay at Cardiff Intermediate School for Boys was introducing a subject-based curriculum geared to a variety of external examinations, Rice continued to develop a more ambitious curricular model, backed by a rigorous system of regular health checks for pupils and aimed at avoiding external examinations. The prospectus which he helped to draw up in 1900 for the 1900/1901 intake of thirty-seven pupils stressed the value of practical work, handwork, music, and visits to galleries and museums. The school did not neglect 'formal studies' especially in mathematics. By the end of the academic year 1900/1901 the school population had expanded to fifty-two, twenty boys and thirty-two girls. Of equal significance was the extension of the age range from eight to seventeen. The school prospectus drawn up in 1901 by Rice's successor, John Russell, was of a more conventional kind, which, while not neglecting the correlation of subjects, gave greater prominence to individual subjects.

The crisis of 1901

How and why Russell came to replace Rice as headmaster can be traced in part to the overly formal and hierarchical relationships between the council and headmaster which lasted for most of Rice's headship. These soon created problems, initially of a minor kind but later of a more serious nature. Letters and visitations were peculiarly inflexible instruments of communication between council and headmaster, particularly in such a small, progressive venture which in all other areas emphasized the value of informal contacts. Council decisions appeared as edicts which they were not always intended to be, and the headmaster, lacking full opportunities for immediate and informal advice and guidance on a range of matters upon which speedy and immediate action was called for, made decisions which could possibly be misinterpreted as unwarranted, arbitrary or highhanded. For some reason it was not until the end of 1900 that the council resolved 'that Mr Rice be requested to attend all Council meetings to assist the Council in the discussion of matters concerning the school', with the sensible proviso that 'he shall withdraw when requested to do so'.

This was a belated move to improve deteriorating relations which had resulted in a resolution being passed at the November 1900 meeting 'that Mr Rice be informed that the Council is responsible to parents for the efficiency of the school and Mr Rice is responsible to the Council'. From very early on in the school's history, the inadequacies of communications between the council and headmaster were becoming apparent. In February 1899 the matter of the headmaster and staff not carrying out 'the object of the society of throwing open the school to all interested in education' was raised within the council. Rather than consult the headmaster informally about the problem, council resolved to set up in the school a reception room for visitors which was to be looked after by 'a young lady'. Nine months later the matter was still rankling when council, after receiving a letter on the subject from Rice, regretted 'any misunderstanding [that] should have arisen and resolved that Members of Council intending to bring strangers to inspect the school are

4. King Alfred School 1899. L to R (top row) Charles Rice (headmaster), (third from his left) Estelle Basden, (sixth from left) Claud Mullins, then Margery Basden and Ida Mullins; (middle row) Enid White Wallis (seated), (fourth from left leaning forward) Mrs Rice, (second from her left) Miss Frood; (front row) (second) Hilda Lowy, (boy seated on the right) Guy Garrod

requested to arrange with the Headmaster the date and hour of the proposed inspection'. It was another year before discussions between Rice and council members took place within the council chamber instead of by letter, by which time several other issues, which could have been easily resolved through informal discussion, had been allowed to develop into points of dispute. These included issues such as Mrs Rice's remuneration for the drawing lessons which she gave and Rice's claim for the subsidy which he said he gave to staff salaries. Such matters were sensitive to deal with even in harmonious times. They were potentially explosive at times of heightened tension. The deliberate retention and constant use of formal channels of communication between the council and headmaster made it almost impossible to resolve problems amicably.

Such was the situation in 1901 when the issue of the future direction of the development of the school came to a head, although at first it appeared that the matter had been resolved by a council majority vote in favour of Rice's plan that the school should be restricted to pupils of fourteen years and under. By 1901 the school was in a critical stage of its development and in February of that year the council asked its staffing subcommittee to consider whether the tuition of the present highest class could be continued efficiently with due regard to the maintenance of coeducation and on a sound financial basis, and, if so, what changes in the staff would be required? Cecil Sharp and many others on council agreed with Rice that the Ellerdale Road school should be restricted to pupils of fourteen and under. Their arguments were both educational and financial. They argued that those who stayed on after fourteen were predominantly girls and thus the coeducational principle would be undermined. Second, the cost of making separate provision for such a small number would be financially crippling; on the other hand, not to make such separate provision, but to mix older pupils with younger children, would be educationally unsound and contrary to the principles of a rational education. Mrs White Wallis, seeing what was largely her brainchild endangered by such arguments, sprang to its defence with all her maternal instincts. She argued that, if the school was capped at fourteen, and parents faced with the difficult, if not impossible, task of finding a post-fourteen education elsewhere to match the rational education provided at King Alfred School, they might prefer not to send their offspring to the school in the first place. The school would then be doomed to slow and painful extinction. To her it was first and foremost a matter of survival. The whole future of the experiment in rational education was at stake.

When the matter was put before the council in March 1901 in the form of the resolution: 'That the maximum limit of age for pupils at 24

Ellerdale Road be fixed at 14', a majority voted in favour, though a powerful minority including Maberly, Mrs White Wallis and the Callards voted against. The latter group was so concerned by the threat which such a decision posed to the whole venture that they called a special general meeting of the society on 25 April 1901. It appears that they went to considerable lengths to ensure that those who opposed the council's decision were present at the meeting. Hickson accused the council minority of engaging in 'electioneering tactics more worthy of an Eatanswill borough than of a reformed education society' but there is no evidence of their having acted unconstitutionally. The council majority was less active in ensuring that its supporters were present at this crucial meeting. The motion which Sharp, on behalf of the council, put before the special meeting was conciliatory in tone and was amended during discussion to turn it into what could have been a generally acceptable compromise. He moved that the maximum age limit for pupils at 24 Ellerdale Road be fixed at fourteen but that the council should have the power, on the recommendation of the head-master, to extend the limit in individual cases. An amendment was accepted that the maximum age limit would operate for the next three years after which it would be subject to review. Thus the age limit was immutable neither in the short term nor in the long term. However, the mood of the meeting did not favour compromise and in a very tense vote the motion was lost by seventeen votes to twelve with six abstentions. Certainly Mrs White Wallis, among others, was not willing to hand such power to the headmaster.

With the council resolution of the previous month having been overturned, the council majority who had voted in its favour were placed in a difficult situation. Should they resign or fight on? In fact, they did both. Four of them submitted their resignations but they hoped that a second special meeting of the society in June would find a compromise solution to enable them to withdraw them. At the June meeting Gilmour, who sided with the council majority, made a skilful but unsuccessful attempt to achieve the fourteen age limit. To Maberly's resolution:

> That the premises of no. 24 Ellerdale Road be used for the purpose of a junior school up to the age of 14 only, so soon as provision shall be made, for the continuation of the education of senior pupils, under the control of the Society in other premises.

he proposed a rider:

> And the council is hereby directed to prepare and lay before a General Meeting of the society to be held not later than the first

week in November 1901 a scheme for a senior school; and that unless such a scheme be approved by that general meeting children over 14 be not retained at 24 Ellerdale Road after Christmas 1901.

Here then was the chance of a compromise which could be extended by further modifications to the cut-off date.

However, Mrs White Wallis had no intention of allowing in by the backdoor something that had been ejected from the front. She objected that the rider was out of order because it directly contravened the society's decision at its previous meeting. The rider was put to the vote. This produced a tie with fifteen voting for and fifteen against. Miall, the chairman, cast his vote against, giving Mrs White Wallis the opportunity to act. She moved that the Ellerdale Road school be kept as an all-age school, a motion which was carried. The former council minority had for a second time proved triumphant over the former council majority.

Rice resigned from his position of headmaster, though the terms and date on which he was to leave remained in dispute. He left to set up his own school, West Heath School in Ferncroft Avenue, Hampstead, though his proposal to link it with the King Alfred School Society was rejected by the society. In 1909, he returned to Bedales. He remained there until 1911 when he decided to train as a doctor, the career he intended taking up just before he was invited to become headteacher of King Alfred. He was replaced by John Russell, whose headship from 1901 to 1920 provided much of the basis of the present school. Gilmour, Sharp, Hickson and Miall resigned from the society and its council. Mrs White Wallis declared that their resignations should be regarded as final so that the society and school could settle down to a period of peace and stability necessary to secure its future.

Thus ended one of the stormiest periods in the history of the King Alfred School Society and its Hampstead school. The new educational movement which had been so united in its aims and policies in 1897 had by 1901 come close to being wrecked on the rocks of division. That it not only survived but prospered was due in no small measure to John Russell whose seventeen years of teaching mainly in conventional day schools had helped him to develop the political skills necessary to deal with the governing body over the next two decades, skills which Rice's years at Bedales from 1893 to 1897 had given him no opportunity to acquire. The irony of a society dedicated to the principles of experiential learning having learnt so little from its constitutional experiences in the years 1897 to 1901 cannot but strike the reader.

Notes and references

1. The years of patient work, undertaken by the KASS archives committee, and especially by its archivist, Mr B. Rance, has left an impressive collection of documents.
2. Quoted in H. A. T. Child (ed.), *The Independent Progressive School* (London, Hutchinson, 1962), 33.
3. Minutes of the founding meeting, 25 October 1897.
4. Published in 1915. Reprinted by Nadder, Element Books Ltd., Dorset, 1986.
5. Ibid., 49.
6. Ibid., 48.
7. *Daily News*, 6 February 1898.
8. *The Highgate Express*, 3 March 1900.
9. Preliminary circular 1897.
10. Extracts from Findlay's letter to Mrs White Wallis, copied into council minutes, 25 October 1897, by the chair, F. W. Miall.
11. See 'Technology, education and industrial and economic strength' in *Journal of the Royal Society of Arts*, 5271/127 (February 1979).
12. In *English Culture and the Decline of the Industrial Spirit 1850–1980* (Cambridge, Cambridge University Press, 1981; Pelican, 1985).
13. *The Times*, 25 May 1900.
14. For a full account of this see R. Brooks, 'Dr J. J. Findlay, first headmaster of Cardiff Intermediate School for Boys, 1898–1903. Instinctive traditionalist or enterprising empiricist', in G. E. Jones (ed.), *Education, Culture and Society* (Cardiff, University of Wales Press, 1991), 45–63.
15. See W. A. C. Stewart, *The Educational Innovators*, vol. ii (London, Macmillan, 1968), 27–9.

Chapter 2

Rebel Cleric's Retreat:
KAS Under Russell,
1901–1920

Russell's headship from 1901 to 1920 began as it ended in fierce controversy during which he maintained a discreet and serene silence. He arrived at King Alfred School when the reverberations of Rice's resignation were still being felt, and departed amidst the threat of mass staff resignations when council chose Joseph Wicksteed as his successor rather than George Earle, who had been a senior member of staff since 1903. But these were momentous years for many reasons, not all of which were directly concerned with Russell or his headship. These were years when the founding principles of the King Alfred School Society felt the cold draught of market forces. The 'no God and no rod' principles remained unchallenged, but the demand for some in-school

5. John Russell ('J.R.') in 1910

preparation for external examinations, especially matriculation, could not go unheeded, particularly after 1907 when University College School transferred from Gower Street to the doorstep (or more accurately to the rear fence) of the Ellerdale Road school. However, the triumph of these years was that the society's flagship school, under the wise leadership of Russell, passed from youth to maturity with its essential principles intact, from the uncertain ranks of an experimental school to the confident status of a demonstration school, whose rationalist message was more relevant than ever to early Edwardian Britain. The Education Act of 1902 had lit the feeble flame of experimentation with the creation of state secondary schools, but it was in danger of being snuffed out by the Board of Education's secondary regulations, which aimed at imposing upon them the traditional trappings of the public schools, and by the rigidly prescriptive requirements of the school certificate and higher certificate examinations, with their inevitable overhaste and overpressure. The King Alfred School Society offered a radical alternative with which some of the Board's own officials, including Michael Sadler and A. J. Mundella, became associated. It may have been a lone, rationalist beacon but it was one which did not go unnoticed in official quarters.

John Russell was the person who gave cohesion, and thus increased effectiveness, to the work of KASS on all its fronts. As headmaster of the King Alfred School, he demonstrated the increasing attractiveness of a practical, rationalist education and pressed for the expansion of the school, first in Ellerdale Road, and then, when 22 and 24 Ellerdale Road became too cramped, at Manor Wood. He was one of the society's chief publicists, at its conferences, at its drawing-room meetings and in the outpost areas where the society hoped to set up other schools.

In 1901, all of this was in the future. In that year, survival not expansion was uppermost in the minds of the council. It seemed for a time that, with its depleted numbers and staff, the whole venture was about to sink beneath the waves of educational obscurity. The captain had gone, only one officer remained, Miss Frood. Most of the crew had abandoned ship, the number left on the school register by the end of the summer term was twenty-seven (eight boys and nineteen girls), some twenty less than was necessary to break even financially and with a gender imbalance which undermined its coeducational basis. However, by the time that the political storms had abated by the end of that year, it was clear that the flagship school had neither broken its back on the

6. King Alfred School in 1901

rocks of political dissension nor run aground in the ideological shallows. The former council majority quickly resigned rather than fight a crippling rearguard action. Isobel White Wallis kept her firm grip upon the helm, helping to put both the society and school back upon an even keel before the year was out. But the lesson was clear to all. Another tempestuous period would probably inflict irreparable damage upon the enterprise. Francis Storr, a member of the new council, fired the first warning shot across the bows of the reconstituted council by making it clear that the first duty of school governors was to appoint a headmaster but 'only once in a blue moon to dismiss him; but, as in the case of the sovereign in a constitutional monarchy, governors would reign and not rule'.[1] Whether the council would heed Storr's advice and take a less dominant role in running the school was dependent in part on the calibre and political skills of Rice's successor.

The council's first concern was to find a suitable successor. It set about the task in much the same way as it had done four years earlier. Appointment to the headship was to be by invitation rather than by competitive interview, with apparently only one person, John Russell, an assistant master at University College School, then based in Gower Street, being considered. An opportunity was missed for considering a broader range of candidates, including women. However, Russell came to the school well-recommended and well-connected. He was initially commended to the society by a former pupil from University College School, the Revd P. H. Wicksteed; thus we have the curious situation of a Unitarian minister (and incidentally father of Russell's successor, Joseph Wicksteed who was author of the school motto) first introducing Russell, a Cambridge graduate theologian, to the selection committee of London's leading rationalist school! Philip Wicksteed, who was also a University of London professor and economist,[2] was well placed to comment on Russell's writings, teaching and wardenship of the Passmore Edwards settlement. Russell was also strongly supported by several members of the council who shared his professional interests, especially Storr, Findlay and Miall. Storr, a prominent member of the Teacher's Guild, gave strong backing to his nomination. Russell worked with Storr at the Guild's Gower Street offices and shared his determination to rescue teaching from the ranks of a decaying trade. They often shared a platform together at public meetings, demanding a more professional status for teaching and teachers. Russell was also a friend of Findlay and of Professor L. C. Miall. He met them regularly in the Guild's offices and joined with them as an acknowledged expert on Pestalozzi, in writing articles on modern teaching techniques in the Guild journal, the *Journal of Education*. The headmaster of University

College School, J. L. Paton, who was himself shortly to move to a new post (at Manchester Grammar School) 'heartily congratulated the society on the gain of his services'.[3] Thus Russell came to the headship of King Alfred School with a wide body of support.

John Russell, the rebel cleric

Russell did not share the pedigree of the other progressive school headmasters of his age. He did not come from the independent progressive school stable. The training grounds of headmasters such as Badley of Bedales and Neill of Summerhill were the classrooms of earlier progressive schools, Badley at Reddie's Abbotsholme and A. S. Neill at KAS (1918–20). The purity of their progressive pedigree was maintained through these incestuous links. Russell's background was altogether different. He had no prior service in a recognized progressive school and came to the cause of rationalist education by a route which was not only longer and more circuitous than that of other headmasters, but which involved the crossing of greater extremes of intellectual terrain, from the Christian convictions of the young Cambridge theologian to the pronounced secularism and rationalism of the skilled writer and dedicated practitioner. Whereas the historical reputation of the exclusive club of first-generation headmasters such as Reddie, Badley and Neill is confirmed in each new published history of the independent progressive schools, that of Russell has declined. As A. S. Neill commented to a former head of KAS, Montgomery, in 1964, 'his name has disappeared from books on education but in his day he was a pioneer'.[4] This chapter attempts to restore him to his rightful position within the august circle of great headmasters and is dedicated to his former students, who through allowing me to recall their school days with them, have helped in this pursuit. Not that Russell would approve of being ranked with the great and the good!

How a theologian came to the headship of a rationalist school takes some explaining, although Russell himself saw the explanation as straightforward. In 1908, he summed it up as follows at the first meeting of the International Moral Education Congress.

> He himself, he declared, had never, either as a boy or even when a theological student, had a glimpse of that inward religious conviction of which Mr Lyttleton [an earlier speaker] spoke. During the twenty-five years that he had been a master, in aiming at the good life he had sought no aid from revealed religion. It behoved all teachers to look from children to themselves. They should teach children nothing that they did not believe themselves.

He could not believe in any personification of goodness, and he held . . . that the influence of prayer was purely subjective. In the King Alfred School – a day school of boys and girls – there was no religious observance, no religious instruction, no religious appeal, but the ideal of the good life was steadily upheld.[5]

However, his path to rationalism was more complex than this explanation suggests, and is worth following for it gave a moral distinctiveness to his headship. Russell was born in 1855 at Wyke (or Weeke), the son of a bookkeeper. He went to St John's College, Cambridge, in 1878, just prior to which he engaged in preaching duties although not as a curate, as sketches of him in the KASS archives suggest.[6] At St John's, when reading for his theological Tripos,[7] he was president of the college debating society, at the very time when Darwin's *Origins of Species* was making its impact upon religious faith. His 'quiet independence of heart'[8] would not allow him to adopt a simple dogmatic approach to the great questions of the day. Dogma, in his view, stood in the way of understanding, a belief which he explained more clearly nearly two decades after he graduated with a second-class degree in theology. In 1895 as warden of the Passmore Edwards settlement in Bloomsbury he explained how 'social dogmatism as much as theological dogmatism' stood in the way of understanding 'the terrible evil of modern pauperism'.[9] Earlier, in 1882, as a young Cambridge graduate who had chosen a career in education rather than in the church, he came to deplore the doctrines and dogmas of Victorian education which emphasized discipline, examination success and rote learning, essentially social goals imposed on education which prevented its alignment with the individual needs of children.

Immediately on leaving St John's in 1882 Russell took up the post of assistant teacher of modern languages and elementary subjects at Islington High School. Although the school under F. P. Barnard did not exhibit the worst excesses of the dominant Victorian educational ideology, his two years there gave him practical insights into its principal constraints on child development. His parting testimonial[10] pronounced him 'competent to discipline and to teach [*note the order of priority*] a large form' so much so that he had 'been satisfactorily noticed by the annual examiners'. However, he did his best to breathe humanity into mass teaching methods which led his headmaster to conclude that 'the kindness of his methods and his personal influence . . . render him unusually valuable as a master', sentiments which were echoed later by his pupils at KAS. Yet, while people such as Reddie and Badley could escape the cramping conventions of Victorian education by setting up their own schools, for Russell there was to be no short cut, no self-created controlled experiment in progressive education. His path to an alternative educational ideology to that prevailing in late Victorian Britain was altogether different. In 1883 he resigned from Islington High School not to set up his own testbed of educational ideas but to seek out alternative educational models on the Continent. He left Islington ostensibly to study 'modern philology' in Germany but principally to experience the new republican ideology which Jules Ferry was introducing in France as part of his policy of strengthening the Third French Republic.

It was not unusual for a teacher of modern languages in England to take up a temporary teaching post in a French *lycée* in order to develop his linguistic and pedagogic skills. What was unusual was the time at which Russell chose to do it, when the young Third French Republic, born out of defeat at the hands of Prussia in 1871, was seeking under its Minister of Education, Jules Ferry, to bring education under secular control. Modern languages in particular and pedagogy in general were at the heart of his attack on the Catholic dominance of education. Ferry gave priority to the teaching of modern languages partly to downgrade the position of Latin in the curriculum and hence to reduce the power of the Catholic Church in France. He also aimed to revolutionize Jesuit pedagogy by replacing rote learning with active teaching and learning methods based upon the Pestalozzian principle of observation. This educational reform had distinctly secular and political goals which the young Russell came to accept. Ferry argued that his

7. The school play with Russell on the last day at Wimereux, 1904

reformed education system would produce 'countless young reserves of republican democracy, trained in the school of science and reason, who will block retrograde attitudes with the insurmountable obstacles of free minds and liberated consciences'.[11] The new spirit in French education influenced Russell for the rest of his teaching career. A quarter of a century later he admitted his 'lack of enthusiasm for Latin' to a team of school inspectors visiting KAS, but a more immediate influence was that of Pestalozzi, whose life and works Ferry had encouraged Baron Roger de Guimps to write and publish. Shortly after his return to England in 1886, Russell translated Guimps's study of Pestalozzi, which, Sir Michael Sadler later claimed, revived the study of Pestalozzi's writings in England. Unwittingly Russell was thus to play an indirect part in founding KASS, whose original statement of aims in 1897 included that of establishing schools 'to give practical expression to the best theories of education extant, and particularly to the theories enunciated by educational reformers, such as Pestalozzi'.

Russell returned from France in 1886 to take up the post of assistant master in what was one of the forerunners of the independent progressive schools, University College School, founded in 1833 as a feeder school for that 'godless institution in Gower Street',[12] University College. Later he became warden of the only settlement in London, the Passmore Edwards settlement, which 'expressly eschewed religion'.[13] Clearly his early religious beliefs had given way under French influence to a secular view of the world. His fifteen years at UCS reinforced this outlook and were a preparation for his headship at KAS in several ways. Above all, it accustomed him to working within a set of constitutional arrangements which resembled those of KASS, where the headmaster and staff were responsible to the school's subscribers and council. He was thus more experienced than was Rice in the arts of diplomacy. But the constitutional preparation was only one reason for Russell's success at KAS. His familiarity at the level of a practitioner for a decade and a half with the enlightened educational ideas of UCS was another. When he moved to KAS in 1901 he had had a long experience of teaching in an institution from which corporal punishment was absent, in which the sciences and modern languages played a major part and in which pupils had a wide degree of choice. The undue haste which characterized schools which prepared their pupils for university entrance was absent from UCS, which still reflected the rationalism of its spiritual founder, Jeremy Bentham.

However, there was nothing inevitable about Russell's move from UCS to a weakened school which was still suffering from the reverberations of Rice's departure along with most of the staff and half of the pupils. KAS in 1901 was by no means a powerful magnet. Why then did he accept the invitation to take up the headship? Part of the answer is to be found at UCS which was also going through a troubled period in its history. By 1900, it was a good school in the wrong part of London. Its numbers had fallen from 512 in 1886 to 313 in 1899; it had an ageing staff among whom teaching duties were generally reshuffled when any-one left. Situated in Gower Street in central London it was far removed from the prin-cipal areas of expanding residential popula-tion, such as Hampstead. The acrimonious debates preceding its move to Hampstead, six years after Russell arrived at KAS, are likely to have played a part in his acceptance of the headship. There were also ideological and personal reasons for his move. Since returning from France he had continued to be one of the principal propagandists for Pestalozzian ideas which were given in-creased publicity in 1896 by the celebration of the 150th anniversary of the reformer's

8. A school magazine title page designed by one of the boys, Charles C. Voysey

birth. In addition, his work as examiner for the National Froebel Union gave him greater opportunity to study child-centred learning in prac-tice. KAS, which was coeducational and strongly opposed to an examination-dominated curriculum, gave greater scope than did UCS for developing a working educational model based on the ideas of the principal reformers. It also had another dimension which was less pronounced at UCS. KAS was not simply a school; it was part of a radical movement which aimed to disseminate through public discus-sion an alternative educational ideology to that which, through restrict-ive codes and effete custom, was fastening itself on the emerging state secondary schools. When A. S. Neill referred to Russell as a 'pioneer' it was because he did not wait for the world to come to his school door. As an active reformer he used to the full the publicity machinery of KASS and other bodies to reach out to the doubters and disbelievers. His was not a cloistered life at KAS preaching to the converted.

Russell's radicalism is also seen in his work as warden of the only non-religious settlement in London, the Passmore Edwards settlement. It claimed to pursue 'different methods and different lines of policy' from the other settlements in London and elsewhere, most of which owed a direct debt to Christian socialism in general and the Anglican Church in particular. However, it functioned in much the same way, encouraging young Oxbridge graduates to live among the poor and to assist in the amelioration of their plight. As a consequence its original council was packed with the great and good from the older universities. Russell took a major part in visiting Oxford and Cambridge to publicize the work of the settlement, and in organizing classes for young people in reading, writing, the manual crafts and drill, but especially in opening up 'the treasure houses of Art, Music, Drama and Literature'. He helped to provide university extension lectures for adults, and entertained its council and former helpers at his country cottage in Woking. He thus carried with him to his headship in Hampstead the belief that schools should not isolate themselves from the social problems and concerns of the age, but should ensure through guided discussion that pupils were made aware of the principal social and political movements and ideas. However, the settlement of which he was the second warden was less successful than many others in attracting residents, and in its educational programme. In his autobiography this comparative lack of success was attributed by Francis Galton to Russell's poor managerial skills.[14]

To Russell, halfway through his career, the idea of a fresh challenge at KAS was attractive, especially as a base in Hampstead would enable him to broaden the circle of people with whom he could discuss his reformist ideas including eugenics and moral education. In this he was not to be disappointed, for he became friend and confidant of people such as George Bernard Shaw and Labour's first prime minister, Ramsay MacDonald. KASS provided him with a platform for publicizing his views whilst KAS offered him the opportunity for turning what was an 'experimental' school into a 'demonstration' school for showing to a wide range of visitors how rationalist educational principles could work in practice.

KAS: years of growth and challenge, 1901–1920

In September 1901, at the beginning of Russell's first year at KAS there were thirty-one pupils on the school roll. When he retired in 1920 the school population was ninety-one. Neither Russell nor the society were entirely satisfied with this level of growth or its nature. Pupil numbers would often increase and then fall back considerably. Such lack of sustained growth made planning difficult but much more of a problem was the fact that growth was not evenly spread across the age ranges or the sexes. Throughout Russell's headship KAS had very few students of sixteen and over. This perennial problem can best be illustrated from statistics in the report of the Board of Education's inspection of the school in 1913 (see Table 2).

Table 2 **Age distribution, 1913**

	<9	9	10	11	12	13	14	15	16	<17
Boys	13	9	7	8	4	–	2	–	–	43
Girls	6	5	6	9	4	4	4	2	2	42
Total	19	14	13	17	8	4	6	2	2	85

Russell explained the reason for this imbalance and its principal effects in his report to council in 1908. It lay in the school's 'failure to convince parents that we are something more than a preparatory school. Plenty of children come to us but too many of them leave too soon, chiefly because our breach with tradition is most conspicuous in the teens.' The disparity between the KAS curriculum for sixteen to eighteen year olds and that of most other secondary schools became more marked after University College School arrived in Hampstead in 1907. Its headmaster, H. J. Spenser (1903–16), deliberately cultivated a more conventional image for UCS, preparing his pupils for an increasing range of public examinations, but especially for

9. Practising the high jump, 1903

university matriculation. Several former KAS pupils recalled leaving KAS in the prewar years for UCS or for one of the nation's prestigious boarding schools. The King Alfred School was operating in an increasingly competitive market, in which the demand to prepare young people for examinations played an important part. To satisfy such a demand caused a greater dilemma for KAS than for any other school.

The society could not turn its back indefinitely upon growing parental demand for examination preparation but it was concerned that such preparation entailed overpressure, overhaste, homework, punitive marks and competitive gradings, a narrow, subject-based curriculum, the downgrading of practical work in favour of abstract theory, rote learning and formal teaching techniques, against all of which KASS had deliberately turned its face. For the first time in their history the society

10. Russell as Alfred in a
school production at
London University,
1912

and school had to respond positively to a challenge to basic principles. Not to make some examination provision would have profound financial and ideological implications. Parents might well prefer to send their children to one of the other growing number of secondary schools in the area rather than face the problems of transfer and curricular mismatch at the age of fourteen or sixteen, thus imperilling the school's financial future. Of equal importance to the society was the threat to its overarching principle of coeducation. KAS was set up primarily to demonstrate the advantages of day-school coeducation in an age dominated by single-sex boarding schools. The case for mixed preparatory schools was, in its view, largely won; the great challenge was to show the importance of coeducation to the healthy development of adolescents. The school's lack of older pupils, and especially boys, seriously weakened its argument. The Board of Education's inspectors in 1913 recognized this when they pointed out 'there is some danger lest it may become a girls' school to which a few boys are admitted'. Parents might well send their daughters to KAS for a progressive education and their sons to UCS or elsewhere for an examination-based education, thus undermining the coeducational principle by fixing in people's minds the idea that KAS was essentially a girls' school. As one former pupil commented: 'The school was not regarded as academic enough for boys.' Sooner or later the nettle of examinations would have to be grasped.

Russell was the first person to grasp it. He recognized that KASS would have to make concessions on at least two of its principles, its opposition to examinations and to homework, in order to preserve and extend another, that of coeducation. He thus pressed for some modifications in council's position in order to enable him to teach older pupils for examinations as part of the regular curriculum. He was assisted by the fact that the society had never been dogmatic on the examinations issue. The school's first prospectus (1898) stated that pupils 'on leaving KAS will be prepared to pass any Public School, University or Technical entrance Examination'. This was a recognition of the importance of examination to adolescents but as the school was to cater for only eight to twelve year olds in its first three years (according to the preliminary circular of July 1897) it did not have to face the issue of examination provision for older pupils. The controversy with Rice brought consideration of examinations a stage nearer for it focused upon the crucial matter of teaching older pupils as part of the student body in the Ellerdale Road building.

11. Russell and the school at Ellerdale Road, 1909

With its colours fixed firmly to the mast of an all-age school, KASS could not delay indefinitely on the key issue of the place, if any, of examinations in the curriculum of older pupils. When Russell spoke to council of the dangers of failing to convince parents that KAS was more than a preparatory school he was hitting a raw nerve.

By the end of his first year, Russell had persuaded council to modify its position so that he could prepare pupils over twelve for the common entrance examination and those over fifteen for matriculation, scholarships or 'other money prizes', but this was to be undertaken 'apart from the regular curriculum'. Russell was able to convince council of the need to make some provision for examinations because he was ideologically sound on the issue while at the same time having had fifteen years' experience at UCS of preparing students for matriculation. It was hoped that this concession, together with the introduction of football for boys and transport to the more distant parts of London, including Bayswater, would help a balanced recruitment. However, it was not a good advertisement for the school when the first pupil to sit the matriculation failed in mathematics and English. Russell reported that the failure convinced him that it was fair 'neither to the pupil nor to the staff nor to the rest of the seniors to carry on preparation side by side with the regular work as we have been doing'. In order not to 'seriously damage the school', Russell had persuaded the parents of Marjory Basden to allow her to remain at KAS for extra coaching.

There was thus pressure on council to make preparation for the matriculation a normal part of the school curriculum, especially after UCS moved to Hampstead. In March 1908, the school committee passed a resolution asking council to approve regulations under which children were prepared for examinations as a regular part of the curriculum. The headmaster's report for the following year showed that this resolution had been accepted by council and that from 1909 the senior class would 'be definitely working for this examination'. Preparation for senior Oxford papers defined much of the syllabus for older pupils in the following year with an increasing emphasis upon homework. The success rate in the matriculation was not always high. As one former student commented, 'I am a little dubious as to whether I would have got my matriculation on KAS teaching.'

Russell's use lower down the school of the papers set by the Cambridge Examining Board met with much stiffer opposition, especially from Mrs White Wallis, who feared that this could lead to cramming, rote learning and a range of undesirable practices. In 1904, Russell reported to council that he had used the preliminary papers of the 'Cambridge Locals' as an external yardstick by which to measure the progress of KAS pupils. The pupils had not been told 'of the purpose of the test or the origin of the papers'. Council recognized the possible undermining of many of the society's principles and issued a

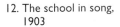

12. The school in song, 1903

13. An early school song

by-law stating that where the headmaster found it necessary to use such papers, it should be undertaken in such a way as 'to avoid impressing upon the children's minds the consideration of marks and places in connection with these examinations'. In the view of Mrs White Wallis this did not go far enough. She saw the use of such tests as indicative of yet another move away from the Findlay curriculum to one which was much more formal and subject-based. She thus led the council's education subcommittee programme of syllabus revision. By the end of 1907 she was fully engaged in restoring 'coordinated studies', having helped revise the syllabuses in geography, mathematics and the sciences.

14. Children of the founders in a hockey team: a page from a school magazine

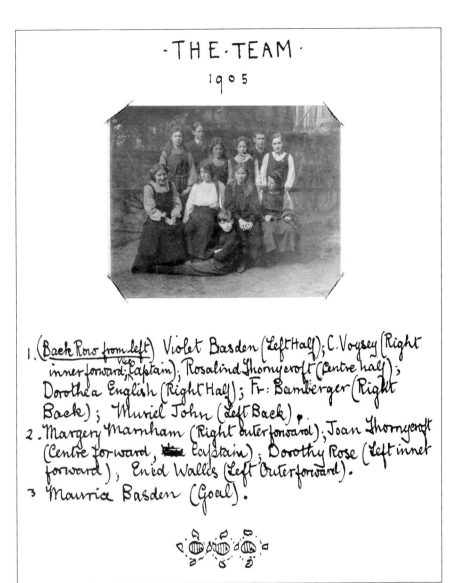

· T H E · T E A M ·

1 9 0 5

1. (Back Row from left) Violet Basden (Left Half); C. Voysey (Right inner forward, Vice Captain); Rosalind Thornycroft (Centre half); Dorothea English (Right Half); Fr. Bamberger (Right Back); Muriel John (Left Back).
2. Margery Marnham (Right Outer forward); Joan Thornycroft (Centre forward, Captain); Dorothy Rose (Left inner forward), Enid Wallis (Left Outer forward).
3 Maurice Basden (Goal).

History and Latin were on the agenda for early 1908. However, her revisionism never fed through to the school curriculum. Although its content was changed during the Russell era, its essential framework of separate subjects remained intact. There were of course concerted efforts to interrelate subjects and to maximize common areas of overlap, such as the teaching of mathematics in science and geography lessons, and the study of literature as part of history, but the definition of the curriculum in terms of distinct lessons and subjects remained a constant feature of the Russell years. The senior timetables for 1913 and 1914 (Tables 3 and 4) illustrate the formality of its framework. However, as

15. Nature study, 1914

16. Coeducational workshop activities, 1914; L to R Florence Fuerst, Alan Rapson, Alan Maberly, Bernard Alfieri

Professor Edgar had pointed out in an inspection five years earlier, much of the originality of a KAS education lay in the way in which the curriculum was delivered rather than in its formal framework.

> About all these subjects as well as about the contents and form of literature, the rules of arithmetic or the facts of science the pupils are encouraged and expected to think; they are not only questioned but they ask questions; not only the *what* but the *how* and the *why* of things are gradually revealed, and the acquirement of knowledge is attended by the development of intellectual interest, and mental power.

In an age when state secondary schools were becoming increasingly conventional and traditional under the Board of Education's code of 1904 KAS had to make some concessions on the curriculum (as it had done on dress with the introduction of a school uniform in 1907) if it were to attract and retain pupils.

Table 3 **Senior morning timetable, autumn term 1913**

		Monday	Tuesday	Wednesday	Thursday	Friday
9.30–10.30						
	A	French	Geo.	French	Geo.	French
	B	Maths.	Maths.	Maths.	Maths.	Maths.
	C1	English	French	Geo.	French	Geo.
10.15–10.55						
	A	Maths.	Maths.	Maths.	Maths.	Maths.
	B	English	Latin	Latin	Latin	Latin
			Drawing	French	French	French
	C1	French	Botany	French	Botany	French
11.10–11.50						
	A	English	Latin	Latin	Latin	Latin
		German	German	German	German	
	B	History	History	English	History	English
		Writing				
	C1	Lab.	Drawing	Maths.	Maths.	Maths.
12.00–12.40						
	A	Singing	History	English	History	English
	B	Singing	Geo.	Lab.	Geo.	French
				Writing		
	C1	Singing	Maths.	History	Drawing	History

The fact that the Board of Education was able to undertake an inspection of the school in 1913 indicates the extent to which the school's curricular framework was conventional. However, the inspectors' report reveals just how far apart were KAS ideals and approaches to teaching,

Table 4 **Afternoon timetable, winter term 1914**

		Monday	Tuesday	Wednesday	Thursday	Friday
2–3p.m.						
	A–1	English	History	History	Lab.	
	A–2	English	History	Lab.	History	Workshop
	B–1	Workshop	Lab.	History	English	⎰ Latin and
	B–2	Lab.	Workshop	History	English	⎱ Singing
	C–1a	History	Arith.	Lab. Wr.	Workshop	⎰ English and
	C–1b	History	Arith.	Lab. Wr.	Lab.	⎱ Singing
	C–2a	Geo.	Geo.	Botany	Gymn.	⎰ English
	C–2b	Geo.	Geo.	Botany	Gymn.	⎱ and Singing
	D	Handwork	Handwork	Handwork	Gymn.	⎰ Handwork and
	E–F	Handwork	Handwork	Handwork	Gymn.	⎱ Singing
3–4p.m.						
	Seniors	Extras and Drill	Extras and Drill	Hockey (Heath)	Gymn.	Hockey (Heath)
	Juniors	Drill and Playground	Drill and Playground	Hockey (Field) Playground	Gymn.	Hockey (Field) Playground

and those of the inspectors who were used only to carrying out strict inspections under the restrictive and conventional code of 1904. The society could not expect the same sympathetic understanding which Professor Edgar of St Andrews had given in 1908, yet KAS required the recognition and the grant which a successful inspection by the Board could provide if it were to meet the increasing financial demands of an expanding school population. The acquisition of 22 Ellerdale Road when

17. J.R., 'The Pied Piper'

the lease fell vacant in 1906 had met the immediate needs of the school's pupils but the inspectors emphasized the inadequacies of the two heavily mortgaged houses when there were eighty-five pupils on the register seven years later. The following brief extract from their report gives an indication of both the physical arrangement of the two houses and the general tenor of their criticisms.

> The School is conducted in two adjacent houses which were built for private occupation. For a school of this size and importance the premises and buildings are unduly restricted. The available rooms provide seven class-rooms, each of which can accommodate about l5; of these two are connected and are used for assembly and other occasions when the whole school is collected. There is a laboratory at the top of one of the houses which may be considered adequate for the science work which is now attempted, a room for clay modelling and a workshop. The latter is very small, is much overfilled with furniture, and in consequence each class has to be divided for carpentry into two or more sets, an arrangement which causes serious waste of the teacher's time. A small room is furnished as a library. A large room in the basement is used for dinner, to which the majority of the pupils stay, and in wet weather for physical exercises and recreation. The Head Master has a small room for his use, and another room is reserved for the secretary, and is the office of the society.
>
> Though the class room is just sufficient, the total cubic area of the building, passages, etc. is too small for the comfortable accommodation of so many pupils and teachers, and the arrangement of the buildings is very inconvenient; there can be no doubt that this adds greatly to the nervous strain which falls on the staff, and particularly on the Head Master.
>
> The provision for the comfort of the assistant staff is seriously defective. It is suggested that the room now set apart as a library might with advantage also be used by the Mistresses, who now have as best they can to use the carpenters' shop when it is not occupied by a class.
>
> The sanitary accommodation is very small, and for the boys is not good; there is no provision for the Masters apart from the boys.
>
> The only playground is formed from the two small gardens at the back of the two houses. It is too small to provide for so many pupils varying so widely in age. A suitable playing field at some distance is rented.[15]

The inspection team of seven, including J. W. Headlam, argued that the school's physical and curricular arrangements were in part responsible for the failure to attract and retain older pupils, though Russell defended both. In particular, Russell's reduction of lesson time to half an hour, introduced in 1904, brought the comment from the inspectors that this was far too short a time for 'real learning' or 'real work' to take place. Though Russell increased lesson time in response, the inspectors' remarks revealed the great gulf between their views on education and those of KASS. The visiting HMIs believed in more passive forms of learning and saw education largely in terms of the acquisition of knowledge. They thus saw the frequent questions asked by

18. The school at Ellerdale Road, 1912

KAS pupils more as interruptions and threats to good classroom discipline than as an essential part of the learning process. As the half-hour lessons which they saw were often, in their view, disrupted by the constant process of questioning they concluded that they were too short, whereas Russell saw questioning as making heavy demands on pupils which should be counteracted by shorter than usual lessons. By 1933, official thinking had caught up with KAS ideals when the Board's consultative committee declared that 'the curriculum is to be thought of in terms of activity and experience rather than of knowledge to be acquired and facts to be stored', but in 1913 the chasm in education philosophy was probably unbridgeable. As a result the staff, consisting of Russell, two assistant masters and three assistant mistresses, were unlikely to receive as glowing a report as that given by Professor Edgar, the sole but sympathetic assessor in 1908.

The staff of KAS had slowly expanded to meet the needs of a growing school. In 1901 Blanche Schooley was appointed to share with Miss Frood, the only survivor from the Rice era, the teaching of the thirty-one pupils, twenty-six having left to attend either Rice's school or some other. The following year, George Earle joined the staff to teach English, woodwork and other subjects, and was to provide much of the stability of the school over nearly two decades. This small, bearded schoolmaster in whiskery tweed, taught English, with an infectious enthusiasm he gained from his father, a Somerset rector, and also woodwork, a craft which he learned from a local carpenter. His teaching at KAS was a success but his first youthful marriage was a failure. He developed a passion for poetry and also, at the age of forty-nine, for Eleanor Farjeon whose home in Church Walks, Hampstead, he shared from 1921. The three full-time teachers were assisted by the part-timers, Ida Varley who taught art, and L. C. Venables who had replaced Sharp as music teacher. In 1907, with fifty-six pupils on the school roll, there was a staff of five, Russell, Frood, Earle, Amy Cryan (maths and science) and Dorothy Willis, Blanche Schooley having left two years earlier. Earle and Miss Frood were given salary increases of £15 and £10 respectively, reflecting their seniority and also the limits of the society's egalitarian ideology.

There were several changes in staff by 1913, one of which followed a disagreement between Russell and the school committee, who wished at the end of 1907 to dismiss Jones, the recently appointed music teacher, on the grounds of the inappropriateness of his 'methods, discipline and personal influence'. Russell persuaded the committee to reconsider but Jones resigned, giving the school the opportunity to appoint a teacher for drawing and singing. Those who faced the rigorous inspection in 1913 were Russell, Earle, Powell, Miss East, Miss Harwood and Miss Poyser. Russell's exceptional teaching abilities were noted by the inspectors and have been fully confirmed in interviews with his former pupils. He had a marked gift for inspiring pupils in English lessons, especially in fostering

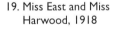

19. Miss East and Miss Harwood, 1918

a love of poetry; his French teaching was also of a high quality, but the inspectors, less familiar than Russell with the direct method of teaching the subject, argued for 'more systematic practice in the reproduction of the French sounds and their combinations'. His teaching of German did not receive a similar criticism. It was Powell's teaching of Latin which drew the heaviest censure, but again the inspectors' lack of sympathy with the less conventional, direct methods of teaching seemed to be at the heart of much of the criticism. As in the case of Russell's teaching of French, the chief criticism was lack of concern with the basics, 'the diligence and accuracy' which should accompany all methods of learning. Earle's teaching of English received mixed reviews from the inspectors. They recognized the taste for reading which he encouraged and emphasized how he and Russell were able to arouse interest in the great questions of the day in informed essay work, but again they pointed to problems with the basics, especially in language and essay construction. One former pupil nearly seventy years later was able vividly to recreate Earle's inspirational English lessons as testimony to his exceptional ability. Even the inspectors could not deny Earle's 'unusually varied and interesting' handwork lessons involving weaving on handlooms and basket work as well as the more usual wood and metal constructions.

The inspection of maths teaching brought to the fore key areas of difference in outlook. The inspectors believed that the opposition of KAS to homework for pupils lower down the school meant that much school time was used unnecessarily in doing 'examples in arithmetic and algebra or exercises in geometry' which could have been done at home. The inspectors favoured the formal teaching of theorems but saw some merits in practical approaches, providing that they were more rigorously linked with theory. Miss East, in reply, expressed her willingness to revise her syllabus to accommodate this criticism. Described by a former pupil as 'grotesque to look at but a delightful teacher', she taught very much in accord with the principles of the society, informing her science lessons with trigonometry and numerical work derived from mathematics lessons. Her companion, Miss Harwood, who was said by a former pupil to be both beautiful and charming, was taken to task by the inspectors on the fundamental point of having no clear views on how to teach reading. Her reply made the reasonable point that, as children came to her from several different schools each of which appeared to teach reading differently, she found it difficult to adopt one single method, which in essence was almost a plea for a national reading curriculum. Her problems were compounded by a relatively large class of twenty very mixed-ability pupils. The history lessons of Miss Poyser made a better impression on the inspectors than on some of her former pupils. Her use of written tests, which impressed the inspectors, may have led to a greater emphasis on the memorization of facts than some of her pupils liked. However, her imaginative use of illustrations received the full approval of the inspecting team.

The matter of religious instruction was not raised by the Board's inspectors but it was hotly debated a few months later at the November annual general meeting of the society. A resolution asserting that 'in the opinion of this meeting the practical application of the second section of paragraph VI of the Memorandum of Association makes it impossible to give religious instruction (as generally understood) in the society's schools' was supported by Mr White Wallis, Mr Jacoby, Mr Brown, Mr Spiller and Mr Davis and was opposed by Mr and Mrs Andrews, Mr Hall and Aneurin Williams. It was carried by twenty-six votes to eleven thus confirming the broad tolerance in religious matters. A subsequent resolution moved by Maberly, one of the society's founders, allowing schools affiliated to (but not financed by) the society to give religious instruction provided that their prospectuses stated the society's position, was lost by the narrower margin of fifteen to eighteen. The maintenance of a strict non-sectarian outlook was thus thankfully maintained as part of a broader freedom of expression. Children from a variety of different backgrounds could mix freely without prejudices creating divisions. It was possible, for example, for pupils from Jewish and Greek Orthodox backgrounds to be taught in an enlightened atmosphere alongside those who professed no religion at all, including the three daughters of the first Soviet ambassador to Britain after the Russian Revolution, Krassin. Such integration extended beyond the Ellerdale Road building, and later Manor Wood, when for example the school friends of the Krassin sisters were entertained in the sumptuous surroundings of the Soviet Embassy. The general atmosphere of freedom also gave full scope for peculiar talent to thrive, such as that of the greatly gifted pianist Solomon, born Solomon Cutner in 1902, who had given school recitals before his first public appearance in 1910 at Queen's Hall.[16]

Behind much of the criticism made by the inspectors in 1913 was an inability to understand fully the importance of the large measure of freedom in the KAS learning process, and especially the reason why the school deliberately rejected the traditional secondary school model. The Board's officials spoke of 'efficiency of instruction', keeping children 'well in hand' and of subject hierarchies, especially the importance of Latin. They were not fully convinced of the value of coeducation and spoke in a chauvinistic manner of the need to recruit more older boys to give the school 'a larger and more bracing atmosphere'. Much of this was in marked contrast to Russell's views. He believed in non-mechanistic learning, the downgrading of Latin in favour of studying modern languages and in a school which had as its 'chief glory' a 'family spirit', whose spiritual economy aimed at 'the education of the child's spirit in its human relations'. Yet Russell set greater limits to a pupil's freedom than either A. S. Neill, who served on his staff from 1918 to 1920 and resigned over what he considered to be the severe limits Russell imposed on self-government, or Joseph Wicksteed, his successor.

One of Russell's greatest achievements in the extension of pupil freedom is said to have been the creation of a school parliament or children's council in 1904. However, Russell's parliament was not a body which shared in the making of school policy. It had no major legislative function for it could not usurp the powers of council. In essence, it was as he described it in his annual report, a system in which pupils 'elected as representatives of their own forms, themselves in turn elected prefects or Cabinet Ministers'. The prefects carried out the traditional function, which he defined as 'to help in maintaining reasonable order'. The system was to encourage pupils to understand that 'no school rule was arbitrary and without reason' and to enable them 'to help govern themselves'. The making of the rules by which the community was governed was not placed in the hands of the pupils. When A. S. Neill constantly asked for 'self-government' he had in mind a parliament in the stricter sense of a body which made laws, not one which was part of the judiciary. It was perhaps because it was so akin to the traditional prefect system, except in its system of election, that few ex-pupils remember it and why, perhaps, parents were willing to send their children to KAS in increasing numbers. What were regarded as major disciplinary matters were dealt with by Russell, who sometimes sought the advice of council. Such an occasion occurred in 1904 when five pupils applied the school principles of observation and experimentation to sexual matters. To Russell this meant investigating a 'rude game' of 'unseemly exposure'. He introduced greater supervision of all pupils, considered suspending the pupils involved but settled eventually for 'a solemn warning'. Even lesser offences did not escape punishment, although this was sometimes undertaken after a meeting of the whole school. Defacing labels or filling inkpots with blotting paper or chalk resulted in a day's ban from hockey. The interrogation during the school debate was often a worse punishment than the exclusion from games. Russell acted firmly in the case of disorder in the school corridors or library, threatening pupils that 'if you can't maintain reasonable order, the staff will have to control corridors and march all to and from classrooms'. He was far from being a libertarian. Even A. S. Neill who argued in favour of greater pupil power was not averse to applying subtle pressure on his classes to encourage them to arrive at the punishment he preferred, which included in the case of one pupil encouraging the class 'to send her to Coventry'.

The success of KAS under Russell can be explained largely by the way in which he maintained the school's progressive spirit while at the same time introducing several formal arrangements in the curriculum, in school dress and in discipline. The pupils' area of freedom was carefully and largely unobtrusively circumscribed to encourage a feeling of security while enabling pupils to develop their individual talents. Russell's was not a concept of rugged individualism where the few could thrive at the expense of the many. He saw KAS as a caring society where co-operation rather than domination and competition prevailed.

Russell's rationalist curricular theory

Much of the school's rationalist theory and practice stemmed from its being the first of its kind, a coeducational, day school. Russell saw his school as a deliberate challenge to the 'cuckooism' of boarding schools, where parents deposited their offspring in the nests of others. Above all, however, the day school principle was seen as a means of extending the family atmosphere into the school, something which Pestalozzi had attempted under more difficult conditions in his school for destitute orphans at Stans over a century earlier. This deliberate policy was the subject of much discussion with parents. Russell looked upon his school as his family, having no children of his own. Of necessity this implied coeducation. He went further than did his predecessor, Rice,[17] in considering the implications of coeducation. As the basic aim of his school was to assist child development, his curricular theory revolved around the needs of children of both sexes and those of the 'intermediate sex'. These needs included sex education in its various forms.

Russell's rationalism ran counter to much Victorian and post-Victorian tradition and started from the basic and often ignored premiss that 'sex everywhere plays so large a part, and often so devastating a part, in all undesigned education is to me reason enough for holding that it should also play a part in all designed education'. The tragedy of sex in the Victorian period, he argued, was the tragedy of a poor education. His mission was to redeem sex through education, to free it from Victorian double standards and to educate for 'vision and joy in sex, as we educate for vision and joy in nature and art'. But his was no libertarians' charter. He argued that sex education should begin at home, where nakedness and the exercise of bodily functions should not be seen as something shameful, secretive or a matter for constant jocularity. Hence before children could be educated the educators must educate themselves and be ready to satisfy the child's spontaneous desire for knowledge about sexual matters as about other things but nevertheless it should be undertaken 'with pedagogic tact' and avoiding 'imposed commandments'. It was, for Russell, a matter of taking appropriate opportunities for frank discussion, for 'well-timed education in sex', rather than having lessons on the subject, for utilizing to the full the advantages of mixed classes to create an informed atmosphere of understanding, away from what he termed the 'male blackguardism' or chauvinism of single-sex schools. To say nothing about sex was the 'risk of silence', which to the humanist Russell was to gamble with the happiness of children and to threaten what he believed was one of the main aims of school life, 'the establishment of beautiful and honourable relations between the sexes'.

In practice, this meant speaking frankly and honestly, of implanting opportunities for discussion in lessons in literature and history, and taking the opportunity in private discussion to consider such matters. What he wanted to do was to sweep away 'the badge of our tribe', the badge of pretence, and discuss sexual matters openly but sensitively. Such discussion should extend, in his view, to 'the intermediate sex', those people 'born as it were on the dividing line between the sexes, so that, while belonging to one sex as far as their bodies are concerned, they may be said to belong mentally and emotionally to the other'. Russell expressed his views on the subject in a review in the *Journal of Education* of *The Intermediate Sex: A Study of Some Transitional Types of Men and Women*, written by Edward Carpenter, a former theologian like Russell, and one of the founders of Abbotsholme. Russell accepted Carpenter's view that society had a duty not only to understand such people but to help them to understand themselves. He went further, to point out that, whereas in single-sex schools friendships with the intermediate sex were 'stifled in an atmosphere which can only be described as that of the gutter', coeducational schools offered more natural opportunities for discussion of sexual variety. It could be seen as part of the growing child's natural curiosity about sex, something which Russell believed the government's Moral Education Inquiry could take on board. Generally speaking, however, he favoured private discussion with pupils, except in regard to subjects such as 'the great scourge of syphilis', but he recognized that as sex education was still in its infancy there was room for a variety of empirical approaches. What he believed all should be working towards was 'a new religion of sex, which worships love too sincerely to degrade it'.

Russell turned to the subject of when sex education should begin and the ways in which it should be presented to the child in a lecture on 'The Eugenic Appeal in Moral Education' to the second International Moral Education Conference in the Hague in 1912. He argued that the 'idea of physical parenthood' should be discussed with young children at the 'first psychological moment' when it would be intelligible to them, and should gradually take on a more definite form as they grew older in order to arm them against 'the pruriency and sex-blasphemy' which was found among Edwardian adults. If a child's religion was not left to the 'ribald scoffer', why then should 'this other holy thing'? Yet Russell was no believer in free love. He was against the 'precocious use of the sex-organs, and sex-dreaming' and believed that the progress of the human race was dependent upon 'a duty to mate eugenically, and sometimes a duty not to mate at all' if this endangered its quality. 'Only a fool would seek grapes on a thorn-bush, but many of us in our spring-time sow our wild seed, and afterwards blame everything but ourselves for the worthless crop.' On the subject of how a child should be made aware of 'the dangers of indiscriminate breeding', he argued that the school should follow the practice of the good home and deal with the matter as a 'private appeal based on frank information'.

Russell's approach to sex education, as a matter more for private discussion rather than for class lessons, has meant that there is little surviving evidence of how (or indeed whether) he tackled the matter. It would appear from the evidence of interviews with his former pupils and from a few surviving documents that his approach was to create opportunities in 'quiet talks' for pupils to raise the matter if they wished. An example of such open-ended yet private discussion is given below, although, in this case, the conversation was more concerned with general preferences.[18]

J.R.	Do y. mind being in a 'mixed' sch?
William	Yes.
J.R.	Don't y. like it?
William	No, I don't like it.
J.R.	Did y. dislike it at first?
William	Not as much.
J.R.	Has anyb. been making y. dislike it?
William	No.
J.R.	If we got rid of all the girls tomorrow wd y. like to stay?
William	No, it wd. be too small.
J.R.	If we turned all the girls into boys?
William	Yes.

J.R.	Do y. want to go to U.C.S?
William	Not especially.
J.R.	What can I do to help you?
William	Leave me to myself.
J.R.	Have you really minded this quiet talk?
William	Not when it's over.

Russell was concerned with the social integration of the sexes, particularly among the older pupils. He believed that coeducation worked well, with the younger pupils, 'the little people who seem to play touch, prisoners' base, kings etc. quite happily and freely together, boys and girls alike'. It was rather more problematic with the older pupils where the boys were outnumbered in the proportion of 7 to 3, with a consequence that the 'elder girls tended to form cliques'. The pre-ponderance of girls in the upper school was always seen as a threat to coeducation. Russell and the society were anxious lest the school be labelled a girls' school, thus causing boys to leave early or not to attend the school at all. The balance of the sexes among the older pupils was to be a problem long after Russell retired.

Though Russell believed that sex education in its strictest sense was largely a matter for private discussion, he was very willing to deal publicly with the broader aspects of the relationship between the sexes. In particular he was willing to argue the case for political equality. 'Co-education', in his view, 'should not be looked on as a single reform but as part of a larger reform – the assertion of equal rights for men and women.' It was something which was practised in the King Alfred School and which he believed should be extended to national life. He saw the relationship between the sexes in his Hampstead school as a 'sex symphony' and wondered why such relationships were so discordant politically at a national level. Why, in particular, 'the mass of women have not felt their disabilities more acutely, have not risen long ago in open rebellion?' His instinctive rationalist response was to blame it upon religion which has 'drugged women with tradition', and upon those who argued that 'woman is too pure, too precious, for politics', which was often a way of disguising a 'cave-dweller' mentality. His basic argument was that if women were so pure then politics would benefit all the more from their intervention, that they 'will certainly upon the whole, make a braver and better fight than men'.

However, the equal political relationships which were so easily achieved at the KAS were not so easily accomplished in national life. Several of its prominent founders were women with formidable political skills, especially Mrs White Wallis who led the council minority which ousted Rice in 1901. Its progressive ethos and above all the preponderance of girls in the upper classes meant that females played a major role in the political life of the school. Russell's problem was in fact the reverse of that in national political life, to ensure that males were not politically disadvantaged. This can be seen from the following extract from the school records in 1903.

> In electn. of *Sch.Officers*, to counteract preponderance of Girls, J.R. has stipulated before voting began, that 1 officer shd. be a Girl & 1 a Boy, thus
>
> | (Sch.Captn. | = Girl. | (Hockey Capt | = Girl |
> |---|---|---|---|
> | (Sch. Vic. C. | = Boy | (Vice   " | = Boy |
> | (Librarian | = Girl | | |
> | (Vice " | = Boy | | |
>
> Proportion between the Sexes also regulated in election of MPs.

The Members of Parliament to which the document also referred were members of the school parliament, a body which Russell instituted during the third year of his headship, 'a ministry of both boys and girls without undue regard to school rank'. A. S. Neill saw things differently. To him, the KAS parliament was not an instrument to achieve equality, but one of repression.[19] No matter how progressive the school was in its treatment of the sexes, he believed that 'the bosses of such schools are naturally selected by the Establishment because they carry on the tradition of suppression. Was in a similar position in 1919 in King Alfred School.' Neill looked upon such things as the 'declaration of allegiance', which was signed by boys and girls elected to the parliament as an instrument of repression in that it insisted that each signatory declare, 'I promise as a school officer to do my best to respect the school regulations myself, and to help others to do the same.' Though by Neill's standard there were few true democrats, Russell's progressivism had strong democratic impulses, which included encouraging pupils to discuss and debate the suffragette cause, and perhaps most scurrilous of all in the view of the Edwardian educational establishment, to read to them his poems about the suffrage movement. Many of the latter were also put to music, including 'The March of the Women' and 'A Song of Captivity', and were usually about particular protest meetings which were covered in the newspaper, thus making their message more poignant for his pupils.

The King Alfred School Society saw Russell's school as providing a progressive model not only for the other schools it intended to found but also for the state secondary schools that emerged after 1902. However, they were on divergent paths, despite the association with the Hampstead venture of eminent educationists such as A. J. Mundella and Sir Michael Sadler who played a prominent part in the development of state education. The rigidly prescriptive secondary school code of 1904 and the ever-increasing pressure of examinations, which resulted in the setting up of the Secondary Schools Examinations Council in 1917, reduced any chances of cross-fertilization. Russell was a faithful propagandist of the society in that in his public declarations he stood firmly against examinations. In an address to the Conference of Educational Associations in 1916 he warned against overhaste in education and urged that school curricula should be based 'not upon the requirements of examining bodies but upon the teachings and warnings of educational science'. He was not, for example, as strong a devotee of correct spelling as were examination boards. It was only with reluctance that Russell taught spelling. In a classroom debate in 1903 over 'gradually and wisely introducing phonetic spelling in England', he commented,

> Men and women would be much wiser and happier if they hadn't to learn spelling. They could do better things; spelling doesn't exercise your brain half as well as many other things; it exercises your memory and certainly *hurts one's reason*; the great *duffer* can spell but a man genius might not be able to – I know one who can't.

His view of phonetic spelling to protect pronunciation reflected the mental set of the Hampstead radical.

> Sylvia: There will always be cockneys who pronounce badly & then there would be a worse muddle than ever.
> John Russell: Yes, always cockneys, though what produced them one does not know, climate perhaps & weak physique.

At the heart of Russell's educational thinking was the experimental method. He recognized that such an approach was time-consuming, 'to do things and to think for yourself takes . . . much time but we who believe in self-education are in no way disturbed', and emphasized guidance rather than instruction, which included 'preparing to try to get the children to feel, to understand, why quiet and order and solace are necessary in certain places at certain times'. Similarly with everyday essentials such as 'punctuality, effort, service, courtesy, justice, and truth' he was well aware that the path of suggestion and guidance was slow, long and difficult and that of command, quiet, short and easy but, to him, true education was self-education. His method called for a large measure of liberty and time, neither of which was available under the pressure of examination where 'the hurry for results' was uppermost in a teacher's mind. For Russell, the educational harvest could not be hurried or even fully anticipated.

The basis of his beliefs was reason, the innumerable warnings by scientists of the dangers of overpressure and overhaste in education. Education should be based not upon society's demands for examination results but upon what psychologists were revealing about the stages of child development. Play, active occupation and comparative freedom were essential, not stultifying testing and continual assessment. Russell discussed this approach to education with George Bernard Shaw and other leading educationists. Shaw's view was the same as that of Russell: 'No one had a right to force any education upon a child except that of a technical nature – technical in the sense of that which would be useful to him. Every other form of education should be the spontaneous outcome of the child's character.' In a broadside at the universities and the Board of Education, Russell commented: 'But the universities still set questions (even in English) to children of sixteen that I can not myself answer at sixty, and the Board of Education still casts the bulk of its boys and girls adrift in the rough, rude world at thirteen.' Russell did his utmost to counter unthinking convention and to ensure that pupils left KAS adequately prepared for adult life.

KAS: a school without peer

Under the presidencies of Professor L. C. Miall and Sir Patrick Geddes, the council of the King Alfred School Society and its propaganda committee, set up in 1902, made concerted efforts to disseminate the principles of the rationalist charter of 1897. The society wisely recognized that the progressive principles which underpinned its Hampstead venture were increasingly relevant to the educational needs of post-Victorian Britain, especially to the new system of day secondary schools that emerged under the 1902 Education Act.

For a short period before these schools took on themselves the traditional trappings and priorities of the nineteenth-century public schools there was a chance, albeit a very limited one, that the coeducational, child-centred model pioneered at Hampstead could influence their development. The society convened national conferences addressed by eminent educationists to disseminate its ideas on such subjects as coeducation, discipline and the relationship between parents and school. Of equal importance was its plan to influence educational practice at a local level. As the state secondary schools were placed in the hands of local education authorities, the society considered establishing peer schools to KAS in various areas of the country to demonstrate to local education committees the merits of a rationalist education. Probably the most ambitious of the society's schemes for establishing outposts were discussed by the propaganda committee in 1911. They proposed to use Miall's connections to help found a school in Sheffield, Findlay's Mancunian connections to set up a rationalist outpost in nearby Altrincham and Alderley Edge, and Geddes' Scottish connections to open a school in Glasgow. However, the society's greatest chance of success lay nearer home, in Chiswick, Hammersmith, Richmond, Gerrards Cross and Ealing, and possibly in southern coastal towns, such as Torquay and Bournemouth, but, despite the strenuous efforts of leading figures such as Russell and Mrs White Wallis, very few of these areas made any response, leaving KAS at the end of the day a school without peer. By 1920 the society was more concerned about moving within Hampstead to a larger site, than with plans to set up new schools outside its catchment area.

Not all of the conferences planned by the council and its propaganda committee had immediate and obvious links with the Hampstead school. One of the first speakers was not an educationist but a celebrated town planner, Ebenezer Howard, who in 1898 had relaunched the garden city movement with his book *Garden Cities of Tomorrow*. Howard gave an illustrated talk on the subject at a KASS conference in 1902 but it was not simply his rationalist approach to urban planning which made his address relevant. The most obvious link between his theme and KASS was the inspiration which it gave to the creation of Hampstead Garden Suburb whose children helped to swell the numbers in the society's first school after 1906. There are several less well-known connections between KASS and the garden city movement in general and the Hampstead Garden Suburb in particular. The suburb is usually said to have been largely the creation of Henrietta Barnett, the wife of Canon Samuel Barnett who served on the society's council for a short period. In March 1906 Henrietta Barnett took up Howard's idea and set up the Hampstead Garden Trust with the assistance of Raymond Unwin and Barry Parker, who provided the first plan, and Lutyens their chief architect. A paper written by Lucille Armstrong in 1985 from her recollections of the time and deposited in the KASS archives attributes much of the inspiration for the Garden Suburb to Patrick Geddes who, at the time when he replaced Miall as the society's president in 1908, was working with Unwin and Lutyens in turning the idea of a garden suburb into a reality. But Geddes was equally interested in education. He had helped to found Abbotsholme and is listed among its first fellows. More importantly for the present study, he was attracted as much to the rationalist principles underlying KASS as he was to the principles of town planning. He thus readily accepted the presidency of the society and brought to it a depth of knowledge and achievement.

There were other less formal links between the garden city movement and the movement for reformed education. Despite the visionary concept of town planning which Howard outlined to the KASS conference of 1902, he had little appreciation of how a system of reformed education could help create a new urban community based on a spirit of co-operation. Ignoring Owen's educational achievements at New Lanark (around 1815) and those of Cadbury at Bournville, he looked upon education in the narrow sense of religious indoctrination and the teaching of the three Rs. Howard could give no assistance to those who had the task of devising a form of education which could develop the humane spirit of the new urban communities. In 1903 they turned to Findlay to provide a scheme of education, similar to that which he had devised for KAS, for the first of the garden cities at Letchworth. In 1905 and 1906 the leaders of the Garden City Association based at Letchworth met at KAS to debate coeducation. They included Badley of Bedales, the Bishop of Hereford who was a friend of Findlay, Dr Foot who modified Findlay's original scheme for the garden city, and John Russell. Russell was about to become the chairman of the Garden City Education Council and hoped to introduce into the schools of Letchworth a modified form of the kind of education which he was pioneering at KAS. However, the residents of the new garden city refused to subscribe to a scheme which would provide for small classes and adequate facilities for practical work. The plan to provide reformed education collapsed under pressure from the Board of Education and the County Council to provide a more conventional scheme of education in the garden city schools. The garden suburb at Hampstead was more fortunate. When it developed after 1906, such education was already being provided at KAS at Ellerdale Road, little more than a mile away. The independence of KAS meant that it was largely free from the purse strings and the dictates of local and central government to provide the kind of progressive education with which the Board of Education had shown little sympathy at Letchworth.

Undaunted by its failure to set up a KASS school in Letchworth, the society refused to turn inward upon itself. It established links with other bodies, including the British Child Study Association, the Sanitary Institute in which Mr White Wallis was a prominent figure, the Teacher's Guild, the Parents' National Education Union and the Froebel Society, inviting several of them to be represented on its council. It continued its series of conferences on topics relating to rational education. In 1906 the former headmaster, Rice, spoke on coeducation and Russell gave papers on children's leisure and the ways in which a rational education helped young people to earn a living. However, in 1906 with the chances of setting up a peer school to KAS at Letchworth receding, the society directed more of its energies to founding schools elsewhere. In May 1906 Russell and Maberly addressed a meeting at Hammersmith on the subject of the principles of a rational education. A local committee was set up to look further into the matter of establishing a Hammersmith rational school with Russell, Miss Frood and Miss Meyerstein representing KASS. Drawing-room meetings were also to be held in Highbury, Kensington and Chelsea as a means of testing feeling in favour of the new school movement. The society was thus reaching out beyond its Hampstead base, and in order to strengthen this move-ment, it considered holding its council meetings in such places as the Teachers' Guild headquarters and the College of Preceptors.

As a guarantor of the society's Hampstead school, Mrs White Wallis was well aware of the need to regulate this expansion lest the society overstretch its financial resources. She believed it necessary to protect the society's interests in any new schools, while at the same time ensuring that each was financially self-supporting. In July 1908 the council approved a code of regulations for which she had provided the initial draft. The principal points were as follows:

> The Council of the K.A.S.S. is prepared to assent to the establishment in various districts of schools to be styled K.A.S. Schools and to be affiliated to the parent society provided:-
>
> 1. A School Committee is to be formed in the district of the proposed school by those people who wish for such a school; the members of this Committee to become members of the Society,
> 2. This local committee elects a certain number of its members to form a Committee or Committees to carry on the management of the school and to be responsible for its finances.
> 3. That the Council appoint the headmaster of the school.
> 4. That the school is formed to carry out the aims and objects of this Society and that it carries out these aims and objects.
> 5. After the first year each school committee may nominate three of its members who are to sit on the Council.
> 6. That the Council have the right to inspect the School at any time. Should it appear to the Council that the School is not being carried on in accordance with the aims and objects of the Society it shall be open to the Council to give half a year's notice to local Committee and at the expiration of that time the school shall cease to be styled as K.A.S. School and to be affiliated to the Society.

7. The local committee shall have full powers, save as expressly restricted above by its elected Committee or Committees to manage school, to raise money by its guarantees, loans or otherwise and to expand such monies on the legitimate work of the School.

8. There shall be compulsory membership of parents.

9. All literature to be issued by the Society.

10. Each School Committee can appoint its own Treasurer, and sub-Committees.

In May 1911 the secretary reported to council that a local committee had been set up at Gerrards Cross to explore the possibility of establishing a school. As at Hammersmith four years earlier, it was found that there was little local support for such a venture. Not enough people had the drive and determination of the society's founders, or were willing to take the great financial risks. The situation in 1911 was markedly different from that of 1898. The new secondary schools which came into existence under the 1902 Education Act and the increased number of independent day schools made extremely difficult the task of attracting a sufficient number of pupils to make the new rational schools financially viable. The expansion of the professions and universities in late Victorian and Edwardian Britain increased the demand for paper qualifications. With the society unwilling to give its full support to teaching for examinations at sixteen and eighteen with its inevitable concomitant, homework, it seemed to be offering a type of education which was increasingly irrelevant to the needs of the age. An education based solely on humane values had a restricted appeal, no matter how hard and how often Russell presented the case for the relevance of a rational education to the world of work. To most middle-class parents such an esoteric education had little connection with the hard-headed business of examination success. Most saw education as a ladder, not a broad highway, and their children would be enabled to climb its rungs by passing highly demanding and extremely competitive examinations. The stringent conditions of the school certificate, which was awarded only

20. The sandpit at the Greenaway play garden

to candidates who passed at least five subjects in carefully defined areas, meant that most preferred a traditional secondary school education for their offspring. Thus the task of establishing KASS schools throughout London and the provinces was an extremely difficult and almost an impossible one even when some concessions were made on the matters of examinations and homework.

Russell blamed the outbreak of war in 1914 upon the intense competitive spirit which dominated nations and their education systems. He condemned the way in which this was disguised by 'an increased flood of cheap emotion, of patriotic insincerities, of organised passion, and of reckless injustice' and hoped that the war would lead to the triumph of those values for which KAS stood. Lloyd George's elevation to the premiership in 1916 and his appointment of H. A. L. Fisher to the presidency of the Board of Education seemed to favour such values but the conditions of war made it virtually impossible for the society to establish new schools. Instead it turned its attention to the growing demand for education within Hampstead. It concentrated upon its play gardens at Greenaway Gardens and Alexandra Road, catering for two to eight year olds, and in 1916 renamed them garden schools. By 1918 only one remained, that at Greenaway Gardens with some twenty-two children. Of greater significance for the future of KAS was the purchase of the Montessori Garden Suburb school in October 1919 from Mrs Mountain Palmer for the sum of £300. The society had already decided to move the Montessori school to Manor Wood, North End Road, where it opened with twenty-eight pupils a few weeks after purchase. The society saw this as a possible preliminary step to the relocation of KAS on the Manor Wood site.

The refitting of the flagship

The war years brought disruption and distress to KAS. Russell had the sad task of reporting the deaths in action of several Old Alfredians to a school which suffered from staff shortages, cramped conditions and the periodic threat of air raids. The final year of the war brought no respite. He hoped that the death of Willie Bamberger, a pupil at the school from 1901 to 1903, would be the last that he would have to announce at the morning callover, or assembly, but he could never be sure. Not long before the Armistice the finance committee was still contemplating laying off teachers because of a decline in numbers and fee income due to the threat of air raids, not just by Zeppelin but also by Gotha and Riesen aircraft after September 1917. By the late summer of 1918 there were some grounds for hoping that the war would soon be at an end and the society began to consider how to meet its postwar problems,

21. Outdoor education in the Greenaway Gardens School, 1911

especially that of the overcrowded buildings at Ellerdale Road, consideration of which it had shelved on the outbreak of war. The flagship was badly in need of a refit, the school roll having increased from eighty-five when the inspectors commented unfavourably on the cramped accommodation in 1913, to ninety-four in 1919 (after the temporary drop in numbers in 1917–18). Furthermore, there was need to find a new captain for Russell was due to retire in 1920, and to find funds to increase the pay of the ratings. The latter's salaries had only increased by 10 per cent during the war even though the cost of living had more than doubled. They received only about half of what was recommended by the Teachers' Superannuation Act of 1918. The immediate postwar years were thus to face the society with a series of new challenges.

Many parents and council members saw the solution to these problems in moving the school to a larger site. It would enable the school to house its pupils adequately, attract more pupils to help raise the £1,330 necessary to bring KAS salaries in line with the Burnham Committee's recommended salary scales, and make the headship of an enlarged school attractive to a number of experienced teachers from whom a worthy successor to Russell would be chosen. Professor Patrick Geddes reported to an extraordinary general meeting in July 1919 that 'a beautifully wooded site had been found at Manor House' and that it was necessary to raise £14,000 for its purchase. The main sum that had to be met was £6,000, with the rest being raised through the proposed sale of the Ellerdale Road buildings and part of the Manor Wood estate, and through a mortgage. Maberly, the sole survivor from the founding

22. Wartime gardening, 1916

group, estimated that the fee income of 150 pupils would be necessary to meet the running costs of the new school. Such sums could also be met in part from grants from the Board but that would involve compromising the school's independence. Professor Watson urged that the Hampstead school should preserve its freedom and not turn to the Board for financial assistance but his resolution to that effect failed to gain any support. The meeting gave its unanimous approval to the proposal

> to purchase the Manor House site or any other suitable site; to provide therein, suitable premises for its Hampstead School and to raise by gift or by loan with or without interest the necessary sum of money and thereby authorise the Executive to take all necessary steps including if necessary the mortgage of the property to give effect to this proposal.

By the time of the November annual general meeting just over £5,000 had been raised through gifts or loans, leaving £15,000 to be met 'on a business footing' to complete the purchase of the site and the building of a new school.

Geddes wanted to move ahead quickly during the summer of 1919 by erecting surplus army huts at Manor Wood so that the school could open there in September. Earle's carpentry and supervisory skills were to be used to expedite the transfer from Ellerdale Road to Manor Wood. Russell argued for a less ambitious scheme and suggested to the 'urgency committee' consisting of Professor Watson, Maberly and Tenney, that

23. Destroying stereotypes: mixed cricket, 1918

only one hut should be purchased and converted for the use of the Montessori school which would be moved from Ellerdale Road. A counter-proposal by Geddes and Unwin, who had planned much of the Hampstead Garden Suburb, led to a compromise under which Earle adapted the Manor Wood stables for the Montessori school but for the time being, KAS was to remain in Ellerdale Road. Henceforth all matters relating to Manor Wood would be dealt with by the building committee which had footed the bill for the conversion of the stables. Even these preliminary moves met with some opposition when the council met on the first day of October 1919. Jacoby pointed out that money was being spent on structural changes before the site had been purchased. There was no guarantee that the purchase price could be found and the building committee had not even been consulted about the work undertaken during the summer. However, the sober voice of caution was ignored and council pressed ahead with the equipping of the Montessori school whose purchase and transfer were fully approved. The services of Mrs Palmer, its former owner, were to be retained temporarily to ease the problems of transfer to the new site. Three weeks later, on 23 October, council began to realize the dangers of allowing the two schemes to become linked. The building committee warned of the dangers of allowing the funds raised for the purchase of the site to be used on the Montessori school, and informed the meeting that it had passed a resolution that it felt 'very strongly that they are not entitled to use any money they hold in trust, for any other purpose until they have secured enough money to pay for the land'.

The shift towards a more cautionary and realistic policy became more evident in the attitude of council towards the new site. When the Orthopaedic Society, with whom the school was to share the site, pressed for the cost of repairs to the roof of the lodge at the entrance to the estate and asked that its part of the site be enlarged to include the greenhouse, council agreed that these matters be left until it was decided whether or not to retain the site. With the appeal having raised only modest sums and the sale of the Ellerdale Road buildings by no means certain, the meeting wisely agreed to hold back from making irrevocable decisions and commitments. Meanwhile, Findlay offered to publicize the appeal at the Conference of Educational Associations to attract those who had a broad interest in educational experiment. C. F. A. Voysey donated his architect's fee of £150 to the building fund, having been paid to produce a plan which would never be carried out if sufficient funds were not forthcoming. Jacoby, impressed by the more cautious policies pursued by the council, lent a substantial sum to the fund.

The society pressed on with the expansion of its Montessori school and took out an option on a clubhouse in Wilkfield Green, which fell vacant in November 1919, for an additional class. Though difficulties over the lease prevented the society from occupying the premises, it nevertheless showed the determination of KASS to promote new ideas and ventures whenever possible. It was not willing to cast its Manor Wood school financially adrift and brought its finances under the control of the building committee which contributed £270 to the conversion of the stables. The Board of Education and Hendon Council were invited to inspect the classes in the expectation that this could lead to grant support. Thus plans for the transfer of KAS to Manor Wood and the expansion of the Montessori school moved forward together. A further point of integration of the two projects was suggested by Mrs Claremont who put forward a scheme for sharing part of the land at Manor Wood with a Montessori training college. Though the idea of a progressive campus at Manor Wood shared by KAS, the society's Montessori school and a training college appealed to the council, it was nevertheless regarded as too ambitious a venture upon which to make a decision before the matter of the purchase of Manor Wood had been settled. Expansion gave way to consolidation. The ideas of a second

24. Visiting Manor Wood, 1919

Montessori class and the training college were dropped for the time being and council concentrated on developing its existing schools. The Garden School was reconstituted in 1920 with its own governing committee and a carefully defined financial independence. The transfer of KAS to Manor Wood became the main priority.

By the beginning of 1920 the purchase of the site was becoming related to the other principal issue which faced the council in the immediate postwar years, that of choosing a successor to Russell. Though he had agreed to stay on beyond his retirement date, the end of the summer term, council set up a subcommittee under Lady Thornycroft to help select a new headmaster for the beginning of the autumn term. As the quality of applicants could be dependent in part on offering the successful candidate the opportunity of running 'a larger school in a larger building, say Manor Wood', then some firm indication of the timescale for the move would assist the selection process. However the January meeting of council was unwilling to commit itself to any definite scheme for transfer with so many key issues not yet resolved. Two leading council members, Aneurin Williams Liberal MP for Consett, Durham, and Director of the Garden City Limited, and Davis were asked to consider a possible way forward through the creation of a syndicate to manage the building and development work on the Manor Wood site. The society was only too painfully aware of the difficulties of raising the finance to develop its share of the site without the additional help of other interested parties.

The appointment of a new headteacher was no less fraught with difficulties. In March 1920 four candidates were considered for the post: Meldrum, Wicksteed, Earle (a senior member of staff) and Miss Hyett. The latter was only available for interview by the selection subcommittee in the afternoon; the evening meeting of the council decided on a motion put by Tenney and seconded by Jacoby to offer Wicksteed the post. Earle received a personal letter expressing the council's warm appreciation of his long service to the school, in addition to an increase in his salary of £60, raising it to £420. Earle and many of his colleagues were outraged and five members of staff tendered their resignations in protest. Russell, however, despite his affection for Earle, believed that Wicksteed was 'the right man'. A special meeting of the council on 31 March 1920 agreed to invite Wicksteed to discuss the matter with them. This took place a week later when Wicksteed informed the council that he 'could fill their places satisfactorily and start the school in the autumn term', whereupon the meeting voted by six votes to four to accept the resignations. Thus for a second time in the school's short history a headmaster came to take up his post with all but one of its staff having resigned. The son of Philip Wicksteed, who had first recommended Russell for the headship in 1901, now succeeded his father's protégé.

Why Wicksteed was offered the headship in 1920 has never been satisfactorily explained.[20] Little was known about Meldrum, one of the three other candidates, and Violet Hyett, a graduate of Girton College, Cambridge's first women's college, suffered the twin disadvantages of being a woman and a Marxist socialist. The society's rationalist principles had severe limits, paradoxically in view of the vital role of women radicals in its formation. Given their prejudices, the real choice facing the selection committee was between Earle and Wicksteed. Possibly the main reason why the latter rather than Earle was invited to become headmaster was that the committee was seeking not just a headmaster but a successor to Russell, who, like him, could play a prominent role in the new school movement. Earle had shown his abilities as a teacher but during Russell's absence because of ill health in 1904 he was not chosen as acting headmaster. Nesbitt, assisted by Wicksteed, had taken much of the lead during this period in addition to teaching at Bedales. Earle's immense love of English literature and rhetorical prose was not as impressive on paper as Wicksteed's reputation as a scholar and literary critic of eminent writers such as Blake. But it was in his involvement in the broader educational movements of the age that Wicksteed's record was the more impressive and possibly made him the more worthy successor to Russell. At the time of his application for the post Earle wrote to Russell, 'it is only because I feel that education opens the ultimate solution to international (as well as other) problems that I can rightly consider further devoting myself to it', but he had never devoted as much time to working with educational movements which could turn such ideals into a reality as had Wicksteed.

Both Earle and Wicksteed were the sons of clergymen. Whereas Earle's father had a comfortable Anglican living in Somerset, Wicksteed's was a unitarian minister whose unconventional views and utopian schemes, including the Labour Church Movement, placed him at the heart of London progressive politics. Philip Wicksteed and the Unitarian wing of the Free Churches had a great influence upon the young Joseph who also shared his father's interest in the Theosophical Society. In 1915, Philip Wicksteed founded the Theosophical Fraternity in Education, the forerunner of one of the most prestigious progressive pressure groups of the interwar years, the New Education Fellowship. Joseph Wicksteed's involvement in the politics of educational reform, his non-dogmatic religion and his strong belief in internationalism made him a fitting heir to Russell. He was two years older than Earle and these few years, together with his greater freedom to play a part in

London's educational movements, no doubt assisted his application. Whether Earle's dalliance with his lover, Eleanor Farjeon, hindered his chances of gaining the headship will never be known.

With Wicksteed's appointment the school was once again in crisis. The departure of Rice in 1901 had led many parents to withdraw their children, and Earle's failure to become headmaster threatened to produce a similar exodus. Council was well aware that its decision had created 'unrest among parents' and it met to consider how to minimize its effects. It considered a proposal for staff representation on the council, in addition to the headmaster who was a member without voting rights. This idea was rejected in favour of having representation by Old Alfredians. This did nothing to lessen the crisis and council took further steps to resolve the situation. In May 1920 it issued a circular to parents asking for their support for Wicksteed and agreed to hold a meeting with parents the following month. Though the outcome of the meeting is not known it seems probable that it had no great impact. Wicksteed would have to wait until September to discover how large or small a school he would lead and whether it would open at Manor Wood. He was willing to do his best to ensure the latter. He offered to buy some land on the estate upon which to build a house for himself, and to lend £850 to the fund providing 'that the frontage was not sold'. He handed on a further £1,000 to the fund from Miss Courtauld. These additions led the building committee to conclude that it was likely that the school would retain the site but the matter of when the move would take place was not resolved. In fact a serious fall in the value of the Ellerdale Road property because of the recession of the early 1920s created difficulties which postponed the transfer. The situation was so grave that council decided to put the houses up for auction. But the worst had yet to come. Council passed a resolution which threatened to wind up the society and school if sufficient financial backing was not forthcoming. Maberly reported the resolution to the annual general meeting in the autumn of 1921.

> That having regard to the financial position the General Meeting on the 25th inst. be informed that the Council has decided that unless donations totalling not less than £3000 can be raised by the end of this year the School must be closed at the end of next term and the Society wound up.

Several ways out of this serious situation were considered, including the sale of part of the Manor Wood estate, an appeal to various bodies, and coming under the control of the Board of Education and asking for fees in advance. Findlay opposed handing control to the Board of Education and favoured the idea of nominating a pupil for half fees if a donation of £250 was given. However, with the unexpected and opportune sale of the Ellerdale Road site, no such drastic action was needed. The school moved to the Manor Wood site in 1921, leaving Russell's successor with the challenge of realizing all of the benefits for which the move had been initiated.

Dropping the pilot

Russell's headship ended as it began, with the school in deep crisis. The conflicts and upheavals of 1901 and 1920 were all the more marked because the years in between were ones of stability and gradual expansion. Despite quite a high staff turnover during these two decades, Russell had built up a core of loyal and dedicated teachers, which helps in part to explain their extreme reaction in 1920 when they transferred their allegiance to Earle whom they regarded as the natural heir apparent. The main body of his long-serving staff had been formed by the time of the Board's inspection of the school in 1913. Despite the society's compromise in its position on examinations, the educational ideals of KASS and those of the inspectors were too far apart for KAS to receive a sympathetic report. It is a tribute to the staff and to Russell that they responded positively to the report whilst confirming their belief in the underlying principles of a rational education. Russell's plea for less haste in the education of children and a greater concern for their individual needs was all the more relevant in the First World War but it went unheeded. In 1917 the Board of Education tightened its control of the examination system. Little wonder that Findlay saw bringing the school under the Board's control as a last resort in the financial crisis of 1920–1.

Russell's progressive thinking was always tempered by a concern for an orderly, but non-repressive school, which alone could provide the security to enable children to develop as individuals. The oft-told story of Russell inviting the school to vote upon whether he should or should not wear a wig is usually seen as an expression of his belief in self-government. Russell believed in open government, in encouraging pupils to understand the need for particular rules, but not in the kind of self-government for which A. S. Neill resigned. His school parliament was designed to encourage discussion of school rules and their acceptance. It was a parliament more in the medieval than the modern sense, with Russell exercising the kind of benign and paternal control of which parents approved. It was democratic in the sense that its members were elected but it did have not have any law-generating capacity. He used its elected members to help carry out the rules which he and the council considered essential for a benignly efficient regime. Under his headship the school became more formal in its curriculum, in its dress code and in its rules and regulations, as one might expect of a school which had trebled its numbers.

What the wig episode signified most of all was his open and affectionate relationship with his pupils whom he regarded as his family. When all allowances are made for the eulogistic tones of retirement celebrations, what shines through in all the accounts of his teaching which were given at his retirement dinner in July 1920 is his total rejection of what Findlay called the 'cold chilly philosophy of (Victorian) education'. Pupils approached him without fear and were inspired by his elevated view of life, 'to be inspired with the belief that life is a high and noble calling, not a mean and grovelling thing to be shuffled through as best we can'. As a mark of the esteem in which Old Alfredians and parents held him, a fund was set up to provide him with a pension. It quickly rose to £1,000 at the very time when the school was also appealing for funds for its building project and enabled him to enjoy a comfortable retirement in Hampstead. He maintained his links with KAS, continued to write poetry and developed closer relationships with many eminent people of his age, including the Labour prime minister, Ramsay MacDonald.

Notes and references

1. *Journal of Education* (February 1901), 112.
2. See *Who was Who* for fuller details.
3. Letter dated August 1901 (KASS Archives).
4. Reprinted in J. Croall (ed.), *Letters from Summerhill* (London, Deutsch, 1968), 18.
5. *Journal of Education*, 30 (November 1908), 776.
6. These sketches are humorously presented, if somewhat misleading.
7. Admissions Register, St John's College, Cambridge, XI (1878) registrant 4729.
8. Referred to by Sir Michael Sadler at Russell's Memorial Gathering, 20 March 1937 (KASS Archives).
9. *Journal of Education*, 17 (September 1895), 384.
10. Dated 31 December 1883 (KASS Archives).
11. Quoted in M. Mayer and M. Rebérioux, *The Third French Republic from its Origins to the Great War 1871–1914* (Cambridge, CUP, 1984), 785.
12. See H. J. K. Usher, C. D. Black-Hawkins and G. J. Carrick, *An Angel Without Wings: A History of University College School 1830–1980* (UCS, London 1981) for full details.

13. W. Eager, *Making Men: The History of Boys Clubs and Related Movements in Great Britain* (London, Collins, 1953), 193.

14. Referred to in J. Lewis, *Women and Social Action in Victorian and Edwardian England* (London, Elgar, 1991), 214.

15. A copy of the 1913 inspectors' report is to be found in the KASS Archives.

16. See *Who was Who* (vol. viii) for fuller details of his career.

17. Rice contributed a section on coeducation to *The Special Report on Educational Subjects*, vol.vii *Board of Education* (London, HMSO 1900) 506–7), at the request of Badley who introduced coeducation in Bedales.

18. KASS Archives.

19. See reference no. 4.

20. Wicksteed stated in a letter to Maberly in 1923 that it was Russell's 'ardent wish to see me as his successor' and that his 'appointment would be almost a foregone conclusion'. He was attracted to the headship by the opportunity to develop his own school at Manor Wood, by the salary and by the secretarial help which Wicksteed's uncertain health required.

Chapter 3

To the Manor Borne:
Wicksteed at Manor Wood,
1920–1933

The euphoria of victory over Germany and its allies was as short-lived as the promise of far-reaching reform held out by Fisher's Education Act of 1918. Both disappeared with the collapse of the postwar economic boom in 1921 and the demands for retrenchment by Lloyd George's peacetime coalition government. But KASS and other reformist groups refused to fly the flag of educational reform at halfmast and demanded bold new educational experiments to meet the brave new world which leaders had promised would rise from the ashes of the old prewar order. Yet the society was handicapped in its efforts to raise its profile in Hampstead and in the reform movement by its financial difficulties in the immediate postwar years. The economic downturn hit the value of its Ellerdale Road properties whose profitable sale it was hoped would finance most of the move to a larger site at Manor Wood. They tumbled in value from £6,000 in 1918 to £3,150 in 1921. Retrenchment hit the society just as hard as it hit the nation. Even the ex-army huts which were to serve as the nucleus for the new school at Manor Wood in the place of Voysey's lavish, purpose-designed buildings were caught up in the economic discontent of postwar Britain. Before they could be moved from Wimbledon Common to Manor Wood they were commandeered by the army to house the troops who were to be used against strikers whom it was thought threatened the capital.

When introducing Wicksteed, the new headmaster, to parents at a meeting at KAS in June 1920 Russell, the retiring headmaster, looked forward to the formation of a 'not very distant Labour government' to reverse the educational cuts and to revive the nation's economy. However, he realized that there could be a sting in Labour's tail for a Labour government might 'immediately close down or nationalise all private experiment in education'. In reality, however, the threat to KAS was financial not political. In 1922, Labour's educational guru, R. H. Tawney, produced Labour's policy statement on educational reform in which he asserted that public school reform did not figure among the party's priorities. Besides, Russell had little cause for concern, for he was a close friend of Labour's leader, Ramsay MacDonald, who, shortly before taking office for the second time, spoke at the society's first annual dinner. Nevertheless, in an increasingly tense political atmosphere where it was rumoured that Labour would end all forms of private ownership, even to the extent of instituting free love in the place of marriage, anything seemed possible.

KASS was not willing to allow any possible political threat or actual financial threat to thwart its plans to move to Manor Wood or to remain a powerful pressure group. Although the cost of the transfer

25. Open-air lessons under the beeches

nearly broke the financial back of the society and school, it pressed on with its plans to move to its new rustic environment at Manor Wood. There, with its suitably converted army huts and Squirrel Hall, a communal building without walls whose canopy rested on the branches of two beech trees, the school became an apostle of open-air education. It was not surprising that one of Britain's chief protagonists of open-air education, Margaret McMillan, who had pioneered such schools in Bradford, was elected to council in July 1924. Perhaps an even more impressive catch would have been Professor Percy Nunn of the London Day Training Centre, who was invited to take up the presidency of the society when Geddes relinquished it in 1922. Despite the intense efforts of a council deputation led by Badley of Bedales in December of that year, he declined the offer and the society turned to its old friend Findlay, who was within three years of retiring from his professorship of education at Manchester University. Nunn went on to exercise considerable influence on curricular thinking, especially on the report on *The Education of the Adolescent* published by the Consultative Committee of the Board of Education in 1926. Two members of council, Alice Woods and Margaret McMillan, had an important input into the Consultative Committee's next two reports on primary education (1930) and nursery-infant education (1933).

KAS extolled the virtues of open-air education but refused to tie its curriculum to the ideas of any one reformer. In 1918, with a new education star, Montessori, rising quickly in the curricular firmament, it seemed that the school, having recently purchased the Garden Suburb Montessori school, was about to turn its back on its non-doctrinal principles. On taking up the headship, however, Wicksteed reminded council of the founders' non-dogmatic position and contrasted it with Montessori's inflexible methods and apparatus. By the end of the 1920s, the shortcomings of her system were more widely recognized. Wicksteed turned instead to a broader set of educational principles and a more flexible programme upon which to base his new curriculum, the Dalton plan pioneered by Helen Parkhurst in the United States. His modified Dalton scheme upon which the morning programme was based gave pupils a great deal of freedom to design their own curricular programmes. Providing each of the school subjects was covered, they were allowed to choose the order of study, visiting the subject bases of their choice for some group lessons but largely to undertake a series of stepped tasks or stages. This new curricular regime, together with the afternoon club programme which allowed pupils a wide choice of activities in which sports at first played a minor part, brought Wicksteed into conflict with the council old guard, who wanted the school run on Russell lines. Narrowly escaping a vote of no confidence, he went on to pioneer this radical form of education which the Board's inspectors in 1922 and 1928 found difficult to assess with their more traditional yardsticks. The new educational order was also reflected in several ambitious building programmes which resulted in the new hall in 1926 and new teaching blocks for science and the arts and a junior block in the years just prior to Wicksteed's retirement in 1933. By that time the school had doubled in size during his headship, to 161 pupils.

The new headmaster

'This is a school for one hundred and thirteen children. The youngest is Frank and the oldest is Mr Wicksteed.' Thus began the ritual, termly essay of a six-year-old pupil, which in its way said more about the school's new headmaster than the more elaborately worded speeches of commendation delivered by eminent educationists at his formal presentation to council and parents in June 1920. The more formal tributes emphasized the points of continuity between Joseph Wicksteed and his predecessors. Like Rice he had previously taught at Bedales. There he had built his own home from discarded railway carriages, some of the simplicity of which he intended to preserve in the home

26. Wicksteed and his Alpha class, 1921

he was building at Manor Wood, and in Squirrel Hall,[1] the assembly point, where his new school was to meet for callover most mornings and afternoons. Badley of Bedales who was present at the June meeting with KAS parents spoke of Wicksteed's idealism. He said of him,

Though by nature more of an idealist than a master of detail, when he devotes himself to any kind of work (as he has done here to schoolmastering) he spares no pains to master it, and shows much ability in this without losing any of that idealism which is his great strength and his great charm. I honestly think that you could not find a better man to carry on your work.[2]

After Bedales, Wicksteed had helped to found a coeducational boarding school at Letchworth and became headmaster of a similar school near Guildford. He had decided to apply for the headship of KAS because, as a day school run by the society, it freed his wife from the heavy responsibilities of helping to run a family-owned boarding school which had so affected her health. KASS had again chosen a male head instead of adding to the small minority, three in all, of headmistresses who ran coeducational day schools.

If in the immediate past Wicksteed had followed a path from Bedales similar to that of Rice, in his earlier career he had much in common with Russell. Both contemplated and were in fact trained for the ministry, Russell at Cambridge, and Wicksteed at Manchester New College after graduating in history at Oxford. Unlike Russell, Wicksteed became a clergyman, a Unitarian minister, for a short time in the industrial north, and then in London where he founded societies for closer fellowship between Unitarian churches in the East and West Ends, and elsewhere. This work was developed through the founding of

27. The coach house, Manor Wood's only original school building

78

a league of religions in which all shades of conformist and non-conformist opinion were represented – and to a meeting of which Russell had once presented his own heterodox views. Like Russell, he had also worked to create a league of nations during the war and after to help prevent a repetition of its horrors, especially through establishing close contact with Colonel House, one of President Wilson's inner circle in the United States. Wicksteed thus followed Russell in moving away from strictly theological concerns to broader moral positions on both religious and international matters. They had both come to KAS around the age of forty-five from similar liberal, progressive backgrounds, taking up the headship, as had their spiritual mentor, Pestalozzi, rather late in life. Russell mentioned this parallel to the audience of parents and governors in June 1920.

> Of the essential similarities between us I put age first – not our age to-day, of course, but the age when I began the Headmastership, and at which he is now about to begin. In that respect there is only a year or two to choose between us, and as these last 19 years have been by far the happiest, and (as I at least cannot help feeling) by far the most serviceable of my life, I see no reason why, assuming that he wins your generous support, that he gets well started at Manor Wood, and that the not very distant Labour government (which I shall do my utmost to help into power) does not immediately close down or 'nationalise' all private experiment in education, – I see no reason why his 19 years to come should not do for him, and for the school, what mine have done for me.
>
> In this connection I cannot help reminding (or informing) you that Pestalozzi, to whom for the last hundred years all reform in education owes so much, was fifty when he was called to his first piece of practical work (he had already of course been dreaming wonderful dreams) and that the greater part of his serious contribution to education grew out of the actual school experiences of the last thirty years of his life.[3]

Yet 'Wicky', as his pupils were soon to call him, differed in several ways from Russell. He was much more of 'a family man' than Russell, with his children around him in school. But above all, though like his predecessor he was 'quietly spoken' and 'easily accessible', pupils generally remember little about him or think of him as a 'grey figure' who tended to 'lead from behind'. This led some pupils to believe he lacked leadership qualities and was not someone to inspire others.

The move to Manor Wood

SKETCH DESIGN for SCHOOL at HAMPSTEAD for THE KING ALFRED SCHOOL SOCIETY

28. Charles C. Voysey's ambitious design for the Manor Wood school

Had the school been able to move to Manor Wood when Russell retired in 1920, before the postwar prosperity gave way to slump, then perhaps in its design it could have approximated more to the visionary plan drawn up by C. C. Voysey. However, when KAS was to the Manor borne it was during the recession and industrial discontent which were already apparent by the end of 1920. The move and preparations for it took place in the shadow of and during the postwar recession. It led to the Voysey plan being scaled down considerably. Partly because of the recession, gifts and loans to the new school came in very slowly and in relatively modest amounts; the Ellerdale Road properties valued at £6,500 in June 1919 when Voysey produced his ambitious plan were eventually sold for £3,150 in March 1922. Even the army huts which were chosen as the new classrooms in place of the more costly permanent buildings were caught up in the postwar slump and discontent prior to their removal to Manor Wood. Before they could be moved from Wimbledon Common the military authorities had commandeered them to house the troops which, under the state of emergency, were to be used, if necessary, against those who were on strike in support of the miners.[4] They were eventually returned damaged, with KASS receiving £67 compensation.

Yet the fact that the move was delayed was not without its advantages for the new headmaster. First, it strengthened Wicksteed's political position and helped to ensure (but not guarantee) the continuation of the Russell concept of partnership between headmaster and council. With the depleted finances available for the new site, Wicksteed was able to become a financial partner in the Manor Wood development by taking out a mortgage on the property with two other members of the council, Jacoby and Brewer. The fact that the number of pupils dropped from ninety-one in 1920 to seventy-nine in 1921 (the first year at Manor Wood) made his contribution all the more important. The fraught relationships of the Rice era had resulted in part from the great political power and authority wielded by Mrs White Wallis as the only mortgagee. As one of the three mortgagees (and as one who also put up buildings at his own expense) Wicksteed now played a prominent part in decision-making, a position which he used to the full from the outset. This was seen in his second advantage, when he intervened in the planning of the Manor Wood site to press his interests and those of his staff. Had the move taken place in 1920, the school would have been built before he arrived. The fact that he was headmaster when the site was being planned enabled him to use his new authority to bring about modifications to the Voysey plan. Originally Wicksteed argued in favour of building a hall and concrete cottages. By spring 1921 these had been downgraded to 'wooden bungalows' and eventually to 'army huts'. What Wicksteed found attractive about the idea of smaller units was the way in which they facilitated the development of an open-air school, which was not easily accomplished under the Voysey scheme, even in its less ambitious form. At a special meeting of the building committee in March 1921, he objected to Voysey's revised plan partly on 'aesthetic grounds' but mainly because it failed to provide sufficient space 'in front of the huts for open air classes'. Raymond Unwin was to consider both schemes and through judicious compromise was to arrive at a final plan which would then be implemented without further delay. In the end it was simply a matter of setting back the huts by about 15 feet 'to facilitate outdoor teaching' but Wicksteed had won his political spurs.

More important, however, was the third advantage of the delayed transfer from Ellerdale Road. KASS, in consultation with its new headmaster, had time to consider what kind of school it should be. Wicksteed insisted that though financial constraints meant the scaling down of building schemes it should not involve the scaling down of principles. At a meeting of the council in November 1920 he strongly opposed the idea that KAS should adopt a system of Montessori teaching. He pointed out that the society 'stood for freedom in experiment with an open mind towards various methods, [which] would not be possible if the school were given over to a prescribed system'. He wished to exploit to the full all opportunities to experiment, without doctrinal constraint. These included using pupils for as much manual work as possible at Manor Wood. The transfer, including the building of Squirrel Hall, essentially just a roof with supports, was seen as part of experiential learning. He saw the Montessori class as a disadvantage for the new school, reporting to the school committee in November 1921, two months after KAS opened on the Manor Wood site, that 'several would-be entrants had failed because there was no junior school not Montessori.' In 1922 the name 'Montessori' was dropped from the title of the junior school altogether.

Wicksteed also used the period prior to the move from Ellerdale Road to sound out parental opinion and that of the school committee on two of Russell's innovations which seemed to contravene the principles of the society, namely the regular use of tests and the increasing use of homework. He proposed a series of modifications which increased the element of choice. 'There were to be no periodical exams – stage tests were optional and could be taken at any time when a child wished to pass to another stage; results were given by remarks only.' The more formal tests employed by Russell and the use of marks in their assessment were seen by Wicksteed as a departure from the good practice set out by the society. The school committee to whom he presented his ideas in January 1921 welcomed his proposals and suggested a few additions which reduced still further the more formalized practices adopted by Russell. They recommended that tests should be used unexpectedly to

29. Squirrel Hall, the school's first new building, 1920

30. Squirrel Hall, built and designed by headmaster and children

31. The rejected plan

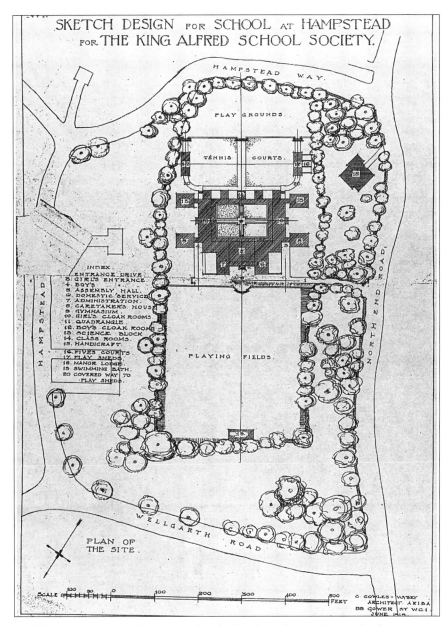

SKETCH DESIGN FOR SCHOOL AT HAMPSTEAD FOR THE KING ALFRED SCHOOL SOCIETY.

HAMPSTEAD WAY.

PLAY GROUNDS.

TENNIS COURTS.

INDEX.
1. ENTRANCE DRIVE.
2. GIRL'S ENTRANCE.
3. BOY'S
4. ASSEMBLY HALL.
5. DOMESTIC SERVICE.
6. CARETAKER'S HOUSE.
7. ADMINISTRATION.
8. GYMNASIUM.
9. GIRL'S CLOAK ROOMS.
10. QUADRANGLE.
11. BOY'S CLOAK ROOMS.
12. SCIENCE BLOCK.
13. CLASS ROOMS.
14. HANDICRAFT.
15. FIVES COURTS.
16. PLAY SHEDS.
17. MANOR LODGE.
18. SWIMMING BATH.
19. COVERED WAY TO PLAY SHEDS.

PLAYING FIELDS.

PLAN OF THE SITE.

WELLGARTH ROAD.

SCALE OF   100   200   300   400   500 FEET

C. COWLES-VOYSEY
ARCHITECT A.R.I.B.A
88 GOWER ST W.C.1
JUNE 1919.

avoid 'cramming and preparation beforehand'; regular end of term tests should be dispensed with. On the subject of homework, the committee suggested sending a questionnaire to parents. The results presented to the March meeting of the school committee showed that only a third of children did any regular homework, and then usually in mathematics and history; two-thirds did some homework occasionally, and then only for an hour at most, either 'to keep up with the class or from preference', whereas 'a very few worked thinking the school expected it'. The survey showed a majority of parents were against homework, although the small number of replies, eight in all, may not have provided any real basis for action or reform. However, it was clear even before the school moved from Ellerdale Road that the new headmaster intended to modify many of Russell's innovations. The break with the past was made easier by the transfer of KAS to Manor Wood in September 1921. It is one of the ironies of history that the Manor Wood site was once owned by one of the major public schools, Eton,[5] whose traditions were called into question by KASS and its Hampstead school.

Just after the school moved to Manor Wood, when the old school buildings were still up for sale, Russell penned a wistful and poignant reminder of their importance to him and the first generations of KAS pupils.

House to Let
(24 Ellerdale Road – December 1st 1921)

O House of Life, whence the door soul hath flown,
Forsaken, silent, sightless, joyless, bare,
But all expectant still, thou standest there,
Awaiting some new soul to make thine own.
No echo left of all the mirth that rang,
No member of the fires that warmed our days,
No flicker of the light that lit our ways,
No single note of all the songs we sang.
Yet may there lurk within thy battered frame
Some thrill of loss for all that thou didst hold,
As those who have outgrown thy narrow fold
Can never quite forget thy magic name,
Nor ever come, old House, and pass thee by
Without a look of love, a smile, a sigh.

J.R.

What then was the new school like in its first few years? The reminders of the war were ever present – the army huts, the 4-feet-high shell-case upon which the change of periods was rung, but especially the wounded who still occupied parts of Manor Wood hospital. A member of the family of the distinguished Dutch historian, Pieter Geyl, who lived in Russell Road, recalled how in 1924 the hospital huts, the other side of the fence on the upper slope, still housed the war wounded. 'It was a sorry sight when their occupants took an airing, (in their distinctive blue uniforms with red ties) the legless, armless and other maimed from the war to end all wars.'[6] The school occupied the other six acres of the site, of which the most original feature was Squirrel Hall. This roughly hewn shelter served many purposes, including a gymnasium where pupils stood 'with flailing arms and healthy chests doing healthy exercises'. Logs provided seats for lessons and an upturned trunk served as a lectern over which the diminutive Wicksteed could just about be seen. There, pupils listened to his talks and sang lustily, especially 'Jerusalem', which, because 'Wicky' was an authority on Blake, was almost as much of a school song as 'Gaudeamus Igitur'. Some ran onto the roof to be chased down by the agile headmaster. Nature's materials, wood, open air and running water provided the basis for a rather romanticized view of a child's educational needs which even the inspectors accepted. Certainly as with most educational beliefs and practices, the concept of open-air education so rampant in Britain at the time did not escape the critical scrutiny of the society. Though eventually the council backed Wicksteed's belief in 'open-air methods', it was not until after some members had pointed out some of their less desirable concomitants: cold, damp and draughts. The buildings committee gave close consideration to the matter, with Mr Bruce Bullock arguing that parents generally disapproved of open-air schools because of their disadvantages. The pupils too remember the cold of the huts with their small stoves in one corner and did not always look forward to folding their tables to carry them to the even greater coldness of the area immediately outside their classrooms. However, as the matter touched upon two basic principles of the society – the health of children which the majority on council and the building committee believed was promoted by open-air education, and the need to experiment, 'K.A.S. was a pioneer school and if it ceased to be one it need not exist' – then it was very likely to gain overwhelming support as an experiment at Manor Wood.

School buildings reflect concepts of learning. Voysey's plan, more coherent and elegant in architectural terms, reflected a more cloistered, formal concept of learning. Its sheer size, close-knit nature and two-storeyed buildings would have overwhelmed a young pupil and his school plan lent itself less readily to the concept of experiential child-centred learning than Wicksteed's. Wicksteed was an educationist whose insistence on open-air learning in a less formal environment was ever present in the arrangement of the wooden, single-storey bungalows in an informal rural setting. Less visually attractive than Voysey's plan, his was better suited to the aims of a KASS education. The minutes of a meeting of school committee in October 1923 indicate the arrangement of the huts: see Table 5. (A kitchen had already been built.)

In addition to the classrooms were the laboratory (30ft), workshop (30ft), cloakrooms (25ft × 2), headmaster's office (11ft), secretary's office

Table 5 **Arrangement of school classrooms, 1923**

Class	No. of pupils	Maximum possible	Dimensions of each room (feet and inches)
Alpha	16	18	26'6"
A	14	16	23'6"
Beta	12	14	20'0"
B	12	15	20'0"
C	16	17	26'6"
D	12	14	23'6"
	82	94	

(19ft), staffroom (13ft) and small classroom (17ft). The space under several of the huts provided a ready refuge for pupils and sometimes their pets, including a mongoose.

The classrooms occupied but a small part of the six-acre site and were in a corner delineated by the upper fence and the road. They were in a natural woodland setting with two large beech trees separating them from North End Road. A small hedge separated the teaching rooms from a sloping rough area of ground, part of which was to be levelled with soil and spoil from the tunnels of the extended underground system. During the process, railway sleepers were laid to help prevent the horse and carts and chain-driven motor trucks from becoming bogged down in the area near the lodge and beyond. The school's parliament, or advisory council more appropriately named, was forced to make rules to prevent personal injury and the breaking of windows through throwing mud and stones. By the beginning of April 1925 the muddy site had been transformed into a level grassed area suitable for most games.

It was not only the mud and stones which the pupils used as weapons. The soil from the underground excavations in Poland Street and Oxford Street contained what were said to be human and animal bones which the pupils used as cudgels, according to a report in the *Westminster Gazette* of 22 March 1924. The bones, fragments of wood and bronze nails, which were unearthed in increasing numbers, were said to have come possibly from a Roman burial ground, although one person who wrote to Wicksteed claimed that the charred condition of the bones indicated that they were the remains of bodies burnt and buried at the time of the Great Plague. He claimed that the bodies, which had been brought by the cartload from the city, were buried in Poland Street on a site later occupied by a workhouse. Whatever their origins, either as the remains of plague victims, or Romano-British settlers, the bones had been used for war games for three weeks before Wicksteed and the teachers learnt of their discovery! One former pupil recalled Wicksteed's 'discovery' of broken pieces of marble and his disappointment on rushing to the British Museum to be told that they were broken pieces of table top from a Lyons tea shop.

32. The 'picturesque huts'

The inspectors who visited the school in 1922 commented favourably on the Manor Wood site, contrasting it with the cramped accommodation which their predecessors found at Ellerdale Road in 1913. They commented that, 'The present site is admirably chosen for the purposes of the School, one of which is to lay stress upon education in the open air. Picturesque huts in the middle of several well-wooded acres make the school attractive.' They would have entered the school through the new oak gates and past the entrance notice board designed and constructed by the woodwork master, Fincham. The freshly gravelled drive from the gate to the shelter adjoining the junior classrooms would have impressed the visitors, as would the rich contrast between the black tar paving of the covered way and the burnt brown façade of the huts. Squirrel Hall where callover was held in the early years at Manor Wood amazed them as much as it did its architect, Wicksteed, a decade later. It was a large hut built around a tree, open to much of the elements and roofed with branches and timbers. In 1930 in his annual report he recalled on the day before the first callover at Manor Wood in September 1921 he had been putting the finishing touches to the construction.

33. Callover in Squirrel Hall

> All the previous afternoon and evening, I had been balancing myself upon the hazardous scaffolding of tables and chairs to put the last touches to the roof – and there it was, sheltering some 80 children and about five or six staff including Miss Hyett, Miss Hibburd, Mr and Miss Rapson (now Mrs Cullen). How we ever survived the next few years is still a mystery.

In 1922 the inspectors disguised their puzzlement at the structure behind the restrained tones of official language (or 'inspectorspeak'). They gave it a special mention in their report but not, of course, by name. 'The present ingenious substitute for an assembly hall will probably prove insufficient' – something of an understatement in view of the fact that there were 81 pupils in the school in 1922. There was a suggestion that it should be converted into a gymnasium by raising its roof but the modifications were too costly for a school already saddled with heavy debts, and it was not very suitable for such a purpose. The provision of stoves, fireguards, chemical fire extinguishers, matting for the floors and bootscrapers for each of the buildings were but some of the costlier items of furniture. The replacement of desks with tables, reflecting a less formal classroom atmosphere, added to the society's expenses, some of which were covered through renting out its buildings in the evening.

By 1926 the total liabilities had been reduced to under £4,000, and with its Manor Wood property valued at £6,000 the society felt that it could begin the process of replacing the wooden buildings with more permanent structures. It could take some comfort from the fact that its debts were less than those at Ellerdale Road whilst its estate was worth double that for which the old school had been sold. The first building to be replaced was the dining hall, which may at first appear a strange priority. However, since the extension of the original timber hall in 1922 it had been used for several purposes, which had added to the school's coffers. Dancing classes, orchestra practice, amateur musical productions, meetings of the Golders Green Federation and educational conferences had been held there. Use by the school and outside bodies dictated that any replacement building would be much more than a dining hall. Hendon Council ruled that any new building should be of a permanent kind, its having grown tired of the constant applications for the erection of temporary buildings on the Manor Wood site. From then on KASS aimed at the complete replacement of its makeshift buildings, an ambitious aim which was achieved by the end of Wicksteed's headship but not on the lines of Voysey's original plan.

The Montessori controversy:
the national debate in microcosm

The 1920s was a decade of contrasts. The recurrent demands for cuts in government expenditure caused much of the Fisher Act of 1918 to be stillborn. In particular, its ambitious plan to provide some kind of part-time education after the age of fourteen for the mass of the nation's adolescents fell foul of the Geddes axe. The predominantly Conservative Coalition government led by Lloyd George demanded retrenchment in education, leaving the mass of the nation's children with a stunted elementary education and few prospects of further education. Russell, when introducing Wicksteed to parents in June 1920, looked to a future Labour government to inaugurate a new era in progressive education.

Labour's new curricular policy had been devised by Professor T. P. Nunn of the University of London, whom KASS tried unsuccessfully to attract to its presidency in 1922. KASS was more successful in attracting other national leaders of the progressive movement to its council and general membership. They included Badley of Bedales, A. S. Neill who was shortly to set up Summerhill, Margaret McMillan, who had pioneered educational reform in Bradford and had helped to devise Labour policy on primary education, and Beatrice Ensor, who with Wicksteed, played a major part in founding the New Education Fellowship (NEF) in 1921. The Fellowship, created to disseminate ideas on educational reform, received strong support from KASS when its new president, Findlay, and leading members including Alice Woods spoke at NEF conferences. Wicksteed also argued that Mrs Ensor of the New Education Fellowship 'provided . . . a first rate nucleus for spreading new educational ideals, and KASS should act in conjunction with her'.

One of the main topics discussed by the new educational forum in the early 1920s was the Montessori system, a system which KASS was among the first to subject to critical scrutiny and to find wanting. When Dr Montessori came to London in the autumn of 1919 to deliver a series of lectures and to conduct a four-month training course, the society on the advice of Russell gave Miss Harwood leave of absence to attend. She was fortunate, for hundreds of teachers were turned away. Fêted by Britain's leading educationists, including H. A. L. Fisher, the President of the Board of Education, Montessori gained many converts including Claude Claremont, who ran her training school and who was the husband of Dr Ethelberta Claremont, KAS's medical inspector who found the Manor Wood site for the society and played the major part in founding the Old Alfredians association. Though the society used the Claremonts' house on at least one occasion for its drawing-room meetings to discuss educational ideas, it never succumbed entirely to the Montessori method.[7] In 1919 it had purchased the Garden Suburb Montessori school and relocated it in the stables at Manor Wood. Within a short time it was found wanting by parents and by Wicksteed. The society had never been one for educational fetishes and took a leading part in subjecting what had almost become articles of Montessori faith to careful evaluation.

The heretical approach of KASS to one of the dominant educational ideologies of the early 1920s had its basis in differences in educational outlook and in its concern to remain financially viable. Parents were already voting with their feet by the end of 1921 and putting the KASS Montessori venture in financial jeopardy. Miss Taylor who ran the Montessori class called a meeting early in that year to explain the system to parents in order to attract more pupils but she was the only one who turned up. In a letter to a special meeting of council in February 1922 the committee of the Montessori class admitted that they faced a problem in that 'there is a certain amount of prejudice in the minds of the general public against the Montessori system and that any school bearing that name therefore starts with considerable handicap'. As the school was one of the two recognized feeder schools for KAS its unpopularity had considerable financial implications which threatened the whole enterprise at the critical time when the society had taken on the financial burden of Manor Wood before it had sold its Ellerdale Road properties. But it was not simply a financial issue. To the Froebelian, Alice Woods, the former principal of Maria Gray Training College who led the attack against the Montessori system within council, it was primarily an ideological matter. Montessori's rigidity, her attack on the Froebelian belief in the value of fairy-tale, fable and fantasy in stimulating children's imaginations, and her constant stress upon the specially designed Montessori apparatus without which her system could not be carried out were all indicative to Froebelians of authoritarianism. The Montessori emphasis upon allowing children to develop at an individual pace, free from the stress of rivalries and from the false incentives of reward and punishments, all of which accorded so well with KASS principles, tended to be lost sight of.

Alice Woods expressed her concern to council about the way in which the Montessori system imposed a 'thraldom on teachers', a charge which Miss Taylor, the Montessori teacher, found it difficult to

34. Freedom of expression

KING ALFRED SCHOOL SOCIETY

Preparatory School

Manor Wood, North End Rd., N.W. 3.
(5 minutes from Golder's Green Station).

NEXT TERM
Begins on

Sep. 20th

Directress:
Miss L. F. Taylor

Assistant Directress:
Miss G. H. Anderson
F. Hamilton

(Certified Froebel and Montessori Teachers).

35. The prep school
prospectus

refute. Although the latter claimed to feel 'a much greater freedom under the Montessori system than under others', she admitted that she had been prepared to modify the system and to improve on it but had been unable to do so. Miss Taylor realized that the issue at stake was one of confidence in the system and argued, with the backing of Mr Claremont, the leading British Montessorian who was present at the meeting, that given better staffing and equipment the class would expand and become 'financially entirely self-supporting'. Alice Woods, however, had the backing of the three most influential members of the committee, Jacoby, a chief mortgage-holder, Maberly, the sole survivor of the founding committee, and Wicksteed. What they sought was not the denunciation of Miss Taylor, in whom the council expressed its entire satisfaction in the first resolution proposed by Maberly, but a reduction in the status of the Montessori system within the society's schools.

The society had always avoided being identified with any one educational doctrine so Maberly's second resolution, carried by six votes to none with four abstentions, was well in keeping with the guiding principles which he had helped to lay down a quarter of a century earlier. It expressed in essence the principal objections against Montessori-ism which were to come to the fore nationally a few months later.

> That the Council is not convinced that the Montessori system contains the whole truth of education and is not willing to bind itself to the uncritical observance of any system so rigid in its tenets, and that therefore though willing to continue the experiment and to await with unbiased interest the result, is unwilling to continue the name of Montessori to a school held on its premises and under its auspices.

Dr Claremont, who had a strong commitment to Montessorian principles, wanted to ensure that the full message of the resolution was observed. She proposed an amendment to the effect that the council while 'recognising that the Montessori method may not be the only method of education' was 'sufficiently alive to its value'. She was clearly afraid that Maberly's resolution was a polite way of burying Montessori-ism but was willing to concede that 'a certain amount' of public antipathy to the method made it 'expedient that the class shall in future be called a Preparatory King Alfred School'. There was to be no hidden agenda as a third resolution made clear. The abandonment of the name was not to lead to the abandonment of the school, only a change in nomenclature and the right of Miss Taylor 'to make experiments especially on the lines of greater freedom'. A resolution to this effect was passed by six votes to one. The last three resolutions laid down the method by which the school's future was to be secured, with representa-tion on the school committee and council with the other preparatory school, and with the financial arrangements and the salaries of the two teachers clearly laid down. The change in status of Montessori-ism within KASS which these resolutions brought about, proved too much for Mr Claremont whose uncompromising faith in the system led him to request his release from 'the legal work of the society'. His wife, however, did not feel so strongly and expanded her work within the school and society. The debate had been in effect a microcosm of the growing national controversy over Montessori and her method.

To the society, however, the matter was not one of personality but one of principle. It had no intention of allowing any one educational doctrine to stifle all other initiatives and developments. One such development was the introduction of a class for Dalcroze eurhythmics in October 1923. While the name of Emile Jaques-Dalcroze has long been consigned to the footnotes of history books, the system of rhythmic movement which the Swiss professor of harmony developed remains popular today in a rather different form. He believed that music could best be appreciated through movement and that children, in particular, feel 'a craving to create', to invent and interpret rhythms and melodies in their movement. When done in association with others, as eurhythmics, he believed that altruistic feelings and qualities were heightened. Thus eurhythmics were much more than dance steps or physical exercises; they achieved a moral or spiritual goal both in the sense of contributing to the individual's all-round development and in that of using instinctive corporal rhythm as a means to promote social harmony. In the interwar years, Dalcroze eurhythmics were widely practised. The King Alfred School being so close to the Dalcroze movement's London headquarters was able to lead the way in bringing its benefits not only to its pupils but also to parents and friends during evening classes.

Dance became an important element in school life with the arrival of Peggy Van Praagh, a gifted teacher who subsequently spent her life teaching and directing ballet (for which she received an OBE). She taught Greek dancing, a form of simple, free, bare-foot dancing based on the position of dancers depicted on ancient Greek pottery. After some pupils saw her dancing with Rambert's Ballet Club at the Mercury Theatre they persuaded her to teach in the afternoon options. KAS considered ballet too formal, lacking the freedom of movement and creative expression of Dalcroze eurhythmics. Nevertheless, the pupils received ballet tuition, many enjoying the science and discipline of it which taught a flexibility, strength, body awareness and body control similar to those of hatha yoga. She also pioneered ballroom dancing, a popular activity during break times.

Wicksteed, Dalton and the crises of 1923–1924

Wicksteed gave his full backing to Maberly and to Alice Woods in their attempt to dethrone Montessori and to reduce her system to a handmaiden of educational reform. His principal objection, like theirs, was her suppression of liberty. Whilst he did not go as far as A. S. Neill, (who assisted Beatrice Ensor in the NEF and played a major role in the Dalcroze movement shortly after leaving KAS) in arguing that the Montessori system was disguised repression, nevertheless, he opposed the authoritarianism and rigidity which he believed lay in her control of her training schools, her total emphasis upon didactic apparatus such as lacing and buttoning frames and weights in sockets, and her refusal to give a child's imagination full scope for its development. As an acknowledged champion of freedom in education he was able to mount an effective challenge in council to Montessori ideology. However, the champion was soon to become the challenged when council undertook an inquiry into the freedom which his modified Dalton plan offered to pupils and which was far greater than was ever available under Russell. It produced a crisis of confidence which only the casting vote of the chairman prevented from turning into a repeat of the situation in 1901, a crisis of whose rumblings even the youngest pupils became aware.

The Dalton learning (as opposed to teaching) plan was pioneered in Dalton, Massachusetts, by Helen Parkhurst and brought to the general notice of British educationists in 1920, the year that Wicksteed succeeded Russell to the headship of KAS. Miss Belle Rennie's account of the Dalton Laboratory Plan in the *Times Educational Supplement* in May 1920 and Miss Rosa Bassett's introduction of the American experiment at Streatham County Secondary School a month later were the catalyst for widespread interest. Wicksteed may not have joined the pilgrims on the road to Streatham but it is likely that he attended the August conference of the British Association in Cardiff which discussed the

Bassett experiment and the meetings addressed by Helen Parkhurst when she visited England in 1921. The time was opportune for KAS to enter another stage in its educational evolution and to serve as a testbed for the latest educational model. The school had an enthusiastic new headmaster who aimed to break away from the more formal teaching patterns and arrangements which had evolved in the last years of Russell's headship. It had a new site at Manor Wood whose temporary huts proved more flexible than permanent buildings in meeting the needs of Dalton pupils, especially in the provision of subject rooms or what Helen Pankhurst called laboratories. Above all it offered an enlightened solution to an ideological problem which had confronted KAS since early in Russell's headship, namely, how to reconcile a rational education with the traditional public examinations for which parents increasingly expected KAS to enter their children.

At the heart of the Dalton plan was an idea which again became popular in the 1980s before the imposition of a national curriculum, that of a learning contract between pupil and teacher which involved rights and responsibilities. What this meant in the classrooms of KAS when the plan was fully developed was that pupils had the freedom to pursue subjects in the order in which they pleased, to go to the classrooms of their choice, but they had the responsibility of ensuring that all subjects with each of their stages were covered over a term. As one former pupil commented: 'Although you had to get through a certain amount of work in each subject in each term, one could select the time one did it and did not have to follow a routine each week.' In the senior school, the forms were social age groups not teaching units. The ex-army huts became subject rooms in charge of specialists in English, history, geography, science, mathematics and French with Latin, each with its own books, apparatus and work schedules. The specialist teachers developed schemes of work to cover the five or six years to school certificate. Each term's work in each subject was planned in a series of ten stages, each with a fixed number of tasks including the reading of passages, memorizing passages and poems, and essays. As each stage was completed it was 'evaluated' and, according to one former KAS pupil, 'I think you got a red, green or another colour and you chalked that up on the proper place on the wall. I suppose it was a marking system but somehow it did not strike us as such.' After each stage was passed and recorded graphically on form stage sheets, pupils passed on to the next, working at their own pace. The abler pupils thus did not have to mark time nor the less able to tackle quickly more than they could manage. It was possible for the slow learner to have part of the work carried over to the next month. During the first part of the

36. Two teachers: Violet Hyett on the right, a keen Dalton supporter

morning (9.30 to 11.05) the pupils attended any subject room they wished for individual work and during the second (11.30–12.40) they followed two periods of group work with each group receiving one lesson a week in English subjects and three each fortnight in mathematics and science. The form master or mistress had an overview of each pupil's work. Competition was eliminated and the child freed from the nightmare of homework. Learning took place in an atmosphere free from stress, fear and anxiety about marks and punishment. The afternoons from 2 to 4 p.m. were also run on Dalton lines and were devoted to private study or to clubs where each pupil had the choice of participating in a wide range of activities including country dancing, eurhythmics, visits to industry, games, photography and handicrafts (see Table 6). They followed closely the games, educational journeys, social gatherings and debates which Parkhurst had introduced in Dalton and New York. Fridays were an exception. On Friday mornings a written test alternated with talks by visiting speakers; in the afternoon there were lessons in either Latin or geography.

This modified Dalton plan was a radical departure from the Russell regime, especially in the relatively small amount of time given to academic studies and in the great freedom it gave to pupils, no subject being absolutely compulsory. It caused much concern within council. As early as May 1922 Wicksteed was defending his new methods in council and was anxious to dispel 'a certain impression that existed among parents and others that the school did not attach much value to serious and steady work'. With pupil numbers at the uncomfortably low level of seventy-eight (thirty-nine boys and thirty-nine girls) he was concerned to let it be 'generally known that KAS aimed at high standards'. He was, however, in a difficult position for many parents associated standards with marks and competition while the school committee was ever watchful for any departure from the founding principles. In 1922 it held an inquiry to ascertain 'to what extent and in what form competition and marks

Table 6 **King Alfred School afternoon choices**

Name:
Term:

Put '1' (or '2' if a second period is possible) after the subjects you want to take.

Country Dancing	Leather
Cricket or Hockey	Needlework
Drawing	Netball
English Dramatic	Photography
Eurhythmics	Printing
Football	Singing
Forge	Swimming
French Conversation	Tennis
German	Weaving
Gym.	Workshop
Industrial Club	Private Work

*Choices Approved, [Signature of Parent or Guardian]

*The Time Table will be made, as far as possible, to give scope for these choices. A change at half term can only be made on a written request from the parent.

existed'. Although the Dalton scheme involved the awarding of three grades, honours, pass or fail (to be replaced in 1927 by a range from A to C) and some league tables were published, nevertheless the school committee concluded that 'no violation of the Society's principle was taking place'. Wicksteed convinced the committee that 'KAS was not working on strict Dalton lines which involved monthly tests and contracting the work by time'. Examinations were only held twice a year and there were no time restrictions. As one former Alfredian put it, 'Competition was not encouraged. Your progress was your own business.'

But the old guard on the council were not satisfied and delivered an attack on Wicksteed and his modified Dalton plan from another direction. This time it was not the restrictions on freedom and individuality imposed by marks which concerned them but the excessive freedom which they believed he allowed pupils. Such freedom they argued was having an adverse affect on pupil numbers and pupil health. In July 1923, when the school numbers had increased slowly to only eighty-four, Riley, seconded by the daughter of the Claremonts, put forward a critical resolution. Wicksteed, like Rice, was facing a council motion which could amount to a vote of no confidence within three years of taking up the headship.

37. The prospectus designed in the print shop

That the council of the KASS note that in the present practice of the School the idea of freedom is being interpreted in a manner not intended by the By-Laws, which is having serious consequences to the health, manners and education of the children and which is giving rise to serious complaints from parents. It therefore requests the Headmaster to change his policy in such a manner as to remove the cause of complaint.

Riley, backed by Maberly, looked back to the Russell era when the headmaster was a continual inspiration and beacon, guiding and uplifting his pupils by example and exhortation. Wicksteed's style was altogether different and his less public profile, together with the greater freedom for pupils which the Dalton learning model entailed, led them to believe that the school displayed 'unwholesome license, . . . general, personal slackness and . . . a carelessness for the feelings and wishes of others'. Such failings, they argued, were injurious to the development of character and to the future of the school. Riley argued that three sections of by-law 37 were contravened, that self-reliance needed to be taught and self-assertion by those of a bullying disposition suppressed, that obedience to a common law ought to be instilled and that the disbelief in the efficacy of any penalties ought to be rejected. Miss Claremont favoured a proactive rather than a reactive headship which 'prevented moral lapses rather than allowing such to occur and then giving treatment'. Their disapproval of Wicksteed's style of headship and of his curricular programme which allowed a great deal of freedom of choice was all too apparent.

Wicksteed was not entirely isolated, for two of the parents who were present, Mr Goodhart and Mrs Close Shipham, expressed satisfaction with the school, the latter requesting that further evidence should be provided if Riley continued to press his resolution. Before the headmaster could make a full reply, Maberly successfully urged an adjournment and consultations with the school staff. The meeting with the school staff on 24 July 1923 failed to produce any evidence for Riley's assertions, and gave full backing to Wicksteed. They argued that there had been no decline in standards of behaviour, health or teaching methods under the new headmaster. The adjourned meeting took place the following day when the matter of his compulsory or voluntary resignation was aired openly. By the casting vote of the chairman, Shipham, a vote of no confidence in his headship was lost and was replaced by one introduced by Mrs Beeton and Miss Alice Woods which acknowledged the differences in style of Russell and Wicksteed but which emphasized 'their identity of purpose'. On this basis they asserted that Wicksteed was steadfast to the principles of KASS and thus worthy of 'their wholehearted support and co-operation in the management of the school'. Their resolution was passed eight to three (with Riley, Maberly and Miss Claremont being the likely minority). However, the division of opinion, unlike that in the case of Rice in 1901, did not lead to resignations or to any permanent divisions within council. Maberly, the council's elder statesman and father figure, wrote to Wicksteed a few days later, stating that he 'would not press any more for any alterations to your method', adding that he 'would much rather send a child to KAS under you than to any ordinary school'. Most of the critics of the headmaster retired from the school committee so that Wicksteed could feel he had overwhelming support for his method.

The crisis was not yet at an end. While those whom Wicksteed had appointed to the staff of the school had fully endorsed his teaching methods and programme in their interviews with council members there still remained one person from the Russell era which, the head noted, had an 'atmosphere (which) would be always a distinct one from mine'. In a letter to Maberly in August 1923 Wicksteed claimed that he had accepted Miss Beddall, his secretary and secretary to the council, because she was popular with the children and he did not want any more changes than were necessary. He found after the clash with the council that the temperamental gulf between them had grown too great to bridge, and was affecting his efficacy. His letter pointed out how much he had relied on his secretaries in the past in view of his uncertain health. He felt he could 'not get from Miss Beddall the kind of help I had originally contemplated'. Wicksteed thus looked forward to 'equipping myself with help more of the character I originally contemplated'. Miss Beddall, probably aware or made aware of the headmaster's feelings, had tendered her resignation.

When Miss Beddall presented her letter of resignation to council in December 1923, the matter aroused considerable debate. The reason for her resignation was said by her to be the headmaster's stated belief that 'her presence was a hindrance in the conduct of the school'. Certainly, Wicksteed's letter to Maberly had made it clear that in view of the council's support for him 'by however narrow a majority' he felt it his duty 'to support myself in every way that I consider possible and likely to improve my efficiency'. He was thus testing the extent of council's support. The last meeting of council in December 1923 showed that such support was far from unanimous. There was a strong feeling of sympathy for Miss Beddall and especially for the view that Wicksteed had himself expressed in the controversy with the Montessorians that differences of opinion and the refusal to follow 'exactly the same educational shibboleths' were the vigorous lifeblood of healthy educational institutions. But the headmaster remained adamant despite appeals by several council members to find some other way out of the situation, other than by resignation. Whether there was an alternative was difficult to see, for Miss Beddall had declared her decision irrevocable. Nevertheless, council voted by nine to four in favour of asking her to reconsider. If she chose not to reconsider then she would be informed of its regret and of 'its entire confidence in her loyalty to the School and to the Society', as well as its deep appreciation of her work for both. She was not willing to reconsider and Eileen Rocke, an Old Alfredian, was appointed in her place. Eileen Rocke, described by a former student as 'a dark, classical-looking, serene, fairly young woman', later became Wicksteed's wife.

The matter did not end there, for a resolution of no confidence and a request for Wicksteed's resignation was put by Maberly and Brewer before a special meeting of council. Findlay backed this resolution if it could be shown that any considerable numbers 'of councillors of standing' had lost confidence in him. However, many parents gave the headmaster their support in a series of letters addressed to council, as did eighty-four 'in a memorial'. Alice Woods and Krohn argued for any charges to be put in writing, with time being given for the headmaster to reply before another special meeting. This was carried and another special meeting was convened eight days later, prior to which a meeting between parents and council would take place. The resolution of no confidence was withdrawn at the second special meeting. Maberly, one of its original proposers and the only surviving member of the founding group, resigned his treasurership, his last contribution being to allow his portrait to hang in the KASS offices.

Thus came to an end the most difficult period of Wicksteed's headship. He had openly acknowledged that neither he nor anyone else could have continued 'J.R.'s school anywhere', either at Ellerdale Road or Manor Wood. However, many councillors had wanted a larger measure of continuity than Wicksteed was willing to permit. They yearned to create something of a Russell tradition, yet to do so would have robbed KAS of the opportunity to take a lead in testing the exciting educational ideas of the 1920s. Educational reform had moved on even in the few years since Russell's retirement. To create traditions and to stand still was to stagnate; to stagnate was to decline. KAS could not afford the luxury of basking in the warm glow of tradition, something which Wicksteed recognized more than members of council. Besides, his Dalton-based curriculum offered immense opportunities for implementing child-centred learning more fully than ever before. Teachers who normally spent their time studying subjects, with the constant nightly pressures of preparation, were now free to study children. Children, instead of studying teachers, could now study subjects with a degree of choice and independence.

'. . . We have come to stay'

The clash of high principle in council contrasted with the squalor which seemed at times to overwhelm parts of the Manor Wood site. By 1923 the comfortable and appealing image of the woodland idyll had given way, especially in winter months, to that of the muddy eyesore. The round-the-clock dumping of soil from the underground excavations had not endeared the school to its neighbours who threatened legal action to stop it. The blue clay threatened their properties because of the drainage problems and pools of water it created. There were floods of various kinds, including one of the preparatory school caused by the blocking of the drain from Manor House hospital 'by bandages and other unsuitable materials'. If Riley was seeking reasons why the school numbers had increased only slowly from seventy-eight in 1922 to eighty-four in 1923 and eighty-eight in 1924 they were not solely to be found in Wicksteed's alleged 'excessive freedom'. Mud rather than Montessori, dirt rather than Dalton, were more likely to dissuade middle-class Garden Suburbia from sending its offspring to KAS, especially as the

38. The school field before development

39. The open-air
theatre, 1923

40. The paddling pool
near the open-air
theatre

playing fields and permanent buildings of UCS, but a stone's throw away, provided a stark and pleasant contrast. But if the transformation of KAS from a temporary to a permanent school was at times messy and always piecemeal it nevertheless affirmed that it was here to stay.

Wicksteed always looked beyond the immediate to the future. The dumping of soil and the felling of some trees bordering houses in the Garden Suburb were necessary to provide the level playing fields without which organized games were difficult if not impossible. The provision of adequate sports fields had a financial as well as an ideological purpose. He saw them as necessary to attract and to retain older pupils, which was one of the constant problems facing the school. When so many other schools in the area with which KAS was in competition for pupils had their own playing fields as part of the school campus, KAS could ill afford to leave its uneven leafy slopes undisturbed. Level playing fields meant inevitable, initial unsightly disturbance but within a couple of years they would prove their worth. Wicksteed also had strong ideological reasons for welcoming the free soil brought by Sabey and other contractors from central London. He had been heavily criticized within council and by Old Alfredians for his excessive attachment to individualism. The Old Alfredians, in particular, looked to organized games to engender stronger corporate feelings to counteract the egotistical impulses of pupils. Wicksteed's daily discussions with the contractors whose task it was to dump and level the soil for a new playing field were all to this end. He thus had better reason than most to welcome the first green shoots which appeared in 1924, a year before Sabey's first contract expired, at the boundaries of the preparatory school. A second contract was agreed to allow dumping over the orchard. Hitherto the school had to use the grounds of the YMCA, parts of Hampstead Heath, the local church hall, Child's Hill and elsewhere as makeshift games and physical education locations.

It could now develop its games curriculum and Mrs Winser, a teacher from Bedales, was appointed to undertake the task. The new fields, including the full-size cricket field brought about by the demolition of the stables, could also generate income when rented out to folk dancing groups and others. The building of a fives court to the north of the dumping area was initially aided by the fact that the Old Alfredians agreed to buy the ground and to give the school exclusive use of it in the daytime. This was not achieved without long-drawn-out negotiations.

To Wicksteed the immediate advantage of these improvements was to increase the attractiveness of the school to older pupils. This was not the only means used. In addition to advertisement in the *New Statesman*, the *Nation* and in the *Times Educational Supplement*, and locally in the lifts of Hampstead station (with pupil-designed posters), he pressed for the publicized introduction of two bursaries, particularly to retain older boys. He still realized that a key problem was that many parents believed that KAS did not give sufficient attention to academic preparation for examinations. As Wicksteed admitted towards the end of his headship, whilst his 'staff were only too aware of the difficulties and compromises which must be made . . . they could not sacrifice the principle that education must come before examinations'. The main problem was one of convincing parents that a rationalist education and examination preparation were not antithetical.

It was, however, difficult to persuade parents that either could be achieved in ex-army huts which were coming to the end of their useful life. Although improvements were made to their furniture and floor covering they could not serve indefinitely the needs of the growing school. Significantly, it was not the replacement of individual classrooms to which Wicksteed and the council first gave their attention but to a building which would strengthen the corporate nature and spirit of the school. Small improvements had been made, some such as seats, fences and gates as memorials to staff or pupils. Mr and Mrs Corbett Fisher, for example, gave new gates to the school in memory of their son. The first major improvement was the building in 1925 of what was termed the 'dining hall' but which in fact served many more purposes, including providing for the staging of plays, rooms for the debating society and even a dark room under the stage for the photographic society. As early as 1921 Wicksteed had asked council to enlarge the dining hut for the putting on of plays and other social events, so that by the time that council turned to the matter of building a permanent dining hall it had become well established that its functions would go well beyond mass feeding. But of equal importance was its symbolic role. As Wicksteed

41. The school entrance
around 1925

said at the opening of the new hall in 1926, 'It will make us appear as if we have come to stay.'

As early as 1922 Hendon Council had begun to reject development plans on the grounds that the Manor Wood school already had 'too many temporary structures'. At that time, with the Ellerdale Road buildings still unsold, KASS could think little beyond plans to alter the dining hut and to add three sheds for coal, bicycles and tools, scarcely improvements which were likely to enhance the school's image in the locality. Even the preparatory school had managed to persuade only six of its forty-four leavers to enter KAS in the years 1923 to 1925. By the end of 1925, however, it seemed to have turned the financial corner. The Ellerdale Road buildings had been sold; pupil numbers had reached ninety-two, leaving a deficit of only £156 which was likely to be turned into a surplus with the plans to close Miss Taylor's preparatory school and to open a preparatory class at KAS for children of five and over. Council willingly took on board the idea that there 'should be a preparatory school on the same site and under the same management as the upper school'. The demolition of the coachhouse and stables which had housed the Montessori school and Miss Taylor's preparatory school meant that a new start could be made. The society could now look more securely to the future and plan for its first major building project, a new dining hall which could cater for the whole school, including its preparatory section.

Believing that stagnation was a prelude to decline, the society moved quickly to appoint Barry Parker, one of the principal architects of the Garden Suburb, to undertake the task. He presented his plans to council shortly before Christmas 1925. Parker estimated that the building of the hall would cost £3,750. This was subsequently reduced to a maximum of £2,500 when Wicksteed approached Gowers, a building firm, for an estimate. By March 1926 the building committee with council approval had appointed Parker as architect and the society approached the bank to increase its loan for the building of its new reinforced concrete hall. In order to make full use of the Easter break to try to complete the building by September 1926, Goodhart, Mrs Corbett Fisher, Mr Jacobs and Mrs Wicksteed agreed to act as guarantors to meet the bank's requirements that £1,000 of the £2,500 loan be paid off within three years.

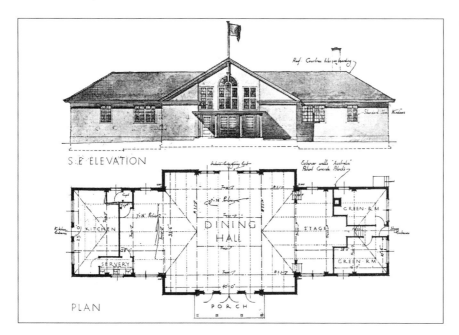

42. Architect's sketch of the new hall, 1925

Some details of the Parker plan were modified, including the proposed glass doors which were replaced by wooden ones painted black. Money was also saved by such means as reducing the amount of gilding on the flagpole, by a more economical gas stove in the kitchen and by making the table tops out of the excess floorboards. Parker's idea of painting the steel roof trusses light green was also modified to include varnishing to improve the tone and finish. In June 1926, with the old dining hut having been removed to be used elsewhere and the building of the new hall being well under way, the building committee, consisting of McGregory Ross, Corbett Fisher and Wicksteed, closely scrutinized the work of Kentish, the contractor. This included giving advice on the type of window catches, on the siting of additional power points and on the provision of an extra stage, and using old gateposts as pillars. Ultraviolet glass was to be used in the large window over the front door as a memorial to Dr Ethelberta Claremont, who had found the Manor Wood site for the school and whose early death robbed KAS of a valued friend.

The plan to open the new building in September 1926 proved to be overambitious. In December 1926 the building committee were still discussing details of furnishings but the scheme was completed in January 1927. Plans were drawn up for relocating classes as the result of the freeing of the old dining hut which was removed to a site below the school hall. It was used by groups E and D. A and its bookshelves were to be situated in the workshop, with B moved to A's former classroom and C to B's. The room formerly occupied by C now became the staffroom. The society and school office and headmaster's study were situated in the green room of the new hall, with the hall also serving as a dining room, a gymnasium, a drama studio, a place to which children could go on wet days, an assembly hall and an examination room. In the evenings, and when not in use in the daytime, it was to be rented out, thus helping to pay off some of the bank loan. The new building was ready for use in January 1927.

By May 1927 the school population had increased to ninety-seven, reflecting the growing prosperity of many Hampstead parents and the more pleasing appearance and appeal of the entrance to the site with its new gate and tarmacked drive leading to the new hall. Efforts were made to improve the rather neglected appearance of much of the hinterland which had been taken over by 'grass and dock leaves in abundance'. The pupils were given the task of turning back the march of nature, while at the same time the long task of dumping, infilling and levelling was nearing completion, allowing what had been termed 'the mud wallows' to be grassed. The new field which resulted enabled the school to meet the parental demand for football, a sport whose popularity grew immensely in the 1920s. By the time that the school numbers had reached 100 in January 1928 council was considering adding to the sports facilities through the provision of two hard tennis courts. The debt incurred in 1926 was reduced by fêtes, recitals by Solomon, a former pupil and world-famous pianist, the production of

43. Birkett and pupils in 'the mud wallows'

plays such as *Pygmalion* and various other activities. The interest on the capital was covered by the letting of the hall to a variety of local groups.

However, council had never waited to clear its debts before embarking on further improvements, something which Wicksteed and the building subcommittee knew only too well. In June 1928, the Board's inspectors indicated in their report areas to which any further building programme should be directed – a larger and more completely equipped laboratory, a geography room, a library, an art room and a more convenient workshop. Exactly a year later, the building subcommittee summoned an extraordinary meeting of council to consider a proposal to borrow £10,000 to pay off the debt to the bank and the other mortgages (amounting to just over half the sum) and to finance the building of new classrooms. Though the building sub-committee did not realize it, the timing of the meeting was significant for it came in the last heady months of the age of unbridled optimism before Britain's economic collapse in the wake of the crash of the American stock market in October 1929. In June 1929 the Manor Wood estate was valued at £17,200, a sum deemed more than adequate upon which to raise £10,000 for the new buildings. Only the arguments for expansion were lacking. These were provided by one of the principal council members and chairman of the building committee, Corbett Fisher, and by Wicksteed, J. H. Badley, Thomas, and significantly for the future, Miss Hyett and Mr Birkett. Corbett Fisher opened on a cautionary note, saying that he had an open mind as to whether KAS could attract sixty new pupils, making a school population of 200 in all, which was necessary to meet the additional annual expenditure of £1,200. His opening remarks provided the other speakers with a theme upon which to enlarge. Wicksteed argued that with the existing buildings KAS was unlikely to be able to compete successfully with local boys' schools, a prophetic remark in view of the

44. Parker's school hall, 1926

45. The big slide, 1936

fact that the coming dark economic clouds would intensify competition. What he believed could emerge from an attractive building programme was a school of 200 'well distributed in age'. He was still chasing the elusive goal of a school with a strong and balanced, truly coeducational upper school, a point which Miss Hyett took up. The accommodation which a building scheme would provide would stem the haemorrhage of

46. Architect's sketch of the library building, late 1920s

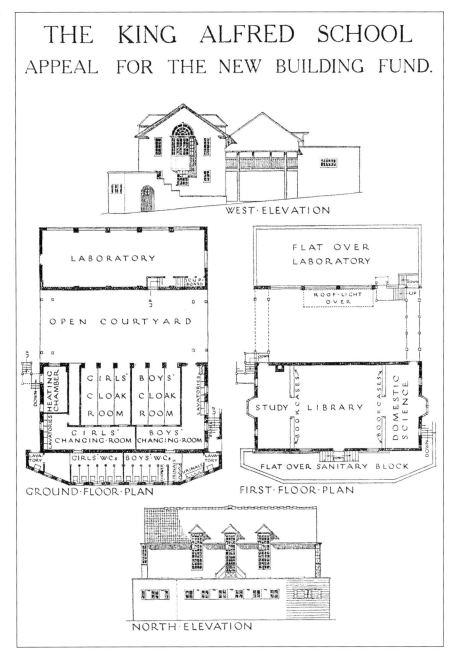

THE KING ALFRED SCHOOL
APPEAL FOR THE NEW BUILDING FUND.

WEST·ELEVATION

LABORATORY

CUP-BOARD

OPEN COURTYARD

HEATING CHAMBER

UP
DOWN

LAVATORIES

GIRLS' CLOAK ROOM

BOYS' CLOAK ROOM

LAVATORIES

GIRLS' CHANGING·ROOM

BOYS· CHANGING·ROOM

LAVA-TORY

GIRLS·W·Cs

BOYS·W·Cs

LAVA-TORY

URINALS

GROUND·FLOOR·PLAN

FLAT OVER LABORATORY

ROOF·LIGHT OVER

DOWN

UP

DOWN

STUDY LIBRARY

BOOKCASES

BOOKCASES

DOMESTIC SCIENCE

DOWN

FLAT OVER SANITARY BLOCK

FIRST·FLOOR·PLAN

NORTH·ELEVATION

pupils at sixteen and enable the appointment of a sixth specialist teacher, particularly in Birkett's view a science teacher. Badley supported Wicksteed and the two future heads when he emphasized that 'the goodwill of the school must gradually deteriorate if it were not reinforced by progressive work in buildings and staffing'. The arguments were sufficiently persuasive to enable Corbett Fisher and Jacobs to gain unanimous support for a resolution in which council, in principle, approved the building of 'a science laboratory, library and classrooms and cloakrooms'. With Miss Hyett and Birkett now reinforcing the building committee, it was unlikely that the scheme would languish. The report of the Board of Education in March had indicated shortcomings in accommodation, especially for art and craft work, and this was taken as good reason for the building committee to include an art and craft block in the new plan.

As in 1926, council turned to the internationally celebrated architect, Barry Parker, to design the new buildings, the plans for which were laid before a sparsely attended extraordinary meeting in 1929 by Hall, Parker's representative. They received general approval and the next step was agreed upon, that of preparing working drawings. In keeping with KAS traditions, the new buildings were multifunctional. The working drawings were tabled in April 1930 and the list of contractors reduced to two, but even before a final decision had been arrived at Wicksteed was asking council to consider erecting a building for two classes on the site of the existing laboratory at an additional cost of £1,000. He gained the general support of council and thus the building programme was extended further to include the replacement of the old laboratories. Without endowments to draw upon or assistance from the state, the additional building, like the main scheme, had to be financed by loans, gifts and increased pupil numbers, which as the nation's financial situation grew worse became an even more difficult task. However, the financial crisis which was to topple the second Labour government was still a year away. The school numbers, which had increased from 143 in July 1930 to 164 in November 1930, still favoured the optimists and expansionists. The din of 'the builder's trowel and the carpenter's hammer' signified progress. With work proceeding well on the original scheme, Parker drew up plans for the additional block in the summer of

47. The library and new buildings, 1930

1930; though Wicksteed struck a warning note by urging that a sustained effort was needed to raise money for the new developments, it was not until the end of the summer term 1931 that numbers declined from 167 to 149, 'largely attributable to the trade depression'. By that time the new buildings had been open for a full academic year and if they did not deliver the rapid increase in pupils which Wicksteed had promised, they helped to slow down the loss by giving the school what he termed 'improved status'.

48. The art and crafts block, 1930

49. The library

The library, with its inadequate heating and poorly filled shelves (though preserving a grand piano), was at first the least satisfactory of the new buildings; the headmaster shared some of its discomforts for his study was located in one of its anterooms, releasing his room in the hall for a much needed staffroom. The covered court which served as an assembly hall and wet-weather play area proved more immediately useful, whilst the science laboratory (which also housed the print unit) and the arts and crafts block rarely failed to impress visitors. The displaced huts which used to house the two top forms of the middle school were a constant reminder that not all pupils enjoyed the benefits of permanent buildings.

The building programmes of 1925–6 and 1930–1 were not an attempt to implement the earlier Voysey scheme. They still allowed much scope for the Manor Wood site to retain a rural and informal freshness which would have been precluded by the severely formal lines of the 1920 plan. Thus pupils could enjoy the benefits of a rural environment in which the school's amphitheatre (enlarged in the late 1920s) was located.

Inspectors and inspected: differences in ideology and expectation

The attempts by KASS to have its Hampstead school placed on the list of secondary schools recognized as efficient by the Board of Education were always problematic. It had tried and failed in 1913 and was to apply again in 1922 with the same result. As Morgan Jones, Labour's new parliamentary secretary to the president of the Board of Education, informed Hopkin Morris, Hampstead's Member of Parliament a little later the term 'secondary school' had a precise meaning which implied 'a certain form of organisation, a certain range of curriculum and a certain age range'.[8] While the society's application was understandable in view of the financial advantages and enhanced status which would accrue if it were successful, most of the school's ten members of staff and seventy-eight pupils were aware in 1922 that KAS was so markedly different from traditional secondary schools that the chances of its succeeding were slight. Had Wicksteed consulted the school's student advisory committee rather than council he might have been dissuaded from initiating the application in the first place.

Violet Hyett, 'the tall, severe history teacher who almost boasted about being plain', was pessimistic about the outcome of the 1922 application on the grounds that the school lacked practical instruction in the domestic subjects usually associated with girls' secondary education, that is cookery, laundry work and housekeeping. In reality, however, the gulf between the inspectors and KAS had as much to do with concepts of education as it had to do with subjects. It is doubtful whether the Board's inspectors understood fully the thinking behind the Dalton-based morning curriculum and the club options which constituted the afternoon programme. Nor was it their aim to do so. The purpose of their visit was simply to see whether KAS made 'adequate provision for instruction' (note the emphasis on instruction rather than learning) in English language and literature, history, geography, mathematics, drawing, natural science, and in at least one foreign language. Other forms of curricular provision including games, physical exercises, singing and domestic subjects came within their remit. The inspectors were thus using a very traditional yardstick by which to measure a markedly non-traditional school.

The work of the junior school under Miss Bristol and Miss Cullis received a brief report which pointed to good standards of reading but with 'considerable variety in writing and spelling'. Perhaps the variations in styles of writing and the varied approaches to teaching spelling were not surprising in view of the great number of preparatory schools which pupils had attended before coming to KAS. The upper school, against which the general standards of the traditional school were applied, was not so briefly or sympathetically dealt with.

50. The staff in the academic year, 1922–3: (back row) far left, H. B. L. Webb; middle, Miss Cullis, J. H. Wicksteed; far right, Miss Bullock; (front row) far right, Miss Hibburd, Miss Hyett

The upper school in 1922 comprised four forms, Alpha, A, Bl and B2, each following what the inspectors described as 'the library method of work' or a modified Dalton scheme. English, taught by Wicksteed and Webb, and history, under the direction of Miss Hyett, were said to have reached a standard 'commonly found amongst children of the same ages in English Secondary Schools'. The theoretical scheme which Wicksteed and Webb had devised impressed the inspectors more than its classroom application, whereas Miss Hibburd's classroom teaching, while judged to be good, was said to lack the broad range of library materials necessary to attain the best results from the Dalton approach. The other subjects inspected, French under Dorothy Bullock, science under Bagnall and mathematics under Miss Hibburd, were severely criticized. Miss Bullock, who had been appointed to teach French a few weeks earlier, was absolved from blame for 'the low standard of attainment'. (She went on to impress her pupils and council with her teaching abilities.) While the mathematics mistress, Miss Hibburd, was described as an 'unusually skilful teacher', her schemes of work were said to be poor. The inspectors were looking for more whole-group teaching, especially in algebra and geometry, which did not accord with the fundamental Dalton principles of pupils working at their own pace with little formal class teaching. The inspectors with their traditionalist outlook favoured homework and suggested that the fact that the Alpha form was more advanced than form A was partly due to the former's homework timetable.

Science, which should have been one of the jewels in the KAS crown, came off badly both in the inspectors' report and in the questionnaire completed by former pupils. The ex-pupils' view that it was 'badly taught' was borne out by the inspectors who found the teaching 'unmethodical' and the record-keeping of the previous teacher extremely poor. No detailed scheme of work for the various groups had been mapped out. The Dalton scheme, which relied heavily upon forward-planning and detailed recording of pupil attainment, had thus not been implemented, with the result that pupils had little 'training in scientific method' and no sound basic 'knowledge of the subject' upon which to build. Despite these deficiencies, pupils nevertheless maintained an interest in the subject area. Though it was Bagnall whom the inspectors saw teaching the upper school it was his predecessor, Dr Eiloart, who was most heavily censured. Garside Bagnall had joined the staff on a salary of £250 per annum in September 1922 and barely had time to outline his work for the autumn term to council before the inspectors descended on the school. Although their trenchant criticisms were directed to the shortcomings of his predecessor's planning, organization and record keeping, Bagnall decided to leave the school at the end of the academic year, on the stated grounds of his inability to find a house in the area. He was succeeded in September 1923 by H. De Birkett who, with Violet Hyett (who taught history and other subjects), was to succeed jointly to the headship a decade later.

Such lapses might, in the view of the inspectors, have been forgiven if KAS had excelled in those two areas which were regarded as the hallmarks of a traditional state secondary education, Latin and games. When, however, we bear in mind that these yardsticks were derived from the great single-sex boarding schools of the nineteenth century, which KASS had been set up to oppose, then it is not surprising that KAS was deemed to 'fall short in both areas'. From the outset, KAS had placed Latin on the periphery of the curriculum and refused to accept the view that battlefield victories were either necessary or were won on public school playing fields. Both games and Latin were optional, which, while not quite making the inspectors apoplectic, drew the retort that after two years of learning Latin, many pupils had 'only a slender acquaintance with the language'. Physical exercises held by a part-time mistress in a nearby school hall, and games taken by the male staff on Hampstead Heath, not only on an optional basis but in mixed classes, drew several cryptic comments about such unusual practices. The mixing of the sexes, in particular, caused a little consternation lest 'the possibility of over-strain (for girls) under such conditions should be . . . overlooked'.

The inspectors found it difficult to reconcile much of what they saw at KAS with contemporary secondary school practice, which, of course, was precisely the difficulty they should have had. The traditional single-sex secondary school, where homework was a regular and important part of the curriculum, where whole-class teaching was the norm, where prizes and trophies were awarded, especially for outstanding achievement in Latin and games, and where examination passes were the bench marks of successful teaching was a world apart from the Dalton-based coeducation of KAS. The failure of the school to gain recognition under the secondary school regulations, while a blow to the school's finances and council self-esteem, confirmed the distinctiveness of the educational venture. Though there was no full reference to school discipline, it was a matter which concerned parents and pupils, some praising the freer atmosphere, whilst others regretted that Wicksteed was not a disciplinarian.

By 1922, however, a growing body of opinion even in official circles was beginning to question the kind of curricular yardsticks used by the Board of Education to measure secondary education. The most prestigious of the Board's own advisory committees, its Consultative Committee, was coming to favour some of the educational practices to be found at KAS and it is difficult not to conclude that had its part-time advisers, such as Professor Percy Nunn and R. H. Tawney, inspected the school instead of its full-time inspectorate the report would have been more favourable. Within six months of the inspection, the Consultative Committee produced a report on *The Differentiation of Curriculum for Boys and Girls Respectively in Secondary Schools*, which endorsed to some extent many of the principles underlying a KAS education, but then perhaps this was not entirely unexpected as Findlay, the society's president and J. H. Badley, a prominent council member, appeared before the committee to put the case for progressive education. Though the Consultative Committee did not give full support to coeducation, it argued in favour of greater freedom from examinations, wider subject choice and a more prominent place in the curriculum for aesthetic subjects including eurhythmics, allowing pupils to play a greater part in organizing their own studies, reducing homework and school hours and of greater awareness of the problems of strain and fatigue. The committee's recommendations were too advanced to be acceptable to the Board's president, the historian, H. A. L. Fisher, and the rest of Lloyd George's peacetime coalition government. Nevertheless, the Consultative Committee continued to give broad circulation to these and other progressive ideas in its famous trilogy of reports on adolescent (1926), primary (1930) and nursery education (1933) when several people who were connected with the society, including Alice Woods, presented evidence.

It was not just the curriculum which distinguished KAS from most state secondary schools and many independent schools, including its neighbour, UCS. It was a young school which was having difficulty growing up. Compared with the traditional secondary school and with UCS it had few older pupils, and very few of sixth-form age. The more numbers increased, the more glaring became the problem, as the percentage of students of sixteen and over decreased. In 1922 13 per cent of pupils were under nine, and 8 per cent over the age of sixteen. With the opening of the school's own preparatory department in 1926, these figures changed considerably. By 1928 no less than 40 per cent were under the age of nine (when the school population reached 113) with $3\frac{1}{2}$ per cent of sixteen and over. Pupils thus saw very few older students who were sitting the kind of examinations usually taken by sixth-formers. This in itself was a disincentive to building up Alpha classes 1 and 2, the KAS equivalent to a sixth form. Wicksteed tried to counter this through his scheme of bursaries particularly for older boys, but it had little effect.

The school was also much smaller than most state secondary schools and had better staff–pupil ratios. Few such schools had fewer than 300 pupils, with many having at least double that figure. KAS reached 100 at the beginning of 1928 without forfeiting its advantageous staffing ratio of about one member of staff to each nine or ten pupils. The pupils also benefited from the small staff turnover, especially in the upper school. The first major staff change in the senior school after Birkett replaced Bagnall in 1923 was the appointment of a new mathematics and games teacher, Mr Rustomjee, a Parsee, in the summer term of 1927. This was a consequence of Miss Hibburd's move to the school office, where she replaced Miss Rocke who went to work in the East End. Changes of staff were much more frequent in the junior school. Miss de Candole was appointed to teach the D form in December 1924 in the place of Miss Bristol. She remained at KAS until the end of the summer term 1927 when she left to teach at St Saviour's in Southwark; she was replaced by Miss Robey, who was assisted by Wicksteed's daughter, Ursula. A year earlier, Miss Cullis, who had been one of the first of Wicksteed's appointments, left with Miss Beeton, who had been at the school for three years, to set up their own school. Miss Caldicott who was also one of Wicksteed's early appointments left in 1926 to work in a school 'recognised by the Board of Education'. She was succeeded by Miss Gillett who, with Miss Ewbank, was the mainstay of the junior school. At the time of the school's third inspection by the Board, in June 1928, Miss Flint was brought in to teach the youngest class, the E class. Thus, the senior school saw relatively few staff changes compared with the junior school which, in view of the fact that the Dalton plan was being developed, was a great advantage to pupils.

If stability was one of the principal features of the upper school in the period between the two inspections in 1922 and 1928, so too was the growing corporate spirit of the school. The feeling that the school was an educational community was reinforced by the development of the activities of the school advisory council to which each form elected a representative to sit alongside members of staff. The greater freedom which the Dalton style of teaching and the afternoon choices offered was thus accompanied by the greater general responsibility which the pupils had in running the school. The representatives attended some of the meetings of the school committee by invitation, helped to find suitable ways of dealing with abuses of freedom such as occurred in 1922 with an outbreak of window and furniture breaking and wall demolition, advised on matters such as school dress, raised money for school funds by arranging dances and other events, and suggested ways of spending it, such as on whitewashing their classroom ceilings. The

51. 1930s piped music

advisory committee also raised matters in council, including a request to be able to discuss religious issues. Thus one of the distinctive aspects of school life which was recalled by former students in later years was the feeling that KAS valued their opinions and that experience on the advisory council taught pupils the basics of committee work including how to chair meetings, deal with other committees and keep minutes. For some, this involvement helped to instil the belief that they were 'pioneers in a great educational experiment', which distinguished KAS and its pupils from other independent schools. Pupils felt a distinctiveness, in particular from 'non-coeducational establishments which housed what they termed "N.E.P.S.Bs" (Nice English public school boys)'.

What also led many pupils to feel that they were special was what one ex-pupil called the fundamental belief 'inherent in a school of tolerance, individual liberty and communal responsibility'. Such values were said to have been fostered by outstanding teachers such as Joseph Wicksteed, Violet Hyett, Dorothy Bullock and Elizabeth Jenkins. The latter joined KAS in 1929 towards the end of Wicksteed's headship, to teach English literature and remained there for a decade. Miss Jenkins found her predecessor Henry Bertram Webb a hard act to follow. Several of his former pupils have described him as 'a real teacher, the kind who instilled a real love of reading and books, a real sense of enjoyment'. They also remember his wife, who spent much time in school looking for him. Her death led to his resignation for shortly after she died, according to one of his pupils: 'Stanley Baldwin discovered her and especially her novel, *Precious Bane*, on the radio; she became famous and I'm sure that Mr Webb got a substantial income, because pretty soon after that he bought a Bentley and married one of his students.' He was indeed a hard act to follow although Elizabeth Jenkins more than matched his teaching and dramatic accomplishments, especially in the teaching of Shakespeare and her annual production of his plays and those of later playwrights. Then in her twenties, she was already a recognized novelist and biographer, especially of Jane Austen and Queen Elizabeth I. She went to a progressive school, St Christopher's, before going to Newnham College, Cambridge. Her comment about her father's choice of St Christopher's reflected the gender-balance problem which confronted Wicksteed at KAS: 'Not my brothers – oh no, that wouldn't have done. Father was prepared to take a risk with me.'[9]

In many ways, KAS was an international community with all the strengths and weaknesses of such. It meant that while tolerance of different outlooks was an ingrained feature of school life and the heightened awareness of different national backgrounds and viewpoints was a natural part of the KAS educational process and experience, the school population was less constant than most, with many such as the Krassin sisters returning to their native countries. The constant infusion of new outlooks, particularly from Central Europe and America, thus had its drawbacks, especially for the Board's inspectorate which operated with a model of the traditional secondary school where pupils spent their entire adolescence in one school. The cosmopolitan character of KAS, with its other distinctive characteristics of being coeducational, placing little emphasis on homework and allowing pupils great freedom of choice, placed the school on an altogether different plane from that which was the normal experience of secondary school children. The influx of German refugees after Hitler came to power was to reinforce its multinational basis.

That is not to say that KAS refused to adjust its curriculum to the realities of interwar Britain. Wicksteed moved towards more conventional practices in some areas. In l926 he introduced what were termed 'test papers'. It became part of the pupils' lot to undertake 'set papers on different classroom subjects', which were 'to be taken in rotation week by week'. This, and other reforms such as the introduction of homework unless parents objected and more 'work' in the afternoons, were part of the preliminaries begun in l926 in preparation for a third inspection by the Board two years later. In some ways, he was returning to the practices for which he had criticized Russell.

There were other moves towards a more conventional secondary school curriculum in the years immediately following the inspection. These included an increased emphasis upon organized games, which, in part, resulted from the provision of suitable fields and courts on the Manor Wood site and from criticisms of the curriculum by Old Alfredians. By 1924, the cricket pitch laid down by the contractor in charge of dumping, Sabey, had reached second XI standard. In 1926 the school committee sanctioned a do-it-yourself approach to improving the tennis courts through the purchase of spades and rakes. Football was added to the curriculum by popular and parental demand, encouraged no doubt, in 1923, by the first Cup Final to be held at Wembley. To ensure that such games did not deteriorate into a 'kick and rush' or a 'hit and rush' approach, Miss Winser, physical culture mistress of

Bedales, was appointed to organize physical education with help from part-time coaches for cricket, tennis and football. Miss Winser was particularly concerned to raise the standard of the gymnasium classes. Rustomjee was also appointed to teach games as well as mathematics, his flexible body and fluid graceful movements as evident in hockey as they were in tennis and cricket. Thus KAS responded to the athletic and sporting demands of the age: this was a natural development in a school whose curriculum had never stood still and whose site was gradually being infilled to create sports fields. Greyhound racing appeared to be the only popular sport of the 1920s absent from the curriculum!

The arts were also well served at KAS. Doubleday experimented continuously in his art classes, with 'tempera and poster colours, with brilliant indian inks, with lino cutting and with clay modelling and pottery'. Peggy Van Praagh was equally outstanding in her sphere of dancing. She had been taught by A. S. Neill and had developed her interest in dancing to the point where she ran classes in Oxford Street. There she taught the dances of the day, the tango, the slow Engish waltz, the foxtrot and the Charleston. She danced with Ninette de Valois and became ballet mistress of the Royal Danish Ballet and later the Royal Australian Ballet. Music was taught by Mrs Martin Shaw whose husband had been an assistant of Cecil Sharp in collecting American folk music. She also produced operas, including *And So to Bed* at the Everyman Theatre, a title misunderstood by some parents who refused to allow their children to attend.

KAS always retained its distinctiveness. What helped to make it different from other day schools was its relationship with the local community. In most independent and state schools parents rarely went beyond the school gates unless summoned. Headmasters often saw their schools as cultural oases in a desert of philistine values and thus discouraged links with the local community. KAS adopted the opposite view, aiming to strengthen its links with parents and the local community. It had after all been founded by the local initiative of a small group of parents and was particularly concerned to increase parental membership of the society in whose hands power ultimately resided. In order to strengthen links with

52. Wicksteed at a production of *The Shoemaker's Holiday* in 1929

parents and to encourage them to participate more fully in school life, parent–staff meetings were held and parents were encouraged to assist in the classroom. Thus another distinctive feature of a KAS pupil's experience was the strong bond between parents and school in the education of their offspring. This was, however, not as strong as the society would have liked. Broader community links came from various societies in Hampstead using the facilities of the school during the daytime and evening, including political groups such as the ILP and the National Union of Labour Teachers, and organizations such as the girl guides and Kibbo Kift. The society's annual dinners, the first of which was addressed by Ramsay MacDonald in June 1928, a year before his second premiership, also served to strengthen the school's links with the local and broader educational community.

In 1928 council decided to apply once again to the Board of Education for recognition. This time it could expect more sympathetic consideration for two reasons. First, it submitted its application not under the classification of an 'efficient' secondary school, with all of the traditional limitations that that implied, but as 'an educational institution of a type not otherwise provided for'. This meant that the distinctive education offered by KAS was not necessarily a barrier to recognition. Second, the inspectorate by 1928 was less blinkered in its attitude to progressive education. By then, it had gained a better understanding of non-traditional forms of education thanks in part to the work of the Board's Consultative Committee and to the propaganda of KASS and other allied educational movements, including the New Education Fellowship. There was thus a better chance of KAS's application succeeding.

That this was so was evident from the way in which the inspectors approached their task, recognizing that different standards and values were not necessarily lower standards and inferior values, a view which was thinly disguised in their previous reports. It is possible to see the inspectors gradually warming to the school and its ideology in their 1928 report – once that is, they had come to terms with its different outlook. The way in which they did the latter was to exaggerate what they thought would be the results of a KAS education – chaos and ignorance – and then to discover that the principal differences were not of kind but of degree, with less orderliness but greater freedom, responsibility, interest, and less pressure (or 'prolonged labour under compulsion') but more lively learning. However, as in the 1922 report, they pointed to certain curricular blackspots, mathematics and science, which they argued were in part the result of the Dalton-style learning programme and, in the case of science, lack of adequate laboratories. In exercising choice, pupils tended to leave work in these two areas to the last, and the subjects were thus 'scampered through in the last part of the term'. At these times the mathematics and science rooms were overcrowded. The other cause of poor achievement in these areas, and modern languages, was said to be the lack of group teaching. For the inspectors it was almost axiomatic that whole-class teaching produced better results than individual programmes of work. The Dalton scheme, however, because of its emphasis on pupils learning at their own pace, rarely produced situations where a large number of pupils were ready to be taught together. Even when group lessons occurred, the 35-minute lesson was regarded by the inspectors as too short, but to Wicksteed and his staff it was a safeguard against overpressure and undue stress.

The report continued with criticisms before becoming more positive in tone and comment. In particular, it expressed its disapproval of the lack of 'hardgrind involved in the acquisition of multiplication tables' in the junior school and the lack of compulsory games in the upper school. The inspectors also disagreed with Wicksteed's belief that 'overcareful correction (of pupils' work) will check the flow of interest and enthusiasm', emphasizing instead that 'children can be trained more and more to be interested'. Here, in essence, was the generic difference in attitude between the traditionalist and the progressive. Miss Hyett's teaching of history with its emphasis upon historical method rather than the acquisition of facts, upon world history rather

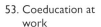

53. Coeducation at work

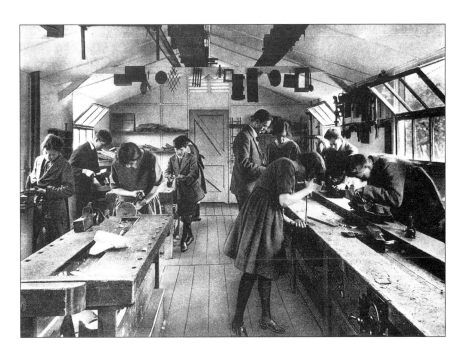

54. Relaxed study: time to sit and stare

than British insularity and socio-economic movements rather than political and 'drum-and-trumpet' history also encapsulated the gulf then as now between the two viewpoints.

Within these and other limits the inspectors gradually became more sympathetic towards the radical experiment. Their comments on the school's disciplinary methods, and especially on the school advisory council, reflected a willingness to take alternative approaches to traditional punishments seriously. Their observation that there was no 'rude or disorderly conduct' witnessed during their visit was not the result of pupils being on their best behaviour. They were impressed by the 'freer and less contained attitude', general friendliness and 'absence of self-consciousness'. The problem which Wicksteed and his staff had to persuade pupils 'to leave the premises than to persuade them to arrive in time' also struck them as unusual.

The key differences of pupils being presented for examinations 'almost by accident rather than intent in the school career', the lack of a subject hierarchy allowing the manual skills to have parity with academic skills, the centrality of parental involvement and the family atmosphere of the school led the inspectors to the irresistible conclusion

55. Young engineers

that KAS could scarcely be classified as a secondary school, a view from which neither Wicksteed nor council demurred. They came as close as they could to giving their approval to the education given at KAS when they recognized that 'no inconsiderable portion of the pupils are receiving great benefit from the School, who in most large Secondary schools would have profited little and might indeed be harmed'. The special attention given to each individual and the careful monitoring of each pupil's progress were seen as being in large measure responsible for the school's success. With these words, the school overcame the first of the hurdles on the path to recognition by the Board.

1928 to 1933: council, KAS and the national crisis

Within a year of addressing the society's first annual dinner in June 1928, Ramsay MacDonald was back at 10 Downing Street, heading a minority Labour government for the second time. However, any challenge which faced KAS and the other independent schools was not political, for Labour, under MacDonald's moderate leadership and dependent upon the Liberals for its majority in the House of Commons, had no radical plans of educational reform. Its only interest in the private sector was one of which KASS approved, that of making sure that boarding schools provided an adequate curriculum and a healthy environment.[10] KAS was under no political threat, evident from the fact that the prime minister sent his sons to Bedales. Its main challenge was to be that which led to the downfall of MacDonald's Labour government in October 1931, the economic collapse which followed the Wall Street Crash of 1929. The school population peaked at 170 at the end of 1930. As parental income was squeezed by the Depression which set in, the number of pupils dropped to 139 early in 1932 (far below the 200 well distributed in age which Wicksteed believed to be the ideal) and only after a slow and painful recovery did it reach 161 at the time of his retirement in July 1933. Even the 'school tailor' went into liquidation. But it was not simply a question of numbers. Fewer boys entered the school as parents searched elsewhere for a cheaper and more examination-orientated curriculum which they believed gave a better chance of securing employment. KASS was also hit by a heavier assessment of its property for local rating purposes. The school fought back by drafting in Old Alfredians to show that a KAS education could

56. Open-air study

provide good employment opportunities, by offering bursaries to boys and by joining the Student Careers Service.

What KAS intended to show in these difficult times was expressed succinctly in the 1931 Annual Report. KAS was not 'a luxury school but one based on fundamental values and as such provides the kind of education which the present critical and chaotic state of Europe proves to be so necessary'. This meant not adopting new aims and educational methods but demonstrating the relevance of a KAS education to a modern world, no matter how difficult the task. It was a time of reaffirmation of belief not of redirection. This reaffirmation found its focus in three areas: in the struggle to retain recognition, despite the financial burden which the Board of Education's regulations entailed; in the determination to continue with major building programmes; and in the continued support given to the Dalton-based curriculum which was seen as the best vehicle at that time for realizing the society's principles.

The matter of recognition was not without its complications as Morgan Jones, parliamentary secretary to the president of the Board of Education, pointed out in an already mentioned letter in March 1930. First, recognition did not entitle KAS to receive grants from the Board of Education and, second, attached to the granting of recognition was the condition that the school should operate a pension scheme under the terms of the Teachers' (Superannuation) Act of 1925. Had KAS been recognized as efficient under the secondary school regulations it would have escaped the pensions regulations but its 'large floating population' had precluded that. It was thus forced to consider the matter of pensions provision when the staff were indifferent to it and when the society faced other demands on its funds, especially its building programme, and at a time when school numbers were likely to fall as the deepening economic crisis hit parental income. In March 1930 council deferred consideration of the matter but bravely adopted the Board's pension scheme at its July meeting. In October 1930 it gave its formal approval, at the very time when the school's numbers peaked before declining to 143 a year later.

In 1929 the Board's inspectors made a follow-up visit. It was particularly concerned with the teaching of arts and crafts, and its report gave council an opportunity to reaffirm its belief in the importance of the building programme, which it was determined to continue with despite the evidence of a slowdown in the nation's economy. The inspectors' report pointed to deficiencies in accommodation, which council was already seeking to remedy, as has been described earlier in this chapter.[11]

The third area in which council refused to contemplate a change of direction during the unprecedented financial depression was in relation to the curriculum. The economically perilous times had given a stronger voice to those parents who wanted a greater concentration on preparation for external examinations to secure jobs. Council refused to alter its curricular course and took comfort from the fact that the school recorded a 100 per cent pass rate in the junior certificate, school certificate and higher certificate in the worst years of the crisis, 1931 and 1932. These results were achieved without sacrificing 'the health and general development of pupils'. While these were not harmonious times nationally, for KAS they were years of growing concord under a number of council chairpersons, including Corbett Fisher, McGregor Ross, Sewell, Mrs Bishop and Mrs Hopkin Morris. A sign of the unity of purpose was seen when Corbett Fisher moved at the end of 1930 that Old Alfredians and members of staff should be allowed to become associate members of council. It was also seen in the way that council gave unqualified support to Wicksteed's Dalton-based curriculum, which was continually being refined. Wicksteed's moves to increase the sense of unity of purpose, including the creation of a lower school council or 'Wicksteed conference' and the development of the school advisory council met with full council support. Council had confidence in him to ensure that his Dalton scheme worked to the satisfaction of parents. He insisted that where pupils were not working well at their stages, they should be given a fixed timetable by their form teacher. Other measures to create a more orderly but not repressive society included the awarding of orange table mats for the week to the table which showed the most civilized dinner table conduct. Surprisingly, this, together with the award of green mats to the second best, was not deemed to contravene the society's insistence that no prizes or rewards should be offered. Other formal procedures, including lining up in a designated area for lunch and the inspection of clothes for the name labels of their owners, were accepted by council. Permits and padlocks also became a regular feature of school life, the former giving permission to stay on the school premises after school and the latter to secure lockers.

It was in a time of growing national optimism in 1933, when Britain appeared to be emerging patchily from the Depression and when KAS was experiencing a financially sketchy but harmonious period in its history, that Wicksteed expressed his wish to resign to give him more time to study psychology. There was a strong feeling on council that what the school needed was continuity and not the crippling change that had caused so much ill-feeling in 1920. Corbett Fisher set the tone by arguing in April 1933 that council should not immediately seek new names but should consider 'the appointment of present members of staff as at any rate a temporary measure'. Wicksteed suggested two schemes for con-

57. Wicksteed just rises above Squirrel Hall's lectern, 1932

sideration, appointing a single headmaster such as Mr Hall or a joint headship of Miss Hyett and Mr Birkett. Nothing was agreed at the meeting, except to write to 'the headmasters of various coeducational schools to ask for recommendations for suitable candidates who could then be invited to apply'.[12]

Initially both schemes were considered, with the first round of interviews of six recommended candidates for the single headship option, from which only Tomlinson's name was carried forward, and the joint-headship option, which after interview resulted in Miss Hyett's and Birkett's names being carried forward. One other name for the sole-headship alternative was added to the shortlist when the post was advertised, that of Mr King. When the matter was brought before an extraordinary meeting of council in July, other possibilities were raised including Mrs Hopkin Morris's suggestion that Miss Hyett be appointed 'with a man of equal academic and educational distinction', presumably not Birkett, the first time that council considered a woman in that light, and Dr Flugel's suggestion of tripartite control with Hyett, Birkett and one other. This, the most expensive option, was rejected. Final interviews under the two schemes went ahead, with King gaining one more vote than Tomlinson. Birkett and Hyett were interviewed jointly, although after their interview Selson proposed a joint headship of Hyett and King if the former agreed. Subsequent discussion, however, resolved the matter. By a count of twelve votes to three on an amendment to Selson's motion it was agreed to offer the headship to Hyett and Birkett, which was confirmed by a unanimous substantive resolution. Whether a joint headship which did not include Birkett would have produced staff resignations as had happened when Wicksteed was favoured instead of Earle will never be known. Council was never made aware of any such radical reaction.

Notes and references

1. This unique construction is, of course, still happily in existence today and provides a meeting (and advertisement) point for the school parliament.
2. KASS Archives, record of June meeting 1920.
3. Ibid.
4. See C. L. Mowat, *Britain Between the Wars* (London, Methuen, 1987), 119–25, for a succinct account.
5. Schedule of the Deeds records, conveyance between the governing body of Eton and M. E. and E. F. Johnston, 26 July 1889.
6. W. F. Geyl, *Geyl Family History* (N. L. Books, 1990), 67.
7. For a fuller discussion see Sue Cohen, 'The Montessori Movement in England', *History of Education*, 3 (1974). Wicksteed's own views are presented in more detail in his book *The Challenge of Childhood* (London, Chapman and Hall, 1936).
8. In a letter dated 25 March 1930 (KASS archives).
9. *Ham and High*, 4 September 1962, 15.
10. The President of the Board of Education, C. P. Trevelyan, set up an inquiry in December 1930 into private schools 'to consider what legislative and other change are desirable for the purpose of securing that the children attending such schools receive an adequate education under suitable conditions'.
11. See the section above entitled '. . . we have come to stay'.
12. Council minute, 20 April 1933.

Chapter 4

The Dual Monarchy in Peace and War, 1933–1945

The appointment of Violet Hyett, the former senior mistress, and of Holland de Birkett, the former senior master, to the joint headship offered a way of avoiding the possibility of 'school quakes' which had characterized previous appointments. As *The Alfredian* commented in its first issue after the new appointments were made, 'Mr Wicksteed has left his school in safe hands'. It was a view which was shared by the older pupils who strongly objected to 'a new K.A.S.' which they believed a fresh-blood appointment would bring. However, a policy of safety first which would have been the sensible course of action for a conventional school was not necessarily the best policy for KAS, despite the overwhelming support given to it by past and present pupils. The school's *raison d'être* was the continuance of experiment in educational method, which does not always accord well with the more immediate goals of safety and security which smack of tradition. Whether the heads would break away from the Dalton framework to continue the radical experiment remained to be seen.

58. Mr Birkett

Two heads better than one?

Neither Hyett nor Birkett fitted readily into the category of leading educational innovator. At best, they (or at least Violet Hyett) seemed capable of repackaging existing KAS practices to meet the needs of the 1930s but not of carrying forward the educational revolution first initiated on Pestalozzian lines by Russell and then pushed determinedly in a Dalton direction by Wicksteed. Birkett, more at home in his print shop than in the headmaster's study, was neither intellectually nor temperamentally suited to the role of educational pioneer. His decayed good looks combined with his large, retired-colonel-style moustache, wayward grey hair which surrounded his bald pate and his approachability to convey an image of geniality and liberality rather than that of revolutionary-in-waiting. The children's cry of 'Birkett, Birkett, how do you work it?' underscores his essentially practical abilities and his easy relationship with pupils (who would approach him through his clouds of vile Empire tobacco smoke), but he was no 'ideas man' like Findlay, Russell or Wicksteed. Violett Hyett, regarded by many as the driving

59. Violet Hyett

force behind the school up to 1939 (after which Birkett's practical abilities were in greater demand during the evacuation to Royston, 1939–45), was made of ideologically sterner

60. Birkett's print shop

stuff. A woman with deep left-wing convictions, she held out more hope of advancing the cause of educational reform during the school's golden years. Not conventionally beautiful, her face tanned and a little lined (not too unlike the high-quality leatherwork for which she was renowned, according to one of her pupils) she affected a donnish image with her large briefcase and studied dowdiness of dress, her tweedy eccentricity, shared by a subset of the middle- and upper-class British women of her time. Her plain but striking face, her dark but not entirely unfashionable, homespun clothes, her smile one of welcome but not of amusement, her glorious Edwardian accent clear but well-spiced with the 'U' words of her age such as 'gal' and 'orf', all helped to project an aura of a person who was very competent, very dependable, just, businesslike and approachable. But was she the natural heiress of Russell and Wicksteed? In the classroom and in politics generally probably so, but in her ability to lead an educational revolution as they had done, probably not. In the classroom, in her history and economics teaching, she focused upon themes, particularly

61. Birkett in Squirrel Hall

revolutions, and used sources far in advance of her time, despite the formal demands of the school certificate. Economics she taught from a Marxist perspective, influencing generations of pupils including Raphael Samuel and Alex Nove. In her meticulous leatherwork lessons she raised the status of an afternoon option to that of a morning academic subject. Her political interests were very much those of the left, in that she shared the fascination of many of her time with the Soviet experiment until it became tarnished with the show trials and purges of the 1930s. She continued to blame Tsarist Russia and its troop mobilization for causing the First World War. She remained a socialist throughout her life, but that which she taught in the classroom was 'not a political doctrine but a question of right or wrong', as Nora Beloff confirmed in her tribute to her.[1] Her lessons were full of 'goodies', the poor and powerless, and 'baddies', the rich and powerful. As one of her former pupils said she took 'no namby-pamby notice of the idea of neutrality and objectivity'.

However, she was unable or unwilling to translate her radicalism into continuing educational revolution. She settled for making Wicksteed's brand of Daltonism more efficient. This decision was understandable and one which council, in appointing her rather than a more innovative head, had endorsed. To some extent her situation was less favourable than that of either Russell or Wicksteed, both of whom were able to institute reform when the forces of age posed no great challenge. By the 1930s, the demand by parents for paper qualifications, for the school certificate and higher school certificate for their offspring, was greater as competition in the job market became more intense. If KAS did not meet their aspirations then state and other independent schools would. It would take a person of outstanding ability and determination to pioneer new methods. This Violet Hyett was unable or unwilling to do, settling rather for refining the Dalton-based teaching programme to meet better the demands of the school certificate.

A new-blood appointment, such as that recommended to council by Selson, was a riskier policy but one which in the long run could have provided greater opportunities for continuing the radical educational experiment. In essence, this was the dilemma which constantly faced KAS, either to restrict its experimental role and risk a descent into its own peculiar kind of traditionalism, or to pass on into new curricular territory with all the risks, disruption and dangers that that could bring. In 1923 many within council had wanted to establish a Russell tradition, and had faced Wicksteed with a vote of no confidence. A decade later it seemed that they had settled for a Wicksteed tradition based upon Dalton lines! There was every danger that innovation would be seen not in terms of curricular advance but in terms of building projects. However even a KAS tradition based upon Dalton was seen by many to be more radical and challenging than that found in most independent progressive schools, and better suited the broad ability range which a school without an entry examination was bound to produce.

Old principles in a new world

Without the disruptions that had marked previous change of heads, KAS quickly settled down to its routine when the school reassembled under its new heads in September 1933. Business as usual was the keynote of the new regime. Continuity was also a key feature of council, with the old faces reappearing at the first meeting in October 1933.

Sewell, Boulter, the Corbett Fishers, Horton, Mrs Marcos, Mrs Maxwell, Mrs Oxlin, Mr Plownar, Dr Polak, Mrs Revell, Mr Spalding and Mrs Vallance welcomed the new heads. They looked to J. H. Badley, rather than to the headteachers to give the ideological lead at the customary January meeting for the propagation of KASS principles, although Miss Hyett was asked to deputize if Badley found attendance impossible. The first prospectus which she wrote with Birkett emphasized the continuity of educational principle and practice with the Wicksteed era. It outlined the Dalton-based curriculum but in so doing emphasized features which distinguished its KAS application from that of other schools. First, no subject was deemed compulsory; second, in direct contrast to the practice of many other schools, as the pupils moved from the middle school, for eight to eleven year olds, to the senior school the curricular framework became less rather than more formal. Class lessons in the middle school gave way to 'work on individual lines' for about two-thirds of the morning, with a minority of time spent on 'fixed group lessons'. The afternoon club activities, drama, photography, country dancing, debating, excursions and swimming, supplemented 'the fixed classes' in gymnastics, music, art, French conversation, handicraft and organized games. The idea of an options afternoon was introduced to the three to five year olds for one day a week. Perhaps the KAS theme of business as usual gave comfort to parents and young people who were well aware of the traumas caused by the unprecedented Depression which the nation was experiencing. Landmarks familiar in the KAS education-scape, but not elsewhere, offered both solace and opportunity to the rising generation of KAS pupils.

But it offered much more. Business as usual was not the unthinking response of two headteachers bereft of an ability to grapple with the intricacies of educational principle. KASS was unusual in the encouragement it gave to its teachers to consider the relevance of its educational principles to the contemporary world. In 1926 it gave Violet Hyett a sabbatical term to visit Soviet schools. By the time she became headmistress in 1933, the authoritarianism of Stalinism had led her to withdraw the broad sympathy with which she viewed the Soviet experiment of the 1920s. Stalin's show trials and purges of 1936–8 destroyed any lingering belief she had in the Soviet system. Her heady idealism gave way to a more sober assessment of the realities of the 1930s. The rise to power of Mussolini in 1922, but more importantly the more efficient fascist regime in Germany established by Hitler a few months before she became joint head, led her to view the KAS curriculum as central to the cause of democracy. The Dalton-based curriculum was seen as a bulwark 'against the mass-mind beloved of Fascist authorities – which accepts what it is told without question, the abdication of personal intelligence and moral authority'.[2] The large element of choice, which carried with it responsibility, offered by Dalton was thus a weapon to counter the darker forces of the age. Eminent figures, including Haile Selassie, ousted from Abyssinia by the Italians, visited KAS to brief pupils on the growing threat of fascism and Hyett and Birkett used the morning callover to show the relevance of the school's principles and practices to contemporary developments. The work of the Jewish Refugee Committee at Woburn House to which *The Alfredian* drew the school's attention, was a constant reminder of the need for vigilance.

There was a danger that in pressing the cause of anti-fascism, the new headteachers would attach more importance to individualism than to social responsibility. However, in their first published statement about the school in *The Modern Schools Handbook* in 1934 they were anxious to dispel any idea that the school represented 'unrestrained individualism and the negation of social ideas'. The book, introduced by an old friend of KAS, Amabel Williams-Ellis, wife of Clough Williams-Ellis, architect of 'the Italian village in North Wales', Portmeirion, offered an excellent opportunity for stressing a view which Fred Clarke, an up-and-coming educationist was to espouse a decade later, that 'the child can only find freedom in society and society can only flourish where its members are free'.[3] The headteachers were anxious to dispel the view held by some Hampstead parents that the school allowed unrestricted freedom to its pupils and that bullying and other forms of anti-social behaviour were rife. The outlook which KAS sought to encourage in its pupils was one 'which stands against oppression wherever it exists. On the other hand pupils are ready to participate and co-operate in social organisation and show respect for any authority which proves itself of social value.' Authority had to earn respect rather than blindly to expect it.

KAS was an extended democracy in which the final authority lay with those who subscribed to the society and voted at its annual meeting. But the democratic process was evident in the day-to-day running of the school. The staff meetings of which Miss Hyett and Birkett had experienced the benefits as teachers in the 1920s continued throughout the 1930s. They represented to Miss Hyett, 'a co-operative type of organisation as opposed to authoritarian methods in which all decisions were arrived at by consent (or sometimes by majority vote) instead of being imposed from above'. The school advisory council to which staff and pupils were elected continued to play an important part in the life of the school through its weekly meetings. Chaired by one of the school captains and representative of both the junior and senior school, with two members of staff present, the advisory council was seen as a valuable training in democracy, although the headteacher kept a right of veto (very rarely, if ever, used). The staff members and secretary of the society did not have a vote.

'The famous KAS mud will soon be a thing of the past'

62. The nursery block, 1933

The tide of mud and clay which had threatened to overwhelm the old army huts, and which was such a source of delight to pupils and of such misery to parents and teachers, was well in retreat by the early 1930s. Much of the mud had been turned into grass by the efforts of the caretaker Wallace and his predecessors. As the tide of mud receded so the number of games played at KAS advanced. In 1924 only tennis, cricket and hockey were played and then usually on borrowed sites. The fives courts appeared a year later and in 1928 a cricket match was played for the first time on a full-size home pitch. Football was added to the games curriculum that year and 1928 also saw the completion of the tennis courts. Netball appeared in 1930 due to the enthusiastic organization of several senior girls. Two acres of well-used, level playing fields had replaced the wilderness of clay hillocks, yet their constant use in bad winter weather threatened to return them to their previous semi-liquid state. By the end of the 1930s, Wallace perpetually rolled and mowed his pride and joy, the cricket square, with manic delight.

Nor did the almost constant presence of builders, nearly as familiar and always more numerous than the staff, help the general condition of the grounds. It seemed in the first years of the new headships that KASS was trying single-handedly to rescue the building trade from the worst depression that had ever hit Britain. Building projects were almost self-perpetuating in that the increased numbers necessary to help finance them soon meant that new buildings reached their maximum capacity. In 1933, the school population stood at 167; by 1935 it was 204 and by 1937, the year of Russell's death, it was 227, two and a half times that of 1920 when 'J.R.' retired.

One of Wicksteed's last duties in 1933 was to report to council that the new junior school block was in use and appeared to be very satisfactory, though to its occupants it still had the somewhat romantic, improvised quality of many of the other buildings. Part of the old building was re-erected on the senior school site. Wicksteed offered the sum of £50 as a parting gift to the school for the erection of a clock on the gable end of Squirrel Hall, a proposal modified to that of a clock tower at the edge of the field, and subsequently dropped. By March

63. Kaufmann's lower school, 1937 (*Architectural Review*, January 1937)

1934 the school committee was concerned with more major projects and reported to council that Kaufmann, a school architect from Frankfurt, was willing to undertake an initial survey, free of charge, for a general replanning scheme, including new buildings forming a junior school. The council stalwarts, the Corbett Fishers, Miss Epstein, Mr Horton, Mrs Maxwell, Mrs Oxlin, Mrs Richmond, Mr Spalding and Mrs Vallance were given powers by council, as a subcommittee, to commission Kaufmann to make detailed drawings of the proposed upper junior school block. They also had the daunting task of raising the necessary funds. By June, matters had moved on so quickly that an extraordinary meeting of council was called to consider the report of the building subcommittee.

Priorities had been established; a biology room was to be the first of the new buildings to be erected, planning permission for this new 'semi-permanent structure' having been gained from Hendon Borough Council, and the lowest tender of £883 from W. Harbrow was favoured by the subcommittee. This plan could be realized fairly easily after gifts amounting to £600 covered the bulk of the costs. On 7 November 1934, the biology laboratory, designed like a tram with rounded ends, was formally taken over. The four-roomed junior block was nominated as the next major project, with smaller projects

64. The biology laboratory, 1934

including the reconditioning of the open-air theatre and the building of netball and tennis courts to occupy the intervening period. By the end of 1934, with a surplus of £1,275, with an expanding pupil population of 191 and with the prospects of a marked slackening in the Depression, council authorized the building subcommittee to take the initial steps in the construction of the junior block. Council was well aware of the dilapidated condition of the existing junior block and the problems posed by its lack of

laboratory and cloakroom accommodation. Miss Hyett and Birkett also pointed out the advantages which could accrue from a new block in terms of the reorganization of the school, with the abolition of the middle school – its two lower forms joining the lower school and its two upper forms combining with the upper school. In December 1935 council, persuaded by the headteachers' argument, and heartened by the fact that KAS now had a waiting list of potential young entrants, took the next step of instructing Kaufmann to prepare working drawings, and of setting up a new building subcommittee to oversee the project and to act in liaison with junior-school parents.

The project was not without its difficulties. One major area of concern was that the four-room scheme encroached on the playing field. The headteachers suggested that the building be placed on the north-east corner of the grounds, a modification that council accepted. Fuller consultation with the staff raised the matter of a covered court for assembly and for 'wet play days', without which the new unit could not be self-contained. Such modifications would add to the debt of £8,500 which carried a heavy burden of interest of £382 a year. However, council had never regarded major expenditure and consequent debt as an insuperable barrier to expansion and simply looked forward to reducing the loan by committing part of the school's surplus. Kaufmann's model of the new junior block provided a choice of construction materials, brick with steel girders, steel or concrete. Whichever was adopted the cost was likely to be £4,000 although the heads aimed at a contract price some £250 less. The rejection of the original plan by Hendon Borough Council, the discovery of the omission of essential items from Kaufmann's original list and matters relating to the financing of the project, were all problems which threatened to delay the construction of the new building. Several members of council gave individual guarantees to the bank which amounted to £1,200. That was regarded as sufficient to secure the bank loan to enable the project to go ahead. Hendon Borough Council also gave the project its approval when the proposed building was moved another 13 feet from the eastern boundary

65. The nursery playground, 1939: Miss Parker in foreground, Mrs M. Montgomery in background

and 6 feet from the northern boundary. This met the objections raised by those who owned neighbouring properties. In his initial estimates, Kaufmann had failed to include the cost of additional soil and drains and other items, a matter which council took particularly seriously. In order to counter the threat of the whole project being abandoned, Miss Hyett and Birkett emphasized Kaufmann's good qualities as an architect and argued that the society was still 'getting excellent value for money', despite the regrettable omissions. Acting upon Selson's suggestion, council agreed to interview Kaufmann whose 'frank and helpful' attitude led to a compromise which resolved the difficulty.

The opening of the new building in January 1935 marked the high point of a golden age for KAS, from 1933 to 1938. The number of pupils increased from 167 in October 1933 to 222 in December 1938. The increased fee income and the consolidation of former extras into the standard fee gave a financial stability which the educational venture had never previously enjoyed. The period contrasted with the uncertainties of the Depression which had preceded it and with the disruption and trauma of war which followed, when the financial and other resources of the society were stretched to their limit. The era of prosperity enabled council to reduce the debt on its Manor Wood estate, and to consider establishing an outpost in the country.

Even at the height of its prosperity council was becoming increasingly aware of the possible effects on the school of unsettled conditions in Europe. Mussolini's invasion of Abyssinia, but more importantly Hitler's reoccupation of the demilitarized Rhineland in 1936, threatened Europe's precarious stability. In October 1936, council showed its clear-sighted thinking, something which Baldwin's National government could well have emulated, when it began to consider ways of preparing to meet the possible threat of war. Miss Hyett put before council the proposal that the 'school would benefit greatly from the possession of a small property in the country which would serve (1) as a camping ground or temporary home (2) to supply fruit and vegetables to the school and (3) as a possible retreat in the event of a war-scare'. She and Birkett had already begun to consider various sites. In March 1937 she reported that she and Miss Else Hibburd were in the process of buying Flint Hall Farm near Royston; council agreed in principle 'to put money into the scheme with a view to making the accommodation for school purposes'. The first pupils attended a camp at Royston early in the summer of that year, thus beginning an association with Royston which was to serve the school well in the war years and beyond.

In October 1937 the heads asked council to consider using Kaufmann for the next building project, but the worsening financial situation and the need to commit more resources to improving the accommodation at Flint Farm led to the abandonment of the scheme. Instead, smaller sums were spent at KAS, such as meeting the demand 'the children are making for warm shower baths'. Clearly the interwar years had bred a less hardy generation. The demands for an improved salary scale and structure, voiced by three male members of staff, Montgomery, Sheppard and Shipham, threatened to make ever deeper inroads into KAS finances. Their request for a definite salary contract involving allowances for children and increments was one which council could not meet. In reply the three indicated that they could not stay on at KAS on their present salaries and also pointed out that working at KAS handicapped them when applying for posts in state schools. The matter was largely resolved, although Birkett made the staff aware that any building projects would take precedence over any revision of salary scales. The priority of the Flint Farm improvements was reaffirmed after Hitler's invasion of Austria in 1938, when the results of a questionnaire sent to parents revealed in May that there was support for evacuation to Royston in the event of war. The Munich crisis of September 1938 put an end to all schemes for improvement. KAS had agreed to rent the school to the publishers Gollancz in the event of war and many of its pupils at Hampstead had elected to go to Royston Farm. The 'famous KAS mud' which had by 1938 largely disappeared from the lives of KAS pupils, was set to make a dramatic reappearance at the new KAS, as the Royston evacuees began to dig trenches as part of their air-raid precautions, and at the old KAS commandeered and vandalized by the army.

Dalton re-presented, misrepresented and appraised

Monarchs came and went in Britain in the 1930s but at KAS Dalton reigned supreme and unchallenged. There was to be no curricular abdication crisis here. While national life was dominated by Edward VIII's attachment to Mrs Simpson, the American wife of a London stockbroker, KAS had long been involved in a love tryst with another American import, the Dalton plan. Even the evacuation of KAS to Royston did not end this long-standing attachment. The curricular continuity from 1933 to 1945, which the appointments of Miss Hyett and Birkett ensured, provided an unprecedented degree of stability and enabled council to proceed swiftly with its building plans.

Much of the time at staff meetings during the 1930s was taken up with evolving more formal procedures for the more effective implementation of the Dalton-based scheme. Montgomery ('Monty'), who was later to succeed Hyett and Birkett, was given responsibility for name boards for the subject rooms. In addition, a fuller series of regulations for their operation was drawn up in 1933. To prevent random or unauthorized departures from the rooms, which could lead to truancy, each pupil was expected to obtain the permission of staff to leave, usually dependent upon the completion of a stage. To maintain a working atmosphere, students were obliged to undertake their stagework only in the relevant subject room and to ensure that all rooms were left tidy after use. KAS also aimed to encourage students to pace themselves, rather than work in strenuous and exhausting bursts, by staggering tests throughout the term rather than by the more conventional method adopted by most secondary schools of devoting one week to examinations in all subjects usually near to the end of term. The longer work periods and the subject-room method whereby pupils rather than staff moved around the campus also facilitated a more rational way of dealing with examinations. Stagework and subject-based rooms freed teacher time to help students who wished to change subjects and so catch up with their peers, and to give additional assistance to those who were having particular learning difficulties. Such an arrangement was particularly beneficial to those students whose first language was not English. In an international school which KAS had become this was particularly advantageous. With the growing number of refugees from Spain and Nazi Germany it served a singularly valuable function. Teachers thus operated on much more of a 'flexi-time' basis giving individual attention to scholars rather than operating on a class-teaching basis with very little time to deal with individual difficulties. The Dalton-based system placed more responsibility upon both teachers and pupils for organizing their time than was usually found in conventional secondary schools.

One former student, Lyndsay Nichols, recalled vividly the effects upon KAS of events in Europe.

> Wicky's departure coincided with something horrific that was happening across the North Sea in Germany. It is now called the Holocaust. A brutal cultural eruption, a social earthquake began to send faint tremors through our peaceful privileged paradise. Hitler had come to power. Soon after, refugees entered the school. Their arrival felt like the first small waves from a cyclone many miles away, but a cyclone which during the next 6 years would come closer and eventually engulf us in the Second World War. These adolescents (mainly boys) never spoke of their predicament. They seemed intent on fitting in and not creating a disturbance. But they were survivors, so they worked with an intensity that in itself

inevitably disturbed the relaxed attitude to study characteristic of a progressive school.

Dalton organization also enabled the staff to give closer consideration to matters of educational principle than was possible in the more hectic environment of the traditional secondary school. In the latter an examination-driven curriculum was axiomatic. At KAS, teachers had greater freedom to reduce the debilitating effects which examinations could have. For example, in the early months of the new headships Miss Jenkins raised questions about the dominant place which Shakespeare had in school productions, a position which would have caused her to be regarded as an arch-heretic in most other schools. She recognized the value for examination purposes of producing the Shakespeare play on the school certificate syllabus but realized that this could possibly be offputting for aspiring actresses and actors in the lower part of the senior school. One way round the difficulty was to have 'a second non-Shakespeare production' under Montgomery and Shipham for the younger pupils but with every effort made to establish the parity of the two projects. Further adjustments were made to the headmaster's essay which Wicksteed had introduced 'to enable him to form some judgement of children whom he did not teach'. As Hyett and Birkett taught the upper school they felt that they had no need for such an essay. Hence it was discontinued in the senior school but maintained in the lower school. One of the main reasons for ending Wicksteed's upper school essay was the increasing demands of the school certificate. Much time at the weekly staff meetings was taken up with discussion of 'examination prospects' and especially in adjusting individual timetables to meet parental aspirations. Latin, which had been placed on the periphery of the curriculum by the clerical rebel, Russell, was now given a more central position. The timetable was carefully regulated to ensure that pupils had adequate examination tuition in the subject. Additional time and attention were given to 'techniques', including handwriting, to try to ensure that all pupils had a good grasp of the basics. The closer co-ordination of syllabuses in the lower and upper schools, especially in mathematics, aimed at improving basic skills and examination results. However, these arrangements did not stop several children dragging their heels and doing less stagework in mathematics than in other subjects. One way round the problem was to give group lessons in the afternoon and devote more time in the morning to stagework. This arrangement did help some students to meet the rule that at least 80 per cent of stagework should be completed before a person was entered for their school certificate, a rule whose value was confirmed in May 1934.

Even with more formalized arrangements to ensure that the Dalton-based scheme worked more efficiently, it was recognized that new pupils entering the senior school from other schools still faced a radically new educational world. Thus staff were constantly reminded 'how essential it is that newcomers should be carefully initiated into our ways of work which are very puzzling to them at first'.[4] To parents and pupils not familiar with 'the new education' which the headteachers described in *The Modern Schools Handbook* in 1934, the principles and practices of KAS must have been difficult to understand.

The popular press took a less considered view of the school in 1934 than that found in *The Modern Schools Handbook*, misrepresenting the KAS philosophy as one of 'study-as-you-please'. It was particularly attracted to the tree house which lasted from 1934 to 1948 where scholars were said to be at their studies. This gave rise to a series of popular cartoons about the subject, including boys protesting they were not stealing apples but doing their homework in trees, fathers remonstrating with the headmaster that they would only have their boys taught in British oaks, lord mayors engaged in classroom planting ceremonies, ex-pupils addressing each other as old bough-mates and tree classrooms declared closed during the nesting season. However, once beyond the school gates and the lightly mocking headlines, even the popular press was able to see the benefits of a KAS education. The 'study-as-you-please' caption of the *News Chronicle* in October 1934 concealed a fairer assessment which emphasized that choice was confined to the selection of subject-rooms where children were often heard asking for more work. The request by a third of the pupils for permits to stay on to study after school hours – for some, a disguised form of 'homework' – illustrated the positive aspects of choice. The school run by Birkett and Violet Hyett was seen as 'happy', where children did not see learning as a burden. Afternoon options, including 'a large gallery of subjects' including weaving, forge-work, piping with bamboo pipes made by the children themselves, painting and sports, drew approving comments from the *News Chronicle*'s reporter.

66. The tree house, 1934

67. Contemporary comment on the tree house, 1934

In many ways the article, together with a *Pathé Pictorial* film in 1937, acted as better publicity for the school than many more formally written presentations. Relationships between pupils and staff, mixed games lessons, the refusal to allow the shadow of examinations to dominate school life, pupil involvement in running the school, the emphasis upon persuasion rather than coercion, and the notable achievements of former pupils especially in the arts, all impressed J. L. Hodson, the *News Chronicle*'s reporter, as did the friendly and frank attitudes of the pupils.

Miss Hyett seized upon the unexpected publicity given to the school to relate the qualities which the reporter detected in the school to the needs of the 1930s. When freedom and choice were rapidly receding in Europe, and especially in Nazi Germany, KAS values should be prized above all. In a series of public addresses she dealt with common criticisms of KAS principles, that 'a freely educated child is said to be insubordinate' and of a KAS education, that it failed to prepare pupils effectively for examinations in particular and for life in general. She recognized that the school could produce rude, self-assertive and occasionally idle pupils, but to her these were 'temporary inconveniences' to be lived through rather than to be suppressed by fear, coercion and intimidation. Friendly reasonings were seen by her as far more effective in dealing with anti-social behaviour, and better suited to an age which needed less not more fear and violence.

In an equally frank manner she addressed the issue of 'the grind of learning' especially for examinations. Her plea was for patience with pupils, especially pre-adolescent boys, who had a 'disinclination to work at uncongenial jobs'. The answer was not penalties and punishments but patient persuasion. Given a completely free hand she believed that sending children to farms or factories on the lines of the Soviet 'polytechnical schools' until they were ready to learn would be preferable, but Hampstead offered little opportunities for such a radical approach! Once they had 'sated their zest for real life avocations', they would naturally turn to their studies. All KAS could do was to offer 'craft experiment' in the place of 'a Soviet multi-bias polytechnical education'. Her particular plea was for a wide range of practical activities to allow children to discover their individual talents which could lead later to expert training. When the craft products brought home by young KAS pupils were seen as inferior to those brought home by children of other schools, this was because the latter objects reflected an overwhelming concern for accuracy in which zest for the job was lost whereas KAS articles reflected enjoyment and creativity which was often dulled by a term's deadening concern for strict measurements and accuracy. Any restrictions on pupils which suited the needs of adults rather than those of pupils themselves were a contravention of KAS principles.

Equally challenging to what Miss Hyett called the 'sick civilization' of the 1930s were her ideas on sex education. Her ideas were concerned not with threats from abroad or from 'the dispossessed classes' which the Depression of the 1930s had helped to create but with the problems confronting the children of the Hampstead well-to-do brought up 'in the artificially sterilised atmosphere of the refined home'. Such children, she argued, suffered 'in ways unknown to the slum child where the psychic sex-life of the working class is saner and sounder than that of the bourgeoisie'. Coeducation to her was one of the main ways of avoiding 'a defeatist attitude towards sex of which D. H. Lawrence makes so much'. The Dalton-based coeducation offered at KAS encouraged a natural relationship between the sexes, thus avoiding the 'definitely pathological consequence of segregated education, most noticeable in boarding school life', including girls' boarding schools, of which she had had experience. The essential happiness and relaxed relationships at KAS greatly assisted 'satisfactory sex-development'. Thus sex education was not primarily or even normally a subject for class instruction at the school, except for teaching the facts of reproduction. Real sex education was, in her view, a product of a healthy attitude towards life, fostered by a non-coercive educational environment. Not all pupils were entirely enlightened. One former student's comments on the school's approach is interesting.

> There was one piece of equipment in Birkett's gloomy laboratory that was riveting. A glass aquarium accommodated a couple of copulating frogs. They seemed stuck like that for days. Conditioned as we were in hush-hush about sex we were confused, fascinated and speechless. Were we really allowed to witness this forbidden sight?

The headmistress also saw the relevance of the Dalton-based curriculum to the broad social and economic trends of the 1930s, which required, in her view, a certain flexibility of mind. The needs of an age characterized by rapid change meant that education ought to help 'people to adapt themselves to changing circumstances not only in practical matters such as choice of career but in mental outlook'. Dogma, authoritarian discipline in schools and the great danger of control by experts were the enemies of the age. The regimentation of public opinion by central agencies including the press and radio could, in her view, only be resisted by developing an independence of mind which was one of the principal goals of a KAS education. Not all of the pupils who experienced the Dalton system at KAS believed that its practice matched such great ideals. While some could not understand why so few schools adopted it there were others who argued that it was too under-resourced at KAS to demonstrate its worth. For example, Miss Hyett's history subject-room was said to have a few wall charts and a shelf or two of the usual books – scarcely the richness of relevant sources necessary to prove the superiority of the 'library method' so necessary to realizing KAS ideals. The constant movement between subject-rooms said by some to give opportunities for a breath of fresh air was seen by others as time-wasting. One ex-pupil raised the question of whether the graph of stage results (with its reds and blues for high achievers and greens for under-achievers), pinned for all to see by the entrance to the form hut, did not represent a form of social coercion designed to shame pupils into working. If that was its aim it was unsuccessful. However, all were in agreement that pupils, in bearing some responsibility for their own programmes, were being treated as 'young adults', something which was felt to be lost by those who transferred to other schools. Whether the Board of Education's inspectors would take such a balanced view of Dalton teaching and organization when they were invited to inspect the school remained to be seen.

In 1938, two months before the Munich crisis and in the growing shadow of war, the Board delivered its decennial verdict on both the junior and senior schools. The school could, perhaps, expect a more informed assessment from the Board of their teaching aims and programmes than they had received in the 1920s, for official thinking, as reflected in the reports on nursery, primary and adolescent education published by its Consultative Committee, had become more sympathetic to progressive education. Indeed, the Consultative Committee's statement in its primary school report that education ought to be considered in terms of experience and activities, rather than of knowledge to be acquired and facts to be stored, showed that progressive aims and practices had made some impact.

The inspectors' report on KAS pointed to the fact that although numbers had doubled from 113 to 226 since the previous inspection in 1928, the general character of the school had remained largely unaltered. Pupils under eleven still predominated, some 61 per cent, and those over sixteen were still a small, if slowly growing minority, from 3 to 6 per cent. Many parents still withdrew their offspring around the age of thirteen or fourteen to send them to boarding schools, traditional day schools or to move abroad. Only about a quarter of the school's pupils who began their schooling at KAS finished it there, some leaving for

68. Birkett's forge in
1936

Oxford and Cambridge but the majority for other forms of further education including schools of art and music. The early loss of many pupils was not attributed to the poor quality of the teachers or teaching, for the inspectors reported that 'the school must be accounted fortunate in its teachers'. Their comments about Dalton-based teaching programme were more critical. While refusing to enter into any discussion about the validity of the method they did point to some instances of incompatibility between 'subject and system which is proving an impossible obstacle to good work' in external examinations, particularly in mathematics, science and Latin, where shorter, more regularly assessed programmes of work were deemed necessary. Either the school would have to abandon the idea of achieving high standards in these areas or compromise 'inalienable articles of faith'. In other areas, the achievement of good standards in the school certificate and the Dalton approach were seen to be quite compatible and 'in some respects actually promotes a good standard of work'.

There were few doubts in the minds of the inspectors about the teaching abilities of the authoritarian but diminutive Elizabeth Jenkins, the elegant, celebrated novelist whose grey fur coat rarely left her shoulders in cold weather, even during lessons. Her teaching of English was highly commended, especially for the way in which she was able to maintain high standards in the basics, especially 'handwriting and the tidy ordering of matter on the page' without inhibiting 'free and spontaneous work'. Her excellent choice of literary texts, her inspirational teaching and the insights which the publication of her novel *Harriet* gave her, made her an outstanding member of staff in the eyes of the inspectors. Her former pupils do not always share this view. To some she did not always fit in well with KAS principles, leaving some with the view that she seemed to prefer literature, especially that of Jane Austen, to children or at least that she was only happy teaching dedicated literati – 'no good for the punters but excellent for the dedicated', as one Old Alfredian put it. There were no such disagreements between inspectors and pupils about Montgomery, under whose careful teaching geography was experiencing something of a renaissance. 'Monty', the charming, handsome, popular, quintessential pipe-smoking, blazer-wearing Englishman, impressed inspectors and pupils alike with his colourful and imaginative blackboard work, including his portrayal of glaciated valleys. The inspectors concluded that he was well provided with visual sources and involved his pupils in much practical work, up to and including higher certificate.

French, under Miss Bullock, neither dowdy nor superelegant in dress, had also experienced a revival, although the fact that she was the personification of KAS in her approach to teaching, was not guaranteed to endear her to the inspectors. Her pupils remember her personally developed and mimeographed French course, carefully colour-coded for each form, and the French plays which she wrote annually for pupils to perform. The inspectors urged fuller development of her course and a higher timetable priority. In their view more time ought to be given to the kinds of class exercises (for which Dalton-style teaching gave limited opportunities) in the basics of translation and of essay writing. Her painstaking work was not always appreciated by her pupils, who sometimes saw her room as 'uncosy' and her teaching 'conscientious but joyless', so further work on the basics would not necessarily have been welcome to them. German, taught by Mrs Birkett, was also seen as undertimetabled. It is difficult, however, to see how an academic timetable confined to mornings only could have yielded any additional time, and non-compulsory homework could have provided further opportunities for much more work in the basics.

Latin under Miss Bullock received an unfavourable report, as it had in 1928. The jewel in the academic crown of most secondary schools had become somewhat tarnished at KAS where the teaching programme was seen as ill-balanced, with progress in the early years being slow and preparation for the school certificate being too excessive in the later years. The novelty of Dalton stagework was seen as poorly matched to the most traditional and prestigious of school subjects. Not surprisingly the inspectors believed that Miss Bullock ought to concentrate more upon class reading and oral work, and upon the history and life of ancient Rome. She was relieved, however, that they made no mention of the lack of Greek, a subject which she had been asked to learn so that she could teach it, but had refused to do so.

Mathematics teaching, which had been heavily criticized in 1928, fared little better a decade later. The need to establish firmer mathematical foundations in the junior school, including more careful and mechanical teaching of multiplication tables,

69. Chemistry at KAS, 1936; Richard Gregory on the right

was regarded as a prerequisite for any improvements further up the school under Shepherd. Again the solution to this problem was found by the inspectors in more class work. They did admit, however, that in certain areas, particularly in geometry, older pupils showed 'an intelligent willingness' to tackle problems for themselves. The initiative which Dalton-based learning encouraged was thus not without its benefits, particularly for abler pupils. One of Shepherd's former pupils recalled plotting a map of the school grounds using a wooden theodolite which Shepherd had made. Other pupils found him entertaining but a bit shambolic, and a person who could not convey mathematics to the ungifted. Michael Selson saw his problem-solving in a different light:

> The mathematical master wears braces
> With pulleys attached at odd places;
> The strain never grows great,
> For they self compensate
> On a complex mechanical basis.

70. Mrs Hettie Barber and her biology class, 1937

The problem-solving approach, noted in certain areas of mathematics, was rather surprisingly said by the inspectors to be little in evidence in the teaching of science by Birkett and Hettie Barber. Pupils were said to have 'little appreciation of scientific methods of thought and reasoning' but had nevertheless acquired much useful information. The fact that practical biology was voluntary and occupied one period on one afternoon a week was, in the view of the inspectors, an insufficient addition to the customary fortnightly double period of experimental work. In biology, chemistry and physics at higher certificate level, the time given to laboratory work and formal instruction was seen as inadequate. However, the existing provision, though inadequate, was a promising beginning.

Mrs Barber, one of the most popular members of staff who openly espoused KAS principles and practices, spiritedly defended herself against the inspectors' criticisms of higher certificate biology, on the grounds that KAS children had learnt how to learn independently and intelligently and thus did not need the same number of formal hours which were given to the subject in conventional secondary schools. The need for a more scientific basis to practical work in the voluntary periods had also been met since the report was presented. However, she regarded much of the usual practical work undertaken in secondary schools as unimportant and so detail-laden that pupils failed 'to see the wood for the trees'. Her approach to biology and chemistry since her appointment in 1936 had in her view shown clearly that under 'the KAS system' pupils could be taught successfully for the Oxford school certificate as the examining board's reports had confirmed. She thus regarded the inspector's views as unsound, but she accepted their criticism that the new biology

71. Shipman inspects hockey sticks, 1939

laboratory's glass construction limited the wall space available for hanging illustrative materials and that the value of the laboratory was also reduced by its being used as an ordinary classroom and as an open-room for general study.

The pupils' views of Hettie Barber were clearly at variance with those of the inspectors. She was a very popular, capable and inspiring teacher who was well able to apply the KAS method in her teaching, which perhaps perplexed the inspectors who found it difficult to get to grips with KAS ideology and methodology. Certainly her science teaching stood in sharp contrast to that of the less well-organized Birkett. The mother of Chris Barber, the jazz musician and KAS pupil,

72. Doubleday's art class: second from left, Gay Thompson, far right, Peggotty Selson

73. Woodwork with Moorish, 1936

74. Using the covered court for a play, 1936

75. Mixed metalwork classes amazed the inspectors: front left, Barbara Keeling, front right, Raja Rosenbluth

she was a very positive, warm and open person who dealt in an unembarrassed, pragmatic way with direct questions about sex which the growing interests of adolescents posed.

Doubleday's qualifications as a pupil of Professor Cizek's class at Vienna impressed the inspectors officially as much as his open-tourer version of the Standard 9 car did unofficially. The products of his inspirational art teaching – linoleum cuts, models of animals and birds and exercises in architectural construction – were laid before and above the inspecting team in the roof trusses. They were glowing in their general praise, although they did observe that the voluntary afternoon art classes of children of widely differing ages wasted much time, a defect they believed to be inherent in the Dalton arrangement. This was not the view of the pupils, who enjoyed Doubleday's discouragement of photographic realism and emphasis upon freedom and originality of expression.

Doubleday was one of ten part-time staff who taught at KAS at the time of the inspection. However, only he and Mrs Birkett, the German teacher, received any extensive examination and comment, despite the fact that part-timers constituted nearly half of the staff. The achievements of most of the part-time staff were summed up in a single paragraph. This reflected the low priority accorded to their subjects in the three-day inspection and the fact that the inspectors failed to understand the central importance which KAS attached to the afternoon clubs and activities. Hence the point in their report that they could not comment 'with assurance' on the work of most of the part-timers. Music, under Mrs Boulter and Mr Coxife, which occupied an important place in school life and in extra-curricular competitions, was ignored by the inspectors. Eurhythmics taken by Miss Bird, and dancing under the direction of a person very eminent in her field, Miss Van Praagh, received no individual assessment. Speech training by a former pupil Renée Beloff (then Mrs Soskin) attracted no mention. Gymnastics and netball under Mrs Lindsay, who had taken over from Miss Porteous when the latter left to get married, were ignored. The crafts, especially metalwork under Mr and Mrs Kelsey and engineering and junior wood-work under Mr Turner, were merely listed as subjects on offer without any accompanying assessment.

76. Leisurely learning in the 1930s

Clearly there was still a wide gulf between the Board's inspectors and KAS on the goals and organization of the educational process. The priority which the school attached to choice, to individual learning, to a less pressurized and more varied curriculum, and to learning in 'accidental' groups which resembled more the age distribution of children in a normal family than that in a conventional secondary classroom, was never really acceptable to the assessors. Nevertheless Dalton-based teaching survived the inspection and the school was passed as 'efficient'. Whether KAS or its educational philosophy would survive the next six years of war remained to be seen.

The lower school

The inspectors saw the lower or junior school at its best. By 1938 it had a strengthened position within the school organization, having acquired two forms from the former middle school, and its new buildings, designed by the German émigré E. C. Kaufmann, which could not fail to impress. They still retained much of their pristine elegance. The L-shaped row of one-storey pavilions, all allowing pupils access to the great outdoors through large steel and glass folding shutters, attracted favourable comments by the inspectors who had come to accept the benefits of an open-air education. In this they had been led largely by the Board's own Consultative Committee which had commended experiments 'in the use of open air classwork and activity' and urged local authorities to incorporate 'the best modern designs when planning primary school buildings'.[5] It also reflected KAS thinking in the emphasis which it placed on 'parents' associations formed in connection with individual schools'. Thus by the time of the 1938 inspection, ideas which had prevailed at KAS since the early 1920s were gradually entering mainstream, official thinking. Though the Board would never come to give any kind of official sanction to Dalton-based learning, it happily endorsed the class-based teaching arrangements of the lower school.

By 1938 the lower school had settled down into a recognizable bipartite form with the two nursery classes, F2 (for the three to four year olds) and F1 (for the five year olds) under Mrs Marriott and Miss Tickle respectively. Both teachers received glowing reports and were highly commended for the manner in which they introduced pupils to reading, writing and number, with a full range of additional activities including stories, poems, singing, music and movement, percussion, painting, craftwork and 'educational games of all sorts'.

77. The junior school as the inspectors saw it

The inspectors produced a rather puzzling and none too favourable report on the teaching in the upper forms of the lower school. E1 and E2 were taught by the strict but caring and respected Miss Robey, whose ample bosom comforted several generations of infant Alfredians, and by Miss Parker respectively. D1 was under Miss Gillett, a comforter and friend to all, who personified KAS principles, and D2 was taught by the first male teacher in the lower school, Mr Powell, who had replaced Miss Russell (she with 'the perpetual startled look') in September 1937 when she went to teach abroad. The inspectors argued that the strict application of KAS principles in these classes did not promote 'altogether satisfactory results'. They went on to condemn the bookish, unadventurous approach to arithmetic. What, in fact, seems to have been the case is that KAS teaching principles with their emphasis upon interesting practical approaches to teaching had not been implemented. The standard of handwriting and spelling was said to be lower at KAS than in 'other types of school'. The reason for this could well have been that KAS principles gave a higher priority to creativity and imagination than to the mechanics of writing and precision in spelling. History and geography teaching, which placed greater emphasis upon sources, was said to lack 'solid achievement'. To some extent these criticisms were counterbalanced by the lower school strengths in art and craft and nature study. Achievements in these areas stemmed in part from expeditions, visits to museums and summer camps. What the inspectors dismissed in a single phrase, 'the happiness and friendliness of the children', perhaps shows the different priorities between the visiting team and the teachers in the lower school. These qualities were to the latter not a by-product but the basic aim of their teaching from which all else stemmed.

KAS in exile: the Royston school in wartime

> Oh come to Royston all of you, all of you
> As good Alfredians always do, always do
> And we'll raise three cheers for the Cottage and the camp
> And never mind the weather if its damp, damp, damp.
>
> (School song to the tune of 'There's a Tavern in the Town')

The departure of Wilson, the chief inspector, and his team in June 1938 marked the end of the school's golden age. This was not because of any negative report. The school received its recognition, and though some members of staff were said to be tense and anxious, the inspectors were immensely popular, especially in the lower school, according to Jack Pole, co-editor of *The Alfredian*. However, the relaxed atmosphere which had characterized the school since around 1933 was not to return, for the international scene darkened as Hitler made known his demands for the transfer of the Sudetenland to Germany as part of his offensive to undermine Czechoslovakia's security.

A crisis in a distant part of Europe could have dire consequences for KAS. If it could not be defused and it led to war with Germany then, as the destruction of Guernica in April 1937 by the Luftwaffe had shown, KAS, so near the heart of the nation's capital, would be in grave danger of obliteration by aerial attack. If the Munich Conference in September 1938 failed to resolve the matter of the Sudetenland then the school would have to leave its London premises for a safer area. Whereas council during the First World War had been forced to lay off teaching staff because of declining attendance partly caused by the threat of bombing, a Second World War would have much more serious consequences. The cost of maintaining a rump school in the country and the Manor Wood estate (even if it escaped damage or destruction) could well be more than the society could bear.

The society's new president, Alice Woods, was faced with the possibility of an unprecedented crisis. Most major crises facing the society had been short-lived and domestic. That facing the society in 1938 was of an altogether different order and was likely to put a great strain on its eighty-nine-year-old president whose health was failing. Few doubted Miss Woods's dedication to progressive coeducation in general[6] or KAS in particular, with which she had worked for over two decades. Her standing within the educational world had recently been enhanced by her publication, *George Meredith as Champion of Women and of Progressive Education* (1937). Corbett Fisher had persuaded her to accept the presidency on Findlay's retirement in 1937,[7] and Miss Woods guided the society through the first two perilous years of war until her death in 1941. She was succeeded by Dr J. C. Flugel, an equally eminent educationist.[8]

78. The school country base, 1937: L to R Mr Birkett, 'Hibby', Mr Amstel (neighbour and parent), Miss Hyett

In the last year of Findlay's presidency, Miss Hyett, ever an astute observer of international affairs, had turned her attention to the advantages of a country base for KAS. This gained the general approval of the school committee in October 1936. The matter was placed immediately before council which received the idea favourably and backed the headteachers in their quest to find a suitable property. It soon emerged that the idea had emanated from Miss Hyett and her friend Miss Hibburd, whose intention it was to buy Flint Hall Farm near Royston, probably for their retirements. The farm, once part of Royston Abbey, was largely derelict and comprised 180 acres on a spur of the Chilterns near Royston in Hertfordshire. 'Hibby' and Hyett persuaded Antony Horton, an Old Alfredian, and Jennifer Horton (née Corbett Fisher) to manage it for them. The finance committee of KAS agreed to put money into the scheme to make some of the outbuildings suitable for school purposes and to meet a general rent of £50 a year. It was thus with a large measure of foresight that KAS decided to provide a base for weekend and summer camps and to plan a safe haven in the event of war.

79. The little barn at Flint Hall Farm, 1939

The farm was approached by a typical, narrow, pot-holed lane from the main road. Beyond the duck pond and at the head of the lane was a small house, in which the Amstels and later the Willises lived. Miss Hyett and Miss Hibburd occupied the cottage beyond. There they were joined by other female staff during weekend and summer camps and wartime. Beyond the cottage was a large square, flanked in part by a small garden but dominated by a large eighteenth-century tithe barn, over 60 feet long and a smaller, yet still quite sizeable, barn with stables, cart sheds and byres. It was thus a site of considerable potential for adaptation as a base for KAS. By June 1937 the small barn had been modified to receive its first guests, sixty pupils in all, most of Miss Sheffield's C form and a group of seniors under the direction of Mr Sheppard. The large barn was left untouched but its smaller companion had been given a concrete floor, windows and a large open brick fireplace, a tribute to the efforts of Birkett and a local builder. Thus at the same time as KAS and Kaufmann were planning the next block at Hampstead, the society was establishing its outpost at Royston.

The growing Nazi menace gave the Royston venture priority over the Kaufmann enterprise. The great influx of Jewish refugees from the Continent which threatened to swamp the school was a constant reminder of German expansionism and of the dangers of appeasement. In July 1938 the school committee reported to council that it agreed to the heads' suggestion of 'circularising parents with a view to ascertaining how many children would be allowed to stay in London in the event of war and how many would prefer to join a country boarding school for the time'.[9] The first step towards changing the function of Flint Hall Farm from a weekend and summer retreat to a reception area in the event of war had been taken. The survey indicated that half of the school population would be willing to go to Royston if the school moved, whereas only 20 per cent would attend if it remained in Hampstead. The additional accommodation, mainly dormitories, sanitary block, kitchen and dining room, was estimated to cost around £1,600. As settlement of the lower school building at Hampstead

80. Flint Hall Farm buildings, c. 1970

81. Sketch map to Flint Hall Farm

necessitated additional expenditure, especially tie rods to prevent further outward movement, the sum required to improve the Royston buildings in the event of wartime evacuation was not easily found. It was hoped that gifts from the parents of children who were to use the Flint Hall Farm would meet most of the cost of partitioning the stables for use as a classroom, of converting the long open-fronted cart shed as a dormitory and common room and of building new living quarters for the pupils on the edge of the field. Without at least £10 from parents whose children were to be evacuated to Royston and £3 from those who were interested, the scheme would have to be dropped.

Emergency measures 'in view of the threatening international situation' were discussed at the September meeting of council. With the outbreak of war appearing imminent, council rejected a suggestion that KAS should join Bedales or Dartington Hall and pressed on with the Royston project, requesting parents to make their contributions. A circular from Hendon Borough Council in October 1938, stating that in the event of national emergency all schools in the area would be closed, gave added urgency to the scheme. The Munich crisis of the previous month had led KAS to test its evacuation plans during the crisis weekend of 30 September to 3 October, and to consider an application by the publishers Gollancz to rent the Hampstead school premises for office purposes in the event of war. A two-year renewable rent was agreed upon at £1,000 per year.

Although the Ministry of Health stated that the school was in a neutral area and therefore 'not included in organised arrangements for the evacuation of children in time of war but with freedom to make private arrangements to this end',[10] those concerned with the running of KAS recognized that if a nucleus of the school was not preserved if war broke out then it would be difficult to revive the school after a war. The school committee, still in the very capable hands of the Corbett Fishers, the Revells, the Maxwells and the heads, was anxious to promote relocation in order to prevent closure. They thus undertook a survey of the school in the interwar years to see if anything could be learned for the future to strengthen the school once the crisis was passed.

It is worth reproducing the details of the survey undertaken on the eve of war. In May 1939 the secretary reported on the number of pupils leaving school during the previous fifteen years (see Table 7). It is a measure of the dedication and wisdom of council and the school committee that at a time of acute crisis they were looking to the distant future and to rebuilding the school.

Of immediate concern was the more adequate preparation of the Royston site so that a nucleus of KAS could be preserved if war broke

Table 7 **Reasons why pupils left the school**

	1936–7	1937–8
Left neighbourhood	11	2
Left England	16	7
Left school	15	15
Went to boarding school	5	10
Left in financial straits	2	7
Left but returned later	3	–
All other reasons	9	11
Total	61	52

Note: No. of pupils leaving each year as % of total no. of pupils in that year: 28.4 (1923–8), 27.4 (1928–33), 22.3 (1933–8).

out. Council was still hoping that war could be averted and pressed on with Kaufmann's plans for a new art block at Hampstead at an estimated cost of £1,350. They were thus covering all eventualities, bearing the brunt of the costs of the Royston and of the Hampstead sites, the Ministry of Health having refused to give any 'assistance to private efforts to take the children out of London' in the case of war. In June 1939 council, having received tenders for the new art block, were forced to shelve plans for the further expansion as school numbers were rapidly declining under the threat of war. Reluctantly the council stalwarts, the Corbett Fishers, the Revells and Mrs Maxwell, accepted the realities of the situation whereby they would be faced with two expansion schemes with no money in hand if Kaufmann's Manor Wood project were sanctioned.

Council rejected the proposed gift of land at Royston by Miss Hyett and Hibburd, preferring to avoid the financial and other difficulties that ownership would entail by paying a peppercorn rent on a five-year renewable lease.[11] This proved to be a wise decision, for at the first wartime meeting of council on 24 September, 1939 it was reported that the Gollancz agreement had collapsed, leaving KASS in a serious financial position with the upkeep of an empty school building. The latter was resolved when the second battalion of the Queen

82. Else Hibburd, school secretary and much more

Victoria Rifles occupied the commandeered buildings at a rent that was half that offered by Gollancz. The question now facing the society was for how long could it afford to subsidize the Royston school.

During the period of the phoney war from September 1939 to May 1940, council had to face the problem of a vastly reduced school population. After the declaration of war on 3 September, many people believed that aerial attack was imminent and as a precautionary measure twenty-eight children were sent to Royston. When the expected attack failed to materialize they returned to London, having only had a four-day camp. By the time that Hitler had launched his attack on the Low Countries in May 1940, KAS had moved to Royston, although its population was only forty-nine. Council tried to counteract the drastic reduction in the size of the school by reducing fees to attract local children, by advertising in the *Times Educational Supplement*, and by reducing staff salaries and numbers. Montgomery expressed a desire to leave KAS for 'a more secure post'. Miss Tickle had already left after being advised by Birkett 'to look for other work'.

The seriousness of the financial situation was evident in the severity of the cuts in the salaries of the teachers. The following extract from the council minutes provides the details:

> Mr Birkett decrease £200 to £400 until his son takes his degree
>   and thereafter to £330
> Miss Hyett decrease 50% to £275

83. The Royston staff in 1941: L to R (back row) Miss Gillett ('Gilly'), Jeff, George Moorish, Mr Birkett (seated), Dina Levin, Miss Hyett, 'Hibby' (Miss Hibburd)

Miss Hibburd decrease £100 to £250
Mr Morrish decrease £60 to £180
Miss Gillett decrease £40 to £180
Miss Robey decrease £55 to £165
Miss Waddington decrease £15 to £165
Mr Montgomery remains at £350
Miss Levin remains at £180.

Though the first two years at Royston started with an overall deficit of some £840, with only thirty boarders and nineteen day children, nevertheless KASS pressed on with making the site habitable. The big barn, cowshed and pigsties (inhabited by two venerable sows, Hunca and Munca) were reserved for farm use but the stables, which formed the other part of the buildings complex which stood nearest to the road, were converted into four subject-rooms, science, history, mathematics and geography, and the print shop. The little barn, with its four adjoining rooms (arks 1–4, for junior form pupils), formed the main junior school room, which was reached by the lane which, by ancient right, passed through the big barn. Beyond, and separated from the small barn by a spinney, were 'the buildings', consisting of an L-shape structure in plan. These were wooden huts, supported clear of the ground by brick piers, and served as the dormitories for junior girls, senior girls and junior boys. These had a mains water supply but cesspit drainage, thus agreeably confining the junior school boys to two baths per week with water no more than four inches deep, marked by a piece of string on the plug chain.

To children brought up in suburban London, Royston offered many compensations for the lack of parental and home comforts. (It is perhaps difficult today to understand the remoteness of a place barely forty miles from London.) There were the usual farm activities such as feeding chickens and harvesting, opportunities to see at close range Flying Fortresses coming and going as the site overlooked a bomber base at Bassingbourn, to pick up the silver paper dropped by German aircraft to confuse the radar, and to meet Italian prisoners of war brought to Royston to work on the land. There was always something of interest to do, riding on the farm tractor with Alf Harwood, the farm labourer, weeding the large vegetable plot presided over by the ever-watchful Barbara, of the women's land army, or bird nesting which could enable pupils to earn money in return for a supply of pigeons' eggs.

Perhaps the flavour of these times is best summed up in the words of Alan Holmes who vividly recalls the entertainments of his junior school days at Royston:

Entertainments on site were mainly of the DIY variety. John Craig had a wind-up gramophone in the junior boys dorm and we listened endlessly to Glen Miller records. The first school play I remember was called *Thirty Minutes in the Street* and took place in the Big Barn, the 'Street' being the roadway through the double doors. Ant's tractor was adorned with the school bell and a ladder to become a fire engine, Mr Turner wore a fur costume to become an escaped gorilla, and much fun was had by all.

Christmas party in the Little Barn involved much preparation work. I recall a life-size dancing skeleton on top of the fireplace and a football-sized spider on a giant web slung from the rafters. On dark or wet Saturday evenings 'entertainments' would be held in the Barn, playing charades or other word games; in summer we played 'Witches'. Will Nickless, one of the senior boys, organised a Wolf Cub pack to which we belonged. We played tracking games extending all over the farm, and once or twice made camp by Half Moonwood.

I remember Hyett and Hibby (they worked together in many things) rented a small field on the farm and grew wheat on it. At harvest time I saw Hyett, who was not a young woman then, cutting the corn at harvest by hand with a scythe. Neither of them were ever seen in trousers, Hibby always had bare legs which went purple in the winter. Hibby made bread, presumably from flour ground from their own wheat, which was not of the most appetizing quality. One day, as no doubt you will hear from many others telling this story, some of the boys got a lump of the bread and kneaded it into a sticky mass and threw it against the dining room wall where it stuck. A notice was pinned alongside 'Call this bread – we don't!' I doubt if anyone told Hyett of this, but Hibby's bread did improve afterwards.

Early contacts with St Christophers at Letchworth to share teachers failed to produce the desired result and KAS came to rely more upon local help, such as that of Dr Dunbar who formed a school orchestra and Mr Whydale, a local artist, who was to help with art and crafts if Doubleday could not visit the school. Some of the old First World War wooden buildings were brought from Hampstead to act as classrooms and as a sanatorium.

Today many of the problems faced by the new KAS at Flint Hall Farm may appear trivial but in the first hard winter of 1939–40 they were serious. Also, some of the costs of improvements to the site may seem slight but to a society whose income had shrunk dramatically and quickly they were critical. For example, the trenches dug early in

September 1939 to provide some measure of safety against air attack had become badly eroded by February 1940 because of the harsh winter. Birkett and Miss Hyett were thus forced to meet the cost of new linings and props. Matters such as whether staff should take children to the trenches or to the dank and forbidding air-raid shelter after bedtime every time a siren sounded were of great importance at such a time of emergency and led to much discussion in council. Corbett Fisher, with his pragmatic approach, wished to leave the matter for the staff to decide upon, although others such as Miss Levin argued in favour of keeping to a policy of making children enter the trenches or shelter whenever the siren sounded in order to absolve the staff from having to make such a crucial decision. Others argued in favour of not removing children from warm beds and of putting up wooden shuttering to protect windows against bomb blast. The matter was put to parents by way of a questionnaire, which returned replies in favour of the latter. The payment by the War Office of £500 rent for the Hampstead

84. The big barn at Royston, 1937

85. The converted stables

premises helped to meet much of the cost but the society found that after only eight months of war its reserves had nearly halved, from £2,622 in August 1939 to £1,439 in April 1940. The twenty-nine boarders and eleven day children during the spring term of 1940 were far below the numbers required to break even, although by the end of the summer term of 1940 with an increase to forty-seven, the headteachers felt confident enough to appoint a new member of staff, Mr Turner, to teach geography and French and to look after a boys' dormitory. By the end of 1941 the financial situation had stabilized and council agreed to raise the salaries of Turner and Morrish. School numbers by then had marginally increased to fifty-three, twenty-nine boarders and twenty-four day pupils. This placed pressure on the teaching accommodation in the barn, and the dining room was drawn into use for teaching purposes.

The relatively few pupils who had left London for Royston led Miss Hyett to raise the matter of reopening the London school, either at

86. Miss Hyett and her class, 1940

Manor Wood if the War Office would release sufficient classroom space, or in a private house nearby if such accommodation was not forthcoming. A meeting at Golders Green of interested parents would be a preliminary step. However, by 30 June 1940, when the school committee next met, British and French troops trapped around Dunkirk had been evacuated, leaving France to capitulate after less than six weeks' resistance. The danger of a German invasion was thus much greater and the society was thinking not so much of opening a school in London but of moving the Royston school to a less vulnerable area of the country, to Painswick in Gloucestershire, where Miss Hyett's family had offered to house it. Further upheaval when the number of KAS pupils was already dropping as the result of pupils being evacuated to South Africa, the United States and the colonies could be disastrous for the school. Only if it became 'a matter of military necessity' would council sanction such a move. There was no guarantee that the school would reopen after its first year in exile.

But open it did the following September with twenty-eight boarders and nine day pupils, leaving a diminished number of teachers with the task of teaching fewer children of a wide age range. Miss Hyett taught history, geography and English, taking on the latter two subjects in the absence of Mr Montgomery (who went to teach at Bembridge boarding school which was evacuated to Coniston) and Miss Jenkins, who stayed in Hampstead. Mr Birkett, using a range of ingenious inventions, taught science, while Miss Hibburd, the school secretary, took Latin, Miss Gillett, one of the mainstays of KAS ideology, biology, and the striking red-haired Miss Levin, French and mathematics. The diminished teaching staff was also obliged to take on heavier domestic duties in accommodation now crowded with furniture from the London school after the nursery block in which it was housed at Hampstead was affected by a landmine blast. The presence of a proportionately large number of under seven year olds also added to the staff's difficulties. The increase in pupils to forty-seven by the end of the academic year in July 1941 had eased many of the financial problems and this, together with the £500 rent paid by the War Office, enabled council to increase the number of staff. A further rise in the number of day pupils to twenty-four, giving a school total of fifty-three, enabled the society to move into a clear financial surplus by December 1941. Such expansion was not without its accommodation difficulties, which were eased by the use of the dining room and an additional wooden building brought from Manor Wood as teaching rooms. Thus the darkest period of the war from September 1939 until the United States entered in December l94l saw the school at Royston gradually moving from a point of great uncertainty to one of moderate expansion. Any plans for expanding the Royston school were always tempered by the fact that the London estate still carried a heavy debt of £7,500 and that society membership, and hence income, was dwindling. Furthermore the number of Royston pupils remained stubbornly around the fifty-three mark (thirty boarders and twenty-three day pupils). By the following December Miss Robey believed that the time had come not to expand the Royston site but to open a nursery school in London. Thus she gave notice of her intention to leave at Christmas 1942. The society believed, however, that the Royston school could be enlarged through the provision of more accommodation for day pupils. Certainly there was no more room for boarders, for two of the senior boys had already been sleeping in a tent for six months, from May until October!

The Board of Education opposed plans for the expansion of the school on grounds of a labour shortage but Miss Hyett and Miss Hibburd had used their ingenuity to circumvent the Board's opposition by purchasing a garage ten miles away, having the pupils and staff dismantle it and re-erect it on the Royston site as a workshop and tractor house. This was later augmented by the purchase of two hen huts whose wood was used for construction purposes. A smaller

87. (Left) Some of the cast of *A Midsummer Night's Dream*, 1942

88. (Right) Some of the principal performers in *A Midsummer Night's Dream*, 1942

89. Cast list for *A Midsummer Night's Dream*, 1942

A MIDSUMMER NIGHT'S DREAM

William Shakespeare.

DRAMATIS PERSONÆ

THESEUS, DUKE OF ATHENS	John Picknett
EGEUS, FATHER TO HERMIA	Patience N. Bell
LYSANDER, ⎱ IN LOVE WITH HERMIA	Ian Thomson
DEMETRIUS, ⎰	Ian Aitken
PHILOSTRATE, MASTER OF REVELS	Michael Craxton
QUINCE, A CARPENTER	Joyce Rathbone
SNUG, (*Lion*) A JOINER	Ruth Laymore
BOTTOM, (*Pyramus*) A WEAVER	Lilith Elkan
FLUTE, (*Thisbe*) A BELLOWS MENDER	Andrew Ciolkosz
SNOUT, (*Wall*) A TINKER	Janet Craxton
STARVELING, (*Moonshine*)	John Tuchfeld
HIPPOLYTA, QUEEN OF THE AMAZONS	Elsie Henrotte
HERMIA, IN LOVE WITH LYSANDER	Anneliese Levy
HELENA, IN LOVE WITH DEMETRIUS	Yvonne Lehmann
OBERON, KING OF THE FAIRIES	Daphne Lee
TITANIA, QUEEN OF THE FAIRIES	Julia Coppard
PUCK, OR ROBIN GOODFELLOW	Janet Morrish
PEASE-BLOSSOM, ⎱	Virginia Snyders
COBWEB, ⎸ FAIRIES	Jennifer Garrod
MOTH, ⎸	Mary Kelemen
MUSTARD-SEED, ⎰	Jeremy Roffey

OTHER FAIRIES:-
Margaret Tabor, Barbara Hawkins, Susan Garrod, Carol Wedd, Jill Willis, Carolyn Parsons, Julian Berrisford, Martin Harwood, Pat Hunnisett, Jill Elbourn, Philippa Parsons.

ATTENDANTS ON THESEUS AND HIPPOLYTA:-
Audrey Hunnisett, (*Amazon*) Janko Kelemen, Ann Garrod, Will Nickless, Audrey Bargas, Christopher Barber, Jacqueline Szpiro, Sean Godfrey, Hugh Wilson.

The play takes place in Athens and in a wood near it.

In accordance with the usual practice of the school the production and costumes follow the Elizabethan tradition.

KING ALFRED SCHOOL, ROYSTON   MAY 30th. & 31st. 1942

Printed by the K. A. S. Printers.

workshop and garage adjoining the school stable had been reslated and provided with a concrete floor and decoration to enable the two senior school pupils to move from their tent into warmer accommodation in the winter. The cart shed, first used as a boys' dormitory, was converted into the junior school building. Council also agreed to purchase an additional house at Flint Hall Farm to help improve the accommodation of the younger pupils. The society was thus planning for a protracted stay at Royston.

The decisive defeat of the German army in October 1942 at El Alamein, however, led council to turn its attention to the distant day when KAS would return to Manor Wood. The following month it gave its support to a proposal by Miss Robey that she should return to London to set up a class for young children. She was greatly helped in this venture by the support of an old Alfredian and KAS teacher Renée Soskin (née Beloff), who had already undertaken its preliminary organization. The family had offered to lend KAS a suitable room at their home in 1 Holford Road where she taught French and drama, inviting several KAS pupils to New Year's Eve parties attended by such people as Mai Zetterling and Sam Wanamaker. Council also assisted by releasing school furniture from the Royston store but insisted that the school would be run by a separate management team with its own finances but with the right to use the name of KAS. This arrangement gave the society a presence in London without any financial commitment. With a debt of £7,500 on its London estate this was a wise and sensible arrangement. It also left the society free to use its rent from the War Office for the London estate to help reduce its mortgage there and to use any surplus from the Royston school to improve the accommodation for the pupils, and possibly to open a kindergarten in Royston. Council, however, recognized that some small sum ought to be guaranteed for its London junior school under Miss Robey. By 1944 plans had been developed to establish a middle and later a senior school under Montgomery in a house, Oakhurst, leased in Branch Hill in North London. With a school population at Royston of eighty-four (thirty-one boarders and fifty-three day children) by July 1944, it was clear that this venture was more than able to cover its costs, and even to appoint two new resident members of staff, Miss Rae to take charge of form C and to teach some upper school geography, and Mrs Ryder Smith to undertake general teaching duties. In addition there were staff replacements, Mr Oblitas succeeding Mr Bullivant.

The successful D-Day landings in June 1944 gave the council increased confidence that its return to London would not be long delayed. Montgomery's appointment as head of a middle and senior

King Alfred School at Branch Hill was confirmed in July 1944. The school was to open the following September. With Birkett and Miss Hyett soon to reach retirement age this arrangement facilitated the peacetime re-establishment of the London school. It also led council to consider the conditions upon which any further schools should be established. Thus with an eye to the future it laid down the conditions for its support of such schools:

1)   One parent at least from each family to be required to be a member of KASS.

2)   Each school to be managed by a Committee of members of KASS at least one of whom must be a member of the Council.

3)   An annual report on the work of each school, together with an audited copy of the accounts to be passed by the Committee of each school and presented to the Council by the head of the school who shall attend the meeting of the Council ex officio without the right to vote. The rejection by the Council of such report shall be understood by the School Committee to involve the abandoning of the use of the name of the Society and the return of any equipment provided by the Society.

4)   Each School Committee to ask for sanction of Council before appointment of new Head.

5)   Each branch secretary to be responsible for collecting membership subscriptions from parents of school children and forwarding same to the secretary of KASS at least once a year, together with a list of names and addresses.

The need to reoccupy the Manor Wood premises became pressing when, in April 1945, Mr Beloff expressed his wish to repossess the premises which Miss Robey was using for the junior school. The first step to the recovery of the Manor Wood premises by KAS would therefore be the reoccupation of the nursery school classrooms and the lodge. The War Office agreed that the Home Guard would vacate these sections of the school. The senior school at Oakhurst, Branch Hill, which, like the nursery school, still faced the threat from V1s and V2s, had rapidly increased in size from twelve in Christmas 1944 to fifty-one by April 1945. Montgomery was congratulated by council on this rapid success, which made a move to Manor Wood even more imperative. Royston had also expanded considerably by April 1945 to ninety-one (thirty boarders and sixty-one day children). This too raised interesting questions about the future. Once the boarding school (always contrary to KAS principles) had been closed and the evacuees returned to

London, what would happen to the Royston day pupils? Council recognized its obligation to continue educational provision for them but saw this as only a temporary arrangement until the local education authority took over. It had no intention of creating a permanent new KAS in the area. Any surplus arising from the temporary venture at Royston was to be distributed among the staff to compensate for salary reductions and extra duties. Miss Hyett and Mr Birkett were to receive a pension of £150 per annum in addition, for they had reached retirement age but were not eligible for a pension under the Ministry of Education scheme. They were thus replaced by B. H. Montgomery when he was formally appointed in June 1945 as headmaster of the school to be reopened at Manor Wood. He reported a great demand for places at the school, with a considerable waiting list, but the dilapidated state of the Manor Wood buildings put difficulties in the way of an early reoccupation of the site. Twenty-nine of the Royston pupils had returned to London by September, making the repossession of the premises imperative. When the Manor Wood school reopened with about 70 per cent of its 1939 total of students, much work had still to be done in making the buildings released by the War Office habitable. By December 1945 there were 164 pupils, seventy-eight boys and eighty-six girls at Manor Wood under Montgomery, and fifty-six pupils at Royston under the care of Miss Hyett and Birkett who expressed their wish to retire from the headship. They were replaced by Morrish but continued to teach at Manor Wood. The Royston school closed in July 1946 when the number of pupils had dwindled to thirty-seven and the Ministry of Education withdrew its recognition. The cryptic comment in the council minutes that 'Plans for the disposal and dispersal of its buildings, furniture and equipment are in hand' marked a somewhat sad end to a brave venture. The gallant efforts of its staff to keep it open had failed. However, although KAS had returned to its Manor Wood site, it did not mark an end to the society's expansionist ambitions, for great interest had been expressed in Stanmore for a school on KAS lines.

90. Staff at Flint Hall Farm, 1944: (clockwise from top left) Leslie Picknett (parent helper), B. H. Montgomery, Mr Birkett, Miss Hyett, Renée Soskin (Gaby on lap), 'Hibby' (Miss Hibburd)

The Hyett and Birkett years in retrospect

Each era in the school's history had been followed by a period of innovative consolidation. The crisis of 1901, which saw the abrupt ending of Rice's tenure of the headship, gave way to the Russell era noted for the formalism of the curricular structure but innovations in curricular delivery. When Russell retired in 1920 many council members had come to accept the essentials of the Russell years as the essentials of KAS. They became alarmed when his successor, Wicksteed, overthrew the Russell tradition through the organizational innovation of his Dalton-based plan which, in their view, handed too much responsibility to pupils for their curricular programmes. By the time that Wicksteed retired in 1933 his scheme had been accepted fully. KAS was ready not for further curricular change but for curricular consolidation. The joint headship of Miss Hyett and Birkett provided this.

91. Notice of auction

KING ALFRED SCHOOL
FLINT HALL FARM,
ROYSTON, Herts.

MESSRS.
NASH, SON & ROWLEY
(W. T. ROWLEY, F.S.I., F.S.A.)

have been instructed to sell by Auction at THE FARM, on

THURSDAY, AUGUST 22nd, 1946, at 2.30 p.m.

A BUILDING

constructed of feather edged boards, with slated roof 128ft. in length giving a floor space of about 260 square yards divided into 4 Class rooms, Kitchen, Lavatories and Stores to be sold as erected. Also adjoining is a

TIMBER BUILT HUT

with felt roof 31ft. in length by 16ft. in width with glazed Verandah divided into 2 rooms.

A Large Quantity of Fittings

comprising a Smith and Welstead double oven cooking range, Century Heater with 75 gall. tank, 3 sinks, 14 hand basins, cisterns with taps, Bath, 6 Lavatory pans and two 400 gall. tanks and two 200 gall. ditto., Anthracite and other heating stoves.

CAN BE VIEWED AT ANY REASONABLE TIME.

Catalogues and further particulars from the
AUCTIONEERS, ROYSTON (Tel. 2112) and
BUNTINGFORD (Tel. 123) Herts.

Under them KAS entered a golden age, although it was somewhat dulled in the early years by the Depression. They continued and refined his Dalton-based scheme, believing that it prepared pupils for the school certificate with its formal examinations, while still enabling KAS to pursue its original principles through handing over some decisions, especially on timing, to pupils and by enabling them to progress at their own pace. The junior school laid the groundwork in basic skills in a more formal class-based manner. So accepted had this formula for progress become that the society and council readily backed building programmes to help reorganize the junior school and to provide more suitable subject bases for the senior school Dalton scheme. The option-based afternoon programme of clubs and other activities extended the pupils' freedom of choice, while at the same time offering additional teaching for school certificate pupils. The dilemma of formal examinations and progressive practice seemed to have been resolved, and the extra-curricular activities of the school blossomed partly as a result of the relaxed relationships between staff and pupils which Dalton encouraged.

All of this achievement in progressive consolidation was thrown into the melting pot with the outbreak of war. KASS had wisely planned in advance, ensuring that a nucleus of the school was maintained at Royston, ready for the day when hostilities ceased. That day came in 1945, by which time Manor Wood had a new headmaster whose task it was to face the challenge of advancing the cause of progressive era in the postwar world. Whether this was to be a new educational dawn, as promised by the attention given to education in the Butler Education Act, or a false dawn, as happened generally in Britain after the First World War, remained to be seen. The place of KAS in the new educational order of primary and secondary education for all had yet to be worked out.

Notes and references

1. *Violet Hyett*, 7–8, a book of tributes to her on her death in 1949.
2. *Brief Notes on the History and Principles of the King Alfred School Society* (1935), 2.
3. Ibid., 13.
4. School committee minutes, 13 May 1935.
5. *Report of the Consultative Committee on the Primary School* (London, Board of Education, 1931), 94.
6. Alice Woods was born in Walthamstow in 1849 to a Quaker family. She was educated at home and at Girton College. She had a long and distinguished career in teaching after gaining a second-class degree in her Girton College Tripos in Moral Science. She taught at the junior department of Clifton, but as headmistress of the coeducational school, Bedford Park, Chiswick (1884–92) and as principal of Maria Grey Training College (1892–1913) had the kind of educational background which made her so valuable to KASS. She wrote several books on progressive education, including *Educational Experiments in England* (1920).
7. Findlay died in 1940.
8. Dr John Carl Flugel (1884–1955) was renowned for his lecturing and writing in the field of psychology. He was an assistant professor at UCL (1929–43), honorary secretary of the British Psychological Society and had been president of the British Psychological Society shortly before taking up the presidency of KASS. His publications included *The Psycho-Analytical Study of the Family* (1921), *A Study of Work at High Pressure* (1928), *Man Morals and Society* (1945) and *Population, Psychology and Peace* (1947).
9. Council minutes, 13 July 1938.
10. Ibid., 1 March 1939.
11. The *Times Educational Supplement*, 10 February 1940, mistakenly reported that the school has purchased the farm three years previously.

Chapter 5

New Age Travellers:
KAS and Montgomery,
1945–1962

During the Second World War, the independent sector had attracted the political spotlight by requesting some form of closer relationship with the state to ease its financial problems. R. A. Butler, the last president of the Board of Education prior to its replacement by the Ministry of Education, set up the Fleming Committee in order to shunt the issue quietly into a siding[1] and not upset his more important plans for reorganizing the state sector. Apart from asking its educational guru and ex-Rugby scholar, R. H. Tawney, to breathe a little ritualistic fire into a report on the public schools, Labour was happy to concur. However, when the Labour Party was elected to office with a landslide majority of 146, the independent schools began to fear that they would be included in the new Labour government's proposals for bringing into public ownership the principal social utilities. Their fears were unfounded. Labour had no intention of stirring up the issue and so intensifying opposition to what it saw as its more important plans to create a national health service and to nationalize the railways and the principal industries. Besides, schools such as KAS, an independent progressive day school, were not seen by Tawney or Labour as part of 'the problem of the public schools'. The challenge to KAS, in the new era of secondary education for all, came not from any radical plans of Labour but from its conservative educational proposals to reorganize secondary education largely on tripartite lines, proposals which in fact brought upon the Labour government the wrath of the left-wing supporters of multilateralism.

The Labour Ministers of Education, Ellen Wilkinson and her successor, George Tomlinson, favoured the strengthening of the grammar schools by making them democratic centres of excellence. With the abolition of fees, they would accept only the top 25–30 per cent, at most, of those who passed the 11+ examination.[2] Labour members of Parliament such as Arthur Creech Jones argued that free selective grammar schools should be developed deliberately to win parents away from the independent sector. KAS, as a day school in close proximity to several grammar schools, could be caught in the particularly vulnerable and difficult position either of becoming a superior kind of fee-charging secondary modern school, catering for a large number who failed the 11+ examination in and around Hampstead, or of turning itself into something approximating an independent grammar school in order to stay in business. In either case its unique character would be imperilled if not destroyed. Two further developments of the late 1940s and early 1950s raised even graver doubts about whether KAS would survive much beyond its half century. The first of these resulted from council's brave decision in 1948 to pay its teachers full Burnham salaries and pensions. In order to do this, the school had to attract even greater numbers of fee-paying pupils, with the consequent pressures upon class size and KAS styles of learning and teaching. The introduction in 1951 of a single-subject general certificate of education in the place of the grouped school certificate added a second, and equally unwelcome, set of pressures. KAS had always sought to minimize examination pressures upon its pupils. However, in the postwar world the demand for paper qualifications, especially for the new ordinary and advanced level certificates of education, grew considerably. KAS found it more difficult than ever to resist the pressure from parents to put academic success at the top of the curricular agenda.

But KAS was not founded just to practise enlightened methods of learning. It had a missionary role which was relatively easy to fill after the First World War when school numbers were small and an educational model, the Dalton-based system of learning, was readily to hand. After the Second World War, with different pressures, larger pupil numbers and no progressive paradigm so immediately available, the role of propagandist pioneer was more problematic. Yet there was an innovatory role for KAS as a long-standing multilateral school to fill in the postwar era. Even though the school could never claim to be comprehensive in the social class sense, it was comprehensive in the academic sense of having within it the full range of abilities. It was therefore well placed to evaluate a variety of teaching arrangements for the slowly growing number of local education authorities which rejected tripartism in favour of multilateral or comprehensive schools. Whether KAS would accept the role of new age innovator, especially in the area of mixed-ability teaching, not just within the Dalton framework, had yet to be seen.

In 1945 all of these great educational issues lay in the future. In the first years of peace the grammar schools were far from confident that they would survive, believing they were caught in the crossfire between the new secondary modern schools and comprehensive schools on the left and the public schools on the right. KAS, without the resources of the state schools and the endowments of the public schools to draw upon, had even more reason to feel insecure in the immediate postwar years. The devastation of the Manor Wood site was so great that it seemed very possible, if not likely, that, having survived the war in exile, the school might expire in the first years of peace, which were described by one former pupil as 'those dreadful Socialist postwar years' in which the freezing cold of KAS was but part of a general chill which settled on the whole country!

Jubilation to jubilee, 1945 to 1948

The surrender of Germany in May 1945 freed the capital from further V2 attacks and meant that KASS could bring home its school-in-exile. Old Alfredians, the school staff and the members of the society had good cause to rejoice, especially as the clamour of applicants for KAS was so great that its finances seemed secure not just to the school's golden jubilee in June 1948 but well beyond. However, for some of the older staff and earlier generations of Old Alfredians, the rejoicing was short-lived and gave way first to unease and then to grave doubts that the war had damaged not just the material fabric of the school but its very spirit. This was not just the natural inclination of the older generation to despair of the next, although probably they had more cause to do so, as the new headmaster, the gentle, self-effacing Baron Harleigh Montgomery (known to his pupils simply as 'Monty') pointed out in his address to parents on the subject of discipline. In his view the large number of new entrants to KAS could scarcely have remained

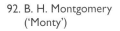

92. B. H. Montgomery
('Monty')

unaffected by the chaos of war and the disruption of evacuation. There was more than a little truth in the accusation that 'the pendulum had swung the other way and the children are ill-mannered, wilful, backward in academic work, and generally unable to concentrate on anything for very long'.[3] Too much neglect or indulgence, too much money to spend, too much cinema-going, these, he argued, were producing a generation of children who, many believed, could only be controlled by good old-fashioned discipline. Mary Gillett, a long-standing member of staff, was renowned for her remark that 'the worst people in the world to have children were parents!' The problem in hers and Montgomery's view was not so much the children as their parents who were beginning to demand 'better' discipline and the 'better' examination results of the new grammar schools. Getting the children through the gates was not the problem facing KAS, for the school population of 213 in the year before the war was quickly surpassed by 1946. Convincing their parents of the lasting value of the KAS approach to discipline and examinations was harder. Sixty-five per cent of pupils completed less than two years in the upper school. Whether the new headmaster had sufficiently effective powers of argument and communication to reduce this high leaving rate in an age which gradually became dominated by the sterner academic values of the grammar schools remained to be seen. KAS, by the time of its golden jubilee in 1948, was in danger not of closing for lack of pupils but of losing its distinctive character by being overwhelmed by children whose parents looked on the school as an inferior stop gap en route to a grammar school or to some other independent day or boarding school, or to a direct grant grammar school. The instability arising from such a situation affected the education of all pupils, of those whose stay at KAS was short and those who stayed on until the ages of sixteen or eighteen.

In the early summer of 1945 it was the material fabric of the school rather than a possibly debilitated spirit that was the greater concern. In June 1945 parents who looked over and through its dilapidated fences must have wondered if the old progressive phoenix would ever rise from the ashes. They had heard rumours that the estate had been commandeered during the war for training the armed forces in demolition work. Given the proximity of the hospital the rumours were unlikely to have any foundation in fact. Most of the damage was casual rather than deliberately inflicted, not by highly trained professional soldiers but by the Home Guard. But the results were equally devastating. Montgomery's report to the general meeting of KASS in 1946 gives a good idea of the extent of the damage:

To give some idea of the work which had to be done I will summarize the chief items:

All the electric circuits (except that in the Hall) had to be rewired. All the central heating plants (except that in the Hall) were useless and needed new boilers and radiators. Several hundred panes of glass were broken. Most of the windows which were not broken were painted over with blackout paint which had to be scraped off. Nearly every window catch, lock, bolt, and door handle had been broken or removed. Many tons of sand had to be removed from the cloakrooms, covered court and fives courts. The two hard tennis courts had to be relaid. All taps needed washers, all plugs in basins had been removed, there were about twenty burst pipes and many other plumbing defects. About one-third of the games field was covered with nine inches of hard core and ash, and the remainder of the field was pitted with trenches and holes – including a concrete pit six feet deep. Every room needed to be distempered to make it habitable. A great quantity of barbed wire and broken glass lay around the grounds. Two wooden huts (used as classrooms before the war) were totally destroyed. The other two huts were badly damaged, the roofs leaked and they had to be re-lined throughout before they could be used. Many cupboard doors were missing and nearly every fixed cupboard had been denuded of its shelves. Nearly all the linoleum had been destroyed. Every room (except the Hall) had an accumulation of several years' dirt and rubbish to be cleaned away.

For council, the immediate consideration was how to speed up the payment from the War Office of the £4,400 claim for compensation. For the headmaster and staff, the problem was one of finding habitable accommodation for the school's 163 pupils and to ensure the early transfer to Manor Wood of Marion Robey's thirty-six nursery children at Oakhurst. For the pupils, repairing the wartime damage was full of exciting possibilities, something which *The Evening News* was quick to report. It described to its readers how children of ten to sixteen years of age were to be seen each afternoon replacing windows, making plaster draughtproof, laying roads and re-lining damaged classrooms. The school tradition dating back to Russell of exploiting the educational opportunities (and cheap labour) of employing pupils to renovate the

93. Postwar reconstruction by Naomi Elkan, Beverly Pease, Anne Fielding, Lorna Lea, Marion Lowenstein, Pippa Jarrett, Jennifer Jackson, Gillian Pugh, Patsy Silver and others

school was part of the prewar curriculum and had been very much in evidence at Royston. It had the sound educational advantage of giving manual work parity with academic study, and most children enjoyed doing something to reduce the damage, desolation and dreariness which Renée Soskin believed characterized the site in September 1945. By the following month 70 per cent of the prewar school was in use, thanks in no small measure to the efforts of the pupils.

Restoration of the site to its prewar size and condition was, however, insufficient in view of the rapid increase in numbers; by September 1946, the number of pupils had reached 232 with a long waiting list. In preparation for the increase, council had sanctioned the building of two new classrooms behind Squirrel Hall, both single-storeyed with the possibility of rooms being built above when finances permitted. The Ministry of Works refused permission for the use of new bricks and fixed a limit of £2,300 for the venture. By the time that Britain entered 'the great freeze' of 1947, the project had fallen behind schedule and the school was also facing mounting costs for repairing frost damage to paths and roofs. One of the two rooms of the new block was ready for use by September, the other being occupied by the end of the term. Forms B2 and C thus found new homes. With numbers having reached 250 (in excess of what Montgomery regarded as the ideal), demands for additional buildings, especially a pavilion, the extension of the lower school and classrooms to replace the huts, were voiced constantly. New buildings competed for limited financial resources with demands for improved salaries and the heavy cost of maintenance. To increase the size of classes from eighteen to twenty to gain the extra funds needed could have undermined the whole aim of a KAS education.

KAS pupils thus witnessed a welcome, rapid change in the physical appearance of the school and a not so welcome, rapid increase in the

94. Pupils (including Alister Pease, Anne Fielding, Lorna Lea, Gillian Pugh) repairing classrooms, 1945

95. Outside the new postwar classrooms, c.1950 (photograph Photoreportage Ltd.)

96. Inside the new postwar classrooms (photograph *Picture Post*)

student body in a very short period of time. The society faced a dilemma; the main way of raising the finance for the construction and maintenance of new buildings and for renovating the old was by increasing numbers. This was a treadmill, in that the increased numbers soon required additional accommodation which was provided largely by increased numbers. There was thus a threat to class size. Increasing staff–pupil ratios would reduce the opportunities for individual learning, but a KAS education was not simply to do with what went on in the classroom. Pupils were encouraged to build dens, to use the grounds to the full for exploration and activity which was seen as a means of individual self-expression. To increase numbers, even if classroom accommodation were available, was thus likely to destroy the balance of maintaining the environment while allowing pupils to use it. Pressure of numbers would also destroy the small-school atmosphere which was regarded as so vital to the achievement of KAS aims. A balance had to be struck between raising the revenue through fees to provide for new accommodation and increased salaries, and maintaining a school at a size sufficient to enable the educational aims of the founders to be realized. Some of the older members of staff began to voice the view that the maximum size of the school compatible with educational ideals had been reached if not exceeded by 1947.

One of the other unsettling features of the period for pupils was the rapid and unprecedented turnover of staff brought about in part by the expansion of the state sector. The Hadow Report of 1926 advocated the restructuring of the state sector into compulsory and free primary and secondary education, which was legislated for in the Butler Act of 1944. The greater opportunities for career advancement and financial reward which these changes offered were a great inducement for KAS staff to move to the state sector. Several of the full-time members of staff who were appointed to KAS in 1945 left soon after as the new state system became operational. For example, Miss Jolliffe left to join the London County Council and Mr Flinn, who was said to be having difficulties with the KAS style of discipline, found a more congenial post in the state sector. Even the stalwart Miss Gillett left in 1947 after twenty years of service to take up a lecture-ship in one of the new emergency training colleges for teachers. In addition there were the retirements of older members of staff. The death of Violet Hyett in January 1949, after much ill health, was another sad blow to the school which left the feeling that the KAS that the older generation of students had known had passed away also. Though Montgomery reported in October 1948 that the period of unsettled staffing was coming to an end, it seemed to some of the remaining staff that the old KAS spirit would never return.

97. Some of the staff, 1947: L to R (front row) Mrs M. Montgomery, Miss Mousley, Miss Hyett, Miss Levin, Mrs Soskin (Anthony and Gabrielle Soskin on the grass); (back row) Mr Montgomery, Mr Roberts, Mr Johnson, Miss Gaylard, Miss d'Eath, Miss Robey, Mrs Barber

The unsettling effect of a rapid turnover of staff on children who had already experienced the dislocation of war was seen in the exam-ination results which hit an all-time low in July 1948. In the age of new grammar schools, KAS could not ignore the accusation that its educa-tional standards were falling. In his explanation of the poor pass rate in 1948, when only half of the eight entered for the school certificate passed, Montgomery pointed to the large number of schools which the entrants had attended and believed that they represented the largest cohort of children who had suffered from evacuation. But the matter was not left simply to chance. The school was already adopting a selection policy to exclude pupils who were unlikely to benefit from the Dalton system and coupled this with a preliminary test in the school certificate year to weed out the likely failures. In addition, KAS became an examination centre for the first time in 1947 to remove the dis-advantage of candidates having to sit the school certificate in unfamiliar surroundings.

Montgomery and council also tried to bring more settled conditions to the school by tackling the question of salaries, something which had occupied his attention in the prewar years. By providing a more attractive salary scale and career structure he hoped to reduce the turnover of staff and to reward more adequately those who effectively put KAS principles into practice. The years 1945 to 1948 saw a lively debate about linking KAS salaries to the Burnham scale. The argu-ments put forward in favour of this linkage were that it would widen the pool of applicants for posts and enable KAS to take into account 'the passing of the Health Act'. Not all staff or council members were in agreement on the issue. Miss Hibburd argued that the system of family allowances built into the existing scale gave married teachers a better deal and that the society did not have the funds to implement the Burnham scale fully. Montgomery was well aware that raising the finance to pay Burnham rates could compromise two basic KAS principles if increased salaries were met by raising fee income by increasing the size of classes from eighteen to twenty, or if deals were struck with government through the direct grant scheme, or with the London or Middlesex County Councils, to gain additional finance. The latter would be at the expense of parental control over KAS. Corbett Fisher stood firm in his belief that salaries must be raised, without surrendering any political independence, a position supported by Mrs Barber, who believed that the KAS scale did not allow sufficiently for qualifications. The matter was finally resolved by an agreement to adopt the Burnham salary structure but to pay only 90 per cent of the Burnham scale, the new salary to be introduced in September 1948. Such a measure, it was hoped, would enable KAS to attract and to keep teachers of the calibre of Miss Hyett and Miss Gillett. One of the first to be appointed under the new Burnham-related scheme was Mrs Hettie Barber, who was appointed co-headteacher in 1948, but full Burnham salaries and Mrs Barber's upgraded salary had to wait until 1951. Council made the decision in March 1948 to regard the 90 per cent rule as a short stepping stone on the path to full parity.

With the rapid influx of a large number of pupils, not all of whose parents fully understood the basic principles and practices of KAS, there was a real danger that the character of the school would change. There was a general social demand, which the new state schools appeared to meet, for stronger discipline in the handling of the 'wayward war generation of children'. Montgomery, in an address to parents and staff in October 1947, recognized, in the postwar world: 'Progressive schools are considered unsound by many people because they do not discipline children in the old-fashioned sense of the word.'[4] Such discipline was deemed by many to be important because the children of the war generation 'are, on the average, unstable, and lacking in purpose simply because they have been raised in a time of instability'. Furthermore, formal discipline, such as that found in the new grammar schools, was perceived to lead to better examination results, which were regarded as vital to a postwar age hungry for paper qualifications. While KAS could attract large numbers of young children, there was every danger that the drift away from the school once pupils reached eleven or thirteen would intensify if parents could not be persuaded that the school offered a superior form of discipline while at the same time delivering good examination results. Renée Soskin was right to point out that the recent publicity about KAS as 'a tree top school' in the press (*Evening News*, 11 February 1946) and cinema (*Pathé Pictorial*, January 1947) tended to trivialize progressive education and to ignore the academic achievements of the school.

Montgomery thus took great care to emphasize that the KAS concept of discipline was not incompatible with achieving high standards in the school certificate. Local rumours about increased bullying at the school and poor examination passes, both of which had some foundation of truth, meant that he was by no means addressing the firm believers in KAS ideology. However, he was uncompromising in his denunciation of the traditional idea of discipline based upon coercion and fear, that which is 'economical of the adult's efforts' and produces 'seemingly well-behaved children conditioned to accept drudgery in their occupations so long as they are still ruled by fear'. Such conditions, he argued, did nothing to develop their personalities or to prepare them to cope with the changing conditions of the modern world. He emphasized the essential aim of KAS which was to assist harmonious development and not 'to rush the natural processes', to encourage the development of individuality through helping children to progress successfully through the stages of childhood and adolescence, which involved understanding periodic revolts, rudeness and bad temper. The latter were to be regarded as 'symptoms of a developing personality or an indication that the child is being overstressed'. Any rules or regulations should be explained to pupils and have their basis in reason. Children should be helped to develop a social conscience through discussing problems of behaviour.

Montgomery was the embodiment of KAS principles in his relationship with pupils. He exercised a quiet, gentle firm authority based not upon fear and coercion but upon quiet persuasion and respect. He was a very patient person, although some regarded him as too retiring as a headmaster. He was, indeed, a rather shy self-effacing person who, even when talking to pupils, appeared ill at ease, hesitantly shuffling papers or his feet. One of his most embarrassing moments must have been accompanying a senior pupil from the school field when, on a hot June day, she decided to strip to the waist. Yet he was always approachable and enjoyed nothing more than registering the sites of camps or garden plots which pupils had chosen around the Manor Wood site. No pupil ever remembered him shouting, even when his bubble car was bedecked with ribbon to look like an Easter egg and placed on the roof of the new common room. He was criticized by some parents for being too weak and allowing too many misdemeanours to go unpunished, yet in the period 1945 to 1948 he was 'the calm still centre of what was a turbulent world'.

98. Watching an eclipse of the sun, 1954

Styles of teaching and learning at KAS were, he argued, open to misinterpretation. Mere effort was to be avoided – to reward it would be to resemble a lunatic who spent so much of his time knocking his head against the wall because it was so nice when he stopped. Purposeful activity was all-important, even if the purpose of an activity was not always immediately obvious to the onlooker. However, for such activity to take place there was need for quiet and order, without making the individual subservient to society, or allowing individuals to disrupt the efforts of others. Monty took two steps to try to strengthen the ideological basis of the school. The first was to amend the entry form to make parents state the age to which they intended their offspring to remain at the school; it was hoped that this would help in the selection of pupils whose parents believed in the school's aims. The second was to reform the advisory council, as described in his annual report of 1947.

> The Advisory Council has had many problems to deal with this year, and it has made some changes in its constitution. The most important is that which alters its name to 'the Council', and its representatives to 'Councillors'. Each form in the Upper School now elects two 'Councillors' instead of one 'Representative', and the 'Councillors' take the place of what used to be 'Form Captains'. The object of this alteration is to spread the responsibility for making and keeping rules over a large number of the members of the School.

Change was also pressing from another direction when KAS celebrated its golden jubilee in June 1948. The following year would be the last under which pupils would be taught for the school certificate and higher school certificate. These examinations dating back to 1917 were to be replaced in 1951 by the single-subject general certificate of education ordinary and advanced levels, a move which was welcomed by the staff but which was likely to keep the standards debate very much alive. More than ever, the new grammar schools were dominating the postwar educational agenda and were seen by society in general as the yardstick by which all other schools were measured.

The jubilee celebrations in aid of the school building fund opened with a tree-planting ceremony by Mr Picknett and Mrs Mason and a recital by the school's most celebrated pianist, Solomon, on 8 June 1948, and ended on 20 June with the last of four perform- ances of *Why Education?*, a historical pageant written by Violet Hyett and Renée Soskin and presented by the Alfredian Dramatic Club. Two plays, *A Gentleman Goes By* and *The Happy Man*, were performed by mem- bers of the junior school. The jubilee fête extended over 18 and 19 June with a pro- duction of *A Midsummer Night's Dream* (in the covered court rather than the amphitheatre because of the inclement weather), displays of art work, country dancing and puppet shows and a number of side shows under 'Monty's direction'.

Thus KAS celebrated its first half- century. Intended as the flagship school it still remained the only one in the fleet. Had the attempts by Morrish and Miss Bullock to open a second school at Stanmore not been sunk by Harrow Council, which requisi- tioned the Woodlands site for housing purposes, then perhaps the best golden jubilee tribute to the school would have been the launching of the second in the fleet.

99. A jubilee tree- planting ceremony by the chair of council, Mr Picknett, and Mrs Mason (Hilda Lowy), one of the first pupils, 1948

KAS at the crossroads

It was understandable that Hyett and Birkett should have continued Wicksteed's Dalton-based upper school curriculum when they suc- ceeded to the headship in 1933. Miss Hyett, in particular, had helped him to pioneer its introduction in 1920–1 and had undertaken the immense task of producing a timetable structure, including individual afternoon option programmes for each student, along the lines advo- cated by Dalton's creator, Helen Parkhurst. Wicksteed supported it at the level of educational ideology throughout the interwar years; Hyett beavered away at making its practical application as effective as possible. It was therefore no surprise that Dalton continued after Wicksteed's retirement and throughout the dual headship. Whether a society dedi- cated to educational innovation and experiment, to giving 'practical expression to the best theories of education extant', could allow a system devised after the First World War to continue after the Second, and remain true to the principles of its founders, was an important but scarcely considered matter when council appointed Montgomery (who had served on the staff from 1932 to 1940 as geography teacher) to the headship without competitive interview in 1945.

Twenty-five years of Dalton had bred a peculiar kind of KAS conservatism in council, which had concerned itself after 1924 more with building programmes than with education policy, and among the upper school staff through the selection policies of Wicksteed and Hyett. That KAS should cling to Dalton after 1945 was entirely understandable for three reasons. First, in its anxiety to return from the Royston outpost to the Manor Wood home base, council found it convenient to turn to Montgomery, after his success at Oakhurst, to rebuild the school and to other older staff to run it. At a time when a speedy appointment to the headship was called for, Montgomery was the obvious choice, being well-versed in KAS ways. The unsettled conditions at postwar Manor Wood left little time for contemplating radical departures in educational ideology or in personnel. Second, there was no alternative progressive curricular model readily available to KAS in 1945 as there had been in 1918 with Montessori, Dewey and Dalton. The New Education Fellowship could have provided a new progressive paradigm but the school's links with it had loosened when Beatrice Ensor moved to South Africa in the late 1930s and the school moved to Royston in 1939. Furthermore, progressivism was not in the ascendancy as it had been in the late 1920s. This leads us to the third reason. The forces of the postwar world were moving more in the direction of traditionalism. The desire to bring order into the lives of children disrupted by war, the pressure on schools to secure employment for children in the uncertain postwar years, the dominance of the new grammar schools which seemed to deliver both of these goals – for all of these reasons progressivism seemed to be in retreat. It was thus not surprising that KAS clung to its modified Dalton scheme as the best hope when the more conventional educational forces of the age seemed to be dominant. Furthermore, the system had shown its benefits over a generation to a school dedicated to promoting choice and responsibility, and to one which was non-selective in its admission policy. The claim made by two leading educationists, Good and Teller, that the Dalton plan 'had been praised far beyond its merits',[5] did not reflect the KAS experience.

The first clear sign to KAS that the star of progressivism was no longer in the ascendancy came when the school received its first postwar inspection in 1949. The Board of Education, which had warmed a little to Dalton in the interwar years, had been replaced by the Ministry of Education under the terms of the 1944 Education Act. The Ministry's officials regarded primary education largely as a preparation for the highly selective 11+ examination, and the secondary system mainly in terms of a hierarchy of schools and subjects with class teaching as the best form of curriculum delivery. The inspectors were more familiar with a view of education as a process of inculcating pupils with an externally defined body of information that demanded the imposition of some measure of coercive order in the classroom. To KAS this was instruction, not education. If the school expected Labour's Ministry of Education under George Tomlinson in 1949 to be any more sympathetic than Stanhope's Conservative Board of Education had been in 1938 it was to be disappointed. Its condemnation of Dalton could not have been more outspoken, even allowing for the language of officialdom.

Even the lower school, where class teaching was the norm, did not escape censure. Lack of adequate control of children in the classroom, lack of a clear, general direction and of sufficiently demanding tasks formed the basis of the inspectors' criticism in the single general paragraph that they devoted to the activities of the lower school. The middle and upper school programme was examined in greater detail, and the general conclusion arrived at that 'strict adherence to the system has introduced a rigidity into the school work which is quite at variance with the school's ideals and desires'. The subject-by-subject analysis suggested that standards were being sacrificed on the altar of Daltonism. 'The time has come', the inspectors declared,

100. Junior school music with Mr Tryggvason, c.1952

> for the school authorities to consider the effectiveness of the present system in its application to each subject, and at each level, and to make the changes necessary to ensure that has always been in fact, the School's aim, namely, that each pupil should receive the education best suited to his or her age, ability and aptitude.[6]

The inspectors went on to consider the 'peculiar difficulties' experienced by teachers and pupils in each subject area, selecting first the subject which most adolescents sought to avoid, mathematics, to illustrate their view. Pupils were said to lose the sequence of Rustomjee's mathematics lessons unless they completed their assignments regularly, which under the open-choice system many failed to do. Without regular class teaching, which under the Dalton system was reduced to a minimum to give priority to stagework, all but the best school certificate pupils tended to flounder, in the view of the inspectors. The 'stage' system led to much purely mechanical work and insufficient experimental work, with overdivision in the subject's component parts. 'Flexibility and liveliness' were lost for all but the ablest mathematicians, reducing the enjoyment upon which the KAS measure of progress depended. Latin under Fuller's stagework had been reduced to 'a series of grammatical exercises' at the expense of 'the enjoyment of literature and the relation of Latin as the language of a people'. In French Mrs Johnson had recognized this problem and had altered the assignments so as to avoid undue emphasis on the written language, with the result that they 'had become indistinguishable from preparation for specific lessons'. The Dalton approach, in the inspectors' view, far from reducing pressure on students, led to an uneven progress in the early years which was only made good by increased pressure later on and the overuse of past examination papers as the basis for teaching.

The inspectors pulled few punches. They could find no merits in the 'stage' system in history, it being declared a restrictive influence upon its teachers, Pole and Johnson, and those whom they taught. It gave little opportunity for pupils to pursue personal interest. Class teaching, on the other hand, produced impressive knowledge and good powers of discussion. There was no doubt where the preferences of the inspectors lay. More class teaching and the removal of the clear-cut distinction between academic subjects undertaken in the morning and the afternoon practical activities, for which they could find 'no sound educational or psychological reason', were implied in their criticisms. In geography as in history, stages detracted from the research value of the subjects, especially when precise page numbers for answering the questions were given in stagework instructions. In French, the 'system' was said to hinder the progress of the majority of pupils. Mrs Barber's science assignments emphasized theoretical issues at the expense of practical work. Their conclusions about the essentials of Dalton organization were thus highly critical of its value. Art, craftwork and music received more balanced comment, although the pervading tone was that 'little serious work' was being done either because pupils lacked a knowledge of the basics or because there was too much discontinuity.

Council and staff rightly refused to be persuaded to change course. The school staff, in fact, believed that 'the criticisms and attitude of the inspectors had been fair and encouraging' and council could be pleased that KAS continued to receive 'recognition'. The school committee argued on the basis of the report that, 'the school appears to have regained its prewar standard in most amenities, except books and handicraft materials'. Perhaps the greatest reason for the school to believe that it was succeeding in its aims despite some apparent deficiencies in its teaching organization was the statement by the inspectors that 'the discipline of the School, as seen at the inspection, calls for no adverse comment'. The attitude and behaviour of the older boys and girls, in particular, were exemplary. A more balanced assessment of the Dalton teaching method came from the many visitors from the University of London's Institute of Education. They continued to be impressed by the school's achievements, and indeed one teacher, the history master, John Handford, left to join the Institute's staff.

KAS had done a great deal before the inspection to make the Dalton-based learning system work more effectively. The staff had spent much time tightening the rules and standards. Laggardly pupils were 'rounded up and helped' and the number of stages was calculated initially on a half-termly basis of five and then on a monthly basis to ensure coverage of each subject area and to give more manageable targets. The system of marking was changed from distinction, credit, pass and fail to a letter scale A, B and C, and an experimental method was introduced of recording stagework results on individual cards rather than a public stage sheet. The latter had been condemned by the school advisory council on the grounds that it embarrassed students. The new experimental method encouraged the private discussion of progress between staff and pupils. Experiment with the curriculum had also taken place within the Dalton framework, with subjects being combined to facilitate project work on the locality, including visits to the library, court and police station. Mrs Ryder Smith and Mr Johnson had urged a more radical plan to create an independent middle school (forms C, B2 and 1) with less open-room lessons and more time devoted to class teaching. The proposal put forward in November 1947, which involved form teachers taking classes before the morning break and specialist subject staff taking the form after the break would essentially have destroyed the Dalton-based approach. The idea was dropped because of timetabling difficulties and because it was recognized that 'the Dalton Plan would cease to operate'. Mrs Barber, the busy, energetic, and to some, awesome, senior mistress, opposed any weakening of the Dalton principle and argued in favour of its closer implementation. The continued support given by the staff to this style of learning, despite the wholesale condemnation of it by the inspectorate, was the result of open staffroom debate and discussion with pupils and parents.

The inspectors had not asked pupils what they thought of the school and its teaching methods. Had they done so they might have been less critical. However, values such as self-motivation, relaxed learning, encouraging pupils to think for themselves, trust and responsibility and acquiring study skills and not just knowledge were not those upon

101. The covered court
in 1948: drawn by
Fred Johnson

which the inspectors placed much weight. While some pupils believed that the Dalton system 'benefited the workers and, at best, entertained the lazy', many appreciated the relative freedom and independence which it allowed. The informality of relationships in which teachers were usually addressed by their nicknames and where pupils were taught by tutorial methods in the open rooms was the hallmark of a KAS education. It could have its difficulties when pupils 'had no sense of the very different standards elsewhere' and when they failed GCE examinations. It could also disguise poor teaching, especially in the sciences, and was in the view of at least one former student rather chaotic and time-wasting in that it was not properly monitored nor did it provide enough rigorous feedback to pupils which the more orthodox tests and classwork was said to do. However, the open-room system was not without social advantages when pupils from different age groups met together. Pupils worked alongside and helped their younger and sometimes their older colleagues, while at the same time having the opportunity of individual help from the specialist teacher.

Pressure of numbers and the need to give greater attention to preparing pupils for examinations in a wider range of subjects caused several modifications to Dalton during Montgomery's headship. There was further tightening up of stagework, with forms 1 to 3 being given weekly instead of monthly targets. With the number of open rooms proving to be increasingly insufficient as numbers expanded, so more 'form lessons' were given in the middle school, especially in mathematics and project work. This had led Mr Johnson to advocate in 1947, possibly for political reasons, an independent middle school (Forms C, B2 and B1) in which pupils would be taught in forms, possibly using the model of lessons with form teachers before the morning break and with specialist staff to some extent after the break.[7] A decade later, this had come about not by deliberate policy but because of the shortage of open rooms. There was still the problem of making the system work more effectively in the upper school. To the suggestion put forward in 1957 by

Fred Johnson that a period be set aside each Thursday afternoon to help the laggards catch up with their stages, Mrs Johnson (formerly Mrs Ryder Smith) added that this could be used not just to help those who had fallen behind because of genuine learning difficulties but also to punish people who came late to lessons. This drew the retort from Mrs Barber, the school's ideological champion, that the latter use would be a direct contravention 'of the principle of the school which set out to encourage the children to want to work. If this had failed then the whole system should be changed.' The system was not changed radically but continued to be modified in a piecemeal manner to allow more teaching and private study to take place in the afternoons, hitherto reserved for options, to meet the needs of those engaged in a wide range of GCE subjects. The shortage of open rooms for stagework had grown so acute by the end of Montgomery's headship that Mr Johnson asked Mrs Barber's replacement, Mrs Paul Jones, if there was 'a deliberate policy to discontinue the open room system'. Her reply showed the growing pressures on staff time and school accommodation. Staff had been given the extra class lessons that they requested, thus causing additional pressures on staff teaching time and school accommodation.

102. Fred Johnson and 'Monty', 1953

Opinion among the staff on the value of the open-room system was becoming increasingly divided. Miss Maxwell and Mrs Tait expressed the view in the closing year of Montgomery's headship that the choice of open rooms in the upper school was inevitably haphazard because of the lottery of staff availability and that 'the combination of young and older children in the same room was not a success'.[8] Roy Greenfield regretted the lack of open rooms on the ground that it reduced the opportunities for remedial work in GCE mathematics. In council, Fred Johnson regretted the reduction in their numbers more on ideological grounds. 'He considered the system had been of great value in the past encouraging children to work on their own. He felt that if the school timetable became like that of a grammar school a valuable part of training in independence would be lost.'

Yet like a grammar school it had (in part at least) to become, as Mrs Paul Jones was only too aware when trying to balance the time-table demands of the various groups within the school. Grammar school headmasters in 1945 had feared that their schools would be marginalized with increasing attention being given to the new secondary modern schools. A decade later grammar schools were regarded as academic centres of excellence, the gold standard, of the state system. As Rée pointed out in *The Essential Grammar School*, published in 1956,[9] the new, greatly augmented middle classes were ambitious, 'they are all expecting at least a Grammar School education for their children'. In particular, grammar schools were trading on their 'day-school qualification', something which set them apart from many independent boarding schools but not from KAS, which could not help but be affected by their competition and ethos. The introduction in 1951 of the single-subject general certificate of education ordinary and advanced levels, which replaced the grouped school certificate, seemed to confirm their paramount position. Schools such as Kilburn Grammar School were the very visible manifestations of the new educational order in and around Hampstead. As Montgomery reported to council after the first candidates had sat the new examination, the Dalton system was expected to deliver even higher standards because of 'the increase in the pass mark' and because of 'the granting of certificates for passing in a single subject'. Perhaps even more significant was the fact that the regulations made it less easy for candidates to sit public examinations a year later than was normal. Hitherto it had been the practice to reduce the pressure upon KAS students by entering many who were older than the usual candidate for school certificate and higher school certificate. The fact that this practice was no longer so easy to adopt might have helped to explain the headmaster's verdict on the 1951 examination that the 'result is depressing for the better candidates'.

KAS, a day school where power rested in the hands of parents, could not simply bury its head in the progressive sand; unlike progressive boarding schools, it was in daily contact with parents. Its ultimate aim was to show that its rationalist education was not a rare plant which would wither with the first cold blast of the new examination system but one which could meet the challenges of the new age without recourse to coercion and mass teaching methods. The inspector's report and the 1951 examination results raised fundamental issues for KAS, which the staff were quick to recognize. In the first general staff meeting of the academic year 1951–2 Mrs Barber opened a discussion on the attitude of KAS to the new GCE, beginning with the basic point that the school had a non-selective entry, 'made up of children whose parents believed in KAS ideals, those who will never be of grammar school standard and children whose talents do not appear until after they have failed the Common Entrance Exam', and also children whose parents like the school for 'its snob value'. It was felt that the number of academically able children at the school was likely to decrease, 'since few parents today can afford to reject a free place in a grammar school if the child wins one'.[10] The staff affirmed their belief in the school's non-selective policy and argued that it should make careful provision for the consequent wide range of ability, which the Dalton framework seemed to assist. There were problems, not least of which was parents expecting their children to be entered for GCE examinations which they had no hope of passing.

In terms of its missionary function, of demonstrating to the world of education the compatibility between the KAS style of learning and the academic demands of teaching the full range of GCE subjects, the school was at the crossroads. As some kind of multilateral or comprehensive school, KAS had a unique opportunity to pilot new methods of teaching for such a wide range of ability. The first staff meeting of the year 1950/1 seemed to reject the adventurous approach of mixed-ability teaching. It concluded that 'with class teaching the presence of all levels of ability at the same time has no justification. There must be either grouping within existing forms or streaming.' It opted not only for segregation of the able from the less able but for a differentiated curriculum for the non-GCE classes based upon social studies, expeditions, surveying and civic studies. Yet the staff also asserted its belief in the need 'to discourage the idea that a subject is not worth studying unless it is taken in an exam'. In the end it gave support to the idea of three separate parallel groups, those studying a full range of ordinary level subjects, those studying a few and those following the alternative non-ordinary level course. What was clear was that the curriculum was becoming GCE-led, with the groupings defined in relation to it. This was, however, the first bite at the GCE cherry and pupils did not need to experience the intense pressure of examinations if they or their parents did not wish it.

The advent of the new GCE raised a whole series of questions which were tackled, half-tackled or retackled over the next decade, such as how far the Dalton-based framework of stagework was the best vehicle for delivering good examination results. Could the full range of subjects be catered for in the morning timetable, leaving the traditional options-based practical activities for the afternoons? How much longer could KAS regard homework as a minor unfortunate necessity for GCE students when grammar schools expected all of their pupils to undertake several hours each evening? Were open-air lessons too much of a disturbance to serious academic effort to merit their retention? Were the traditional approaches to marking and standards too lax? Ultimately these questions boiled down to the overarching question of whether KAS principles and teaching methods, as they had been understood and practised in its first half-century, were 'workable in a school which was not isolated from the examinations pressure of postwar Britain'. Homework, competition, streaming, overstrain and worry, rewards in the form of high marks and punishments in the form of additional work seemed to be alien to the school's very being. Then there was the matter of the sixth form. Should KAS specialize in the subjects which it offered or should it provide the full range of advanced level subjects, often in very small groups? Should it have a non-academic sixth form?

In many ways the school became a more serious and earnest community, with more rules and regulations which seemed to govern most aspects of school life, although contemporaries who had never experienced KAS in previous decades would not have recognized this. The use of biros was forbidden and fountain pens strongly recommended; spelling tests, spelling books and spelling lists became a feature of everyday life; marking (including the use of symbols) was standardized, restandardized and scrutinized. Little wonder that some of the older staff expressed the view in one of the weekly staff meetings that 'the original traditions of the school had been lost in the war and none had been built up since to take their place when they were having to deal with increased numbers and a wider age range'.[11] It seemed to them that in the quickly changing postwar years, the school was losing its way.

One of the staff meetings in October 1951 came to the conclusion that the existing division of the day into academic study in the mornings and options/activities in the afternoons, and the principle of Dalton-style learning were still excellent and well-suited to KASS ideology. The meeting concluded:

> A uniform grammar school standard can not be achieved by all pupils in a non-selective school, and in any case, the leading principle is to help children in such a way that they learn to study for themselves and are not driven by any arbitrary standard.

Nevertheless the search for a new ideological synthesis to meet the needs of the 1950s, and especially the challenge of the grammar school, continued at KAS and at many other progressive schools, as a meeting of such schools at Frensham Heights in 1955 to engage in collective discussion of these issues demonstrated. KAS, however, was able to carry the debate forward more vigorously than many of the other progressive schools because of the central role which parents played in its power structure.

In 1954 a group of parents appointed neither by council nor the school committee gave focus to what it saw as a standards debate in a report which it forwarded to Miss Hibburd for consideration by the school committee. Although not representative of the majority of parents,[12] they appeared to voice some of the general concerns of many parents who had an active interest in the school's affairs. The openness of KASS to discussion of contemporary issues and the eminence of many of the subscribers to the report meant that the report could not be ignored or quietly shelved. The parents prefaced their statement of concerns with a general pledge of support for the fundamental principles of the society. In fact, so concerned were they that KAS should not be subverted from within by the wishes of parents who were out of sympathy with or not interested in the aims of the society, that they argued in favour of only selecting pupils for KAS whose parents were clearly in agreement with the school's progressive aims.

They were also concerned that the ideals of the society were being undermined from within by 'a cult of individualism which could be described as a feeling among these children that to take responsibility for what others do is contrary to the spirit of the school'. As a corrective they argued in favour of giving responsibilities to the upper school and ample opportunities to practise such responsibility through the school council, committees and form officers, and of extending out-of-school activities and societies to meet the problems of the increased size of the school. Clearly they were loyalists not subversives.

Their concern for standards extended to the crucial area of examination results, around which the standards debate of the 1950s was being largely conducted. The academic high fliers were not their concern but 'the standard reached by the average child – by far the majority' in a school which was largely non-selective. To raise standards they attempted to focus the in-school debate on the issues of greater controls and incentives to ensure that pupils worked to their full capacity, to the creation of a quieter working atmosphere and of more intensive preparation for examinations. This was not, however, an all-out attack on Dalton, more of a plea for more class teaching, loose streaming, and concentration on the basics in the lower part of the upper school and for closer organization of stagework for thirteen to sixteen year olds. They believed that class lessons for the latter group wasted much of the time of the gifted pupil. They thus advocated through a series of questions a bi-focal perspective with more formal classwork for ten to thirteen year olds and a more rigorous Dalton structure for thirteen to sixteen year olds. The standards debate also raised questions about the general antipathy to homework during both term time and vacations. The group expressed its concern 'about the absence of all homework as a matter of principle' and the lack of 'guided reading on holiday tasks'. To meet the needs of the new age of the GCE examination the school ought to rethink its teaching strategies but not reject Dalton entirely. What both the parents group and staff wanted in the mid-1950s was further fine-tuning of existing practice to ensure that pupils did not underachieve in the new examinations. This led to homework becoming more prominent when, for example, in 1958 the school committee sent a circular to parents of middle school children advising them of the amount expected.

But the new examination was not intended for the vast majority of the school's pupils. Mrs Barber reported to council in 1951 that the pass standard at GCE was roughly equivalent to credit standard in the old school certificate, the pass mark having been raised from 40 to 45 and expected to go even higher. The examination tail was thus in danger of wagging the progressive dog, as the new examination was designed for the top quarter of the ability range. Changing examination boards from Oxford to London (and subsequently to Cambridge) and selecting easier option papers, for example the set-books paper in English literature, only made small inroads into the problem. The staff had to face the question of 'the best way of providing for the education of children who were not suitable candidates for the new external examination', by far the majority. The school remained remarkably conservative in its approach and could think in the early days of the GCE only in the rather conventional curriculum-differentiated terms, contrary to the intentions of the founders and subsequent KAS tradition. This involved differentiation, for example, by providing a domestic science course for girls 'who were not likely to develop on academic lines', and curricular hierarchies in which GCE examinees received an academic education and non-examinees a more practical, craft-based education. The essentials of Dalton-based learning with its concept of freedom of choice were thus undermined. The implications of bilateralism and gender bias for progressive education were not considered. This was perhaps because the distinction between the two groups, examinees and non-examinees, was not great in the years immediately following the intro-duction of GCE in 1951, with the GCE pupil sitting only an average of three GCE subjects.

Mrs Barber, Montgomery's very able co-headteacher, spent much time from 1954 onwards dispelling the idea that KAS was a kind of bilateral school which provided 'the intensely academic curriculum of the grammar school' for some, and 'the defeatist practical curriculum (and attitude) to be found in many secondary modern schools', for the many. Shortly after the introduction of the GCE she pointed to a fact that others, including the eminent educationist, William Taylor, came to recognize later,[13] that 'far more than the twenty per cent who find places in grammar schools can, given time, good training and hard work qualify themselves for courses of training in a variety of careers'. KAS developed a fast track, whereby pupils in their fourth year entered GCE, and a slower track, the more usual two-year course found in most grammar schools, but almost without exception all pupils undertook some GCE courses with a third moving on to advanced level. More than half of ordinary level candidates at KAS had 'either failed in the 11+ examination in another school or would certainly have done so if they had entered' yet the school nearly always exceeded the national average in its pass rate and by the mid-1950s candidates were gaining four or five passes as a minimum. Little wonder that very few children trans-ferred to other schools. Interestingly she pointed to the reason for this. The old idea that 'anyone can pass School Certificate' was replaced in 1951 by 'the discouraging idea that the GCE is only for able children'. This, in KAS, had given way to 'a new attitude' that, with the deter-mination to work hard and given individual encouragement through the Dalton scheme, all pupils could achieve some measure of success. Many of the older pupils were already curbing their afternoon options volun-tarily to undertake private academic study for the GCE, although no pupil was coerced into such an arrangement. KAS was thus maintaining its experimental role in its approach to some of the problems presented by the tripartite system and the General Certificate of Education. In particular, in Mrs Barber's view, it illustrated 'what can be achieved in a school in which selection at 11 plus is eliminated'. What is perhaps of greatest significance is the insight which she offered into the 1944 Education Act, which introduced the system of secondary education for all. In inspiration she believed that the Act was more in line with the KAS conception of education, which emphasized parity between various forms of education and assisting all children to achieve their best. The rigidly divided bipartite or tripartite system based upon selection at eleven which was introduced and reinforced by the GCE examination which limited the educational opportunities of the majority rather than enhancing them, in her view denied the very intentions of its authors, especially R. A. Butler.

Examinations and other developments in the 1950s also high-lighted another area of difficulty for KAS, that of science teaching. Despite the best efforts of Mrs Barber and other science teachers, science remained a perennial problem for KAS, as for many schools, a problem which was highlighted nationally by Britain's continuing industrial decline and by the shock of the Soviet launching of Sputnik in 1957. Science and technology failed to glow white-hot in KAS. This was partly a problem of attracting good, qualified science teachers, partly because of the cost of equipping science laboratories which state schools could more easily afford and partly because of the weight of KAS tradition in which the humanities had always occupied a more central position, as each of the reports by HM Inspectors had shown. The founding of a science society by Mrs Barber failed to reverse the trend. Council was alert to these difficulties, which were not unique to KAS, as the single-subject GCE system revealed. Thus when council discussed spending priorities the claims of science teaching, including additional allowances for science teachers and ring-fenced allocations for equipment and training, were high on the list. The school was willing, for example, to pay for a residential course on teaching method for a science graduate who was thought to be potentially a good teacher but who lacked a professional qualification. There were, however, only eight or nine candidates for physics O level a decade after the new examination was introduced, and council was all too well aware that 'Most children want craft work and numbers to be catered for are large.'[14] Nevertheless, this kind of detailed concern for the needs of minorities as well as the majority was characteristic of council's approach to postwar challenges. Spending priorities within a very restricted budget inevitably raised matters of educational policy and priority.

But it was not simply the new GCE examinations which posed problems for KAS. There was also the matter of the 11+ examination. KAS had long insisted in its prospectus that it did not coach pupils for the common entrance examination, success in which gave access to other independent schools. It was now faced with the problem of the new 11+ system of selection for grammar schools. As in the case of the common entrance examination, it opposed preparing pupils in any specific way for the new examination. The school was not going to be 'haunted by examination preparation'. Its reasoning was the same in both cases. The school prospectus issued each year insisted that 'The School is planned to promote a continuous and harmonious development of boys and girls from infancy to maturity, and the junior department is not intended to prepare children for other schools; it is an integral part of a unified scheme.' KAS thus refused to act as an 11+ centre or to provide a pressurized 11+ preparatory course. Nevertheless, parents of KAS pupils sometimes entered their offspring for the 11+ in other centres. In 1952, for example, six pupils were entered elsewhere and all six passed. Such a development could have a deleterious effect on the school in leading pupils to go elsewhere who could show that a

103. Sixth-form teaching in the open air, 1950 (*Picture Post*, photograph by Raymond S. Klebee)

KAS education was not incompatible with examination success and by reinforcing the view that a KAS education was suited only to younger children and the less academic. The school thus began emphasizing in its prospectuses from 1954 onward that it offered the full range of grammar school subjects and the annual reports highlighted the number of GCE passes at ordinary and advanced level and the subsequent successes of Old Alfredians at university, drama school and elsewhere.

In the early 1950s few considered the possible damaging effects of the 11+ and the new GCE on KAS. The more immediate threat to its distinctive kind of education was seen as coming from another direction, the threat to increase the size of classes in order to meet the cost of paying full Burnham salaries to teachers. Dr Davidson, who was only on council for a short period, highlighted the matter by expressing his opposition to 'any break with tradition of small numbers in classes which would increase the difficulty of providing a progressive form of education for an unselected body of children'.[15] 'State teachers', he added, 'were often harassed and overburdened.' Higher fees and economies such as the purchase of reconditioned, guesthouse cookers for the kitchen in place of new ones, were the only alternatives to introducing into KAS some of the excesses and formalism of the state sector. State aid, a topic which was then being discussed in the correspondence columns of *The Times*, was ruled out by Montgomery because of the strings which would be attached. Income tax relief for parents who paid school fees, which more than one correspondent advocated, was seen as the best form of indirect assistance. Thus council and staff remained firm in their defence of the essentials of a KAS education in the face of the mounting pressures of the age. A concession on the no-homework principle was all that had been made. Yet there always remained a threat to the school if it relied mainly on fees for its income. Dr David-son emphasized this difficulty when he expressed his doubts[16] whether KAS 'could ever become a school on the same footing as state-aided schools unless it were willing to accept pupils selected solely for their great wealth'. Selection by wealth entailed accepting pupils whose wealthy parents might not be wholeheartedly in sympathy with the aims of the society while rejecting children whose less wealthy parents wholly endorsed KASS principles. Mammon was scarcely a god to be worship-ped by a society dedicated to a rationalist education. Nevertheless, KAS had to make concessions such as that of increasing the size of classes to twenty.

KAS was faced with a fundamental problem. It had no financial cushion of endowments. This meant that at times of heavy financial pressures, particularly increased salaries and building programmes, its main recourse was fees, but there were limits to fee increases. The alternative was to increase the number of pupils, a strong temptation when there was a long waiting list but pressure of numbers could quickly undermine the very goals at which the school aimed, by swamping individuality, and by making Dalton and the choice-system unworkable. Such were the real-life issues which faced the school and the society. By the beginning of the academic year 1953/4 numbers had increased to 280, raising the question of how long a small-school ideology could be maintained. A grammar school of even twice that number was not seen as a hindrance to an effective education but even 280 pupils in a pro-gressive school of KAS's type was seen as problematic and a threat to its principal aims. Educational experiment to enlarge the scope for individual development was quite possible with the size of school which Russell, Wicksteed, Hyett and Birkett ran, but was becoming increas-ingly difficult for Montgomery, who was having difficulty holding the progressive line. The school surplus for 1951/2 was equivalent only to the fees of three children, a position which was increased to that of twenty-one children in 1952/3, but this still left the whole enterprise dangerously vulnerable to any downturn in the nation's economy or to any swift increase in basic costs, especially salary increases in line with the Burnham scale. If the latter included equal pay for women, which KASS despite its radical ideology had opposed, then the financial situation could become dire, as council recognized in 1954. It agreed that parity of pay was to be achieved over six years, although annual increments at Burnham rates was a major drain on income.

Nevertheless, the continued success of the venture relied upon attracting sufficient pupils. For the moment, time appeared to be on the side of KAS. As the report of the finance committee to council in July 1955 pointed out: 'It was recognised that as state schools improve in quality and accommodation their competition will be an increasingly strong factor but reliance was placed on the statement that the "bulge" will not be met by them for the next five years'.[17] However, demographic trends did not favour the nursery department, with numbers falling from fifty-nine in 1953 to twenty-one in 1955; most nursery schools were badly hit, according to council's chairperson, Mrs Jobson, who believed that 'educational theory also has turned against nursery schools'.

If nursery schools were out of favour in postwar Britain, sixth forms were seen as a major part of the educational revolution and the visible expression of high academic standards. KAS, which had nailed its colours firmly to the mast of an all-through four-to-eighteen education since the clash between council and Rice in 1901, had no intention of abandoning its sixth form in the age of the grammar school. Yet it faced two kinds of challenge in making sixth-form provision. First there was the problem of numbers, inevitable in a largely non-selective school. In 1958, the school had 288 pupils of whom about 150 were over the age of eleven. Of the latter, fifteen went into the sixth form. They studied ten subjects between them, in very small groups, together with a general course. Second, science facilities were a particular problem which the school committee tackled in great detail in 1959. KAS faced the financial challenge of providing for small sixth-form classes, especially in science, while at the same time maintaining the distinctive education for 'academic' and 'non-academic sixth-formers' of which the school was justly proud. By 1960, however, the sixth form had increased to twenty-four.

Thus in the postwar years KAS was determined to maintain its progressive ethos and curriculum while at the same time meeting the requirements of an age in which the grammar school, based on British traditional education, was seen to set the standard. Yet it was not easy to resist the erosion which resulted from increased costs and numbers and from competition from the grammar school. For example, Montgomery announced in July 1959 that from the following September 'there would be more afternoon lessons which would further limit children's choice of individual occupations'. The school committee, which by September 1959 had transformed itself into the Joint Consultative Committee, was to embark on a series of discussions about educational policy and the curriculum and a reappraisal of the 'basic principles on which the school was started', together with an investigation of the conduct of the school and discipline. The forces of the age, no longer generally sympathetic to progressive education, were combining to make the school and society contemplate the first truly radical reappraisal since both were founded. However, as Mrs Paul Jones, the school's co-headteacher, reminded council just before Montgomery's retirement in 1962: 'KAS is not a grammar school and any change which forced it to a selective entry would be a reversal of its hitherto type of education.'[18] Discussion of 'the expansion of the school in scope and for numbers' was deferred until after the appointment of Montgomery's successor. Whatever emerged, it was clear that the old KAS had gone and gone forever under the impact of postwar changes and developments. The First World War, which had caused such massive destruction to populations and empires, had led to fewer postwar difficulties for KAS than had the Second World War. Yet in some ways the school's difficulties were created by its success, in particular its ability to attract sufficient numbers to cover its escalating costs. This put pressure on average class size, which by the end of Montgomery's period as headmaster stood at twenty. Staff were questioning whether such a number was compatible with the 'open-room' system which lay at the heart of the Dalton experiment. Already the afternoon options system had been modified to allow for academic studies which hitherto had been confined to mornings. As Mrs Barber pointed out in a perceptive paper, the school could not 'under present conditions' run without loss if the numbers fell below 270 and it was 'not as easy as it was before the war, when there were rarely as many as 200 children to try new methods of teaching and social relationships'.[19] She might well have added that in the more complex educational world of postwar Britain it was becoming increasingly difficult to maintain its prewar progressive practices. Perhaps what was happening was that the new educational order based on the 1944 Education Act and examination reform was forcing KAS to move into new areas of educational experimentation. It could not simply be a new age traveller. It aimed to help direct the new educational order, not to establish a detached alternative educational commune.

Chiefs, co-chiefs and indians

Had the postwar renaissance of KAS been accompanied by the political upheavals which characterized its early years, the school would not have survived to its golden jubilee. That it did so was largely the result of the political calm in which Montgomery succeeded Hyett and Birkett. Not that there was any real opportunity for protest, for Montgomery, the London-based heir apparent, was formally appointed head in June 1945 before the rest of the staff had returned to the capital. The immense and pressing problems of rebuilding Manor Wood helped to ensure that the years from 1945 to the golden jubilee remained an era of good feelings. The society, council and staff had to pull together or the whole enterprise would pull apart. Montgomery's informality and friendly manner with pupils soon won them over to the cause of regeneration of the site and school.

The society was fortunate in its officials. Dr J. C. Flugel, the eminent psychologist who had succeeded Dame Alice Woods in 1941, remained the society's president until 1950 when he was replaced by Lady Thornycroft (1950–7) and briefly by Mrs Corbett Fisher (1958) after which the office remained vacant during the rest of Montgomery's headship. KAS ideology was also reinforced by a galaxy of distinguished vice presidents including Sir Leonard Hill, the distinguished physiologist, J. H. Badley of Bedales and two who had connections with the founding years, Lady Thornycroft and Mrs Voysey. Contact with the War Office and world of journalism was provided by Colonel Aylmer Vallance, formerly of the *New Statesman* and presently at the War Office, and with the broader political world by the radical Liberal, Murray MacDonald. Providing both continuity with the prewar years and funds for the many building schemes was the veritable giant of the concert hall, Solomon, who unstintingly gave piano performances to swell the coffers of the building committee. Continuity was also the key characteristic of council which played the major part in re-establishing KAS at Manor Wood after the War Office derequisitioned it in stages in the summer of 1945. Anthony Horton of Flint Hall Farm, an Old Alfredian and member of council, assisted the transfer at the Royston end while a core of members from the prewar years, led by the Corbett Fishers and including Mrs Maxwell, Mrs Dennis, Mrs Cowen and Mr Picknett, worked untiringly in London to ensure that the school opened for the autumn term, a major part of which was the formal appointment of Montgomery as headmaster. Mrs Corbett Fisher chaired most of the meetings during these critical months when the matters of war damage and repairs dominated most of their meetings. It was she, in particular, who was also willing to press first for revised salaries for the staff and then for Burnham salaries soon after the initial problems were resolved. It was perhaps natural that the energies of council in the years to the school's golden jubilee in 1948 should be absorbed with matters relating to war damage, new buildings, staff salaries and pupil numbers but this had been at the expense of its role as guardian of ideology and advisers in curricular matters.

This may well have been because council felt that these matters were safe in the hands of the school committee, which reported its

104. Miss Robey at the head of the nursery class, 1949, with Mrs Meddemmen assisting

105. The cast of *Pride and Prejudice*, 1950: L to R Hans Kohn, Eva Lucas, Marion Goldwater, Pat Essex, Peter Wasserman, Richard Thomas, Raphael Samuel, Sylvester Bone, Barbara Hawkins, Julie Heyting, Rachel Davis, Fred Johnson (staff), Anthea Ionides, Sheila Woolf, Bunty Essex, Pauline Hutton, Donald Neal

discussions at each council meeting. The school council, chaired mainly by Corbett Fisher (who also chaired the finance committee) until 1948, represented a partnership between the staff and council, the professionals and lay people. As most of the staff representatives on the school committee were long-standing teachers at the school, council could leave curricular matters in their hands while it dealt with the more pressing postwar matters.

When the school reopened at Manor Wood many of the old faces reappeared, a little more weatherbeaten from the war years at Royston and a little more lined with the anxieties of what the insecurities of the postwar years would mean for their charges. Montgomery's predecessors, Violet Hyett and Birkett, returned on a part-time basis, the former to teach senior history until just before her death in 1949, the latter to organize the print shop. Miss Levin, a rather formidable lady in the view of some pupils, became senior mistress and mathematics teacher until she left to join the staff of a state school. Mrs Barber, one of the champions of an undiluted KAS ideology and remembered by several of her pupils for her motherly concern and her patient expositions of KAS principles, returned in 1946 to teach some biology. She was soon to provide the more efficient organization and administration which the school needed. Miss Gillett, one of the 'pillars of the old KASS spirit', returned as head of the lower school until her appointment to a lectureship at Bletchley Park Teacher Training College in 1947, after twenty years of service at KAS. The magic of drama reappeared with Renée Soskin, who also provided speech training. Her force and drive became legendary, with more than one student recalling how the school shook when a pupil inadvertently broke a prop in the amphitheatre. Mrs Ryder Smith, noted for her sense of humour, infectious smile and immense love of teaching and of children, came back to Manor Wood in its first term to teach French and Latin. She was seen by some 'not as an inspired teacher but a capable one if listened to'. She was shortly to marry Fred Johnson, who succeeded Miss Levin to the headship of the lower school. Miss Robey's return with Oakhurst

Pride and Prejudice

by
Jane Austen
(arranged for the stage by Renée Soskin)

CAST

Mr. Bennet	F. C. Johnson
Mrs. Bennet	Anthea Ionides
Jane Bennet	Rachel Davis
Elizabeth Pennet	Barbara Hawkins
Mary Bennet	Pauline Hutton
Kitty Bennet	Bunty Essex
Lydia Bennet	Pat Essex
The Rev. William Collins	Raphael Samuel
Mrs. Hill	Stephanie Harris
Charlotte Lucas	Sheila Woolf
Lady Lucas (Friday)	Shirley Anderson
(Saturday)	Marion Goldwater
Sir William Lucas	Hans Kohn
Mr. Fitzwilliam Darcy	Sylvester Bone
Mr. Charles Bingley	Julie Heyting
Miss Bingley	Eva Lucas
Mr. Wickham	Richard Thomas
Lady Catherine de Bourgh	Molly Rubin
Colonel Fitzwilliam	Peter Wasserman
Mrs. Gardiner	Naomi Elkan
Mr. Gardiner	Felix Moore
An Innkeeper	Donald Neal

Stage Manager: Audrey Barber

Set designed by Mary Lou Jennings,
- painted by Peter Norland.

nursery section was delayed until September 1946. The matronly Marion Robey remained on the staff until the end of the autumn term in 1960, many generations of KAS pupils having experienced her maternal, bosomy warmth. She died in 1974.

Together, these staff formed a rockbed of stability at a time when the head was despairing of the rapid turnover of staff among the new younger members, who quickly became aware of the expanding opportunities in the state sector as the new system of primary and secondary education was put in place or who found the KAS style of discipline not to their liking. To their number, however, were soon added several who gave valuable service to the school over the next decade, including Hazelden in charge of games and physical training, the slim, elegant Miss d'Eath who became the form mistress of the C form and Montgomery's wife, and Fuller, an Oxford graduate who quickly established a reputation for his English teaching. The latter, a gentle, quietly spoken person proved to be an imaginative inspiring teacher until he left in 1954 to pursue his literary career. A rapidly growing school in which the traditional KAS style of discipline was not so easily maintained needed a solid core of teachers dedicated to the KAS ideal in order to retain its distinctive character. To outsiders used to the dress codes and political values of the grammar schools and public schools, the teachers were often seen as subversives. Most were indeed left wing in their views,

107. The staff in 1956: L to R (back row) John Handford, John Tryggvason, Harry Kemp, Philip Haselden, Malcolm Manwaring, Fred Johnson, J. Rustomjee, B. H. Montgomery; (middle row seated) Rosalind Johnson, Kathleen Montgomery, Margaret Maxwell, Hettie Barber, Marion Robey, Ruth Wiseman, Winifred Marsh, Kay Clifford, Janice Smithells; (front row on grass) Cynthia Walker, Pat Bulman, Mascha Gardner, Grace Low

particularly several female teachers including Deana Levin, an active communist, who persuaded some pupils to join the Young Communists League and who left because she felt the school was too privileged. The impression that the school was a hotbed of radicalism was reinforced by the way in which many teachers dressed, most males suitless, tieless, wearing baggy trousers and open sandals, and women teachers in long flowing dark skirts without stockings. There were exceptions. Among the men, Malcolm Manwaring and Ronald Fuller projected an entirely different image, the former in a flamboyant blazer with a green sports car, the latter in a sober suit, quietly supportive of struggling students of English. The tall, charismatic Scot Ian Carnegie, 'a little too large for the history room', and the excitable Welsh woodwork teacher, simply known as 'Dave' to his pupils, also demonstrated the individuality of the staff. Among the female teachers were equally strong role models, something which benefited the school greatly. The painstaking teaching of the academic, bespectacled Margaret Maxwell encouraged many to go on to university. Renée Soskin, who had 'the roar of a lion' when needed, encouraged many aspiring young actresses and actors. These and many other staff were intentional subversives with an educational philosophy totally at variance with the growing traditionalism of the 1940s and 1950s, and one which suited what was essentially a tolerant international community where learning was deliberately intended to be fun.

108. Dave Thomas supervising the building of the games room, 1957

And then there was Miss Hibburd, 'Hibby', the school secretary and much more who played a key role in the practical transmission of the KAS culture. She has been caught in a beautiful cameo by an Old Alfredian:

> While my mother discussed the practicalities of the school's day for a five year old she stood answering mostly with her eyes shut or flickering half shut, as she always did. Appearance unforgettable: faded fair (reddish?) hair in a thick untamed mop but cut shortish, skin, pale. Eyes blue, I think, (it's the aura I remember not the details). She wore shoes, heavy walking shoes with no stockings or socks, and her legs were thin . . . In the winter her ankles looked blue. Her clothes were long, long skirts or tunics, or baggy dresses, mostly autumnal colours.

She also acted unofficially as school nurse using the guideline of the smaller the pupil, the larger the plaster.

The staff were alert to the need for in-service training to reinforce and develop the KAS approach to education. Hence, experts in various areas were invited to address staff meetings. Dr Hallam, for example, gave a talk on the psychological development of children to help the new members of staff especially to understand the KAS approach to discipline. Montgomery was not averse to expelling difficult pupils – six 'awkward boys' were 'removed' in May 1946 – but if possible other ways of dealing with them were preferred. For example, one boy's 'bad behaviour' was attributed to his feeling insecure, which called for sympathetic handling of the problem, including allowing him to take more woodwork, a subject which he liked. However, there were occasions when the staff felt that the headmaster expelled pupils too readily without full consultation. Staff training was put on a systematic basis when a committee comprising of Montgomery, Mrs Barber, Miss Morisley, Miss Robey and Miss d'Eath was set up to devise an ongoing programme. Much of the training revolved around the matter of record-keeping, something which a larger school in the era of the grammar school necessitated, although the issue of intelligence testing figured large in their deliberations, as did that of child guidance.

The formalizing of staff training was a necessary consequence of the increased size of the school staff and a fairly large measure of staff turnover in the early years. In 1947, two stalwarts, Miss Levin and Miss Gillett, left and seven new staff, Messrs Kemp, Fuller, Flinn, Roberts, Vickers and Miss Bamford and Miss Joliffe were appointed. By 1950 only the first two of the 1947 intake were still on the staff. The fairly rapid turnover slowed down in the early 1950s as full Burnham salaries came into effect, with the result that by the midpoint of Montgomery's headship a clear pattern of staffing emerged (see Table 8). The earlier trend reappeared in the late 1950s, so that only a small core of the old staff remained by the end of the decade (see Table 9); they did not include Rustomjee who retired in 1956 having given twenty years' service to the school in full- and part-time roles.

The growing number of assistant staff led Miss Hibburd in September 1951 to raise the question of their adequate representation on the school committee. As a result the composition of this committee was altered in 1952 and 1953 to accommodate their increased number. Three members of council, Epstein, Garrett and Robins, wished to take the matter much further in order to bring the assistant staff into contact 'with the body that has executive power'. Their argument was essentially that, as the society owned only one school and was unlikely to own

Table 8 **List of staff, November 1954**

UPPER SCHOOL AND MIDDLE SCHOOL		
Upper Sixth	H. V. Kemp, MA (Cantab.)	Mathematics and Physics
Lower Sixth	Mrs H. M. E. Barber, BA (Cantab.)	Chemistry
5	B. H. Montgomery, MA (Oxon.)	Geography
5a	Mrs R. C. Johnson, BA (Lond.)	French
4	R. J. Handford, BA (Lond.)	English and Latin
3	Miss B. E. Nicholls, BA (Lond.)	History and Latin
2	F. C. Johnson, B.Sc. (Econ.) (Lond.)	History and Geography
1	Miss W. Marsh, B.Sc. (Lond.)	Biology
1a	Miss K. I. d'Eath, NFF	

LOWER SCHOOL		
B	Miss R. Wiseman, NFF	Head of the Lower School
C	Miss C. Walker, M. of E. Cert.	
D	Miss P. Bulman, NFF	
E	Mrs D. Chadwick, NFF	

NURSERY SCHOOL		
F1	Miss M. Robey, NFF	Head of the Nursery School
F2	Miss A. M. Sanford, NFF	

Masters and Mistresses without Forms

Miss L. F. Bradish	Craftwork
Miss D. Egerton, LRAM	Music
Mrs M. A. Fagan, Chelsea Coll. of Physical Education	Physical Education and Dancing
P. H. Haselden	Games
Mrs V. Mitchell, Dip. of Fine Arts, Slade School	Art
Mrs A. Monro, BA (Goucher College, USA)	Craftwork
J. Rustomjee, BA (Cantab.)	Mathematics
Mrs Soskin, LRAM (Eloc.)	Dramatic Work
D. R. Thomas	Woodwork
J. Tryggvason, Royal Academy of Music	Music
R. Taylor	Physical Education

Secretary: Miss E.M. Hibburd, BA (B'ham)

any more, there was little point in having a school committee and a council as their functions overlapped. The three thus recommended the abolition of the school committee and the creation of subcommittees with clearly defined functions, which would report to council. One sub-committee would be entirely concerned with staff matters. The matter was not resolved immediately. It was reviewed again in 1959 when it was recognized that the staff could only be present on council in an advisory capacity. The charity status of the school did not permit salaried employees to be full members of the executive. The discussions resulted in the school committee being replaced by a new joint consultative com-mittee. Its first meeting took place in September 1959.

The joint consultative committee was to concern itself with broad matters of educational policy and the curriculum, the reappraisal of the

Table 9 **List of staff, November 1959**

Upper School B. H. Montgomery (Headmaster), Mrs Paul Jones (Headmistress)

Upper 6	Mrs E. M. Tait, M. of E. Cert.	Biology
Lower 6	Miss M. Maxwell, MA (Oxon.)	English
5	Mrs A. B. Paul Jones, BA (Bristol)	English and Philosophy
	R. Greenfield	Mathematics
4	M. J. C. Baker, BA (Cantab.)	Mathematics
4a	Miss E. Rosenthal, BA (Lond.)	French
3	I. H. Carnegie, BA (Lond.)	History and Latin

Middle School

2	F. C. Johnson, B.Sc. (Econ.) (Lond.)	Head of Middle School
		History and Geography
1	M. G. Manwaring, BA (Lond.)	English and French
1a	Mrs K. I. Montgomery, NFF	Mathematics

Lower School

A	Mrs G. M. Lamond, NFF
B	Miss C. J. Parsons, M. of E. Cert.
C	Miss C. Walker, M.of E. Cert.
D	Miss J. P. Bulman, NFF
E	Miss E. M. Knight, NFF

Nursery Class

F	Miss M. Robey, NFF	Head of Nursery Dept.
	Assistant: Mrs D. Kothari	

Masters and Mistresses without Forms

Mrs M. A. Fagan (Chelsea Coll. of Phys. Education)	Physical Education and Dancing
Miss E. Hawes, LRAM	Music
Mrs V. Palmer, MA (Oxon.)	Latin
Miss S. J. Russell, ATD	Art
J. Sofair	Mathematics and Chemistry
Mrs R. Soskin, LRAM (Eloc.)	Dramatic Work
R. Taylor	Physical Education
D. R. Thomas	Woodwork
J. Tryggvason (Royal Academy of Music)	Music
Mrs D. M. Wilson	Craftwork and Needlework

Secretary: Miss E. M. Hibburd, BA (B'ham)

basic principles upon which the school was started, the conduct of the school and discipline, and liaison with the society. The staff representation on the new committee was substantial and included the head, the deputy head, the head of the middle school, two elected representatives for each of the senior and junior school, and a representative from the nursery section. The treasurer and architect became ex-officio members for the time being. In addition to the joint consultative committee under the chairmanship of Mr Strange, the finance committee and buildings and maintenance subcommittee continued to function and to report to council. The newly formed committee had the two great advantages of giving strong representation to the staff and of bringing to the forefront of debate the founding principles of the school and society. The staff, who at their separate and joint meetings had always made the review of KAS ideology a major item on their agendas, could now expect its broader discussion by the joint consultative committee, half of whom were parents. Their views were now likely to be presented more fully to council.

One of the recurrent problems of the 1950s was that of relationships between senior management, which rarely appeared harmonious for long. In 1948 Mrs Barber was appointed senior mistress, a position which was turned into co-head in 1952. In the Hyett–Birkett era the joint headship had worked well for two reasons. First, that is how the headship had been conceived from the outset, and second the interests and abilities of the two heads fell into distinct areas, which enabled each a large measure of independent action. In areas of joint concern Violet Hyett's immense ability and astute skills of diplomacy meant that her will usually prevailed but not always obviously so. Montgomery's headship was altogether different. By the time that Hettie Barber became co-head, Montgomery had had seven years as sole head. It is perhaps not surprising, therefore, that there should have been some initial problems in defining areas of responsibility. What perhaps is remarkable is that the matter came before council and that council felt obliged to intervene. Just a few weeks into the co-headship, in October 1952, it was reported to council that difficulties had arisen between the two heads over areas of jurisdiction. The precise details are not known but Mrs Barber felt that the matter was so unlikely to be resolved that she began to look for a post elsewhere. Whether the difficulties were the result of Montgomery's lack of powers of communication, as some alleged, or of a possible overreaction on the part of Mrs Barber is not known but council came to the conclusion that they were 'unwilling to contemplate the loss of either head'. Mrs Barber's understanding of KAS ideology and her great ability to translate it into effective teaching would certainly have meant a great loss to the school had she resigned. Council expressed 'their confidence in the headship, in the individuals composing it and in their ability to make it work'. Epstein's judicious and tactful investigation of the matter for council led to a gentle directive from council which encouraged more harmonious relationships. Mrs Barber withdrew her threat of resignation and remained in post until 1957 when she left to become head of an approved school for girls. She was noted as 'a warm person, busy and efficient in manner'.

In 1958 KAS reinvented the wheel. They revived the post of senior mistress to which Mrs Ros Johnson, another long-serving member of staff and the only survivor from the Royston years, was appointed. Montgomery's argument that 'the joint headship is a difficult one in itself and tends to waste time and energy' gained the support of a majority on council; it became one of Monty's chief concerns in the restaffing arrangements when Mrs Barber left to replace the joint headship with the position of headmaster and senior mistress, even though council did not give the idea unanimous support. Less than halfway through her first term as senior mistress Mrs Johnson resigned her post. Mrs Jobson, who chaired the crucial meeting of council in February 1958 at which the matter was discussed, interviewed Mrs Johnson and reported to council that her resignation was partly the result of her being informed that the May meeting of council had not given unanimous backing to Montgomery's restaffing plan. To this were added other factors, including 'the weakness of her position from the start', probably further weakened by her being called before council, conflict of personality and emotion (according to Mr Norden), ambition and the inevitable difficulties of reviving the senior mistress position at the close of the joint headship (according to Mr Epstein) and the long-standing problem of areas of jurisdiction. This heady mixture of reasons had produced deep divisions and feelings which Montgomery could see 'no way of righting'. If the matter was one of the Johnsons and Montgomerys jockeying for power, as one observer claims, then it is not surprising that the matter appeared irresolvable.

Mrs Jobson recognized that the duties of a senior mistress varied 'at the entire discretion of the head who assigned them'. Given such a position, council could do little other than accept her resignation from the position if she did not withdraw it. For the future it was agreed that the senior mistress should be invited to attend council meetings and recommended that members of staff holding posts of responsibility should meet for weekly discussion. Mrs Johnson withdrew her letter of resignation, but the matter did not rest there. It was agreed that the post of senior mistress as revived for the current year should lapse and its duties be divided with Mrs Johnson as careers mistress and responsible for social and welfare activities, with Miss Maxwell (who had expressed willingness to accept the post of senior mistress) as sixth-form mistress and responsible for examinations and university entrance, and with Fred Johnson, head of the middle school, deputizing for Montgomery during the latter's absence. An extraordinary meeting of council was held at the beginning of the academic year 1958–9 to decide on the future pattern of senior management. Ten members of council and three members of the joint advisory committee recommended 'the early appointment of a woman joint head from outside the staff of the school'. Montgomery staunchly opposed the creation of a joint headship, believing 'it had inherent difficulties of divided loyalties and was apt to create a hazy position in staff and children'. He added that there were insufficient duties to share out in a school with only 150 pupils over the age of eleven and doubted the wisdom of considering the woman co-head appointed as a future head of the school. To strengthen his argument, he urged that the obvious choice would be a scientist but these were rare, expensive and could entail the dismissal of the existing head of science.

Montgomery's spanners were insufficient to cause the seizure of the works, for his retirement was only a few years away. The extraordinary meeting was not dissuaded in its plan for a woman co-head and countered Montgomery's arguments, Mrs Soskin arguing that neither subject offered nor salary should stand in the way of an appointment and Mrs Jobson urging the appointment of someone of Mrs Barber's calibre who 'would give attention to the outside world of education', something sadly missing since Mrs Barber's departure. Mr Johnson's position and that of Miss Maxwell would have to be reviewed when the new appointment was made. The meeting was determined to press on with such an appointment, with Mrs Jobson and Mrs Mitchell being delegated to deal with the advertising and short list. However, it was agreed at the following council meeting that initially the new appointment would be to a deputy headship which, after a successful period of probation, would become a joint headship. This was to ease the problem of terminating an unsuccessful appointment and to help the appointee to gain a headship elsewhere.

Five applicants for the post were called for interview, although Mrs Paul Jones did not attend. After a second interview Miss Hann was offered the post, subject to a satisfactory reference and her willingness to accept it after its scope and difficulties were explained fully. Nothing proved to be straightforward, for her reference was regarded as unsatisfactory and Mrs Paul Jones was interviewed by council and offered the post on 8 December 1958, partly on the basis of her three years' experience with the Association of Teachers in Colleges and Departments of Education. Not surprisingly these twists and turns in the history of the senior management of the school caused consternation among several parents, who wrote to council urging it to assume a more active and positive role in the leadership and administration of the school. In their view it had delegated too much of its authority and met too infrequently to enable it to intervene effectively in the running of the school. It should now make the greatest possible efforts 'to solve the problems which are strangling the school'. The resolution of the difficulties would have been a fitting tribute to the president and one of council's most dedicated and longest serving members, Mrs Corbett Fisher, who died in January 1959, and to Wicksteed, who died in November of that year in his ninetieth year. The successful division of responsibilities between Montgomery, the Johnsons and Miss Maxwell was an important initial step in this direction prior to the wholescale revision of duties when Mrs Paul Jones joined the staff. The more permanent division once she had taken up her post was a more difficult matter to resolve, for it raised questions such as the position of Mr Johnson as head of the middle school. There was also the issue of whether the deputy head should attend council meetings. The latter was resolved by inviting her attendance until, as joint head, she was entitled to attend. Mrs Paul Jones joined the staff in April 1959, her previous headmistress agreeing to release her for the summer term. At the end of the term Mrs Johnson resigned after nineteen years' service. Her replacement summed up this period of tension and her task as follows:

> I started at the school in Easter 1959 . . . His former co-head, Mrs Hettie Barber had left the school to take up a new career some months earlier. The dissension which accompanied the appointment of a successor had ended in strong feelings and bruised egos. My job was to help the head to heal the breach.[20]

These political issues which dominated the closing years of Montgomery's headship disguised the fact that, while the chiefs were often in political dispute the indians remained loyal and largely unperturbed. Of the fifty-five staff who were appointed between 1945 and 1960, twenty-four were still in post in 1960, with an average length of service of ten-and-a-half years, nine had left to get married, four had left for career advancement and three at the request of the school. In July 1961 six men were invited for interview as Montgomery's successor in a co-headship with Mrs Paul Jones but none proved to be acceptable. In October 1961 it was agreed, after re-advertisement, that Mr Alan Humphries should be offered the post, which he accepted and took up in October 1962. He could not, however, call upon the services of the school secretary, Miss Hibburd, who retired at the end of the summer term after thirty-five years' service.

KAS culture and the youth culture of the 1950s

Shortly after the end of the First World War, Sir Percy Nunn (whom KASS had tried unsuccessfully to attract to its presidency) laid down in *Education: Its Data and First Principles* (1920), the canon of education which KAS followed in the interwar years, that the 'true aim' of education was to 'cultivate individuality'[21] 'to encourage free activity, not negative, to confine or to repress it'.[22] During the Second World War, the new high priest of curriculum theory, Fred Clarke, pressed the claims of society in his slim book *Education and Social Change* (1940). It was with the new orthodoxy in mind that his wife visited the school in January 1946 to report her observations about the experiences of KAS pupils to the weekly staff meeting. She was impressed by the way that children 'were called by name and treated as individuals'. The number and variety of individual afternoon activities drew favourable comments but she believed that 'the things that develop children in a group and as a group required a more important place in the curriculum'. Quoting her husband, she argued that the main function of the school was to intro-duce 'the child into society'; it was really 'a matter of exchanges between the school and the outside world'. She recommended such activities as surveying and local studies as ways of achieving this.

While Montgomery was willing to modify some of his stagework to include some of these new curricular activities, he was not willing to modify the essentials of Daltonism or the afternoon activities. He and his staff dismissed the view that the goal of education should be that of fitting people into society. This they did for several reasons, not least of which was that society as they saw it in the late 1940s and 1950s was so shot through with deeply unattractive characteristics that it would be a betrayal of their trust and KAS ideology to pursue the goal advocated by Mrs Clarke. The first staff meeting of each term was usually devoted to a discussion of basic principles and at the first of the summer term in

109. A lower school play in the open-air theatre, 1950 (photograph Gene Shelley)

1946 Mr Glover outlined what he believed to be the weaknesses of postwar society, its greed, its low standards of honesty, its commercialism, and 'overconformity', its low spiritual values, and its lack of security. This list received the general approval of the staff. This was just one of the problems the staff had with Mrs Clarke's approach; they believed that her whole perspective was gravely flawed. The basic tenet upon which the school had been founded was that of fostering the talents of each individual in accordance with what was known about child development. Dalton received the general support of the staff, despite the increasing problems of implementing it (and the afternoon activities programme) in a growing school, because it offered the greatest opportunity of maximizing choice and individual responsibility. There were of course dangers in this, as Mrs Soskin pointed out in her attack on 'the cult of individualism' which she believed had grown up in the school in the 1950s.

It was the freedom and diversity of experience which the popular press and film producers found interesting about KAS during Montgomery's headship. *Picture Post* visited the Oakhurst school in June 1945 and produced a series of striking photographs with a brief commentary on the nursery school experience. The children were seen busily and very happily engaged in their 'clay lessons', making snakes and various animals. *Picture Post* returned around Christmas 1947 to ask the pupils what toys they liked. Again the photographs, although obviously carefully posed and selected, revealed the openness of pupils in their responses and their uninhibited joy in explaining the practical qualities of the toys they selected. *The Observer* around Christmas 1958 showed a series of lino-cuts, line prints and collage work by pupils in order to demonstrate that it was possible to create Christmas cards and presents without having to succumb to the commercial pressures of the age.

Some of the other distinctive qualities of a KAS education also seized the imagination of the popular press, particularly roll call in Squirrel Hall, the advisory council and the more unusual afternoon activities, including type-setting in the print shop. The more sensational stories focused on 'The Pupils Rule This London "No Cane" School' and 'School in the Tree Tops'; the latter also proved popular in 1947 as a *Pathé News* item. Occasionally, visiting photographers were disappointed, as when the picture editor of *Picture Post* reported to Montgomery that the photographer had returned with pictures 'the complete normality of the scenes of which makes it difficulty to realize that the children have matters in their own hands, very reassuring for a prospective parent but it just doesn't give us a story!'[23] Not all publicity was acceptable, especially when a former pupil sued the school for damages in 1961 claiming that the school was negligent because two boys tipped her off an electric heater on which she was sitting. Her claim was rejected, even though the headmaster recognized that such an act could be regarded as 'hooliganism', but believed that no punishment would be suitable for such a happening.

Clearly, the view of the press was that KAS offered a very different kind of educational experience from most schools of the 1950s. But how different was the pupil experience of the 1950s? Probably Alfredians of the interwar years would have regarded the school as less distinctive in the 1950s as the growing school roll resulted in a more regulated society, if only to protect the Manor Woods grounds and environment from the effects of heavier demands upon them. Even the use of the tree hut had to be regulated: the first five to arrive could claim it for the ensuing break. Pupils were asked to be careful not to damage the fruit trees. However, the freedom that was allowed was much greater than that in other London day schools. Pupils were allowed to swing on ropes, light fires with staff permission, carry knives (provided they were not a danger to

110. The tree-top school, 1945 (photograph Keystone Press Agency)

others) and to build dens. Climbing and even skating on the chemistry laboratory roof were allowed. These were the natural activities of growing children which surprisingly resulted in no major accidents. With all these freedoms came responsibilities, especially to ensure the safety of others and the protection of the environment. Inevitably some pupils did not accept all of these responsibilities all of the time, but the reaction of the staff was not to forbid the use of school facilities because of this. The usual approach was to consult the offenders or the advisory council about such matters.

The school advisory council was reconstituted when KAS returned to Manor Wood, with its membership and functions closely defined. Two staff representatives were elected each term to join the representative from each of the upper school forms, and the two girls and two boys from the two senior forms, 'the school four'. They met usually each

Monday morning at 9.45 and to increase interest in its deliberations the agenda was read out at callover and publicized by 'the school four' visiting each form during the weekly form hour. The heads and Miss Hibburd could attend meetings but could not vote. The school council chose the head boy and head girl each term, unlike many grammar schools where they were selected by the staff or headmaster on an annual basis. Pupils were thus encouraged to participate in the politics of school government and to learn about committee procedures, including the creation of subcommittees such as the games and party committees and the school fire brigade, the taking of minutes, and the presentation of and amendments to motions and how to gag over-talkative members. Matters such as school uniform, 'ragging' or bullying, the use of the library, the running of callover, behaviour during school dinners, dust fights in Squirrel Hall, school parties and open day appeared regularly on the school agenda. Matters such as religious teaching and homosexuality less so. While some who served on it believed its powers to be 'largely illusory', most believed it was 'not window dressing but did have substance'.

Enhancing pupil participation in areas of school life was not without its problems. There was the possibility of matters of school principle being affected by vote in council. The election process could also foster 'a spirit of competition' which some members of staff believed was 'alien to the spirit of KAS'. Montgomery was particularly anxious to involve as many pupils in the committee structures as possible and to restrict the chances of their being monopolized by a few. To strengthen the corporate spirit of the school Mr and Mrs Johnson pressed for the

111. Mixed hockey in the 1950s: L to R (back row) Francis Morland, Michael Kerr, David Schackie, Gad Simon, John Williams, Philip Leuw; (front row) Jack Kendall, Elspeth Munro, Karen Weaver, Barbara Hawkins, Robert Munro

building of a common room. A common-room committee was formed in 1959 and as a result of gifts and money-raising events the building, costing about £500, was officially opened in November 1961 by Mrs Ros Johnson. It had a wide variety of uses from providing a place for indoor games for fifty to sixty on wet afternoons to afterschool activities, including meetings of the debating society and of parents and staff. It was both a snack bar and a common room, as the film which was made about the project showed.

Mrs Johnson warned against the idealization of the school council and of viewing it as an instrument for dealing with those aspects of school life which should be the province of the staff. Matters relating to punctuality, behaviour in the library, tidiness in dress, good manners, and respect for property were, she believed, ones which concerned adults and for which pupils had little feeling. It was thus the duty of the staff not the pupil council to deal with such matters by maintaining consistent standards and inculcating good habits. Though KAS opposed punishments in principle, it used mild punishments in practice to achieve such ends. Pupils who were persistently late were made to clean up the dining room after lunch as a deterrent. They could also be denied permits to stay late after school, which was one of the privileges which many enjoyed.

In 1945 in his defence of coeducation in KAS Montgomery asserted that, 'if boys and girls remain in touch with each other during the vital years of adolescence they are less likely to form exaggerated sentimental and idealistic pictures of the opposite sex'.[24] At KAS he noted the development of healthy boy and girl friendships, 'not always platonic but certainly healthy'. In the 1950s in KAS there was a much more sexual intimacy than in the interwar years, when sex was largely seen as an activity for Old Alfredians. Miss d'Eath expressed her concern at the awakening sexual interest of boys when they spent much time in the library during private study examining photographs of semi-clad African tribeswomen in the *Geographical Magazine*. At least she did not resort to banning the magazine or to pasting brown paper over the nubile maidens, which was sometimes the practice elsewhere. KAS could scarcely expect to remain unaffected by the changing outlook of the teenagers of the 1950s. Doris Day had yielded her position of purity to the more open sexuality of Marilyn Monroe and Brigitte Bardot. Elvis Presley, Cliff Richard and James Dean provided a rather different role model from Noel Coward, Pat Boone and Bing Crosby. Little wonder that KAS was affected in 1958 by an 'excess of sexual excitement' which the staff hoped the cold weather and requests to the girls to wear cardigans over their off-the-shoulder dresses would help to abate.

Not everything was left to the vagaries of the British climate. Mrs Paul Jones recognized the need for human intervention in sex education. She acknowledged the change in attitude in the 1950s towards sexual ethics and argued in favour of a positive response.

> A senior girl or boy (and more often it is the girls who are articulate on the subject) will ask, 'Can you tell me, apart of course from the risk of disease and pregnancy, why sexual intercourse with different people is wrong, or unwise?' It is practically useless to say bluntly, however much you may believe it and want them to believe it, that all sexual experience outside marriage is wrong. Though very few teachers and even fewer parents wish to face the possibility, it seems clearly indicated already that generations now growing up regard the older views on virginity and continence as outmoded. They have, as a whole, a freedom to put their ideas into practice which has been hitherto unknown, and it seems likely that this freedom will increase rather than decrease. It is therefore of the greatest importance to try to give children, while they are still young enough to benefit by it, some idea of the necessity for personal dignity and integrity in their emotional and physical relationships with others.[25]

Sex education, where KAS should have led the way, was largely ignored or seen simply as a matter for biology. In consequence, at KAS as elsewhere, most sex education came from peers rather than teachers, behind the bicycle sheds, on the chemistry room roof or at camps or other places, rather than in the classroom where the habits-of-rabbits approach was regarded as immeasurably less exciting.

John Handford, of the University of London Institute of Education and a former history teacher at KAS (1951–6), summed up the value of the school's curriculum and general ethos when he wrote to Montgomery in the year of the latter's retirement:

> In talking to our first-year students, I have, as you can imagine, laid a great deal of stress on freedom in education, genuine coeducation and children's responsibility. When asked where such methods are to be seen, I have to admit that it is very difficult to find them within the state system.[26]

Not all of the students who visited KAS understood fully its operating principles. As the person in charge of teacher training in Bishop Otter College, Chichester, commented when her students returned from a visit to the school: 'We unfailingly find that King Alfred's promotes discussion, some astute and some so blind.'[27] Yet KAS provided valuable teaching experience for students from a large number of training institutions including the Rachel McMillan Training College, Goldsmiths' College and Hampton Training College.

The elements of freedom and responsibility were a key feature in the structure of the curriculum not only in the morning selection of open rooms and in the responsibility of undertaking the required stagework but also in the afternoon options programme. By the time of Montgomery's retirement the number of afternoon choices stood at twenty-two.

Art of Pottery	Needlecraft
Basketball	Netball
Bookcraft or Basketry	Nursery School
Common Room	Printing
Country Dancing	Recorder
Cricket	Rounders
Current Affairs Discussion	Choir
Estate Work	Speech Training &
Football	Dramatic Work
Hockey	Tennis
Music Appreciation	Woodwork

Not all pupils shouldered the responsibilities which went with the choices and Montgomery spent much time each afternoon winkling pupils from various hiding places in the school grounds.

The broad education which KAS offered was not confined to the daily curriculum. There was a host of extra-curricular activities, ranging from the occasional grand event such as the school's participation in May 1951 in 'Top of the Form', when KAS beat a Swedish school but lost to one in Denmark, to regular and annual events. The annual film show was used to raise money to purchase the following year's film stock. The pupils filmed within the school (winter and summer sports, the classroom activities of the younger children and the school council, etc.) and outside (the swimming galas, school holidays in Holland and elsewhere, etc.). By the time that Montgomery retired, the tired black and white films had largely been replaced by colour. Music festivals, visits to and performances of plays, and school camping and skiing holidays became a regular feature of school life. In the late 1940s there were trips to Geneva and Guernsey and in the 1950s to Switzerland, France, Scotland and the Lakes, Guernsey, Royston, the New Forest, the Isle of Wight and Austria. The amphitheatre provided a splendid venue for music festivals and for plays such as *Rogues and Revels*; the wealth of contacts which the school had with the world of drama meant special opportunities to see London and Stratford productions, including David

112. The school field, 1951

Kossoff's *Man on Trial*. Mrs Soskin's presence on the staff meant that drama played an important part in the lives of many, if not most, pupils.

KAS did not seek to train pupils for any particular occupations but did provide special classes to assist pupils to enter the occupations they wished to take up or to go on to the university of their choice. For example, Latin was provided for aspiring medical students, pharmacists and those wishing to enter particular universities. Medicine was a popular career and boys went into science, engineering, journalism and teaching. Girls tended to take up a career in nursing, teaching, art school and the stage, with a few entering banking, publishing, and the civil service. The gender divide, although of a lesser extent than elsewhere, was still very apparent even in KAS. However, the type of education which the school offered was neither intended to encourage such a divide nor to fit pupils for particular social or occupational roles. The 1950s were a time of great change, as Mrs Paul Jones recognized in her discussion of a KAS education in H. A. T. Child's edited work *The Independent Progressive School* (1962):

> At one time it may have been possible to produce people suited to a particular social environment. Today that is not desirable. We cannot afford to produce in our children an attitude of mind which will fit them only for work in a certain profession or life in a certain circle, and which leaves them unable to apprehend the thoughts and mentalities of people outside their immediate environment. It

113. The winning KAS team in *Top of The Form*, 1951: L to R (seated) Simon Ryder-Smith (15), Naomi Elkan (17), Wynford Vaughan Thomas (question-master), Julie Heyting (15), Sylvester Bone (17); (standing) Mrs H. M. E. Barber (KAS head-mistress), Mr F. P. Thomson (managing editor of *English Illustrated*) (photograph BBC)

is therefore essential in our view that they should be enabled to encounter and assess the value of views and convictions which differ from their own.[28]

A time of change, a time of challenge

Montgomery's headship[29] was thus a period when several of the educational features of the old KAS landscape suffered such erosion that few of the pupils of the interwar years would have recognized its flattened contours. The modified Dalton curriculum, the key feature of the interwar curricular framework, received so many revisions under the pressure of increased pupil numbers and the demand for a more recognizable grammar school curriculum that it had all but disappeared by 1962. The youth culture of the 1950s was also a pressure for increased uniformity. Yet KAS still offered a distinctive education to its pupils, particularly when counterposed to the grammar schools of the period. Relationships with teachers were much more relaxed and informal; discipline was interpreted very differently, with no resort to any kind of corporal punishment. A teacher was dismissed for slapping a pupil, something which was unlikely to happen elsewhere. The school offered a rich cultural programme in the afternoon and afterschool activities. Yet the school under Montgomery could never return to the prewar pattern. The brave decision of council to pay teachers Burnham rates meant that the numbers needed to fund the scheme inevitably made the school a much larger and more regulated body.

Notes and references

1. Lord Butler, *The Art of the Possible* (London, Hamish Hamilton, 1971), 120.
2. Ministry of Education, *The Organisation of Secondary Education* (Circular 73), 12 December 1945.
3. 'Discipline: An Address given to a meeting of parents and staff at King Alfred School', 20 October 1947, 4.
4. Ibid., 5.
5. A. G. Good and J. D. Teller, *A History of American Education* (New York, Macmillan, 1956), 420–1.
6. Report of HM Inspectors, June 1949, 7.
7. Minutes of the staff meeting, 11 November 1947.
8. Ibid., 23 October 1961.
9. H. A. Rée, *The Essential Grammar School* (1958), 14.
10. Minutes of the staff meeting, 8 October 1951.
11. Ibid., 14 February 1951.
12. *King Alfred – A Pilot Experiment* (1954), 4–5.
13. *The Secondary Modern School* (London, Faber and Faber, 1963), 5.
14. Council minutes, 21 February 1961.
15. Ibid., 13 February 1952.
16. Ibid., 2 July 1952.
17. Ibid., 7 July 1955.
18. Ibid., 21 February 1961.
19. *King Alfred School – A Pilot Experiment*, 11.
20. *Guardian*, 1 April 1993.
21. *Education*, 249.
22. Ibid., 250.
23. Letter to Montgomery, 20 July 1950.
24. 'An Address on Co-education given at a parent–staff meeting at Holford Road' (1945), 4.
25. H. A. T. Child, *The Independent Progressive School* (London, Hutchinson, 1962), 93.
26. Letter from John Handford to Montgomery, 8 January 1957.
27. Letter from Phyllis Jenkin to Montgomery, 8 October 1960.
28. Child, *Independent Progressive School*, 9.
29. Obituaries in *Guardian* (1 April 1993), *The Ham and High* (2 April 1993) and *The Times* (10 April 1993) provide further insights into his headship.

Chapter 6

School and Society:
The Swinging Sixties
and Swingeing Seventies

In many ways it was fortunate for KAS that Montgomery retired in l962. His quiet, reserved, almost hesitant style of headship would have been ill-suited to deal with the impact upon the school of the rapid social and political changes of the swinging 1960s and with the severe financial and demographic pressures of the swingeing 1970s. The new forces of the age tested to the full the common bond between council, headteacher and parents which had grown up under Montgomery and in the 1960s produced a major crisis of understanding and communication[1] with which the 'unworldly Monty' would have been unable to cope, if the views of many of his former pupils are to be accepted.[2] However, one piece of advice that he could have offered the new headteachers, Alan Humphries and Nikki Paul Jones (who became Mrs Nikki Archer in October 1964), was that the most obvious challenges to the school were not always the most serious, especially when they emanated from Labour's political rhetoric as they had done in 1945.

The Conservatives, who had been in government for almost a decade when Nikki Paul Jones joined the school in 1959, were rapidly running out of steam. Labour appeared threatening, especially as its long-term plan for the reform of the independent sector took on greater urgency after the publication of Anthony Crosland's *The Future of Socialism* in 1956. He rejected 'flat proscription' and the argument that, left to their own devices, private schools would 'wither quietly away as redistribution (of income) bites further into the higher incomes and as the State schools improved their standards'.[3] For him the way forward was to push on vigorously with the Fleming Report's recommendation of 1944 for integrating such schools into the national system by 'sending a really large number' of state scholars to them. The threat to KAS was not simply that Labour's rhetoric had been stiffened with such words as 'infiltration' and

114. Alan Humphries with 'Monty' (B. H. Montgomery), 1965

'democratization'. The new heads and council were faced with a much more real threat than Montgomery and council had been in 1945. Crosland intended to keep the matter at the top of Labour's educational agenda when it came to power (as it did in 1964) and to use legislative powers to achieve his goal if the private sector refused to co-operate. Shortly after becoming Education Secretary, Crosland set up the Public School Commission under Newsom, and Crosland's successor, Patrick Gordon Walker, extended its power under Donnison to consider schools such as KAS. It seemed that Donnison was about to pass sentence and all that was necessary was for a fusillade of legislation to end the life of the condemned. Council with its wealth of experienced people from the professions refused to be panicked. In its 1968 plan for the future of the school, the year that Donnison reported to Wilson's government, council disregarded 'the political factor', no doubt recognizing that Labour lacked the political will to tackle the independent sector. They also took heart from the fact that Fred Willey, Labour's Minister of Land and Natural Resources, sent his three children to the school. There was no fusillade, just a deferment of sentence until Labour returned to office in 1974, followed by a single shot, a *coup de grâce* which felled not the independent day schools such as KAS, but the part state-funded, direct grant schools, which by and large bequeathed their bodies (and their high academic standing) to the independent sector.[4] Council had been wise to concentrate its energies on more pressing problems. It was left to Nikki Archer on the eve of her retirement, and of the 1983 election, to pass on the watchwords of 'eternal vigilance' to her successor, Francis Moran, but by that time Margaret Thatcher had given the private schools a copper-bottomed guarantee about their future. There would be no political predators at large in Manor Wood for a long time to come. In fact, the Thatcher years were to extol the virtues not just of freedom of choice which they believed the independent sector represented, but the kind of parental power in the governing of schools which lay at the heart of KAS.

If Labour's attack on direct grant schools caused most of them to join the independent sector, its other main plank of education policy, the drive under circular 10/65 for a national system of comprehensive schools, helped to swell the number of pupils who wished to attend such schools. Some of the lesser private schools faced with the threat of closure due to falling school rolls suddenly found themselves saved by Labour's attack on grammar schools and its policy of comprehensivization. To KAS the advent of the comprehensive school was more of a mixed blessing. Had KAS simply been an independent school with a high academic reputation it would have welcomed the influx of refugees from grammar schools, but it never aspired to being an independent grammar school. The 1968 subcommittee of council looking into the future of the school recognized that KAS was likely to become increasingly attractive because of its small classes and its ability to cater for a wide ability range, including former grammar school pupils. Yet it also saw a major danger in that the advent of comprehensive schools could reduce the body of parents whom KAS regarded as its lifeblood, not those who saw the school as a substitute for defunct grammar schools, or who enjoyed the social prestige which they believed might accrue from sending their children to a school attended by the offspring of stars of the world of entertainment (such as Peter Sellers, Bob Monkhouse, Dennis Norden, Albert Finney and Humphrey Lyttleton), but those who truly believed in a non-selective school with progressive ideals. The subcommittee realized that its bedrock of ideologically committed parents could be weakened if 'its true devotees found the progressive education in the socially varied, non-selective comprehensive school more attractive',[5] especially if it was free and better resourced in the crucial areas of modern languages and Nuffield science. KAS was first

115. The new joint heads, Nikki Archer and Alan Humphries

and foremost a non-selective school in the academic sense. Escalating fees were already affecting the core of KAS devotees, and should this treasured group be further diminished then the school would be more open to pressures from parents who wished to push it further from its basic catholic ideology, and turn it into a quasi-grammar school or a school for 'problem' children. As a school dependent solely on fee income it was very much subject to market forces.

The main challenge and stimulus to KAS in the 1960s and 1970s came not from the direct or indirect consequences of deliberate government policy but from other directions. The change in the style of the headteachers' reports to council from 1966 provides valuable insights into the interaction between KAS and the wider world and they would not be out of place on an educationist's bookshelf as an example in microcosm of the bewildering and rapid changes which hit schools during these decades.

School and society: redefining KAS progressivism

The reason for the change in the perspective of the headteachers' reports to council was summed up by Alan Humphries in 1966: 'Anyone reading these reports in the future should be able to feel something of the spirit and condition of the school and know more about relationships and beliefs which are the basis of its work and life.'[6] Why each year the heads believed it was necessary to engage in searching the progressive soul and in rethinking the progressive role of KAS is explained by their constant need to respond to the rapid social changes of the period (which is the subject of this section) and to the equally rapid spread of progressive ideals in the state sector (which is the subject of the section which follows). As a consequence of the latter, the school became a net importer rather than a wholesale exporter of progressivism. Whereas Neill at Summerhill was not prepared to develop his school's ideals to meet the educational challenges of the age but remained in a not-so-splendid isolation,[7] Nikki Archer and Alan Humphries, by choice and circumstance, constantly re-aligned their school's ideology to the new social and educational thinking.

116. The 'Why Education?' pageant, 1968: Malcolm Manwaring, a parent and Nikki Archer

Society in the 1960s and 1970s differed markedly from that of 1898 and the much enlarged parent body differed as much in outlook as it did in number from that of the founders. The 230 families who provided KAS with its pupils were part of a society whose values had changed markedly since the late Victorian period and to which the heads and council had to respond positively, without either jettisoning essential principles or destroying the delicate balance of trust upon which the effective functioning of the school ultimately depended. The essential question was not simply that of whether the heads, council and parents could agree on a new progressive synthesis. Society continued to change rapidly; the parent body and council changed over time; KAS ideology was never monolithic but contained several elements whose priorities at any given moment in time were always the subject of debate. Arriving at and sustaining a consensus of opinion on how to meet the many complex challenges of the age, which refused to appear singly and in sequence but appeared in awkward combinations which seemingly demanded very diverse responses, was a test of political skill and diplomacy which none of the early headmasters or councils had ever had to face.

By the mid-1970s, Mrs Archer was in no doubt about the most important change in the social experience of Alfredians since 1898 and which had become increasingly evident since she became co-head with Alan Humphries in 1962:

> As well as financial and political pressures, we are now facing the more intangible threats which arise from the increasing instability of our society. As an independent school we urgently need to redefine what it is to be progressive today. We all know what our founders thought it was in the apparently permanent stability of middle class Victorian England. At the time generations of religious belief had re-inforced and supported the ethical codes, which were passed from one generation to the next and provided a useful pattern for young people to model themselves on.
>
> The conventional authoritarian society from which 'King Alfred', and the other self-styled progressive schools first emerged as enlightened pioneers, has long since disappeared. The vital need, as they originally saw it, was to open up a narrow and inflexible system of education which was preventing the normal creative energies of children from developing. Today the attitudes of society as a whole, and, hence the function of schools, are very different and we shall do our children less than justice if we fail to recognize this.[8]

For the KAS children growing up in 'a divided and increasingly violent society' a more ordered and directed environment was necessary but how could this be reconciled with the essential character of the school? When society provided the corrective counterbalance, KAS could provide a less controlled form of education. With that force having been largely removed, the school 'must provide the balancing factor'. It was therefore necessary, in her view, to redefine the progressive experience, a matter which, given the political sensitivities inherent in the constitutional arrangements of the society, could cause controversy either because some felt that no redefinition was necessary or because some disagreed with particular reformulations. The Archer–Humphries

117. Upper school concert performers, 1978

reformulation entailed a public declaration against overpermissiveness to dispel the 'lively folk legend' still at large in Hampstead that the school found all rules and restraints unnecessary. Hence both were seen by pupils as 'new brooms'. Some of the pupils from the Montgomery era found 'the increased intervention' irksome. To counterbalance the increasing permissiveness of the sixties and seventies, the headteachers found it necessary to assert the need to impose limitations on children's freedom. Their views sounded conventional and certainly would not have been acceptable at Summerhill or at KAS in the years to 1939:

> Although we regard children's needs as a constant priority, we must not fall into the trap of assuming that whatever the child wants is necessarily the right thing for him, or her, at that particular stage. It is often easier and pleasanter for both parents and teachers to say yes than to say no. A too permissive attitude can be a real disservice to young people. Teachers must take the responsibility of fulfilling an adult role and not feel that the child's view is the only valid one. In this respect we need constant support and backing from parents.

However, the three basic conditions deemed necessary to a suitable form of progressive education at KAS for the sixties and seventies involved no radical departure from the basic tenets of the previous eras but more a shift in the direction of formality without undermining fundamental principles. The first was defined as,

> . . . an orderly and peaceful social environment, which can ensure that the educational experiences basic to young people's growing needs can take place. To achieve this environment a respect for the rights of others, and a willingness to accept responsibility for one's own actions, are both imperative. Equally important is a recognition that this school is a place where education, in the formal sense of the word, must have priority.

This first priority was emphasized to counter the growth of what was believed to be the increasing irresponsibility and self-interest of a society where violence and commercial greed were becoming the norms. The reference to formal education, which raised some eyebrows, was intended to show where council and the heads stood in general in the standards debate of the 1960s and 1970s, to dispel the idea that children at KAS were 'prepared for exams with reluctance and passed them without distinction', and to act as a corrective to the opinion expressed by some, but not a majority of parents in the lower school, that the emphasis upon 'standards of work' was incompatible with progressive education.[9]

The second emphasized the need 'to offer a wide range of subject-based study and to see that the highest possible standard of teaching is offered to children in order to ensure that they have every opportunity of developing their individual potential to the full'. A broad, balanced curriculum, including the sciences, was deemed to be an essential, especially as these decades witnessed a curriculum revolution in content and delivery. The need to offer opportunities for pupils to develop their abilities to the full and to enhance their employment prospects was an important priority. Yet some former pupils believed that gender bias tended to reduce choice, with girls, for example, not expected to take science other than biology.

The last of the conditions reiterated a basic concern of KAS since 1898 without which its distinctive kind of education could not be achieved.

> Thirdly, we must maintain the kind of relationship between adults and children in the school which creates trust and co-operation as well as the personal confidence which helps the teaching and learning process to take place. All this demands a high degree of professional commitment and expertise and is very hard work.

The relaxed relationships between staff and pupils were regarded as so vital that over the years several teachers who found it difficult or impossible to work in a non-authoritarian atmosphere either resigned or were dismissed. It was only within the framework of such relationships that

118. Relaxed relationships: Mr Salter with a group in the lower school covered court, 1966: L to R (front row) Timothy Jones, Alison Berton, Ruth Rose, Danielle Elichaoff, Julia Weekes, Catherine Elliott, Oriel Sullivan; (2nd row) Julian Haines (laughing), Michael O'Kelly (side face); (back row) Adam Kops, Martin Treacher (photograph I. G. Tremayne)

the aims of the school could be achieved and change could be managed. Change did not involve scrapping the old and replacing it with the new. As the school evolved, 'the new aspects grow out of and are related to the old; new parents and new children, new staff, buildings, equipment and techniques are all assimilated and become part of it and the essential character of the community'.[10]

The annual reports offer some general insights into the changed and changing nature of society to which the school had to respond. The minutes of council meetings provide more precise detail. The former pointed to pressures, especially commercial pressures, which forced children to forfeit their 'real childhoods' and to become adults at an earlier and earlier age. Nikki Archer used the illustration of twelve- and thirteen-year-old girls wanting to play 'childish games in break'[11] but the physical limitations of high platform soles and long skirts, dictated by adult fashion, denying them the freedom to do so. Even worse were cases in the junior school of children 'whose sophisticated appearance as little copies of mother may be appealing to an adult eye' but which were a ruthless denial of childhood. KAS culture aimed to oppose contemporary culture in giving children the opportunity to grow through and enjoy their childhood, and not cut it short. The increasing portrayal of violence on television and in the cinema, negative parental attitudes, and 'obsessive individualism' were roundly condemned in the headteachers' annual reports.

The minutes of the council meetings of the period provide a different perspective and show some of the dilemmas which faced the headteachers and council. Political threats from Labour, real or imagined, and adverse economic trends meant little to most pupils. Social developments meant much more, for the Carnaby Street culture was essentially a youth culture, a development of the popular culture of protest which had grown up since Bill Haley first rocked around the clock in the mid-1950s. A school which encouraged choice and freedom of expression as KAS did inevitably felt the full blast of the new, youthful, cultural spirit more strongly and more immediately than many of the more traditional independent schools which frowned upon dissent and saw it as an obstruction to good academic results. Shortly after Alan Humphries joined Nikki Paul Jones to form a new joint headship James Hemming addressed the school's staff–parent committee on the revolution in morals, a matter which raised two important but related issues for the heads. First, in the past the school had pursued liberal policies safe in the knowledge that broader social constraints acted as a counterbalancing force for most pupils. In the 1960s many of these constraints were weakened or removed through what Hemming termed 'a growing social permissiveness'. This raised the issue of whether the school itself should become less liberal and more traditional in its attitude to discipline, in order to avoid what some parents would see as a descent into libertarianism. Certainly a school which was perceived to be a hotbed of anti-social values and which was seen to place little value upon academic success and firm, traditional discipline would find it difficult to sustain itself in an age of high inflation by attracting only those parents who

119. The staff/pupil cricket teams, 1962: L to R (top row) David Elster (p), Nicky Isaacs (p), Charles Posner (p); (3rd row) Bruce Pitt (p), Alan Humphries (s), Ian Carnegie (s), M. Wetherall (s), Malcolm Manwaring (s), Dave Thomas (s), Roy Greenfield (s); (2nd row) Richard Willey (p), Nick Wright (p), Jonathan Myer (p), Hugh Pearman (p), Mike Hellyer (s); (front row) Tony D'Arcy (p), Rodney Myer (p), Paul Shackman (p), David Jacobs (p), Andrew Elton (p), Nicky Norden (p), Alan D'Arcy (p), Harvey Flinder (p) (p – pupil, s – staff)

wanted a progressive education for their offspring. This had a direct bearing upon a second and related issue. As parents and members of council had differing expectations of the school, some wanting a firmer stance on matters such as underage drinking, smoking and sex than probably they were willing to adopt at home,[12] others favouring a more relaxed response more in keeping with KAS traditions, and with the majority supporting intermediate positions depending on the particular issue, the heads could expect a rougher ride than their predecessors.

And so could the pupils, who soon became aware that the new heads meant business. A school without a uniform was open to one being imposed from nearby Carnaby Street; so it happened during the joint headship when a pupil, acting as fashion's advance guard, walked through the gates in a bright red tunic. Sergeant Pepper had arrived at KAS earlier than at any other independent school. Faced with the choice of yielding to Carnaby Street commercialism or restricting pupil freedom, the heads chose the latter. Progressivism seemed to have slipped a notch. The red tunic was quickly shown an equally vivid red card. To be progressive was almost to be reactionary, as Nikki Archer commented to John Izbicki of the *Daily Telegraph*. An American student attired in trousers, string vest and an enormous horse blanket was not allowed to 'ride roughshod' over general dress requirements. The heads would not allow the school to look foolish and so damage its reputation in the neighbourhood. Even a proposed fund-raising performance by the Beatles in 1964 after their successful American tour was rejected, despite support within council. A previous appearance by Billy J. Kramer at KAS for a photographic session for his record 'Little Children' had led to an outbreak of hysteria by some pupils. As a consequence the headteachers turned down the offer of a Beatles' concert on the grounds that 'it would not be good for the school to be associated with the kind of mass hysteria which surrounded appearances of the

Beatles'.[13] Their decision led to some boys declaring in a strongly worded letter to Alan Humphries that he was destroying the school's progressive ethos. Furthermore the appeals committee, which saw itself as much 'the guardians of the school's conscience' as a fund-raising body, supported the pupils. Council also gave added support to the concert in a vote of twelve in favour, two against and four abstentions. Nikki Archer and Alan Humphries were probably the only headteachers in the country who ever declined a performance by the Beatles. They also vetoed a biographical film about Churchill on grounds of political bias, despite council expressing its support for showing it. The need to oppose rampant and exploitative commercial pressures and to assert standards in dress, behaviour and political balance had produced the new progressives of the 1960s, willing to exercise their authority in order to allow pupils to develop through what they saw as the natural stages of childhood and adolescence. Of course, there were limits to their influence, especially on sixth-formers. As one former student recalled 'smoking was not a problem, or drinking – we went to the Bull and Bush for that'.

The headteachers believed that parents were as much in need of guidance through the turbulent social times as were pupils and it was within the continuing tradition of parental involvement and enlighten-ment that KAS developed its staff–parent seminars, often inviting experts to address such meetings, to which sixth-formers were some-times invited. They covered a wide range of subjects and reveal many of the issues with which the school had to deal. Dr Faith Spicer, Medical Director of the London Youth Service and Chairperson of the Lewis-ham Juvenile Court, introduced a general review of problems of adoles-cence. Mrs Archer spoke on the social problems of nine to twelve year olds in 1965. Dr Derek Miller examined the key area of 'Freedom and Permissiveness' in 1966. This was followed in later years by such topics as 'Forms of Addiction', 'Drugs and Children' and 'The Generation Gap'. The parent–staff committee also organized larger conferences such as that on 'Ethical and Moral Values in Education' in April 1966.

But how did the school handle the problems about which the many eminent professionals spoke? In 1968 the school faced its first 'drugs incident', the result of which was the offender's suspension. Though the boy was receiving psychological help it was decided not to readmit him, Dr Miller arguing on council that '14 year olds tended to test out the reactions of adults and if he came back it would appear as if his action was being condoned.'[14] This kind of conservative response was also evident a year later when Mrs Archer, admitting that she was still 'feeling her way', raised doubts about Mrs de Peyer's suggestion on council about giving 'professional talks about modern problems such as drugs, safety on roads, sex and venereal disease on a straight informational basis'.[15] Mrs Archer employed the traditional counter-argument that this 'might raise the desire to experiment', though she recognized that the school had 'a responsibility in this field, but the heads were not sure how to discharge it'. The heads did, however, distinguish between the use of drugs and mere drug experimentation.

Further drug-taking incidents and other aspects of the moral revolution, including underage drinking, at least one couple making love in the grass, underage smoking (which on one occasion set fire to a hollow tree which later fell into a neighbouring garden), graffiti, vandalism, swearing, glue sniffing and increased petty theft, led the school to develop a more positive response than was found in many independent and state schools. Except at the end of term, when the heads could do little more than pray (although even this was severely circumscribed in a rationalist school) that those leaving would not transgress to excess, the school came to adopt a more considered attitude to the problems of the age. First, it recognized that such activities were subject to fashions. 'Three years ago drug taking had been the fashion, now it was drink. The 12 year olds seemed to be particularly vulnerable,' declared Mrs Archer at the end of the summer term in 1975. Second, in her view, the head's disapproval 'must be expressed firmly but notice must also be taken of the pupils' state of mind that prompted this behaviour', for example, the pressure of examinations. Individual counselling and discussions with parents could be required but, in any case, any action taken would need to be backed up in the classroom by films and talks. Furthermore, as KAS adopted a rationalist approach, it could not accept any inconsistency in the measures taken. It could not take measures against underage drinking and yet tacitly permit underage smoking.

The school did not rely simply on an appeal to reason, although as Roy Greenfield, the deputy headteacher, argued, training children to be responsible people was part of the role of teachers. It also took practical steps to deal with these problems, such as discouraging staff from drinking with sixth-formers, and increasing vigilance by the staff to prevent theft. KAS was thus evolving a new form of progressivism of a more authoritarian kind but one which nevertheless still kept faith with the basic tenets of the society. It could not use the practices of the 1930s to deal with the problems of the 1960s, something, which, as Alan Humphries pointed out in his condemnation of Summerhill's insularity, did a great disservice to education. If progressive schools were to serve the educational needs of the nation then they should develop their ideals and practices no matter how painful this was or how much this seemed to transgress the gospel of the early pioneers. What they had bequeathed was not holy writ but a series of guiding principles. Summerhill's strict faithfulness to the Neill ideology was a disservice to the educational community, a rather barren form of luxury in the views of Alan Humphries and Nikki Archer. Of course, to KAS pupils who had never known the 'Monty' era, the regime still appeared relaxed, caring and informal, despite its evolution during these decades.

It is not surprising that Alan Humphries, described by one of his former pupils as a 'clean-shaven charmer' and by others as resembling an Anglican chaplain or army officer, and Nikki Archer, seen by many as a 'more attractive version of Mrs Thatcher', were not always 'viewed with enthusiasm'. The general ethos of the school under Montgomery had been strongly against authority. Under his successors, according to several of the former pupils who experienced the headship of all three, 'although outside, the school was viewed as very progressive and liberal,

120. Upper school concert players, 1978

on the inside it did not feel like that'. Montgomery was not seen as a strong enough leader to inspire the school community forward into the 1960s, yet 'Alan Humphries and Nikki Archer seemed controlling rather than visionary and inspiring to many pupils'. However, as one former pupil perceptively argued, 'no head could win'. Alan Humphries was a 'neater and more conventional' head of a progressive school than some expected, and Nikki Archer was much more determined and businesslike than Montgomery, remembered by many people as a father figure giving out passes for camp registration after locating and marking them on a map of Manor Wood. His retirement was a watershed for the school as many pupils recognized. The new heads led from the front. No one could have mistaken them for the school caretaker as happened in the case of Birkett when a parent slipped half a crown into his hand for showing him to the headteacher's office, his own!

Curricular winds of change

When Harold Macmillan, as Conservative prime minister, made his famous 'wind of change' speech to the Cape Town parliament in February 1960 he was largely unaware of the benign breeze which was beginning to rustle through the classrooms of England and Wales. The following month, at Westminster, his Minister of Education, Sir David Eccles, signalled revived government interest in the school curriculum, quietly handed over to teachers and local education authorities by Lord Eustace Percy in 1926.[16] He promised to sally forth into 'the secret garden of the curriculum' but in actual fact showed no intention of commandeering the curriculum as Kenneth Baker was to do in 1988. A few months before Alan Humphries joined Nikki Paul Jones to create a new co-headship, Eccles set up a Curriculum Study Group of professionals to consider curriculum reform. Just before the Conservatives left office in October 1964 this body was reconstituted by Sir Edward Boyle as the Schools Council for the Curriculum and Examinations. During their joint headship (1962–70) and the sole headship of Nikki Archer (1970–83), the Schools Council launched many curricular initiatives to which KAS as a progressive school felt bound to respond. Boyle also set up the Plowden Committee to enquire into primary education. Its report, *Children and their Primary Schools*, published in 1967 and much maligned by later generations of Thatcherite Conservatives, represented the high point of state progressivism. Thus the curricular winds of change were already gathering in force before Macmillan and the Conservatives handed over office to Wilson and Labour in 1964.

It seemed, at last, that KAS was about to become at one with its age as the ripples of progressivism grew wider and wider. This convergence was perceptively described by a former Alfredian, Jennifer Armitage, as follows:

> When I attended the school in the years 1952–62, the education we had there was most unusual for its day. By the late sixties and the seventies many of the ideas that KAS and schools like it pioneered (primary and junior teaching in small groups, children grouped round tables and not in serried ranks, and emphasis on creative art expressive abilities of children) had begun to be seen more widely everywhere. They became the norm rather than the exception.[17]

Writing in 1995 she went on to point to the stark contrast with recent years when 'we have seen an alarming return to conservatism . . . in education, with the introduction of more exams and more formality'. Revealing by contrast the essence of KAS philosophy, she continues,

> it is a great pity that the status quo and conservatives (with a small c) are always so fearful of encouraging interest, enthusiasm and intelligence in children. They fear it will lead to revolt and so suppress it. The suppression, of course, always has the opposite effect to what it is designed to do and, I believe, produces a sullen

and listless generation, quietly mutinous though rarely openly so, because what motivated them, as children, has been quashed, at an early age.

I make no apologies for quoting her words at length for they provide a valuable perspective on these years.

In terms of the teaching of particular subjects KAS had little to export and much to import. The direction of much of the curricular reform of the 1960s and 1970s was evident long before the Conservatives left office. The shock waves sent out by the Soviet launch of Sputnik in October 1957 were much stronger than its sound waves. Britain responded in part by pressing for the modernization of the science curriculum which, true to tradition, was left to the independently funded Nuffield Foundation. KAS was in no position to take any leading part in any of the very early Nuffield projects, lacking the necessary resources, buildings and leadership. Under Montgomery, science teaching had failed to thrive, although council hoped that his successors, given the necessary backing, would bring science from the periphery of the curriculum, where it had always had a precarious grip, towards the centre.

However, there were obstacles. First, neither of Montgomery's successors were scientists, although Audrey (Nikki) Paul Jones (later known as Nikki Archer), a philosophy graduate, promised to help out with biology when appointed, and Alan Humphries, a graduate in English literature, had studied mathematics and science at Oxford before the war interrupted his studies. Despite lacking a full scientific background, they realized the importance of bringing science teaching into the 1960s and together they established close relations with the Nuffield Foundation, the fruits of which Alan Humphries was able to use in the British School in Brussels which he left KAS in 1970 to found. Second, KAS lacked the immediate resources to implement Nuffield science. The cost of equipping the school for ordinary level Nuffield physics alone was £4,000, even if adequate buildings were available, which they were not. As Mr Kartun pointed out to council in January 1966, 'The difference between the 60s and the 20s and 30s was that magnificent things could be done then without money but not now.' Third, the early teaching programmes devised by the Nuffield Foundation in science, mathematics and modern languages were targeted at the top 20 per cent of the ability range. KAS, a non-selective school, had relatively few pupils suited to such courses and science teaching at sixth-form level was in the costly teaching ratio of one member of staff to two students. At a time when spending priorities were constantly under review (for the school relied on fees and appeals only for its income), the huge financial demands of science teaching for the few seemed to suggest that it would have a low priority. Yet, in true KAS tradition, council, urged on by many parents, was willing to back the headteachers in their bid to raise the status of science and science teaching in the school. They refused to accept the view of one former student that 'in a school like this, it should not have been there at all'. Fourth, Nuffield science was teacher-led and in an age when suitable heads of department were few in number, KAS was fishing in a very small pool with very little attractive bait. A small sixth form and a limited career structure in comparison with grammar and comprehensive schools were disincentives. These difficulties were compounded by the need to find a head of science who was also in sympathy with the school's general ideology, particularly after the sitting tenant was dismissed by the heads during their first year in office on the stated grounds that he lacked such sympathy,[18] a decision that was opposed by some parents but supported by council. As council was in the process of devising plans to improve facilities for science teaching, including building a new science laboratory, the matter of a replacement became urgent. Despite the general shortage of science teachers, the school was able to make appointments in physics, chemistry and maths but the departure of Mr Brain in 1964 left the school's science department under strength with further replacement staff difficult to find. The appointment to the science headship of R. Chapman, who had served in the educational department of the RAF and in a large Wandsworth comprehensive school, appeared to offer much needed stability, but his sudden departure and replacement by John Pounds, a Cardiff chemistry graduate, left the school's science department in an unsettled condition for a little time. The fact that Nuffield science was not generally well taught left some of the pupils who went on to science degrees and to teach science with the feeling that they had been disadvantaged.

In a school lacking both a strong tradition in good science teaching and large financial surpluses which could be devoted to upgrading science facilities, the matter of modernizing the science curriculum was not easily resolved. The finance subcommittee of council heard a hard-hitting report by Nikki Archer in December 1965 about how the research sponsored by the Nuffield Foundation in co-operation with the Department of Education and Science would affect not just equipment and buildings but the approach to science teaching throughout the school. The latter was an area in which KAS had been the least progressive, with the traditional chalk-and-talk teaching methods given priority. As the heads pointed out to the appeals committee, the school could not let the revolution in science teaching pass it by. 'Well-qualified staff were not willing to jeopardize their careers by teaching in old-fashioned schools with obsolete equipment.'[19] It was left to Mr Morgan to point out that adequate facilities for teaching the modern hands-on approach to science were necessary for the survival of the school. In terms of an investment in the school's future, Nuffield science was thus essential, especially as it 'seemed to provide a scheme which would not too quickly become out of date and in which physics now takes the leading part with biology and chemistry close seconds'.[20] Council were all too aware of the wider issue of spending priorities which modernizing the science curriculum involved. Mr Lush, adviser to council on architectural matters, had already agreed with the heads to sacrifice the gymnasium in the new building programme to provide the immediate finance for an expanded science department.

All of this seemed to be a catching-up process rather than a pioneering one. However, Nikki Archer recognized that the school could make a distinctive contribution, not perhaps in the mechanics of the new science teaching, but in the development of 'literate and cultured scientists'. This was not a new aim; for generations KAS had trickled pupils into science and medicine with the broad outlook to life which KAS had deliberately fostered but it did seem particularly relevant to the late 1960s and 1970s when intense specialism seemed to be the order of the day. Experts from Nuffield science projects could guide the school on the details of implementation and inform the parents about its general principles through addressing the parent–staff committee, but the broader liberal philosophy of the school would provide the framework in which to develop not narrow, expert, hands-on scientists, the kind of civil engineers who looked at life through the wrong end of a drain pipe, but to nurture scientists of a rounded, Renaissance outlook. Mr Myer, a leading bed manufacturer on council, was not willing to let the matter rest. He welcomed the new twin pillars of KAS science philosophy, combining practical understanding and experience with breadth of perspective and balanced understanding. The aim was to produce neither 'cultured dilettantes' on the arts side (which KAS, like many other progressive schools, was unfairly said to have produced in too great abundance in the past), nor myopic scientists. 'Society in the next twenty years', the heads declared in 1966, 'will demand highly educated men and women who are technologically literate, with sufficient breadth of outlook to ensure that they are not corrupted by an increasingly affluent society.' A KAS education with its emphasis upon all-round development, coeducation, avoiding undue pressure and fostering natural and responsible relationships needed refocusing slightly, not replacing.

Such a philosophy had many practical implications, including the provision of suitable in-service courses of training for teachers in the junior school (as was the case for example in March 1966 when the junior school staff went to St Paul's Junior School for a training day), and a willingness by council and the heads to provide sixth-form Nuffield science, no matter how small the numbers. Moving over to Nuffield science also raised questions of an ideological nature, as was pointed out by parents in a memorandum for discussion.[21] The memorandum was a response to a statement of 'The Aims and Principles of King Alfred School' produced by Alan Humphries in May 1966. In the politically charged atmosphere of early summer 1966 when the greater democracy debate was under way,[22] some saw a contradiction between the head's statements that children progressed through the middle school 'unshackled by other considerations than the educational needs of the individuals' and more importantly that 'always the individual will be seen as an individual, not being measured always against a norm', and the requirement of the Nuffield science that pupils reached a certain standard in mathematics, and other subjects, before they would be able to follow the course. As KAS was a non-selective school with an emphasis upon individual learning, would pupils be debarred from beginning the course until they had reached the required standard or could they begin it without doing so and find it 'above the heads of some'? Clearly imported innovations could create difficulties but then the school had never been sufficiently strong in science to pioneer its own home-grown programmes. This was essentially KAS's own standards debate, a standard imposed from without or that which the pupil by his or her own hard efforts could achieve. This was in many ways a parallel debate to that surrounding John Hertslet's headship of the lower school.[23]

The discussion paper, beside highlighting the problems of possible mismatch of ideologies brought about by imported innovation, pointed to a possible broader innovative role for KAS in curriculum delivery for mixed-ability classes, towards which the authors argued some comprehensive schools were moving. Under the joint headship, the stage and open-room system had seen something of a revival, though at the expense of increasing inroads into the afternoon options programme. At a time when some 'state schools are experimenting with unstreamed classes and in Sweden the state system is in the process of changing over to unstreamed classes . . . have they anything to learn from us?', enquired the well-informed document.[24] The device of set lessons in the first part of the morning combined with open-room choice after the mid-morning break facilitated mixed-ability teaching, even though it was becoming increasingly necessary to use afternoon periods to ensure that each subject had an adequate representation. Such a system suited schools of the size of KAS, though even it was soon to find difficulty in continuing the system as numbers increased to meet escalating costs. Nevertheless, the school tried to use the choice system whenever possible. Even in 1974 when numbers had increased to 429 (from 298 in 1962), council was welcoming 'the return to KAS traditions of choice subjects and open rooms to relieve examination pressures'. A report produced by the middle and upper school curriculum group in 1982 reiterated the importance to KAS of a return to 'choice' afternoons during which no examination subjects were timetabled and of strengthening the system of open rooms which were 'available for study to all children in a particular year and . . . staffed by teachers from each department'.

121. Icons of the 1980s: a common room mural being dismantled, 1987

Along with science, modern languages were to cause acute problems. By 1968 there was insufficient space for two modern languages on the timetable and the curriculum innovations found in the state sector of starting modern languages in the primary school and of using audio-visual technology, were not easily incorporated into KAS teaching programmes. Lack of both experienced staff and finance were serious handicaps but there were strong demands from parents for the introduction of the Nuffield languages project. Again, innovation had hit the school at one of its weaker points, in the teaching of modern languages which had long experienced difficulties, particularly with the rapid turnover of staff. Failure to provide sufficient and adequate teaching of more than one foreign language is a common criticism made by former students.

In the early 1970s the matter of the closure of the school was raised in council as an option for dealing with the mounting financial difficulties brought about in large measure by increases in teachers' salaries. Behind this suggestion was also the mistaken belief that KAS had little or no role in an age of progressivism. Council quickly and rightly dismissed the idea, on the grounds that it overestimated the financial problems, underestimated the growing opposition to progressive ideas and practices, and exaggerated the extent to which progressive principles were to be found in the state sector. KAS still had a role as a demonstration school. Even before Alan Humphries left for Brussels in 1970 a reaction to progressive ideas was setting in, born but a stone's throw away from the school on Hampstead Heath. There in 1969 Brian Cox of Manchester University and Anthony Dyson, of East Anglia and formerly a lecturer at the University of North Wales, Bangor, planned the opening shots in the counter-offensive in a series of *Black Papers*. The need to defend progressivism and to continue to provide in the locality a distinctive kind of education which could not be replicated in its entirety elsewhere were seen by council as more than an adequate justification for finding ways to deal with the grave financial situation. Shortly afterwards the *Black Paper* anti-progressive cry was to be taken up by the Labour Prime Minister, James Callaghan, in his Ruskin College speech (in 1976), thus confirming council's belief that the storm clouds were gathering and the school should be outspoken in its defence of child-centred education.

While the pupils were generally aware of some of the deficiencies in the KAS curriculum, and largely unaware of the broader political issues, mostly they were impressed by the breadth of the subjects on offer and by the different teaching styles and characters of the teachers. Roy Greenfield, the deputy head, was appreciated for his approachability, the ease with which he listened to pupils, possibly being a better listener than the head. Margaret Maxwell was seen as totally committed to the liberal ideology of the school, while at the same time showing that it was perfectly compatible with high standards in English teaching. The KAS ethos enabled teachers to develop distinctive styles and approaches, though as one pupil explained, generally the teachers 'with

122. The progressives of the 1970s: KAS staff in 1976: L to R (seated in front) Nikki Alexander, Katie Munden; (front row) Jane Pare, Ivor Thomas, Dave Thomas, Lindsay Talmud, John Peisley, Sarah Rosen-Webb, Roy Greenfield, Gordon Davies; (2nd row) Jane Epstein, D. M. King, Stella Magarshack, Margaret Maxwell, Nikki Archer, Naomi Hull, Liz Yates; (3rd row) Frank Hammersley, Sydney Buckland, Margaret Barlow, Shirley Blakemore, Shirley Hamper, Clare Smallman, Eva Goodliff, Hilary James; (4th row) Pat Block, Sarah Palmer, Katherine Smyth, C. B. Thompson, Tony Wallis, Jack Buxton, Joe Keating, Julian Ritchie, S. Dow, Denise Gibbs, Françoise Burford

the stronger personalities were the better teachers. The classes were interesting and they put their subjects over with great enthusiasm.' Hilary James, for example, was seen as an outstanding history teacher, whose left-wing views led her to discuss 'black issues . . . not well known then'. Others recalled with a little less affection included Dave Thomas, the woodwork teacher, whose style of discipline was not always thought to be entirely consistent with the relaxed ethos of the school or even with the school's attempts to reduce gender bias in the curriculum. The many excursions, camps and festivals greatly assisted in the development of relaxed relationships between staff and students. The drama festivals, visits to London theatres and camps in Wales, the Isle of Wight and elsewhere were regarded as an integral part of a KAS education. Yet it was not an education which ignored the basic skills, as the following section shows.

The lower school and the standards debate

Educational historians have tended to present the *Black Paper*–progressive debates as an epic struggle between two entrenched opposing camps, fighting over but never sharing any curricular ground. Such a view is understandable for the exaggerated language used by Cox and Dyson in the first two papers, and the images used on their covers, convey the idea of a great adversarial contest. *Black Paper* academics such as Max Beloff (who in fact was a pupil at KAS from 1920 to 1926) tended to confirm this picture, whereas classroom practitioners, such as his sister, Renée Soskin, who was a pupil at the school from 1924 to 1934 and who taught there for twenty-five years, suggest there was more common ground than at first appears. Writing in *Black Paper* 1977 she felt that her former colleagues at KAS would brand her a 'reactionary',[25] but there was little with which Alan Humphries, Nikki Archer or others of the senior management in the school including Margaret Maxwell would have disagreed, especially as she ran a school of her own on lines not too dissimilar from those of King Alfred School. In her article in 1977 she described what was essentially the Alfredian educational experience of the 1960s and 1970s, in small classes with children of varying abilities, working in an atmosphere of reasonable quiet and calm under a flexible timetable, and where children were encouraged to

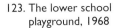

123. The lower school playground, 1968

achieve high standards. The learning of the basics, reading, writing, spelling and punctuation, with unobtrusive testing, was not seen as inhibiting children's creative powers but as a crucial means to the expression of natural creative ability. In her view, as in that of KAS, special provision for children with learning difficulties involved more careful teaching not less. Above all, Renée Soskin argued, the idea that 'children will learn when they want to' was not the *laissez-faire* model that was sometimes implied. Children should be encouraged to learn through the creation of a stimulating environment but never coerced as under the old elementary school regime.

That KAS was largely in tune with the ten essential points which Mrs Soskin laid down as an alternative to 'sterile political dogma' was not simply the result of her many years of teaching there at a senior level. Even in the few years since she had left KAS in 1962 the school could have chosen to follow a more radical progressive path after Montgomery's retirement. That it did not do so was a matter of deliberate choice, involving the resignation of the head of lower school, John Hertslet, in 1966 who wished to realign the education of the lower school with the ideals of the founders. A. S. Neill in 1918 clashed with the headmaster, John Russell, in wanting to push the school further down a more radical path, that of self-government. Unable to do so, he resigned and went on to set up his own boarding school, Summerhill, a few years later, where he implemented his ideas. In some ways, the South African Hertslet was a latter-day Neill, but interestingly he resigned to take up a post in the state sector at the nearby Hargrave Park School, where he believed his progressive thinking was more acceptable, prompting Alan Humphries among others to ask 'Who are the progressives now?' This was a question which was asked increasingly in the 1960s, particularly after the publication of the Plowden Report in 1967, and lay at the heart of the standards debate. To the students who moved to KAS from other progressive schools, the school in these decades was a very orderly, even disciplined, environment by comparison.

When the Plowden Committee was engaged in its enquiries between August 1963 and October 1966, KAS and council were conducting their own standards debate, precipitated by the appointment of John Hertslet. Prior to his appointment as head of lower school in 1964, council had expressed its concern about the lack of close supervision of that part of the school. The heads had initially opposed the creation of the post of head of lower school but had yielded to Mrs Jobson's arguments in council. She argued for the closer co-ordination of syllabuses, thus preventing 'each teacher rather arbitrarily teaching according to her own interests'.[26] Though a strong supporter of child-

124. An outdoor art lesson, 1964: L to R Simon Lee, Richard Gilbert, Simon Jeffries, Steven Lyttleton (photograph Reg Wilson)

centred education, she also argued that while some subjects should 'not be kept in watertight compartments . . . maths and English must be taught in a continuous and orderly manner; and spelling, for instance, cannot be abandoned'. Mrs Archer also expressed her concern about standards, that the school should ensure that 'the academic level of the classes (was) being raised with the age levels'. She was particularly concerned about the standards reached by those who were about to transfer from the lower to the middle school. 'An increasing number of them', she argued, 'will be 11 before they reach middle school but, unless the curriculum is changed, they will be no further forward than the 10 year-olds have been in the past.'[27] Spelling tests and other checks were seen as an important part of raising standards.

One of the key features in the background to Hertslet's appointment was thus a growing body of opinion in favour of more orderly progression through the school and the need to give children 'enough to bite on'. However, the heads stood firm in their resolve not to press 'academic standards' to the exclusion of other equally important values and not to 'imitate grammar schools'. A general sympathy with KAS methods, whatever they might be in the changing world of the 1960s, was deemed essential for all staff. What was evident, however, from the opening remark of the headteachers in a parent–staff committee discussion of 'Misconceptions about Progressive Education' in October 1963 was that high individual standards of achievement and progressive education were not just compatible but something at which the school ought to aim. In May 1964 the appointment of John Hertslet to the post of head of lower school from September was announced to council. Exactly a year later the school's standards debate was being conducted around his philosophy of education and his consequent style of teaching. Mrs Jobson, who had earlier emphasized the importance of a traditional framework for the teaching of the basics, first raised the issue in council of his suitability for the headship of the lower school. In the ensuing discussion, Alan Humphries put his finger on the very issue which was to be at the heart of the national standards debate: 'In the early pioneering days of progressive education', he argued, 'the emphasis was on the emotional development of the child. There were still two streams – those who emphasise personality development and those who seek high academic standards. Mr Hertslet was perhaps a little old-fashioned in that he considered emotional wellbeing the more important.' The answer to the immediate problem was seen to lie in sending him on a training course for junior school teachers. If this was intended to be a process of re-education it was remarkably unsuccessful for he remained as unrepentant in his views in 1965 as he was when interviewed thirty years later. He believed that preparation for tests and classroom-bound education, whatever form they took, were the antithesis of progressive education. True progressivism lay in the full use of the Hampstead environment and in giving priority to a child's emotional development. By May 1966 his unwillingness to change his teaching methods and educational priorities was evident to all. He felt obliged to resign, stating openly that 'he could not take examinations or preparations for examinations seriously, nor therefore formal lessons or a formal curriculum'.[28]

When Anthony Dyson in his *Black Paper, The Sleep of Reason*, three years later spoke of the romanticization of the idea of 'self' and condemned the emphasis upon unregulated self-expression, he was conveying to readers in a somewhat exaggerated way the same set of ideas which Alan Humphries had attributed to those who, like Hertslet, believed that 'personality development' was the sole aim of the education process. It might appear strange that progressives such as Alan Humphries and Nikki Archer could share some of the ideas of the contributors to the *Black Papers* but, in reality, this was nothing unusual, for many headteachers believed in mixing 'formal' and 'informal' methods and 'formal' and 'informal' aims. The difficulty was that in a school with KAS's constituency such a practice was bound to lead to opposition from one wing or other. Some parents believed that Hertset's view of education was nearer to the true ideals of the founders than were those of the heads and council. They were anxious for assurances that the headteachers' emphasis upon academic standards was not a backdoor means of turning the school into a grammar school. It was not difficult for the headteachers of a non-selective school to give such assurances but it still left some KAS parents asking the question on the lips of many educationists in the 1960s: 'Who really are the progressives?'

As far as many parents of children in the lower school were concerned the immediate question was 'How progressive was their own child's educational experience?' Measured by the standards of that of

Alfredians of the early years or even of the interwar years, it would seem that education had become more formal, but these early experiences are not perhaps the best yardstick. Judged against the best practices described in the progressives' bible of the sixties, the Plowden Report published in 1967, the lower and middle schools could still be regarded as forward thinking. Its status as arbiter of progressivism was enhanced in the eyes of some KAS devotees when Donald McLachlan, the former editor of the *Sunday Telegraph*, writing in the *Black Papers*,[29] condemned both the Conservative Minister of Education who initiated the Plowden inquiry in August 1963, Sir Edward Boyle, and the Labour Minister to whom Lady Plowden presented her report in October 1966, Anthony Crosland, for their 'egalitarian sentiment'. What perhaps is more important is the fact that though the Plowden Committee never visited the school nor requested written evidence from council, nevertheless many of the report's recommendations reflected ideas and practices which were already a normal part of the everyday experience of young Alfredians. While the *Black Papers* argued that even if children in progressive schools were happier, the price they paid in underachievement and future failure was much too high,[30] Plowden and KAS saw the happiness of pupils as a prerequisite to successful learning, which extended well beyond the *Black Paper* concentration on the three Rs. It also extended well beyond the school. In order to maximize pupil achievement Plowden argued for a stronger partnership between teachers and parents, something to which few headteachers gave a high priority during the Plowden inquiry but which was of paramount importance at KAS. The school believed that the harmonious development of the abilities of its pupils could not be achieved solely in the classroom; schools were not teaching shops but were in the very active business of transmitting sound values and attitudes, the effectiveness of which required the partnership of parents. Most KAS parents recognized with Plowden that the atmosphere of the school was of paramount importance and that a basic determinant of a friendly co-operative atmosphere was the need to let children enjoy their present. 'The best preparation for being a happy and useful man or woman', Plowden declared, 'is to live fully as a child', an idea that had long been the basis of lower school teaching.

The Plowden Report placed a great emphasis upon the school being a community in which children of all ages lived together. KAS as an all-age school from four to eighteen was peculiarly well suited to achieve this. One idea which the headteachers adopted from the report in order to strengthen the family atmosphere of the school was that of vertical or family grouping – a form of organization frowned upon by the *Black Papers* contributor D. M. Pinn from the nearby Henrietta Barnett Junior School.[31] As Plowden pointed out, having an extended age range within one class rather than having all children of the same age was not a new practice but went back to 1931 (when the Consultative Committee produced its report on the primary school) and beyond. In many ways it was a return to the first form of class organization at KAS and an extension of the ideas underlying the open-room system. Its revival suited many of the particular needs of the late 1960s. It made it easier to provide for children who were exceptionally able and those who were 'retarded'. It made it easier for newcomers to be absorbed, as classes with an extended age range could well include brothers or sisters. It also helped the informal learning process, with younger children being attracted by some of the materials provided for older children and with older children with learning difficulties being ready to talk and to play with younger children. Such a mode of classroom organization imposed great demands on teachers and its mixed-age and wide ability range made it unworkable, in the view of the *Black Papers*, except in the hands of very gifted teachers.

By 1969 with plans afoot to introduce a two-form entry into KAS, the headteachers were willing to experiment with the system which would add a new dimension to the experience of pupils. In October of that year, Mrs Archer outlined to council the practical and ideological advantages of family grouping in that it allowed 'flexibility in numbers and educationally would help the policy of allowing children to develop at their own pace'. The staff were reported to be enthusiastic about it, provided it was adequately resourced in view of the competition from science for limited funds. She was thus willing to take the matter a stage further by consulting training colleges and schools already running such a system. Mrs Aitken gave the head her support in council, arguing that 'it altered the whole perspective' of the education of the younger child, and agreed that the matter should be brought before a meeting with parents before the end of the month. By May 1970 plans had been drawn up for five, six and seven year olds to be placed in family groups from the beginning of the new academic year, with a view to introducing children aged eight and nine to the system the following year. As was usually the case with new schemes, the new grouping system was to be reviewed at the end of its first term. Not surprisingly, perhaps, its future was said to be in doubt, not because of its lack of educational value but because of the shortage of accommodation. Nikki Archer, now acting as sole head after the resignation of Alan Humphries, argued that, unless adequate accommodation was forthcoming, it 'could not be extended, nor even continue as at present'. By January 1971 doubts about its sur-

125. Lower school pupils on the roll bar

vival were growing, in view of the need for considerable expenditure on additional accommodation for art facilities, although new staff, including Patricia Heller, were appointed to share in family-group teaching from September. In the year in which Marion Robey died, 1974, it was fitting that the lower school to which she had contributed so much was finally declared to be secure in its vertical grouping system, although the problem of encouraging children of different ages to mix together was still unresolved. Nevertheless, Nikki Archer was ready to extend the system to the middle and upper schools. Ivor Thomas, with experience of family grouping in state primary schools, was appointed to develop the system but the staff were more enthusiastic at first than the pupils, who were not sure what was expected of them. Escalating inflation by the mid-1970s and the great amount of time needed to develop the system in the middle and upper schools caused the idea of extending it to be dropped.

It continued in being in the lower school, receiving support in council at the end of the decade from Mr Miller-Bakewell among others, who argued on the by now familiar lines that 'it enabled the pace of the children to be more flexible', thus being 'a help, not a hindrance' to the realization of KAS aims. There was a sense in which it also continued for part of the time at least in the middle school. The Dalton-type stagework still used in that part of the school brought children of different ages together in open rooms and in some class lessons. Thus the idea borrowed on the face of it from the Plowden Report was, in essence, a development of the system used by Russell, refined by Wicksteed in his Dalton system and accepted by headteachers since. Its pedigree therefore was pure KAS. It remained in place after the retirement of Nikki Archer in 1983. A description of the lower school around 1983 showed how for the most part each class spanned two age groups, though French, mathematics, music, movement and games were taught in single-age classes. One of the major developments of the headship of her successor was the abandonment of family grouping after an extensive inquiry into its value. Progressivism for KAS was a process, that of subjecting modes of organization and styles of teaching to constant review, not a fixed unchanging set of objectives. The organization of the lower school into family groups can be seen from the following description in the 1980 school prospectus.

Lower School

The junior department is generally known as Lower School, and accommodates approximately 200 children organized into eight 2-year classes and one entry group of 4–5 year olds. The arrangement is as follows:-

Reception:	(one class)	4–5 years
Infant:	(two classes)	5–7 years
Lower Junior:	(three classes)	7–9 years
Upper Junior:	(three classes)	9–11 years

The main entry points are at 4 years and at 7 years

The value of family grouping to the lower school was discussed in council in the last few weeks of Nikki Archer's headship. By the 1980s the matter of bullying was being more openly discussed in educational circles and KAS found family grouping one way of tackling it. It was said to promote greater interaction, tolerance, understanding and responsibility. It also had the value of easing the problems of children who needed an additional year in a lower group or who, though younger, were ready to move up to the next group. The system thus enabled staff 'to make the best decisions they could for each child on the basis of their present stage of development and tackle problems when they occurred rather than anticipating difficulties that might never happen'.[32]

126. The first pre-fab classroom in the lower school, 1970

In the changing educational landscape of the 1960s, King Alfred School was less conspicuous than it had been in the past. In an age of separatism it had been an all-age school; when most pupils attending the carefully segregated primary and secondary schools of England and Wales belonged to the indigenous population, it drew on an international clientele; when schools selected pupils on grounds of ability, it maintained its non-selective intake. In the 1960s society and educational ideology caught up with KAS. London's schools became multi-ethnic and comprehensive and because of the latter the distinction between primary and secondary became less marked. This, together with growing financial problems, led to some on council to consider the closure of the school. Although much of its outward distinctiveness appeared to have gone, there were others on council who recognized that the school could maintain and even develop its curricular difference not simply by importing Nuffield and Schools Council projects such as integrated humanities, but by improving the quality of the school experience in a number of ways. These included developing remedial education, assisting transition between the parts of the school, developing the relaxed style of teaching which helped immigrants to settle down and to make the most of their educational opportunities and to assist all those who wished to secure places at university or elsewhere. Whereas many London schools had begun to gain experience in some of these areas, KAS had considerable experience in all of them. The aim of the heads and council was to develop within the context of the 1960s the traditional aim inherent in the school's very nature, of a good mixed-ability school with opportunities for children at all levels to achieve their full potential; and resisting 'the wayward elements of the most vocal members of the community' to 'swing from one aim to another'.[33] To

127. Guy Christianson, head of lower school, 1977–1982

many outsiders the school was still regarded as 'alarmingly liberal', particular to those parents who sent their children to nearby independent schools. However, KAS was not 'all sex, drugs and rock and roll' as some believed.

One area where KAS could excel in the age of the comprehensive school was in developing further its already abundant expertise in helping pupils with learning difficulties in a small-school environment. This obvious course was not without its dangers, as the heads and council recognized, for it carried with it the possibility that the school would be seen in the neighbourhood as one which specialized in helping such children to the disadvantage of pupils who were more gifted. This perception of the school was nothing new but neither was it easily dispelled, despite the annual publication in the heads' report to council of examination successes. It was as much alive in the early 1980s when the examination performance of most mixed-ability schools of all kinds was shown to be constantly improving as it was in the mid-1960s when it was thought that the demise of the grammar school would lead to a decline in standards. Yet as the curricular policy statement of 1964 recognized, remedial education needed to be given an even higher priority than before, not simply to enable pupils to attain their best individually but to help ensure that lower school pupils reached the middle school adequately 'prepared in the funda-mentals'.[34] The move towards a two-form

128. Fred Johnson, head of middle school, 1957–1968

entry advocated in a memorandum on the future development of the school drawn up in June 1969 made increased remedial provision imperative.

Thus one feature of school life which was more noticeable to pupils and parents during the lower school departmental headships of Hertslet's successors, Jennifer Jones, Frank Hammersley and Guy Christiansen and the middle school headships of Fred Johnson, Jennifer Jones, Malcolm Manwaring and Ivor Thomas, was extended remedial provision, which was made free to pupils below the age of nine, instead of eight, from 1971. The year before, the school had begun to pioneer ways of assisting dyslexic pupils and by the time that Callaghan made his Ruskin College speech in October 1976 about declining standards of literacy and numeracy, pinning the blame on the progressives' disregard of the basics, KAS could rightly declare that central to the pupils' experience at all levels were reading, writing, spelling and mathematics, always taught in a manner 'to avoid producing anxiety in the children about their own levels of achievement'.[35] By 1976 remedial education had become a regular part of the curriculum for which no special fee was charged.

One major reason why KAS was developing the remedial side of the family-group system was underlined by one of the team of school inspectors who addressed council at the end of the 1970s. In answer to a question by the chair of council, Jack Black, about the changing character of the student body, the lead inspector pointed to 'the increasing number of foreign children . . . KAS is becoming increasingly international, as were many other independent schools. The KAS ethos is attracting more overseas people.'[36] The lack of command of English of many such pupils placed heavy demands upon teachers but, the inspector concluded, 'Remedial work at KAS was very good.'

The mixed-ability classroom where some children were given additional remedial help was easier to maintain in the lower and middle schools than in the upper school, though in the first two years of the latter there was no immediate noticeable difference in the composition of classes. In the third year, however, some selection was introduced in science, mathematics and French. By the fourth year differences were more marked when pupils embarked on ordinary level courses or those for the certificate of secondary education, in the case of the latter against much parental resistance.

The preceding survey of the lower school (and to some extent the middle school) during these years shows how misleading the label 'progressive' had become during the 1960s and 1970s. The *Black Paper* dons and Conservative and Labour ministers refused to look behind the label, finding comfort in the reports in 1976 on the William Tyndale Junior School, where education was said to have 'stultified into a late sixties style of informal progressive recession',[37] and in the initial conclusions of Neville Bennett's research into 'Teaching styles and pupil progress'. The facts that William Tyndale was not a typical school and that Bennett's conclusions that formal styles of teaching delivered results superior to informal styles were later revised to show little difference were conveniently ignored. Above all what Bennett's research revealed was what KAS teachers had long since known. It was extremely difficult to identify 'formal' and 'informal' classrooms. They were not that static, and varied according to particular activities, and at different times of day and even to the extent that some pupils in the same classroom could be said to be engaged in

129. The new nursery playground, 1981

the more formal tasks of learning the three Rs while others could be engaged in more informal activities. Even Bennett's 'mixed' classroom suggested a more stylized approach to teaching when, in essence, the activities were so blurred as to defy even this generally more appropriate description of the KAS method. In terms of standards, the Hertslet episode in the mid-1960s showed that the heads were not willing to sacrifice standards of attainment in the basics on the altar of an uncompromising progressive ideology and the increased emphasis upon tests of various kinds, including spelling tests, was sufficient evidence to parents and inspectors of this intention during the period 1962 to 1983.

'Politics is a passionate business.' Discuss

Sixth-form Alfredians faced with this kind of general studies examination question at the end of Nikki Archer's headship in 1983 could have found much upon which to base their answers from the national and the school experience of the preceding twenty-one years. Even before Alan Humphries left in 1970 there was much evidence that national political life and that of the school had changed considerably. This was particularly evident after 1965, with the end of grousemoor Conservative politics, when Wilson's Labour government appeared to usher in a more democratic age. Tony Blair, the Labour leader at the time of Wilson's death in May 1995, argued that Wilson was to the politics of the 1960s what the Beatles were to its popular music. The northern lad from Huddersfield and Merseyside's Wirral Grammar School for Boys, with his Liverpool Huyton seat, appeared to symbolize, with Liverpool's 'fab four', a new democratic age, a spirit of protest, Wilson having resigned with Bevan in 1951 against Gaitskell's budget proposals to introduce NHS charges for dentures and spectacles. The 1960s promised to be as exciting politically as they were in popular culture. For Wilson they were probably too politically exciting with crises in economics, over Rhodesia and in trade-union relationships; with demonstrations against British government support for the United States in Vietnam; and with student unrest, particularly at the London School of Economics (LSE), from 1967 to 1969.

In politics, as in most things, when Britain sneezed, KAS quickly caught cold. In the 1960s political activity tended to focus upon the relationship between council and parents in 'the greater democracy debate' influenced in part by Labour's electoral victory and Hertslet's resignation; between council and staff over the latter's representation on council, caused largely by the increased power of teacher unions and the enhanced status of the profession through its leadership of Schools Council projects; and between council and pupils over the powers of the pupil council, affected indirectly by heightened student political activity at the LSE and elsewhere. In the 1970s and early 1980s the focus shifted more to council itself, to its size and composition, partly a response to the national drive for greater efficiency in management, and to the relationship between council and head, a hardy perennial which tended to flower quickly when watered liberally by sudden political storms. The passion which had been missing from much of the political life of KAS in the Montgomery era returned with a vengeance in the joint headship of Nikki Archer and Alan Humphries (1962–70) and in the sole headship of the former (1970–83).

KAS was not simply a school community; it was a vibrant political community, which on occasions led some members of council to believe that parents who sent their children to the school for 'the wrong reasons' were sometimes preferable to those who sent them because of its progressive ethos and who campaigned hard to maintain what they thought it should be. Camouflaged conservatives were certainly often easier to handle than strident progressives! A school for political scandal KAS never was but, as the constitutional statement of October 1966 pointed out, council as a whole 'has always welcomed discussion and even controversy. Indeed, this is at the very heart of our constitution.'[38]

At times of heightened political activity and controversy in national life, such as that around and following Labour's narrow election victory in October 1964, one group or another tended to become impatient with the normal democratic processes of the society. Members of the society elected the school council in which executive power was vested and it was thus open to parents who were the main body of the society to seek to change policy through the usual democratic procedures at the annual general meeting or specially convened statutory meetings. For most of the time this system was recognized as entirely appropriate and adequate for the expression of parental opinion, especially as the school also had a parent–staff association and the heads were easily accessible. As Nikki Archer has pointed out, at KAS 'the constitutional powers of parents had always been absolute but by common consensus only exercised in areas deemed appropriate. Most parents (recognized) that power games and conflicts were alien to the KAS tradition.'[39] Occasionally, however, such as at the time of John Hertslet's resignation, a few parents wanted a more direct say in school affairs, or so it appeared, even though it was totally impractical and undesirable for every matter concerning the school and its staff to be put before the parent body. Although Hertslet's resignation was essentially a matter for him and the heads it was thought by his small but vocal group of parent supporters that it involved important ideological and constitutional issues, that the school was in danger of being turned by the heads into a more formal educational institution on the lines of a grammar school, something which in fact was neither possible nor desired, and that council was out of touch with parents, something which could appear to be the case because of its emphasis on the confidentiality of its discussions and the fact that it usually only met about five times a year. A meeting with parents in June 1966 chaired by Mr Kautun, a member of council, clarified the issues though it did not resolve them for all present. A small group of 'radical militants' wanted council to define its responsibilities and relationship to the heads and parent body more clearly and to 'improve the operation of democracy by promoting discussion of the current problems of the school instead of general problems'.[40] Mr William Wood, another council member, regretted 'the air of bitterness' which had pervaded the discussion and argued that a few were seeking to use the occasion to make personal attacks on the heads, which led Alan Humphries to threaten to resign. Council was criticized for its poor leadership and the heads for their education policy. What was necessary, above all, was to restore good relations, and in order to try to achieve this, council, led by its chairman Roderick Garrett, set up a subcommittee. The subcommittee recommended the publication of a bulletin for parents about non-confidential policy decisions. The bulletin could also provide a forum for parental opinions. In addition, it recommended more effective use of the parent–staff association for discussion of matters of immediate concern. It suggested that at annual general meetings and on other occasions council members should wear badges to identify themselves. To deal with the immediate matter of 'the dissident parents' it was suggested that a meeting between them and council should be arranged prior to the annual general meeting. By the time that William Wood had replaced Roderick Garrett as chairman of council in 1967 much of the heat had gone out of the debate, leaving the bulletin as one of its most visible achievements.

By that time other interest groups were becoming more vocal in their requests for more open government and greater consultation in the running of the school. One such group was the staff, who as employees were debarred under the terms of the society's charitable status from full membership of council. The 1960s saw the growing professional strength of teachers and their unions, reflected in the fact which Mrs Archer reported to council in May 1969 that 'staffs of some maintained schools were asking for representation on governing bodies'.[41] The way forward in her view was for the staff to have policy discussions with council on an annual basis. The proposal still left the staff under-represented and very much on the periphery of the decision-making process. The first step to bringing them in from the cold came with the creation of the educational consultative committee, a forum of teachers and council, which first reported back to council in March 1970 and recommended the appointment of a male deputy to assist Nikki Archer on the departure of Alan Humphries. However, membership of the educational consultative committee did not bring with it direct membership of council. Council was not persuaded that staff representation was necessarily a good thing in that it raised many problems, including that of confidentiality in staffing matters and that of a non-parent body electing members to council. The matter was left in abeyance until

130. Ivor Thomas, head of middle school, 1972–1979

March 1973. Again the problem of charitable status precluding membership with voting rights was raised but the possibility of staff representatives without voting rights was briefly considered. At the council meeting four months later the matter was taken further when the chairman, William Wood, gave his backing to the idea of staff as non-voting members of council who would be excluded from reserved items. In December 1974 the first four staff representatives, Mrs James, Mr Mortensen, Mr Peck and Mr Ivor Thomas, joined council but staff membership remained subject to annual review. With staff representation on council the educational consultative committee met less frequently.

These years, particularly towards the end of the 1960s, were ones of student power. A school such as King Alfred which deliberately fostered freedom and independence of thought among its pupils could scarcely expect to remain unaffected by the student unrest of the times. 'Why are you so secretive?' the sixth form asked council in l969, picking up the torch of 'greater democracy' which the small group of parents had laid down two years earlier. As in the case of the previous group of 'dissidents' they were said to be 'a vociferous minority'[42] whose 'mood was that of the prevailing questioning of authority'. But no matter how much of a minority they were, council's response was, as in the previous debate, open and constructive with the chairman and other council members meeting the sixth-formers for an exchange of views. The desire for political change overflowed into the pupils' council which suspended its constitution in order to experiment with a more democratic system, an open assembly which replaced the system of elected form councillors and which anyone could attend. Those who attended had a vote. The experiment which was to last a term was extended but according to the annual report ended the year after in 'acrimony and dispute, in a near state of disintegration'. The prevailing ferment also led sixth-formers to request that they need only come to school for classes, in reply to which the heads agreed that they could absent themselves for one part of the day only, morning or afternoon, providing they had no lessons. The most extreme proposal put forward by the student body, however, was not met with favour, that any disciplinary action concerning pupils should be referred to the pupil council or assembly which would have the right to decide on and implement its own punishments. This infringed the powers of council and the head and had ideological implications. In reality, as Nikki Archer pointed out in an interview for the *Times Educational Supplement*,[43] there was only a small area where the pupil council could make decisions. Although the pupils had a debating assembly, unlike many other schools, an assembly which gave them practical experience in committee matters and open debate, nevertheless their actual powers were not much more than those of prefects in state secondary schools. They were far less than the powers which the pupil assembly enjoyed at Summerhill under Neill. Nor were pupils represented directly on council.

Most of the former students who replied to questions about the pupil council tended to appreciate the concept but recognized the limitations in practice, particularly in the heady days of the late 1960s. It was obvious to them that in testing the boundaries of their power they were likely to lose and that there were no real opportunities 'to challenge the system'. There was also a complaint common to many committees that 'Those with the loudest voices get what they wanted.' It would seem that the understanding they gained of group dynamics and the limitations of power was probably one of the greatest values of the council, despite the fact that one respondent concluded gloomily that by 1968 it was 'empty of purpose and power'.

John Hertslet's resignation had thus signalled a vigorous debate by various groups within the school and the society about the parameters of the political power of the heads and council and about open and responsible government. The debate extended to the heads and council who considered their respective powers in relation to the hiring and firing of heads of department in particular and of staff in general. In the wake of Hertslet's resignation in 1966, Mr Elliott raised the question in council of whether the heads should share the responsibility for the appointment of heads of department. Mrs Archer felt more strongly about the matter than did Alan Humphries, who said he would not mind so doing but would not ask for it. She argued that a key factor in the choice should be whether or not a person could work with the rest of the staff and that this 'was a matter only the heads could judge. She would prefer to take her own responsibility.'[44] There was of course the problem of council not accepting the heads' recommendations, but their contracts seem to deny the possibility of a clash for according to them the heads proposed and council ratified, though there were doubts about whether this applied to

131. The two deputy heads, Roy Greenfield and Gordon Davies

heads of department. The following year, under the new chairmanship of William Wood, council considered the matter of the parts played by the heads and council in the dismissal of a member of staff, in particular the case of changing the duties of a teacher to the extent that it could be interpreted as dismissal. If council, on appeal, did not support a decision by the heads then there was the danger of an open break if the heads themselves also refused to change their minds. The constitutional position thus always left the door open to difficulties unless as was required constitutionally there was close discussion between council and the heads before a member of staff was dismissed. If council and the head disagreed at that stage then the matter remained unresolved but if they supported the heads then, according to Mrs Archer, 'they must be prepared to follow it through'. However, there were members on council who firmly believed that council must feel free to hear an appeal if it were made, that the appeal could be the first time when the 'true facts of a case were heard' and thus the heads' decision could be overruled despite prior discussion. These thorny matters remained for the future for in the case in point a change of duties was sanctioned. While a dual headship remained in being the joint authority of the heads speaking in unison on council or largely in unison was a powerful factor in the political dynamics of council discussion. With the departure of Alan Humphries for Brussels (where, incidentally, he faced a tougher governing body of diplomats and industrialists), the position of the head was weakened and Nikki Archer became the school's first sole female head, with a deputy, Roy Greenfield.

The pressure of interest groups for increased representation in the running of the school did not abate with the coming of the 1970s and a change in the character of the headship. The 1960s witnessed a general enhancement of the professional status of teachers which was reflected at KAS with their being given representation on council. It was as a consequence of this step that the staff requested the privilege of placing items on the council's agenda and the right to participate in planning the school's expansion, especially in the controlled introduction of the family-group system. Thus these decades were in many ways a golden era in terms of their political representation, being given as much say in the running of the school as the constitution would allow, and possessing great autonomy as teachers. The latter was outlined in council by a teacher representative, Mrs James, by chance a few days before Callaghan's Ruskin College speech in October 1976 which was to begin the process in state schools of transferring control of the curriculum from teachers and local authorities to government. She pointed to the freedom of KAS teachers who 'with meetings and discussions, and an organized syllabus . . . had both support and scope for their ideas'.[45]

Not all groups were so happy with their representation. The school four, expanded to the school six in 1968, were far from pleased with their role, which they felt was too much like a janitor's, and the limited influence they exercised on school policy. In 1973 half of their number felt that the system was archaic, in that it was drawn from the whole school when it should be drawn only from forms 4 to 6 with emphasis in particular upon the sixth form. A positive step was taken to enhance the power of the school six when they were invited to attend parent–staff committee meetings. Their request that the pupil council should, like the teachers, send representatives to council was not supported by the parent–staff committee, which recommended instead that the chairmen of the various council committees should attend the pupil council meetings when it was appropriate to do so. Council gave its support to the latter idea but was unwilling to take the truly radical step of student representation on council, a measure which would have helped to meet student criticism that 'the school was neither sufficiently democratic nor enough of a community'.[46] It would have been the ultimate vote of confidence in the merits of a KAS education without conceding to pupils the immense powers they had at Summerhill. In a letter to council, the pupils' council put forward several recommendations of a radical nature, including reducing the size of the school by a third, achieving a wider cross-section of society in the school by a sliding scale of fees to help poorer families, allowing all subject classes, except in English and mathematics, to be optional at all levels and to permit pupil observers on council. However, by the mid-1970s, the heady days of the movement for increased representation were passed in KAS as in the nation at large. The battle then was to focus on maintaining the broad representation that already existed, not on expanding it still further.

The passion of the greater democracy debate had evaporated in the cold draught of financial crisis. Escalating inflation and substantial salary awards for teachers among other things created more pressing concerns for the country, and for KAS. Expansion, greater democracy, teacher autonomy and increased student rights rapidly became out-dated concepts with a curiously antiquated 1960s ring about them. The watchwords of the mid-to-late 1970s were accountability, efficiency and value for money, heralding the ideology of the Thatcherite 1980s. James Callaghan, who replaced Wilson as Labour prime minister in March 1976, lost no time in saying what he believed this meant for teachers, teacher trainers and for state schools. In the coded language of his speech at Ruskin College, he expressed a series of concerns, about low standards of numeracy, science teaching, the lack of able students, especially girls entering industry, and informal teaching methods, though in the case of the latter he was anxious to emphasize that this was not 'a clarion call to black paper prejudices'.[47] Behind his speech were the twin themes of accountability (teachers 'must satisfy parents and industry'), and the more efficient management of existing resources, particularly through the overhaul of the government and management of schools. He called upon his Education Secretary, Shirley Williams, to launch 'the great debate' into the curriculum and allied matters through a series of regional conferences, a move which has been interpreted by some historians[48] as a thin smokescreen to cover a bid by a small group of politicians and civil servants to assert their control over the curriculum and the education system while giving the impression of open government and debate. The constitutional reforms advocated by a small but powerful group within council were seen by other council members in a similar light.

The issues of efficiency, accountability and perceived threats to open government came to dominate council politics in the late 1970s and early 1980s. While the national debate inaugurated by Shirley Williams proved to be something of a damp squib, that within council led to intensely factionalized politics and ultimately to the resignation of the headmistress in l983 and to the request by her successor, Francis Moran, that council set up a working party to consider what went wrong. On its past track record, council by 1979 was long overdue for a period of heightened political tension. That it began around that time and was so protracted was the result of the confluence of several factors: a shift in the national political climate away from increased representation to greater efficiency through placing decision-making in fewer hands; a desire to make KAS more attractive in an age of adverse demographic trends and economic recession; the arrival of a group of newcomers to council who were anxious to preserve its tradition of open government; the strong individualism of many council members and the presence on council of a headmistress whose firmness of resolve would not allow her to stand aloof from the political arena when the future of the school was at stake. These factors combined to provide an extended period of political faction and controversy worthy of a Tudor court or parliament. That the apparently innocuous request by the headmistress that the school should be inspected for the first time in thirty years unleashed forces which led to the tragedy of her resignation, was an irony of Shakespearian proportions.

The origins of the conciliar crisis can be traced to the year following the short-lived and unspectacular 'great debate' when council, caught up in the new national mood of efficiency and accountability, agreed in February 1978 to Nikki Archer's suggestion that the school should be inspected 'to give the opportunity to remedy anything we are doing incorrectly'. She thus hoped to leave the school in a good position when she retired in 1985. Recurrent economic crises in the 1970s and downward demographic trends made it essential for the school to maintain if not increase its population through increased attractiveness. The subsequent report, not as in the past by DES inspectors but by School and Charity Consultants Ltd. of Canterbury, was no more, and probably less, critical than those of earlier decades. Had it not been for its timing and council's handling of it, it would probably have gone the way of earlier reports: limited discussion in council, contents noted, pledges made for future action, followed by particular and piecemeal implementation as finances permitted, and finally relegation to the school archives for the curiosity of future historians.

In essence, the 'Survey of the Organisation, Work and Buildings of KAS' delivered to council in May 1979 by the Canterbury consultants was not unduly critical, possibly because it was undertaken by a body of inspectors more favourable to the school's aims and objectives than were the school inspectors of early decades. What it said about shortcomings in the teaching of English grammar, mathematics and science had all been said before, and the positive aspects, especially the quality of the lower school and French teaching, were more pronounced than in the 1948 inspectors' report. Above all, it recognized that the school had kept faith with the founders' educational philosophy. However, by coincidence the report was presented to council in the run-up to the general election of May 1979 which saw the return of the Conservatives to power under Mrs Thatcher and during which the Conservatives vied with Labour to assert the importance of the effective teaching of science and the basics. Callaghan handed on the torch of educational orthodoxy to Margaret Thatcher, marking an end to the progressive era in state education and asserting the importance of traditional discipline and a core curriculum in those precise areas which the consultants had found wanting. Though the preliminary references in council to the report made no mention of the consultant's comments on the teaching of the basics and on school discipline, the fact that members were invited to scrutinize it to put points to the consultants meant that these areas could not be ignored. John Izbicki, council member and education editor for the *Daily Telegraph*, raised the matters of school discipline and the comments on the standards of English when the consultants attended the September meeting of council. The modest progress of pupils in mathematics and science was also reviewed, though the head was unwilling to discuss the former 'at present' and the latter was said to be the result of a misunderstanding of the work by the inspectors and the difficulties of finding physics graduates to teach physics. The inspectors pointed out that they were reporting 'on a good school which could be even better' with 'a firmer structure',[49] which was a fair assessment of their conclusions, though the prevailing national concern for improving standards in the basics gave a heightened awareness to their comments on English and mathematics.

It was not just the content of the report which aroused debate. Three years later, in discussions about the reform of council which caused much heated controversy, it was claimed that there was something strange, if not constitutionally improper, about the way in which the confidential survey was not circulated immediately among council members and about the creation of a small working group to consider it.[50] Though the council minutes for the period do not entirely bear out the first claim, they do demonstrate that many members 'were perturbed by some of its conclusions' and some members, especially among the newer recruits, were uneasy about the *ad hoc* working party. In between the September and October meetings of council a working party (not mentioned in the September meeting and therefore probably not sanctioned by council) was set up, which led Phillip Kossoff to question its status and to suggest that it would be preferable to 'make it a Council Sub-Committee': that is to bring it within the terms of the constitution. It appeared to some members that it represented a threat to the collegiate style of decision-making and an unwarranted delegation of council's responsibilities. Kossoff exercised his legal expertise in drafting a resolution for the December meeting to regularize the position of the working party as a subcommittee of council, which was carried by a large majority. Before the meeting had ended, however, the honorary treasurer and member of the working party, Bernard Igra, had handed in his resignation, feeling that conditions were insufficiently congenial to carry on the work. A special meeting of council in January 1980 chaired by Sir William Wood sought to resolve matters relating to the resignation and to the working party. The minutes of council show how deeply opinion was divided on the status of the working party, with the chairman expressing his concern that the resolution had been passed when he, as chair also of the working party, was unable to attend. The working party saw itself not as a subcommittee of council but as 'a small group of people with expertise on education and the day-to-day working of the school',[51] what the former treasurer termed a think-tank 'set up on an informal basis without a rigid constitution' and reporting to council, a group in fact not without precedent. After further discussion the motion passed at the previous meeting was rescinded, but whether feelings of 'underlying suspicion' would now disappear remained to be seen, particularly as the treasurer in withdrawing his resignation repeated his belief in a smaller council which met more frequently.

Whereas the democratic impulse of the 1960s had led to the demand for wider representation and hence a larger council, the emphasis in the late 1970s and early 1980s upon balancing account-ability and efficiency led to a move on the part of some members to reduce its size, an issue which was likely to create passionate debate. KAS was never a school which sought a quiet life above all else. The fact that proposals for constitutional reform emanated from the working party set up initially to consider the consultants' report only served to intensify division, with some arguing that this did not involve 'the usurpation of Council's authority' but others questioning whether the working party, now with a much wider brief, was proper under the constitution. At the very least, according to one member, there was need for a formal policy of delegation.

And so matters rolled on without the matter of the constitutional position of the working party being resolved to everyone's satisfaction. In March 1980 the working party presented its proposals for a smaller council of eleven to replace the existing one of twenty-one, bringing to the fore a clash of ideologies between those who believed it reduced democratic representation and those who argued that it enhanced administrative efficiency, and enabled council to act as 'an effective decision-making body without delegation to committees or subcom-mittees'[52] while improving communications with staff upon which the working party put much store. The latter position was fully endorsed by the headmistress who also believed that 'teamwork between Council and Head' could be much improved through the creation of a smaller council. On the matter of the reduced representation of parents, the working party said that they had considered the idea of keeping council at its present size but delegating executive authority to a smaller man-agement committee. However, as an earlier memorandum had noted, 'many nerve endings are so raw that it is difficult even to ask questions about powers, responsibilities and delegation without apprehension being apparently felt that one is trying to twist someone's tail'.[53] This was as true of the head's area of responsibility as that of council, making it very difficult for members to approach the matter with the 'open mind' which Sir William Wood asked for when proposing the working party which consisted of three officers of the society and three professionals. The slimmed-down council was said by its supporters to lead to improved decision-making and policy formation, co-operation with the head and staff, and responsiveness to the views of parents. Large councils in their view resulted in matters being decided and redecided, with the same issue being chewed over meeting after meeting. Opinion was divided, with some arguing that the proposed reforms would be too drastic, distancing parents even further from the executive, and others arguing that a council of twenty-one was confusing to new members and wasteful of their enthusiasm, and unbusinesslike with time wasted on trivia. Discussion inevitably brought to the fore perceived shortcomings of the existing council, including the allegations that some members of council had been denied adequate information by a smaller inner cabal. The vote at the end of the meeting, with eight members in favour of a reduced council, eight voting for a council of twenty-one operating through a single management committee and no one in favour of streamlining the existing structure with a minimum number of committees and subcommittees, left the working party to consider its proposals further. Constitutional reform was not going to be easily achieved, if ever. So far the debate had generated more heat than it had light.

The series of special council meetings continued into the summer of 1980, with that of July reiterating the working party's support for a smaller council and its lack of support for the alternative, which had in fact gained equal support in council a few months earlier. Debate was all the more vigorous because of the working party's unanimity. Doubters were still concerned about the responsiveness of a smaller council; the working party and its supporters extolled the virtues of a smaller, more businesslike council with close links with the parent–staff committee in particular. The vote at the end of the July meeting showed more agreement, with ten in favour of a council of eleven, six in favour of numbers ranging from thirteen to fifteen, one in favour of twelve and one in favour of twenty-one. It seemed that the matter of principle had been won and the question was now one of degree, a matter which was again referred to the working party. Consistent with past practice, the working party stuck to its guns at the September meeting of council, supporting its previous proposal for an eleven-person council, and continuing with its work of consulting interested parties, including the staff. But the matter was far from over. The constitutional changes had to be placed before an extraordinary meeting of the society; a resolution to that effect was passed by a very narrow majority of two with one abstention early in 1981, indicating that some who had supported the changes the previous year were now reconsidering their position – a point used by proponents of the smaller council to support their argument for a more effective decision-making body! However, the narrowness of the majority led the chairman of council, Jack Black, to leave the matter open for further consideration, ruling out the immediate opportunity of placing the matter before an extraordinary general meeting of the society when the previous resolution so to do was rescinded by an overwhelming majority.

The attempts to 'reconcile democracy with efficiency' continued apace with the idea of a council of twenty-one gaining a little ground, though still strongly opposed, partly on the grounds that 'democracy could be its own worst enemy – there could be too much talk'.[54] However, on a vote of ten in favour, eight against and two absentions council admitted that there was insufficient support to justify the reduction in size, and agreed to invite written expositions of the various cases for a special council meeting in June. At the June meeting the deadlock appeared even greater with an equal number voting for and against the working party's small executive proposals, and for and against taking the matter to an extraordinary meeting of the society, although the rules allowed any fifteen individuals to put the matter on the AGM agenda. The staff representatives who were without voting rights had good reason to be disappointed with progress for they had given their full support to the idea of a smaller executive, sharing the general view of the working party that such a body would produce 'quicker and more effective decisions',[55] be able to deal more directly with detailed matters and make council more accountable through the system of annual elections, even though the staff would lose its representation. It was not until April 1982 that the matter of constitutional reform came before an extraordinary general meeting of the society.

Such root-and-branch reform was not without its critics, who gathered their views to put before the meeting. Ten members of council opposed constitutional reform on various grounds, not least of which was the belief that it did nothing to tackle the real causes of any malfunctioning of council, which were that council was not being conducted according to accepted committee rules and its committees, especially the finance committee, were making policy decisions appropriate to council. Council members were said by the opponents of the scheme not to have been given the essential information necessary for them to play their full part in the decision-making process. Reduced representation and a shift towards oligarchy were in their view not the best way forward. It could lead to parents with children at KAS actually being in a minority on the executive, and to a narrower range of skills, expertise and educational beliefs upon which council could draw. Such a position was at odds with the moves in the state sector to increase parental power and to widen the range of expertise at a school's disposal. The strength of the case put forward by the opponents of the new constitutional framework lay in their line by line consideration of the proposals as well as in the broad objections on grounds of principle. In their opinion, 'new parents' would be prevented from standing for election; dissent on council could be suppressed, proxy voting could make the chairman or any other member overpowerful; a life presidency in place of annual election could possibly lead to abuses of the position; teacher representation could be weakened rather than enhanced and the parent–staff committee would be subject to the patronage of council. A small council without subcommittees would in their view seriously weaken the democratic nature of council and damage the school.

These views were sent by the ten members of council opposing the scheme to each member of the society prior to the emergency general meeting in April 1982 to help ensure that those present would consider all sides of the argument. Those who backed the proposals, though perhaps not engaging so enthusiastically in pamphleteering and lobbying, were willing to modify their views on proxy voting, and on the size of council (allowing the AGM to vary it between eleven and twenty-one) and on other matters. However, it appears from the account of 'an innocent member of the society'[56] that these amendments and the general arguments in favour of the scheme were not clearly and effectively marshalled during the meeting. It seemed to many at the well-packed and acrimonious gathering that it was a matter of choosing between warring personalities rather than arguments and that in the end the threat that if the resolution were not passed there would be several resignations actually tipped the scales against the resolution. With the case for the proposition not apparently being as clearly presented as that against, emotions were given a freer rein. Against the head's advice, the chairman and several leading council members relied upon their authority rather than published statements to win the day. Had those who proposed the changes broken down their resolution into its constituent parts, then perhaps the essence of their case, a reduction in the size of council and the elimination of subcommittees in conjunction with the formalized strengthening of the parent–staff committee, would have secured a majority. However, the resolution was defeated, leaving many with the view that the intensity of feeling, fractiousness and factiousness were inappropriate in the governing body of school dedicated to rational principles and were 'a canker which must be removed from the body educational'. A general meeting should not have been expected 'to fight the battles of the individual council officers and members'. Council's decision to allow the minutes of the extraordinary general meeting to consist only of a formal record of the resolution, the names of the speakers for and against and the result denies the opportunity to historians of ascertaining whether such statements accurately reflect what took place. However, those whose resolution was defeated were anxious that the vote should be seen as one against a particular resolution and not one 'in favour of any alternative set of proposals'. The existing system of a council of twenty-one with teacher representatives and subcommittees thus remained in force, at least for the time being. For some this constitutional arrangement offered opportunities for broad representation and wide expertise. In the view of at least one member of council it still left in existence 'an oversize body of interfering parent-governors' intent on turning 'the place into some form of cooperative'.[57] If such were the situation then the controversy which had begun over the handling of the consultants' report and which had merged into proposals for constitutional reform, would possibly refocus on the position and power of the headmistress, Nikki Archer, whom a report for the *Times Educational Supplement*[58] recognized as having a great deal of power and few qualms about using it when necessary, and who would resist any attempt to reduce the powers of headship. She would not hesitate to provide a lead when council was too divided to do so. The dinner tables of Hampstead and Highgate awaited further developments with eager anticipation.

In 1983 that same unnamed reporter contrasted the settled calm of KAS with the turbulent early struggles of other independent schools without apparently realizing that the school had just been through a controversy over the headship no less bitter and divisive than that of its early years and those of other schools. The controversy in 1900 and 1901 involving the school's first headmaster, Charles Rice, was echoed in the years 1981 to 1983 in that surrounding the school's first, solo headmistress, Nikki Archer. Both resigned, the latter as the longest serving head of a recognized progressive school.

A head who could be tough-minded when she believed that the interests of the school were at stake and a fractious council were a heady mixture, as earlier history had shown. Despite resignations and the efforts of conciliators, council seemed to lurch from crisis to crisis in the years 1979 to 1983, while making protestations about the adverse effects on the school of bad publicity! At a time of inflation and adverse demo-graphical trends, the school could well have done without the negative image generated by a council in constant crisis. Burying past differences was not an easy process but should have been achieved sooner rather than later in the true interests of the school. The buck should have stopped with council there and then. Unfortunately council had one further painful process to undergo before any semblance of unity could be achieved – an early parting with the headmistress. This was not unavoidable, for Mrs Archer was close to retirement in any case, but in a situation in which acrimony flourished, in which school rolls were declining and good teachers were leaving, it seemed a likely step.

Constitutionally and historically heads at KAS were generally in a more vulnerable position than in most independent progressive schools. Clashes, however, were less likely when joint headships existed, giving the heads a stronger position on council as in the years 1933 to 1945 and 1962 to 1970, or when a single head such as Montgomery followed the advice of a largely united council. When council was in a prolonged state of bickering and division, thus unable to offer the kind of consistent guidance that a head and school had the right to expect, and the head was of a much more dominant personality than Montgomery, more of a leader making decisions than a simple facilitator, then the relationships between the head and council (or to be more accurate, some sections of council) were likely to be tense. That they became tense to the point of council agreeing a package for Mrs Archer's early retirement is not in dispute, but the reasons for the deterioration in relationships remain unclear. Even the working party set up by council to meet the request of her successor, Francis Moran, for an explanation of 'what went wrong' produced neither minutes of its meetings nor an agreed report and was disbanded by council rather than revive acrimony. The strength of the feelings generated by her early departure was evident from a letter sent by the staff to council which asked 'We appeal to you to let Mrs Archer retire with dignity, support her as Head of School until the end of term and not completely ignore her and recognise her as Head.'[59] The politics of school government were, indeed, a passionate business. Whether this was partly a reflection of Conservative reforms in the state sector, which were giving school governing bodies increased powers and which as a consequence were limiting the traditional power of heads, is not clear but it is certainly instructive to consider the breakdown in the relationships between the head and certain sections of council at the dawn of parent and governing-body power in the state schools.

The paucity of official records dealing with the dispute and the partisan nature of the few that have survived make it difficult to arrive at many, or indeed any, definite conclusions but they do point to some of the sources of misunderstanding and the lack of mutual trust between the head and some sections of council. A large part of the difficulty was seen by some of the working party to lie in the way in which council worked. To some, including newer members, council meetings appeared to be run rather differently from what they expected, with an alleged air of secrecy and a perceived lack of normal meeting procedures, such as the placing of resolutions upon which council could vote. The apparent deviations from the norm were also seen to include the lack of an effective subcommittee framework. The net result of these perceived shortcomings was said to be the denial to council of full information, of full consultation and of a full role in decision-making, leaving a small group, including the headmistress, in an overpowerful position.

Not surprisingly these views did not go unchallenged, especially by those who saw government by consensus rather than by votes and resolutions as a more normal part of committee procedure (and who regarded constant resort to the latter as symptomatic of division and disharmony) and who were less wedded to a set and constant system of committees or subcommittees. To such members, a more flexible system of subcommittees, including those of an *ad hoc* nature, such as that set up to consider the consultant's report and constitutional change, was preferable. Only a finance committee merited permanence; others should remain in existence only so long as they served a useful purpose. The headmistress inclined to the latter opinion on the matter of committee procedure and subcommittee arrangements, arguing that eclecticism and 'ad hockery' were entirely consistent with consensus perspective. In the fraught atmosphere of council meetings those who opposed these views did so on the ground that they gave undue power to a small group. The defeat at the emergency general meeting of the working party's proposals for constitutional change (to which the head gave full and open backing) was seen by them, rightly or wrongly, as a rebuff for government by cabal and a victory for open government. Hence the comment by one member present at that highly emotional meeting that those present were being expected to choose between warring personalities rather than between constitutional frameworks. The way forward after the meeting in April 1982 was likely to be fraught with difficulty unless several members stepped back from the confrontational positions they had adopted.

Intransigence would only prolong divisions at the very time when council needed to improve its public image to help overcome the inflationary and demographic pressures which were affecting the school. Counter-measures to the poor public image, always a matter of concern to the head, and declining school rolls were urgently required. Strategies to cope with the effects of inflation on school fees required immediate consideration. Continued soured relationships could only harm the school. Much thus rested on the response of council in general and the head in particular. Council had to work better and the head had to play a major role in its discussions if speedy, effective action was to be taken to halt the school's decline.

However, divisions ran too deep for an early end to the disagreements. Some of the members of the working party on 'What went wrong' believed that the head's co-operation was far from wholehearted but judging from the reaction of certain sections of council to the style and content of an advertisement to boost the recruitment of pupils, there was still a tendency to niggle. The mutual re-establishing of trust was still a long way off. The proposal to create an education policy committee and a publicity committee, certainly well within the constitutional powers of council, needed perhaps more careful discussion with the head than council had the time and possibly the inclination for. To at least one observer, the education policy committee acted more like a star chamber. Whether the head would fully endorse such changes was doubtful, especially after the urgent matter of producing a prospectus for publicity purposes was taken out of her hands. Thereafter the events leading to her early retirement from the position of head to take up that of educational consultant took a rather 'painful and laborious course', with her ex-gratia payment and the school's contribution to the purchase of the house for the new head adding to the financial burdens of the society. She could have stayed to fight by appealing to the parent body as a whole, as some encouraged her to do, but as she says, 'She chose to resign to preserve the stability of the school.'

The 1980 Education Act had given statutory recognition to the right of parents in the state sector to choose a school for their children and to be involved in its management. KASS had been founded on these principles and had practised them for nearly a century, yet in 1983 it seemed poorly suited to offer itself as model to the state sector although the head wrote to John Silkin and to Shirley Williams to point out the relevance of the experience of KAS.[60] Council had not fully worked out its relationship with its teachers or its head as later attempts to clarify such matters were to show. Yet though no unanimous report emerged from the working party on the breakdown in relationships between council and the head, there was a general realization, as in 1901, that, having looked over the abyss, with closure more than a remote possibility, systems on their own, whether old or new, would not work unless there was trust, goodwill, openness and close consultation at formal and informal levels. This was one of the principal reasons, but not the only one, why the headship of Nikki Archer, like that of Charles Rice, was followed by a long period of relative political calm, representing something of a golden era in the school's history, despite the pressures of the First World War in the case of Rice's successor, John Russell, and those of the national curriculum in the case of Mrs Archer's successor.

To any KAS sixth-form pupil faced with the bland kind of examination question posed in the title to the section, the 1960s, 1970s and early 1980s, with their passionate debates over representative government, offered exciting illustrative material for discussion. To Nikki Archer's successor, Francis Moran, the lesson was clear.

> Rows of one sort or another, seem very much a pattern of the history of K.A.S. I have no intention of provoking one . . . I see my job as protecting, maintaining the school, whatever blood letting may be going on in the Society . . . I set my own personal sights on retiring . . . in the year of what will be the school's centenary; I intend to achieve that.[61]

Had members of council consulted the minutes which record earlier conflicts and crises they would perhaps have been more aware of the factors which caused such damaging downward spirals. Perhaps one of the key elements in their future training ought to be an opportunity to study these documents, although the decision not to record in full the events of the emergency general meeting of April 1982 would handicap their full understanding.

Building for the future

Several members of the 1983 review group on the relations between council and the head were critical of the way in which, they believed, a small group in council, together with the head, had come to direct the school's expansion since 1968. Nevertheless, they recognized the extent of this impressive achievement: 'doubling its size, increasing its curriculum and improving its academic standards'.[62] The part which the head played in upholding KAS ideology and in helping to provide the material and curricular scaffolding for expansion was described in the national and local press between 1981 and 1983.[63] However, both the more guarded tribute by some of the review group and the fuller recognition in the press failed to emphasize the importance of developments in earlier years, and the parts played by a great number of people on council and elsewhere in the years prior to and after the opening of the arts and science block in 1968. Nevertheless, it should be recognized that the optimism and high demand for school places in the 1960s made it easier to contemplate expansion. The economic difficulties of the 1970s followed by the economic recession and the falling birthrate of the early 1980s (which was predicted to drop by 40 per cent in Inner London by the following decade) made planning more difficult and less certain. It is indeed a tribute to parents, council, head and staff that major projects continued to be planned and implemented when the times were far from favourable.

One of the key problems facing council and the heads in the 1960s was how to provide the facilities which the new educational ideologies and growing school population demanded without destroying the school grounds and environment which played such an important part in a KAS education. This was not a new problem but one which was becoming more acute. The first year of the joint headship of Nicki Paul Jones and Alan Humphries witnessed a gradual increase in the school population from 290 to 298. By 1966 numbers had risen to 313. Even during these years of modest increases the heads were pressing for a building programme in addition to the smaller improvements that had been made during their first year, including new paths and driveway, the filling in of the covered court, a new staffroom, the creation of a sixth-form study room and an enlarged library. The vacating by the heads of the two rooms at the rear of the stage helped to meet accommodation needs. Even in 1964 when the school population stood at a relatively modest number of 292 (154 boys and 138 girls), they argued strongly in favour of a building plan costing £51,000. At its last meeting of that year council gave unanimous support to Mr Elton's proposal that the

132. Building for their future (photograph Adam Kossoff)

full building programme be embarked upon, involving an increase in fees and a high-profile appeals campaign, which was already operating at a modest level. By February 1965 the appeal fund stood at nearly half of the total required, when council agreed to retain the services of Mr Harvey, who was shortly to be replaced by Jack Dribbon, as full-time professional fund-raiser. However, even with more applicants than school places and half of the total amount for the project already resting in the appeal coffers, council had to decide on priorities. Pride of place was given to a new nursery classroom costing £6,000 with a sixty-year lifespan and erected during the summer of that year to double the nursery intake. The main aim of this was to avoid an intake of pupils around the age of eleven or twelve, which gave rise to educational problems when pupils were not familiar with the KAS style of teaching and learning. This was followed by a single-storey double classroom five years later to assist the expansion of the lower school.

In 1965 a new factor came to play an important part in planning. That was the brave decision taken by council and the heads against substantial parental opposition to change to Nuffield science, which required new well-equipped laboratories at a time when little was known nationally about its accommodation requirements. The delays to and the adjustment of the building programme necessitated by the switch to Nuffield science caused further frustration among parents, especially when events such as recitals by John Williams, the classical guitarist, Mrs Easton, the eminent soprano, and later Julie Felix seemed to add substantially to the appeal fund. There was some resistance also from pupils who argued that a better heating system for the library and classrooms ought to have been given first priority. As a result, council found funds to renew the central-heating plant and replace the ageing night storage heaters. (However, the abiding memory of many pupils is that of cold classrooms and sitting on radiators!) Matters were not helped by the fact that the cost of the new arts and science buildings had increased to £64,000 and government credit restrictions made it all but impossible for council to raise a loan. Only voluntary covenants, personal influence in the banking world and consideration of whether part of the scheme for the arts and science building designed by Mr Lush could be built, enabled the plan to stay afloat until building got under way in June 1967 with the necessary but unfortunate tree felling. The new building was officially opened on 30 January the following year, one of the few projects to start and finish on time at the set cost. It was not until 1976 that the debt incurred by its construction was paid off, and this despite the extra expenditure of repairing damage to twenty class-rooms caused by the great summer flood of 1975. Its construction

133. The new science and art building, built in 1967

134. Cricket, 1970s style: Toby Wynn and Pedros Santos

freed much needed additional accommodation. The old physics and chemistry laboratories were converted to a staff common room and one end was partitioned off for main offices for the administrative staff, Mrs Bassett and Mrs Whitehead. The old craft room now relocated in the new building became the music department, while the old art room was converted into a sixth-form common room. The work of Mr Morgan, who had taken over the chairmanship of the appeals committee, and the appeals committee itself had borne much fruit. Not everyone appreciated the new building. It was referred to later by one former pupil as the 'dreadful new art and science block built in the late 60s! Awful! Couldn't see out, couldn't see the teachers, without straining your neck.' Such a view, however, was rather exceptional.

One of the perennial problems facing Cecil Lush and the building committee was Squirrel Hall which was rapidly approaching its half-century. Its poor condition, especially its roof, raised the question in 1969 of whether this last architectural link with the move from Ellerdale Road to Manor Wood should be demolished. It was described by one former student as 'atmospheric but unsafe'. There was a strong feeling against its demolition and true to the original spirit of its creation, staff, pupils and especially parents set about repairing it on weekends during the summer months. By the beginning of October 1974 it was largely watertight but it took a further three years of part-time work to renew its seating. Such timely measures ensured that it remained as the only visible symbol of the early school at the time of the school's centenary. Whether it will survive to see the centenary of the move to Manor Wood in 1919 remains to be seen.

It was not, however, by preserving the symbols of its past that KAS would survive into the twenty-first century. It had to acquire the facilities which parents and pupils had come to expect of modern independent

schools. The mere addition of more classrooms, such as the single- and double-
storeyed classrooms erected in 1970–1, was
insufficient. KAS could only remain
attractive, Nikki Archer told council in
1976,[64] if it had modern sports facilities.
Thus at a time when the school entered a
very difficult period in its history, with high
inflation, increases in teachers' salaries of 30
per cent and significant rises in interest
payments on loans for the construction of
the science and art block, council was under

135. Rebuilding Squirrel
Hall, 1973

pressure to develop those facilities which historically were the most
neglected. It had the advantage of the fees of a vastly increased pupil
population which had risen from 292 in 1963, to 356 in 1968 and 429
(203 girls and 226 boys) in September 1974, a dozen short of what was
regarded then as its optimum size. Through careful budget controls and
increased fees the school was able to move from a balanced budget in
1974 to a modest surplus in 1976. By 1976 the school recorded a
surplus of over £1,200 which trebled by 1979 before falling back to
£1,941 in 1980. Such sums, however, did not enable KAS to finance
major building projects out of fees even in relatively prosperous times,
and sports facilities were particularly costly. In February 1976 council
considered a proposal by the building committee for a gymnasium,
including a badminton court, and a 16- or 20-metre heated indoor
swimming pool with changing and lavatory accommodation.

This scheme was the first major project for nearly a decade but its
launch came at a very difficult time, leaving the choice at best between
the gymnasium costing between £40,000 and £50,000 and a swimming
pool at £70,000 with heavy annual running
costs. The treasurer, Mr Igra, could
certainly not recommend the total
expenditure of over £150,000 out of school
funds. Of the two, the staff backed the idea
of a swimming pool because it would be
used by all sections of the school, but even
scaling down expenditure for a cheaper
enclosure which would be satisfactory in
appearance still left the project well out of
financial reach. It was a scheme which the
treasurer recommended be dropped for the
time being. The idea of a gymnasium thus

136. The new
gymnasium, 1981:
Geoffrey Hautman,
left, and Richard
Essex, right

137. The Green building and common room just before demolition in 1987

became more attractive, especially as it was believed that physical education teachers were leaving because they felt that the school lacked commitment to their subject area. The gymnasium project was thus given the green light although some support still remained for a swimming pool. At the end of 1980 the contract for the gymnasium was nearly ready for signing, but by then it cost nearly one quarter of a million pounds, with the money to be raised partly by debentures and covenanted donations and partly from reserves. The scheme was to be paid for by deferred terms; the building was to be ready by Christmas 1981 by which time, in fact, school numbers were in decline. After a full year of use, the head was able to comment on its value to the school, particularly in realigning the cornerstone of KAS ideology, 'the ability to concentrate our energies more fully upon each individual'.[65] It also served to enhance relationships between staff and students with staff and sixth-formers making a determined effort to get fit, and between the staff of the various sections of the school with badminton, volleyball and table-tennis matches. Council had thus taken a major step forward in raising the status of sport throughout the school.

Blow winds blow, but the ship sails on

The two decades (or so) which mark out the joint headship of Nikki Archer and Alan Humphries and the sole headship of the former stand out as a unique and interesting period in the history of KAS. At no other time was the school so deeply influenced by the social, educational, economic and political forces of the age. For KAS, a day school in the capital, there was no hiding place. Nor did it wish to seek a quiet solitude, some kind of quiet haven, having deliberately turned its back on the kind of tranquillity and detachment which rural seclusion, boarding status, remote government and rigid academic selection gave to many independent schools. However, this meant that when the winds of change blew, and blow they did with unprecedented, continual, vigour and speed throughout the period, no less in the early Thatcherite 1980s than in the Wilsonian 1960s, KAS quickly felt the blast.

At times it appeared as if the school had dragged its progressive anchor, as some of the rebellious crew were quick to point out. The reaction of the heads to the social changes, emanating from Carnaby Street and elsewhere, seemed unduly repressive to some of the ratings, the pupils, and even to some of the officers. The educational changes inspired by the Schools Council based in Great Portland Street seemed to highlight the weaknesses, particularly in the sciences, rather than the strengths of KAS. Yet attempts to align the schools with these curricular changes, especially in Nuffield science, brought the complaint from some of those who had bought passages for their offspring, that the school was sacrificing its progressive ethos. The Hertslet debate of the mid-1960s, reminiscent of the Neill–Russell controversy of 1918, involved the passionately argued case by some parents that the school was drifting towards the rocks of formalism and thus in danger of having the keel ripped out of the progressive ship.

Then there were the effects of inflation and recession which, it was claimed, would raise the price of a progressive passage well beyond the reach of those who would most likely be the most dedicated and involved of

138. The Green building just before demolition in 1987

the ship's complement. In addition, the cost of constant refits and of the improvement of facilities seemed at times to overwhelm the venture. But the officers kept their nerve and trimmed their financial sails to keep afloat. They were sometimes inclined to mutiny, as when some felt they were being left in the officers' mess while a few on the bridge were believed to be intent on getting their hands on the ship's wheel. Again, as in most clashes which the strong winds of ideological change brought, there were some who defended the old-style progressivism, with its emphasis upon broad representation and consultation and those who, influenced by the more right-wing Thatcherite progressivism, emphasized slimmed-down executives and more efficient decision-making.

But the ship sailed on, sometimes under a flag which was less progressive than its founders would have recognized. The essentials were still there, mixed ratings, who were allowed a large measure of freedom, ownership still in the hands of a parental co-operative, no bible readings by the appointed captain, and a powerful officer class, replenished at regular intervals. Though KAS was still the only ship belonging to the society line nevertheless it had, through its considerable refits in the sixties and seventies, increased its tonnage. The ratings for whose benefit it continued its journey through calm weather and tempest had increased from 298 in 1962 to 410 in 1983, when a newly appointed captain mounted the bridge, after a drop to 380 in 1982. The longest serving captain retired, having helped to plot the ship's passage with a certain panache through this turbulent period. It was a retirement which left an indelible impression on at least one crew member. 'I can remember Nikki's farewell callover. She danced high kicks up the catwalk to the stage, dressed in fishnets and a leotard. I remember thinking she was amazing to do this', recalls one of her grateful students who valued the freedom and happiness which she experienced under Mrs Archer's headship.

Notes and references

1. See the section on the lower school and the standards debate.
2. Many of the replies to the questionnaire on his headship emphasize his low-profile approach and his difficulty in dealing with parents which is traced to an inherent shyness.
3. A. Crosland, *The Future of Socialism* (London, Jonathan Cape, 1956), 212.
4. See B. Simon, *Education and the Social Order 1940–1990* (London, Lawrence & Wishart, 1991), 439 and R. Brooks, *Contemporary Issues in Education: An Historical Perspective* (London, Longman, 1991), 127–34. Of the 154 direct grant schools, only 51 (mainly Roman Catholic schools) elected to join the state sector.
5. Council minutes, 5 December 1968.
6   Annual Report, 1966, 5.
7. Alan Humphries contemplated writing a book on the harm done to education by A. S. Neill.
8. Annual Report, 1975, 8.
9. See the following section on the lower school and the standards debate for a fuller discussion.
10. Annual Report, 1969, 8.
11. Ibid.
12. Council minutes, 8 July 1964: 'There was a feeling that they (the parents) were too permissive.'
13. Ibid.
14. Council minutes, 5 December 1968.
15. Council minutes, 10 December 1991.
16. See J. R. Brooks, 'Lord Eustace Percy and the abolition of the compulsory elementary curriculum in 1926', *Contemporary Record*, 7

(1993), 86–102.

17. Jennifer Armitage in a reply to the Montgomery questionnaire, January 1995.

18. Council minutes, 7 May 1963.

19. Council minutes, 24 January 1966.

20. Statement by the heads on the future of the school, April 1966, 3.

21. At a meeting on 27 June 1966.

22. See the later sections of this chapter on the lower school and political developments.

23. See the following section.

24. Parents' memorandum, 3.

25. 1977 *Black Paper*, 21–2.

26. Council minutes, 12 March 1963.

27. Ibid.

28. Council minutes, 9 May 1966.

29. *Black Paper, Fight for Education*, 44.

30. 1977 *Black Paper*, 25.

31. *Black Paper*, 2 (1969), 2.

32. Council minutes, 21 June 1983.

33. Council minutes, 9 April 1981.

34. 1964 curriculum policy statement, 2.

35. Annual Report, 1976, 3.

36. Council minutes, 18 September 1979.

37. Quoted in 'The Open University – William Tyndale File', Course E200, sections 12–15, 1981.

38. The Constitution of the King Alfred School Society, October 1966, 1.

39. Letter to the author from Nikki Archer, 15 December 1995.

40. Special Council Meeting minutes, 5 July 1966.

41. Council minutes, 20 May 1969.

42. Ibid.

43. *TES*, 1 July 1985.

44. Council minutes, 6 June 1969.

45. Council minutes, 12 October 1976.

46. Annual Report, 1973, 5.

47. Ruskin College Speech, 5.

48. For example B. Simon, *Education and the Social Order 1940–1990* (London, Lawrence & Wishart, 1991), 45.

49. Council minutes, 8 May 1979.

50. In a document entitled 'Background to the present dispute for the extraordinary general meeting', April 1982.

51. Council minutes, 8 January 1980.

52. Council minutes, 18 March, 1980.

53. 'Suggestions for making council work better', 6 October 1981.
54. Council minutes, 31 March 1981.
55. Letter to the chairman of council, 5 February 1981.
56. Letter to Sir William Wood, 1 May 1982.
57. John Izbicki, *Daily Telegraph*, 29 October 1984.
58. 'Daring to be Different', *TES*, 1 July 1983.
59. Council minutes, 10 May 1983.
60. Nikki Archer also sent a deposition to the Taylor Committee pointing to the value of the KASS model. The school had behind it eighty-five years of 'experience of parent management over which time the parameters of partnership and collaboration, especially the definition of the acceptable limits to the collaboration of parents' (letter to author, 15 December 1995), had been worked out.
61. Annual Report, 1983, 4.
62. Memorandum by Xenia Bowlby, 15 September 1983. The doubling of size was an exaggeration.
63. *Daily Telegraph*, 25 May 1981; *TES*, 1 July 1983; *Hampstead and Highgate Express*, 25 March 1983.
64. Council minutes, 17 February 1976.
65. Annual Report, 1983, 13.

Chapter 7

Etonian Progressive in the Era of the New Right:

The Headship of Francis Moran

The headteacher who led the school for most of the last two decades of the twentieth century, Francis Moran, shared much in common with the celebrated John Russell, who was its head for the first two decades of the century after the crisis of 1901. At first sight neither was an obvious choice for the headship of a progressive school. Both came to KAS from the kind of traditional independent school which the society had been created to counter, single-sex schools whose curricula seemed domin-ated by the narrow goal of academic success; yet both were appointed unanimously by council when there were other candidates available of proven progressive pedigree. In the case of Moran, the other two short-listed applicants were from Bedales and Dartington Hall, both well-known independent progressive schools.

Was it that council was suffering moment-arily from some kind of severe mental aberration brought on by the deep bouts of extreme political division which gravely up-set its judgement or can the explanation for their unusual choice in both cases be found elsewhere? Certainly, Russell, who rejected his theological background to engage in the secular progressive movements of late nineteenth-century and early twentieth-century London with Ramsay MacDonald, the future Labour prime minister and others, was the kind of person who seemed peculiarly suited to lead the rationalist educational cause in Hampstead. After all the bourgeois rebel cleric fitted as easily into the drawing rooms of Hampstead with his literary and musical tastes as he did into its school for gilded youth. But what of Moran, whose first appearance as head caused something of a stir among students not only because he failed to fit the preconceived

139. Francis Moran, head from 1983

picture of an Etonian beak but also because he contrasted with the elegantly dressed Nikki Archer? One of his former students recalled his arrival: 'I remember Nikki Archer as a formally dressed lady, whereas Francis Moran arrived wearing Jesus sandals, thick glasses and a beard (appearing to be a seventies hippy throwback).'[1] Though this description is exaggerated, especially in terms of the new head's footwear, it does reveal contrasting perceptions of the out-going and in-coming heads.

He also appeared very different from the tweed-suited, bewigged Russell, but despite these differences in appearance and the sixty years which separated their headships they had much in common. Both came to KAS from Cambridge by circuitous and unexpected routes. Both experienced disillusionment after working initially in less privileged sectors of education, Russell in Islington and Moran in Dagenham, Buckinghamshire and Norfolk. Both found their progressive feet in or near the Bloomsbury area of London, Russell in the university settlement movement working with Philip Wicksteed, Mary Ward and others, Moran at the University of London's Institute of Education, with Jimmy Britton,[2] Nancy Martin (who suggested he apply for the Eton post), Harold Rosen and their progressive coterie. Both came to KAS with strong literary backgrounds, having taught in traditional public schools, Russell at University College School soon to move near to Manor Wood, Moran at Eton which had once owned the Manor Wood estate.

What is crucial to an understanding of why each was appointed is the fact that both were regarded as mavericks within the traditional educational establishments in which they had worked. A decade after Moran's appointment the chair of council, Kara Conti, underlined this point in the society's annual report:

> Ten years ago the school was in a bit of a mess. We considered a Head of English from Eton . . . of all places. The colleagues and friends who recommended him to us all described him as 'not a true Eton and establishment man'. One called him 'an acceptable rebel' – (thank God! we thought) and please Francis feel free to be unacceptably rebellious on the odd occasion.[3]

Like a latter-day Russell, 'the social democrat, Guardian reader'[4] had ploughed unconventional furrows in traditional fields. In particular, the arch-heretic 'successfully dealt with the entrenched Eton classics establishment and . . . finally got the English Department recognised as a major academic department'. However, his achievement was not simply that of rescuing English from the hands of the classicists whose relatively weak examination record demanded a change. It also lay in the direction in which English teaching at Eton went after he became head of its English department in 1977. To have replaced poor traditional English teaching by classicists with good traditional English teaching by graduates of English would scarcely have revolutionized its position, which was his ultimate goal. In his bid to modernize the study of English at Eton he had three advantages when he joined a small group of radicals in 1967: the climate of the 1960s which encouraged curricular experimentation; Eton's name and prestige which enabled him to drive a coach and horses through the ordinary and advanced level regulations of the Oxford and Cambridge Examination Board; and the trust of the headmaster. The English department was able to set its own GCE syllabuses (often, Moran claims, never officially submitted to the board for approval) and to experiment in their teaching, sometimes excluding poetry in favour of the kinds of literature which they believed would interest their pupils, including Icelandic sagas and European literature in translation. The examination board trusted their respectable and venerable institution and allowed the English department to go its own way, especially with its coursework and new syllabuses. The newly founded English department was well positioned to take advantage of the progressive ethos and favourable climate for experimentation which the Schools Council encouraged.

140. Sue Boulton, deputy head from 1985

Thus, in many ways, Moran had been able to share more fully in the reformist spirit of the age than many of the staff in independent progressive schools. This experience, together with his personal qualities, especially his depth of understanding of how children learn most effectively, led council to select him for the post above the staff choice of the candidate from Dartington Hall.

When he moved to King Alfred School the political pendulum was beginning to swing against progressivism. Just before the Conservative victory in the 1979 election, the ex-Alfredian, Max Beloff, had promised the Conservative party conference that the Tories would curb its worst excesses, beginning by abolishing the Schools Council 'within one week of returning to power'.[5] Though such dire threats were not immediately carried out and some of the policies of the New Right were by no means unacceptable to KAS, nevertheless Beloff's words heralded a decisive shift of power away from the teaching profession and local education authorities to the centre, a process which Labour under Callaghan had already begun. While in July 1983 council appointed a man of the left, the nation had just made a further lurch to the right when the Conservatives won the election with an impressive overall majority of 144. The Schools Council had been abolished the previous year and it was clear that the reforms of the Secretary of State for Education and Science, Sir Keith Joseph, were not going to stop there now that the Conservatives were firmly in power under Margaret Thatcher. His successor, Kenneth Baker, though at the DES for a shorter period (May 1986 to July 1989) pressed on with even more ambitious plans for extending control over the curricula of state schools. Changes to examinations at 16+ and the imposition of a national curriculum on the state sector were bound to affect KAS either directly or indirectly.

New era, new head – new thoughts, 1983–1988

In 1898 Professor Findlay urged the King Alfred School Society to avoid state entanglements and to guard jealously the independence of the schools it set up. With the exception of coming to terms with the system of public examinations this it was largely able to do. Certainly the three principal inspections by HMI showed how much out of sympathy official thinking was with KAS ideals and practice and how wise council and the heads were in heeding his advice. Even when the society was particularly financially stretched it turned a deaf ear to the siren voice of governments to compromise its independence in return for state aid. In the 1980s and 1990s, however, isolationism was a position less easy to sustain even if it wished to do so. The educational reforms of the New Right were so numerous and far-reaching that it became increasingly difficult for KAS more than most independent schools to escape the fall-out even before the advent of the national curriculum and GCSE in 1988.

In general, as far as KAS was concerned New Right reforms fell into four categories: those which could possibly affect the relationship between the school and the state, particularly the assisted places scheme and grant-maintained status; those upon which KAS felt it could usefully offer Conservative politicians advice, especially in the extension of parental involvement in the running of schools; reforms from which KAS found it difficult to escape but to which it gave a general welcome, especially the General Certificate of Secondary Education (GCSE); and those whose fall-out was so widespread and educationally polluting that KAS maintained a staunch opposition, particularly the national curriculum. Not that the head expected the school to fare any better under Labour. Death by liquidation through Labour's threat to remove charitable status was, in his view, no better than death by a thousand national attainment targets and tests under the Baker Education Act of 1988.[6]

Two years before Moran's arrival council had taken the decision without fanfare of trumpets not to take part in the assisted places scheme launched by Sir Keith Joseph's predecessor, Mark Carlisle, in the Education Act of 1980. The first of the New Right policies which was said to assist working-class pupils to enter independent schools was such a political hot potato that, without any recorded discussion and before Moran took over the headship, council decided not to participate in the scheme. Moran agreed with this decision, arguing three years after his appointment that funds taken from the state sector would be used mainly to provide places not for those for whom they were officially intended,

141. Maintaining tradition: open-air study in the 1990s. L to R Lily Ridett, Claire Vincent, Natasha Ockrent

working-class children, but for the sons of middle-class parents fallen on hard times or whose 'creative accounting' techniques[7] worked in their favour.[8] Moran's arrival and his declared intention of continuing the Archer–Humphries practice of using the reports to the society's annual general meeting for commenting on 'educational policy and educational possibilities at both a national and parochial level' rather than the 'numerous minutiae of the school year' meant that the response of KAS to national developments was more likely to be openly debated and recorded than had been the case with the assisted places scheme. He lost little time in commenting upon Sir Keith Joseph of whom 'penetrating insight (was) not quite the hallmark' and upon the idea which the Conservatives carried forward from Labour's last education secretary of the 1970s, Shirley Williams, of some kind of common examination system at 16+. He clearly thought more of the reform than he did of its purveyor.

The General Certificate of Secondary Education was generally welcomed by Moran, who said it was a principal means of restoring some of the more progressive methods of teaching and examining which he believed parental pressure (not necessarily from the majority of parents) had caused the school to jettison along with the Certificate of Secondary Education (CSE). He recognized the anomaly of a so-called 'progressive' school with a wide-ability intake being forced to provide most of its courses[9] only to GCE ordinary level designed at most for the top 25 per cent of the ability range. Parents shunned not only the CSE designed for a much broader ability range, but pressed the school to offer GCE 'in its most traditional guise – mode 1: that is a syllabus externally set and externally assessed',[10] when more liberal examination modes were available. In a report to council in October 1985 he compared his experience at KAS with that at Eton:

> I was once sceptical . . . but two years experience has shown me that however non-academic a child may be the typical parent here will still force that child to O level and will discount any pleas by the school that the child who takes a public exam should take one more suited to his ability. In this respect more traditional schools are better placed to protect children from the ambitions of their parents.[11]

A common examination system at 16+ would, he hoped, avoid the problem but, above all, its full value would only be realized if KAS adopted mode 3, where the school set the syllabus and the examination which were moderated by the examination board. He saw coursework used as a part of mode 3 schemes as one of the ways to allow 'high fliers' to fly high while allowing 'low fliers' to get off the ground. Whether or not the New Right would favour the more widespread use of mode 3

142. The coeducational principle: mixed football teams at the International Games in France, 1996; L to R (back row) Sasha Nedeljkovic, Andrew Hadji-Michael, Jonathon Salmon, Heydon Prowse; (middle row) Billy Allen, David Southwood, Nik Engineer, Nicky Menzies, Jonathon Krantz, Alexis Neokleous, Jamie Shamash, Tim Martin, Sam Sugarbread, Martin Lawley; (front row) two French mascots, Buster Turner, Kate Luck-Hille, Rachel Frazer, Jake Panayiotou, Tom Boltman, Samuel Potter, Jake Schaverien, Sam Engineer, Jack Mosse, Josh Sugarbread

and coursework, always viewed by *Black Paper* authors as leading to a lowering of standards, remained to be seen. Even if by some strange chance such progressive practices were given official encouragement KAS would still be left with the anomaly of its sixth form which was geared only to advanced level without a non-academic side which a non-selective school seemed to require.

But would the DES sanction the new examination progressivism? Moran detected mixed messages emanating from the DES with Sir Keith Joseph at one and the same time giving his support to a GCSE which offered all modes of examination and which followed the more enlightened practices of the old system and yet opposing a wide variety of syllabuses in favour of greater uniformity. The Education Secretary had the immense problem of squaring the circle, of persuading the Tory right that the old standards could be preserved in what was essentially a new exam. Little wonder that the criteria-referencing of the grades, upon which the whole of the illusion rested, was delayed and thus teachers, already embittered over matters of pay, were left in confusion up to and into the year when they were expected to teach pupils for the new GCSE examination beginning September 1986. Even the determined efforts made by the new examination boards to equate the top three grades of the new examination with those of the old failed to make up the ground, so KAS, like most schools, felt ill-prepared to introduce the new schemes of study. The government refused to delay its introduction, a refusal which left the examination boards with quiet instructions not to penalize candidates in the first year of the examination for matters which could be put down to inadequate preparation. The great increase in the number of pupils gaining grade C and above, seen by the right as a mark of declining standards, thus came about.

KAS like other schools was able to record in 1988 the beginning of a trend of escalating pass rates, which, in fact, was witness to achievement in a wider range of skills than the limited traditional, well-drilled, essay techniques of ordinary level. As Moran pointed out in his report to KASS in 1988, 'GCSE is more demanding on both students and staff than its predecessor. It is also, by and large, a more appropriate exam for the majority of the age groups concerned.'[12] However, the new examination left KAS with a problem which the more selective independent schools did not feel so acutely. GCSE was a poor preparation for advanced level which had failed to jettison most of its traditional approaches. The mismatch was not so much of a problem to abler students but to schools such as KAS with a wide-ability intake it could make the transition a tremendous hurdle to many students. There was also the problem of GCSE being part of key stage 4 of the national curriculum, whose traditionalism many on the extreme right were intent on strengthening under the Education Act of 1988. KAS could be dragged into the national curriculum if GCSE was at its apex. In 1990 the chairman of council, Ari Zaphiriou-Zarifi, pointed out that no matter how enlightened the examination regime there was an important matter of principle for KAS which stemmed from measuring the school by its examination results. He was 'sometimes frustrated by the degree to which some (parents) don't recognise that some of the more exceptional liberal qualities do occasionally clash with the educational demands that you put on pupils and staff'.[13] Even parents who were liberal in outlook when their children entered the school became more conservative as their offspring progressed up the school so that by the time they were sixteen the main criterion by which many parents judged the school was examination success.

However, though this was a much narrower yardstick than many on council would have wished, it was a fairer measure after the introduction of GCSE than before, in that it accorded better with KAS aims and the nature of the school. The outcome in KAS, as in most schools, was a steady improvement in examination results. Instead of being pleased with the success of the new examination the government became alarmed, partly because it conflicted with its notion of declining standards upon which the whole of the national curriculum ideology was based, and partly because of its suspicion of innovation, especially coursework. The result was that through the controlling examination body, SEAC, government placed severe restrictions on how much coursework would count towards the final assessment, usually in the region of 20 per cent. In the head's view this would scarcely affect the ten or so pupils of the 'grammar school' type at KAS but it would affect the vast majority and undermine the positive aspects of the new examination 'to show what a pupil can do'. Further penalties for poor spelling which Kenneth Clarke and other education secretaries pressed the examination boards to implement were also likely to reduce the positive qualities of GCSE. In his annual report for 1991, Moran concluded:

> the reduction in coursework means less flexibility for schools, less fitting modes of assessment to the abilities of pupils, and finally uncertainty yet again about what we're going to teach. The final insult; we have to find out changes in educational policy from the media – as do the Exam Boards! And lest anyone here considers I am knocking one political party, let me remind you that the formally adopted policies of the other two are still anti- the private

sector. Both support punitive financial action against independent schools, introduced by modifications to Charitable Status.[14]

With the reversal of the liberalizing trends of the GCSE which had in his view allowed 'our moderate children to flourish even in exam time',[15] he predicted a decline in the school's examination results. His forecast, however, proved to be wrong. Results continued to improve.

The new examination at 16+, even with its revised coursework component, left a mismatch with advanced level which was felt more acutely at KAS than at most independent schools. Ordinary level was part of an examination-centred approach to education which had been viewed since its inception in 1951 as a stepping-stone to advanced level. The advent of GCSE, which stood nearer to the school's student-centred tradition, paradoxically left KAS with a problem. As the head pointed out, most students of 'the grammar school' type would find little problem in studying at advanced level despite the removal of the ordinary level stepping-stone, but KAS with its non-selective intake could not expect many of its students to achieve the transition from GCSE to advanced level without great difficulty. There were three possible ways forward. First, the school could hope for a similar revolutionary change at advanced level which would broaden its basis. Had Sir Keith Joseph remained as Education Secretary then even this distant prospect could have become a vague possibility but the rejection by his successor, Kenneth Baker, of the Higginson Committee's recommendations for streamlining advanced levels put fundamental reform out of the question. Advanced levels were to remain the gold standard which even advanced supplementary levels, the only associated reform the government introduced, had to approximate. The size of the bar could be halved but the purity of the gold was to be unadulterated. Given government intransigence KAS could choose a second path and introduce a non-advanced level side to the sixth form or thirdly it could move towards a broader examination such as the baccalaureate. The education policy committee raised the question of the value of students spending two years in the sixth form with low or no advanced levels to show for it but nothing was, or could be, resolved immediately. Parental resistance, lack of finance and low numbers were obstacles to change at sixth-form level, and council refused to bite the bullet, no doubt because of its other priorities and a lack of clear viable alternatives.

The anomaly of a selective sixth form in a non-selective school thus remained. Given that fact, Moran remained clear in his view 'that if sixth formers come back they come back to do a proper programme, and they must be seen to be doing a proper programme – not simply to be here for the ride'.[16] Perhaps not surprisingly, therefore, many of those who were at school during the headships of Nikki Archer and Francis Moran agreed with one former student that 'he did not appear to be part of the Alfredian spirit'[17] and was more conservative than his predecessor with 'his Eton background'. When Francis Moran arrived, concluded another, 'everybody knew (or was told) things were going to change; everybody knew he was the new head; and he seemed to play a role in everything we did'.[18] A 'throwback to the seventies' he might have been in appearance, but he was certainly intent on taking the school forward into the 1980s and 1990s, into the era of league tables and serious academic study. Parents of some pupils in the fifth form received letters advising them to make provision for their offsprings' advanced levels elsewhere, a practice which was seen by at least one student as being unacceptable in its timing, giving little time to seek a place elsewhere, and in its presupposition that advanced level would be beyond their ability. The privilege of the sixth-form teaching day when the sixth-formers took over classroom teaching remained but other privileges were removed or circumscribed. In particular, the very recent tradition of the sixth form being seen as the equivalent of a sixth-form college where students could come and go at will was ended. The sixth form were now expected to spend more time in school, which resulted, in Moran's view, in the pupils' council having more 'drive, energy and maturity'. Greater involvement in the school in general and their studies in particular resulted from his less liberal attitude to the sixth. The sixth-form rules of 1986, which were presented as a series of expectations,

143. Examinations: a higher priority

showed how much closer the KAS sixth form was to that of a grammar school than those of some other progressive schools. As 'volunteers' in the sixth form, students were expected to organize their own study schedules, making the best use of their time and resources. To reinforce such 'expectations', lessons and tutorials were made compulsory and students were allowed off campus for only three periods a week with the remaining non-timetabled study to be employed positively in private study, 'choice' activities, school duties or extra-curricular activities. They were reminded that they had a particular responsibility in that 'young pupils will be looking towards you as models for their own behaviour and attitudes'. They were thus perceived by the head more as Thomas Arnold's moral storm troopers than as A. S. Neill's 'senior democrats'.

Central to New Right policies was parent power. For KAS too it was the foundation stone. Parents were not simply on council; it was they, by and large, who elected council, the governing body, at the annual general meeting of the society. Theirs was the ultimate direct control as the founders intended, and not just the indirect control of forcing the school into bankruptcy if a sufficient number of aggrieved parents withdrew their offspring. Parental power at KAS had always been much more than market forces making ultimate decisions, and not surprisingly as Moran pointed out in his 1987 annual report, if the school was partly a partnership between staff and parents, often the former never felt they were equal partners.[19] Yet, the head, like his predecessor, was amazed that no one from the DES had bothered to visit the school to study its rich and colourful history of parent power. Nor was government willing to learn lessons from its experience as a day school to help guide the newly emerging grant-maintained schools, the recipients of government largesse to encourage them to opt out of local authority control. Dogma rather than carefully considered and researched reform appeared to be the order of the day.

The limits of the New Right's belief in open competition and market forces were seen, according to the head, in the government initiative in relation to city technological colleges. The creation of such colleges was announced by Baker at the Conservative party conference in October 1986. They were to be financed by his department with private-sector sponsors making a considerable contribution towards the costs. Such a substantially funded initiative scarcely offered a level playing field for independent schools. Moran recognized the threat to KAS and the contradiction to the government's declared market philosophy. 'Look', he told the 1987 annual general meeting:

> here we are launching an appeal and desperately trying to get money to refurbish our antiquated buildings stock; the Minister decides he's going to plonk a C.T.C. down next door to us. We can not of course protest because this is the day of open competition (but) . . . the Minister will not stand aside; he will do the fund-raising for the C.T.C. and use his enormous power and influence to make sure that millions come from the biggest of big business.[20]

Thus, directly or indirectly, KAS could not escape the effects of New Right policies.

'The zoo on the hill': myth, reality and the quest for identity

'People used to ask me if all the teachers were stoned and did we all sit up trees barefoot in lessons.'[21] This recollection by a former pupil bears witness to how much more fascinating and potent myth was rather than fact in views about the school, even in the more conservative Moran era. To the historian it reveals interesting insights into the nature of myths about KAS. Rarely were they monolithic. More often they were an evolving mixture of strong residual elements of tales from long ago (in the above anecdote from the distortions of *Pathé News* items from over half a century earlier), of dominant and fairly constant strands usually taken from rumours or sensational headlines about various forms of excess (including that above relating to the drug culture of the sixties and its associated language and a headline in the *Hampstead and Highgate Express* in 1987, 'Pupils tore building apart'), and of emergent elements which usually related the school to the latest social fashion or educational fad. These elements combined to give myths about KAS a certain piquancy and potency which were capable of constant expansion and variation. In 1993 the new chair of council, Kara Conti, argued: 'Gone is the hippy drop-out image of the sixties',[22] but it was more likely that it had been recast by Hampstead's mythmakers rather than buried. When the school was working on its legend project in the 1990s it could well have examined those to which KAS had given rise over the previous century rather than national or international myths and legends.

A concern to distinguish myth from reality was one of the reasons behind the two surveys which were launched in the 1980s. Though each had its own immediate aims and objectives they nevertheless reflected general concerns about progressive education dating back to the first month of the new headship. Hardly had Francis Moran settled in his study when he felt obliged to respond to an article on progressive schools by Michael Dixon in the *Financial Times*.[23] Dixon argued that progressive education was in decline because of the increasing demand for higher examination grades and qualifications by industry. He thus could find only three truly progressive schools in Britain which had not succumbed, Summerhill, Kilquharity House in Scotland and the Inner London Education Authority's White Lion Street Free School in Islington. They still allowed pupils rather than examination requirements to have the 'decisive say in what they did at school'. Not only was KAS not included in this premier list, it was not even mentioned by name among schools such as Abbotsholme and Bedales (the immediate predecessors of King Alfred) which Dixon ranked as 'no longer progressive but merely liberal'. Initially it appeared that the chair of council in 1983, Professor Lewis Keeble, would write a reply using a brief memorandum which an unnamed but prominent colleague on council prepared for him, emphasizing the school's increasing roll, its adherence to progressive ideals, as well as its ability to 'get paper qualifications like Summerhill from an unselected entry', and like 'conventional schools', without losing 'the mutual trust and respect' which represented 'a different kind of relationship' from that found in traditional schools. It was, however, the new head[24] who replied to Dixon's article, pointing to the inherent romanticism of defining progressivism in terms of 'democratic organisation' and using the main points of the memorandum to provide a positive counterbalance. The emphasis which Moran placed upon taking 'seriously the job of giving an individual student power over her or his life', often despite pressure from ambitious parents, could not, however, disguise the fact that in the running of the school the pupil council counted for very little and students were still without a voice on council. Answers to the 1988 questionnaire suggested that the pupil council was a broad training in 'the lesson in democracy' in general, in terms of elections and debating procedures, but not in the specific terms of actual power-sharing within the school,[25] a point to which the head was possibly alluding when he pointed out in his letter that progressive schools were not perfect.

However, increased pressure from parents and industry for even greater success in examinations was but one dimension of the problem of the control of education slipping away from schools into the hands of those whose main concern was not the needs of individuals. Of equal concern to KAS was what Moran called 'the national curriculum and its attendant horrors'[26] to which Baker asked independent schools to conform. The reaction of KAS to the national curriculum and the 1988 Education Reform Act will be dealt with fully in the following section, but one of its effects was to lead the school to define more clearly those qualities of its experience which could be lost if control over the curriculum and its delivery was compromised.

Thus the school had several reasons for looking more closely at itself and how others, including past generations of Alfredians, perceived it. Dispelling myths and correcting inaccurate views about KAS was one important reason, in view of the market forces which determined the school's existence. However, there were others, particularly the ideological need to demonstrate that KAS still ranked highly among the important independent progressive schools and to counter the government-directed attack on progressive education upon whose perceived shortcomings the whole of the national curriculum edifice was erected.

The two surveys conducted in the 1980s were undertaken by different bodies and aimed at different groups. The first in 1986, undertaken in the aftermath of the 1982–3 crisis and the earlier decline in the school population, was directed at parents, partly to assist in the marketing of the school, and was a high-profile study undertaken by the education agency, Gabbitas Thring. The second, entitled 'What is KAS?', was largely a matter for existing and future teachers and arose out of an attempt to define what kind of school KAS was through a questionnaire sent to former students from each of the decades of the twentieth century. After a second trawl the Gabbitas Thring survey produced a response from about half the parents and revealed that most of them had learned of the school from friends. This did not explain fully why they sent their children there, particularly if negative images and myths about the school abounded in the neighbourhood. Fortunately, more positive views of the school were also in circulation and the two decisive factors which attracted parents were its concern for individuals rather than academic competition and its concern for the social and emotional development of children. Quite close behind, and very much connected with these, were the relaxed staff–pupil relationships, the coeducational nature of the school and the extent of parent–teacher co-operation. There was, however, a variety of responses and expectations on particular issues, for example on expulsion. While most would accept it for severe disruptions such as bullying, many were against it on principle, though a minority would accept it for regular swearing. Even on the issue of academic competition there was a variety of responses, possibly reflecting the point which their children had reached in their education. Some parents believed the school was not academic enough while others believed it was becoming too academic. The head concluded that, while all views ought to be listened to, the school ought not to 'be chivvied into action simply because of a small, vociferous parent group'.[27] He also considered the matter of parents' knowledge of school practices being outdated; for example, lower school maths received a critical response from a significant minority, despite the recent heavy investment in the subject, including a supernumerary member of staff. Part of the answer to the problem was seen in terms of better publicity about innovations. However, not all of the answer lay simply in better communication. The classroom facilities were seen to be superior to sports facilities, despite the provision of a new and up-to-date gymnasium. In the 1980s improved sports facilities of many kinds were a feature of many independent schools and, in the face of such parental expectations, the provision by KAS of a new gymnasium scarcely seemed to be a major acquisition.

The survey also considered parental attitudes to smoking and drug-taking, matters which figured large in many of the myths about KAS. Parents were against smoking in school by any of the pupils. On the subject of drugs, most parents felt the appropriate action would be to notify the parent and suspend the pupil, although a fairly large number favoured counselling. A small minority felt it was a matter for the police, which, in fact, was the legal position facing the headteacher. These specific issues raised the more general one of the relative importance of the happiness of the child at school and the school's norms of behaviour and other factors such as success in external examinations. The latter factor was rated higher than the former two by many parents. The major conclusion that Moran drew from the survey was that the school should make greater efforts to reach the whole of the parent body, especially in explaining what the school stood for and where it was going.

However, what the school stood for in the increasingly complex educational world of the 1980s was not obvious to the staff. In their first INSET (in-service training) day in September 1988 they found it difficult to arrive at a consensus on several issues relating to existing practice and future directions and objectives because they found it difficult 'to describe what KAS was with any degree of unanimity'.[28] At the first general staff meeting of the new academic year it was agreed that a working party should be set up to help define KAS and in October a strategy to help achieve this was decided upon. This included broadening the working party to include representatives from the parent–staff committee and the pupils' council, and devising a questionnaire which was sent to 424 former pupils covering as many generations as possible. The 110 replies were analysed in the period January to June 1990 by individuals or small groups concentrating on the cross-generational responses to one or more questions.

On the matter of democratic organization, which as mentioned earlier, Dixon used to distinguish the progressive from 'the merely liberal', the replies on the status of the pupils' council appeared to confirm Dixon's conclusion about the evaporation of one key aspect of the progressive spirit. Up to 1960 there were only five negative responses but in the following decades they increased greatly, with disillusionment following the heads' veto and fewer pupils taking the pupils' council seriously. It lacked credibility, which was regarded as a major loss by at least one former student when it could have been such 'an important facet of KAS'.[29] As the school regarded it as an important part of its tradition, dating back to Russell's creation of a school parliament with cabinet ministers and boys and girls having equal

144. *Bugsy Malone*
musical, 1992: L to
R (front row) Amie
Berman, Chloe
Camber, Zoe
Hoffman, Serena
Levrant; (back row)
Eleanor Simpson,
Grace Davidson,
Gemma Mudu,
Sophie Dahl, Carly
Martin, Reina
Alexander

voting rights predating national women's suffrage, the result of the survey came as something of a surprise, although little was done to enhance its status, except for giving it representation on the parent–staff committee. It still remains the Achilles' heel of KAS progressivism in that the veto remains and students have no kind of representation on council or committees other than the parent–staff, leaving perhaps the impression that the self-confidence, self-reliance and assertiveness (which several former students saw as a major benefit of a KAS education in their answers to a later question) could be a political embarrassment. Political hierarchies and the distribution of power left pupils rather powerless, something which was possibly felt more as the school increased in size. This fact is difficult to reconcile with the image of student excess which forms part of many myths about KAS but does accord with the perception by pupils that there was less freedom in the seventies and eighties.

Though KAS was less liberal than some state schools of the period in the political representation which it accorded to its pupils, it was more progressive in its attitude to staff–pupil relationships and in its general ethos. Good relationships between staff and pupils, based on co-operation not fear and fostered by small classes, an emphasis on individuality, a relaxed school atmosphere and a concern for the disadvantaged, were rated highly by students throughout the twentieth century. Students were encouraged to question, to have enquiring minds, to be happy and to enjoy their studies, to develop good communication and social skills, and to show their initiative – all qualities which their replies to the questionnaire emphasized.

The disadvantages of a KAS education were equally important to those who wished to discover what KAS meant to its former pupils. Some of those listed ran contrary to KAS principles, such as the lack of religious education, and insufficient emphasis on competition, formal discipline and strong academic drive. Others were matters over which the school had little or no control, including high fees, a closed environment and limited social mix and a small sixth form. The school did its best to limit fee increases and encouraged students to engage in community projects, which, as the headteacher reported to Neill's biographer, Jonathan Croall, in 1991, were not always as wholeheartedly undertaken as he would have wished,[30] and to enlarge the sixth form through advertisement and bursaries. The criticism that the KAS ethos and emphasis on self-discipline led some to underachieve was an inevitable consequence of a curriculum which was not primarily examination-driven. Those who wanted more formal discipline and a higher priority for preparation for public examinations were perhaps in the wrong school. Not surprisingly, when asked how the school could be improved, many of these respondents made suggestions which could have affected the ethos, if not the viability of the school. Certainly, many parents felt that the highest priority should be given to a child's happiness and that this was not necessarily antithetical to academic achievement if the latter were approached in a calm and rational manner. It would appear from the answers to the question about whether former KAS pupils would send their children to the school that a growing proportion were more willing to do so in the seventies and eighties than in most previous decades, though the combined numbers throughout the century showed a rough balance. Even when respondents replied in the negative, most did so on grounds of cost or the innate élitism of the school rather than its ethos, although a significant minority believed that the school was insufficiently academic or competitive for their children. For example, in 1987 it was reported to council that a pupil was being transferred from KAS to 'a properly structured and academically serious school'.[31] There were others who believed the opposite, that KAS had 'lost its way' in attempting to become more academic. Such were the conflicting opinions of some of the former students, now often parents.

The respondents to a third questionnaire, distributed in 1995 in connection with the present book, do not generally accept this latter verdict. They measure the school's success in terms which Alfredians in the early part of the century would have recognized. They tend to emphasize its value in developing individual confidence. As one former Alfredian put it: 'Academically it was not brilliant but I am glad of this as

I had more chance to develop my personality and my true strengths than people at other schools.'[32] As a non-selective school it is perhaps not surprising that its examination results did not always match schools which selected their entry on grounds of ability. The positive side of this was that KAS students were not cowed by authority. They were not 'scared into working'[33] and hence the difference in the atmosphere and in teacher–pupil relationships encouraged the development of a more assertive and balanced personality. The emphasis on the latter did not, however, prevent the headteacher from running 'a tight ship with capable staff'. Teachers such as Keith Moore played a major part in the transformation of pupils, in one case changing 'a shy, weedy little boy to a confident and reliable one', partly through the policy of sport for all, now a permanent feature of the KAS programme.

Not all parents of course agreed with the school's emphasis on aims which were difficult to quantify and whose outcomes were by no means certain. One discontented parent believed that it could be plausibly argued that 'these individually developed, emotionally nurtured, paragons are more loutish, more uncaring, less civil, than their peers in other more traditional schools'.[34] Perhaps not surprisingly he chose to send his son to what he believed to be a nearby 'serious academic institution'. Generally, however, the three surveys tended to show a rather different picture, of a school in the eighties successfully coming to terms with the growing emphasis upon good examination results while maintaining its traditional concern for the development of the individual within a relaxed, happy school atmosphere. Whether this balance could be maintained in the nineties when the educational world became increasingly dominated by the national curriculum and its tests and league tables of examination results remained to be seen. It was by no means impossible, especially when KAS is compared with other progressive schools. One former pupil recalled, 'I left KAS to go to Bedales for the sixth form but came back after six weeks . . . ; I found the lack of privacy and the rules a step backward rather than forward.'

Living with a GERBIL

The attempts in 1986 to discover what was distinctive about the school could not have been more timely. This was underlined in Areta Hautman's report to council on Kenneth Baker's address to the Governing Bodies Association (GBA). In the spring of 1987, the Education Secretary was preparing the nation in general and schools in particular for his Great Education Reform Bill (widely referred to as his GERBIL), and his talk to the association reiterated the kinds of argument which Callaghan had used a decade earlier in his Ruskin College speech. He felt, in the words of Mrs Hautman, that 'there was a swing of opinion in the country for the return of sound old-fashioned standards in education' and 'that employers had appealed to him for literacy and numeracy in prospective employees'.[35] The national curriculum, by which he believed state schools could be made to return to basics after the mischief perpetrated by progressive educationists of the 1960s and 1970s, was one of the main planks of New Right policy announced in the Queen's Speech at the end of June 1987. His GERBIL and the bill on the poll tax were the Tory flagship legislation of the new session and were unlikely to meet much effective opposition in parliament with the Conservative majority of over 100. The poll tax was later dropped and played a part in the downfall of Margaret Thatcher, but Baker's Education Act provided one of the principal elements of continuity between the Thatcher period and that of her successor, John Major. It remained the backbone of Conservative education policy throughout the 1990s, long after Thatcher and Baker ceased to be forces in British politics, and also provided New Labour under John Smith and Tony Blair with much of its education policy.

KAS and council welcomed the election result in that the school's charitable status remained secure. However, Baker's GERBIL was such a hybrid creature that it was bound to evoke a mixed response. In theory KAS could maintain a detached position, for the so-called national curriculum was in fact a curriculum for state schools only, but, from the outset, the head felt that there was more than 'official encouragement to the independent sector to comply'.[36] There were pressures of various kinds emanating from the DES which could compromise KAS progressivism. Baker's successor, John McGregor, in a letter to the *Guardian* on 14 November 1989 argued that 'parents who choose an independent school will expect at least as much for their money as the Education Reform Act will secure in the maintained sector and they will look elsewhere if they don't get it'. To Moran, this was a backdoor attempt by government to impose the national curriculum on independent schools. There were also more direct pressures to conform, as publishers directed their output to the national curriculum and GCSE became an integral part of its key stage 4, building upon its earlier stages.

Moran, using the observations of Richard Aldrich of the Institute of Education,[37] noted several similarities between Morant's 1904 Regulations for Secondary Schools, introduced when Russell was head, and Baker's national curriculum.[38] The lists of ten subjects to be taught were virtually identical and reflected a certain arbitrariness, which Russell could ignore in the case of Morant's Regulations but which Moran found difficult to overlook, for Baker's list omitted the key areas of information technology, computing skills, drama, economics and photography. Moran discerned a peculiar mix of the 'prescriptive' and the 'elastic' in the subject list when its details were subsequently published, with technology encompassing craft, design and technology and drama being included as a kind of catch-all subject to be used as an integrating force. The idea that the highly prescriptive list could leave sufficient time to cover important aspects of a KAS curriculum, such as careers and personal and social education, was also seen as a sleight-of-hand arrangement, particularly as the main subjects were to be examined by a barrage of standard assessment tasks at seven, eleven, fourteen and sixteen. With ten levels of attainment being tested and with each subject having a range of skills to assess, he estimated that a primary school teacher with a class of thirty would have about 6,000 assessment procedures to undertake. In KAS things would not be quite so bad if the scheme were adopted, for it would only amount to 4,000 procedures because classes were smaller! There were, he argued, certain areas of the national curriculum which fitted KAS tradition, particularly the ideas of continuity from five to sixteen, of the integration of subjects and that many skills are common to a diverse range of subjects. The view that records should be formative, summative and evaluative also fitted KAS practice.

The declared intention of the government was that the publication of the results of the tests would provide parents with information which

145. Craft, design and technology expanded by Stephen de Brett. Clockwise: Bob Rowland, James Ingram, Stephen de Brett, Tom Griffith, Gur Benshemesh, Grace Davidson, Joe Beattie, Katy Bower, Xulia Duran, ?

they could use to choose a school, though, of course, not the curriculum. The concepts of parental power and parental choice were ones with which KAS felt perfectly at home, as was the notion of schools being responsible for their budgets. Financial delegation to schools, giving schools a greater measure of independence through the opportunity by parental ballot of opting out of local government control and opening up schools to market forces, were all areas in which KAS had had nearly a century's experience. Through such methods Baroness Young told the GBA in 1988 that 'she was hoping to get parents in the maintained sector as interested and involved in their schools as in the independent sector'.[39] Although she wondered if the independent sector could help in training the parent governors and headteachers of the new state schools of the future, KAS was never approached by government to share in the task, probably because it was not the kind of independent school which ranked most highly in government estimation. The school remained unapologetically progressive and was willing to implement the research findings of other bastions of progressivism, including London

146. Learning activities in the lower school; L to R Buster Turner, Jessie Marre, Duncan Mann

University's Institute of Education. To help raise reading standards, the lower school implemented the results of the Haringay experiment run by Hewison, Tizard and others based in the Thomas Coram Unit of the Institute. The project had examined ways in which the home could supplement reading programmes initiated by the school. To KAS, which was always trying to increase direct parental involvement in keeping with the 1897 founding principles, implementing its research findings was a natural extension of informal practices already in being.

The school's interest in research projects, rather than in blindly following the untested and untried ideas which were beginning to emerge from Conservative politicians in the mid-1980s, also reflected the scientific outlook of the founders in their view of the curriculum. Moran and his staff refused to leap aboard educational bandwagons set in motion by government or by others, but engaged in a closely considered assessment of how research findings could possibly help the school to deal with its problems. Certainly John Peisley's review of the curriculum introduced when the new head took over would have raised Conservative eyebrows, especially his analysis of the causes of underachievement by pupils and his proposed remedies. John Peisley, head of science, argued in a paper presented to council in 1986 that 'There is still too much esteem for academic ability. For instance, there is pressure for all subjects to be 'O' level (and CSE is seen as second class) although GCSE may help to change this.'[40] While his analysis was not as radical as Herstlet's in the mid-1960s, he was concerned with many of the same issues: lack of continuity between lower and middle school; lack of cohesion and co-operation between subject teachers; the failure of integrated studies due largely to timetable constraints; and the difficulty of achieving a balanced curriculum when the most able sought to take nine subjects and avoid arts and crafts, and when the less able and too many girls sought to avoid science. In his view, pupil and parental expectations were often too great, the goals of two-year courses were too remote and subjects existed 'in their own world'.[41] The language of the curricular debate at KAS was clearly very different from that of government ministers, as were the sources of help to which Peisley turned to help resolve difficulties. In particular, he turned to John Holt's book *The Common Curriculum* and to Hargreaves's report on the schools of ILEA, an education authority destined for abolition under Baker's GERBIL. It was the latter which provided Peisley with most insights into problem areas, particularly those of transition to the secondary school and the curriculum for fourth- and fifth-formers. During the transition from the primary to the secondary school, pupils could lose motivation and momentum, leaving some pupils with the ability to judge just how little they could do without being reprimanded. Hargreaves's answer, which

147. Pottery, a traditional KAS activity under Jan Bradley: Kelly Malkin, Jan Bradley, Isis Godfrey

Peisley rightly thought worthy of consideration, was not to erect systems to trap unwary pupils but to encourage teachers to adopt a more coherent teaching style across the transition years and to educate teachers through a programme of integrated studies rather than separate-subject teaching, thus providing greater continuity and a more coherent pupil experience. Fragmented subjects with a variety of teaching styles would be replaced by more coherent areas of study with a closer identity of teaching modes, a point which Findlay had made in designing the school's first curriculum in 1898. The idea of more immediate goals (half-term units assessed either by 'graded tests, profile or similar'), accelerated courses for very able pupils, a large core of compulsory subjects, and a broad science course were regarded as key considerations for improving courses and the course structure leading to the examinations at 16+.

Peisley believed that KAS had made a mistake in going for an option scheme in 1983 which, while allowing choice, the essence of progressivism, often denied coherence and balance to programmes of study and tended to produce timetable complications to the extent that, in his view, it resulted in the timetable 'dictating how we teach and not vice versa'.[42] He thus argued for a review of the whole curriculum, with a large common curriculum and limited options in the upper school, and with modules and unit credits to provide more immediate goals.

148. John Peisley, Head of Science, in the physics classroom, 1991, with (clockwise from Peisley) Kelly Panayiotou, Jemma Konrad, Jacqui Chanarin, Mischa Brearley, Balpreet Gujral, David Chivers

This kind of pronounced professionalism was not unique to John Peisley. The Moran era was notable for the encouragement which the head gave to his staff to define their curricular goals at a time when government was seeking to impose goals on state schools. The increase in the size of KAS, however, made it ever more difficult to match means to ends. In September 1983, the school had 380 pupils; in 1989, the number had increased to 489. Such pressures encouraged the staff to set up working parties on the curriculum but the headteacher was concerned that debates should not be confined to the staffroom. He thus initiated a programme of reports to council by teachers as part of a scheme of training for the former and encouraging the latter to clarify their views. As their combined thinking on curricular matters helped to define pupil experience it is worth considering a little further how heads of department in particular viewed their task, before examining how pupils saw the curriculum and its delivery.

John Peisley's report to council was thus not unique, though perhaps it was unusual in that it was a broad overview of the whole curriculum. Other curricular statements to council included that by Rita Murray on integrated studies with special reference to the MACOS scheme (man: a course of study) initiated by the Integrated Humanities Association. What perhaps was significant about this was that while the government was pushing the nation's schools towards a subject-based national curriculum on the grounds of alleged deficiencies in education brought about by the Plowden progressivism of the 1960s and 1970s, KAS was considering adopting the MACOS scheme because its thinking was very much in line with 'the Plowden philosophy about the primary school'.[43] The scheme involved employing the skills of English, geography, history and maths or science in considering topics such as the sea. Such a theme would also include music and art. Before any steps towards its adoption were taken, teachers visited schools, including Countesthorpe, where the project was already in use and took part in workshops in the use of MACOS materials. The idea of following the MACOS scheme was eventually dropped because of what was seen to be its lack of balance.

KAS resistance to national curricular stereotyping and to overconcentration on examinations and league tables was evident in other presentations. One particular concern was remedial teaching, a report on which was given to council by Francis Daniels and Olive Peet and upon which Denise Gibbs, Mike Young and Francis Moran had already made their comments. In a non-selective school, remedial teaching had a higher priority than in schools with a highly selective intake and an eye to high positions in league tables. (Bedales, for example, had gone down the academic selective path.) Visits by staff to other independent schools known for their strong remedial departments raised a number of issues, including restricting intake to prevent the school being swamped by pupils needing remedial help, the forms which remedial help should take, the transition from the lower to middle school and the monitoring of student progress. What the staff were generally opposed to was the creation of a large-scale remedial department on the lines of Millfield School, Somerset. They favoured a more flexible system to include not just remedial provision but 'special needs' assistance for gifted children. With the latter in mind the school joined the National Association for Gifted Children. One of the strengths of KAS was that it combined a concern for gifted children with that for those who were less able. At any one stage 20 per cent of children were receiving special needs help, many of whom would not have qualified for such support in the state sector. A result of this, as one former pupil recalled, was that pupils were never stigmatized by their peers for receiving such help.[44] However, the school felt it had to impose a quota on children needing remedial help entering the first year to prevent KAS being swamped by requests for such assistance and being seen as a school solely for remedial children. Remedial help was made even more imperative because of the parental pressure on the school before 1988 to enter their children for ordinary level, even in such subjects as drama, photography and electronics which began their life as non-examination courses. A course in child development, so appropriate to a school such as KAS, was one of the few to be successful in resisting such pressure. However, it withered away because fewer and fewer pupils opted for it.

By 1991 a 'special subjects' department had come into existence, giving support to about 30 per cent of students with a wide range of learning problems, from mild difficulties with spelling, handwriting, organizational skills and general understanding to moderately severe dyslexia. A testing programme in the middle school enabled the team of four to detect those whose learning difficulties might not have been picked up at an earlier stage. They also moved into the area of working with mainstream departments by providing additional extension work for the particularly gifted student. This provision was delivered more and more through in-class support, although particular and acute problems usually meant withdrawal from lessons. The latter was particularly the case in French around 1990 but not in maths when most children with learning difficulties wanted to be withdrawn, thus creating an impossible situation. The general extension of lesson times to seventy minutes and the abolition of the traditional open rooms were regarded as unhelpful to 'special needs' work.

The richness of pupil experience was also indicated in other reports to council. One area which had witnessed a remarkable resurgence in the 1980s and 1990s was drama. Under Tony Grounds KAS was selected for the finals of the Sunday Times National Student Drama Festival, the first London school to achieve that feat. In April 1987 at the week-long Wakefield Festival a group of fourth- to sixth-formers shared the joint accolade of best company for their part in Grounds's play, *Holiday in the Sun*. His aim throughout the school was to encourage pupils to feel that any drama production was their project. Prior to this success pupils had performed in a play called *Coal*, which took as its theme the recent miners' strike, in yet one other which Grounds had written, *Waiting for the Hovercraft*, staged in March and May 1985, and at Swansea in 1986 in his play *The Play's The Thing*. The subject was an element of 'choice', and was also taken at ordinary level where 30 per cent of the examination was a practical. He hoped to extend it to advanced level. The pupils had also been able to take *Waiting for the Hovercraft* to the Lyric Theatre, working with the theatre's actors. Clearly a subject which was being pushed to the periphery of many state schools by the many other demands of the Baker curriculum, or was represented by an annual production, had taken on a life at KAS which was so in tune with the school's founding principles, especially in encouraging the kind of individuality which was not so easily expressed elsewhere. Curricular experimentation remained very much a central part of the school's tradition.

The emphasis upon resisting academic drift and upon catering for the personal and social needs of students was evident also in Sue

Boulton's paper to council on personal education. Whether these needs could be best met in the formal curriculum or by the extension of the form system was the principal area of discussion at KAS. The list of suitable topics for inclusion was almost endless but it was developed around a core of themes, principal among which were charities, children's rights and responsibilities, careers, national issues, records of achievement, bullying and the functions of the pupils' council. To help develop this part of the school's curriculum she had prepared starter packs of materials. The whole aim was to develop those aspects of a child's education that were largely neglected or only paid lip-service to in those schools whose curriculum was dominated by preparation for public exams. In his editorial to the 1989/90 edition of *Which School?* Francis Moran argued that progressive schools were 'the last bastions of anti-cramming'.[45] The school was there for the child, and not the child there to maintain the school and the examination system. Within this philosophy the kinds of programme developed by Tony Grounds, Sue Boulton and others played a major part. They were seen as vital to the school's health and balanced curricular diet and fitted in well with the great priority which parents attached to social and emotional growth in the Gabbitas Thring survey.

Their work was seen very much as building upon KAS tradition in the more recent as well as distant past. For example, a few months earlier, Peter Andrews, head of the English department, had explained to council the scheme of social, personal and community education, known by the acronym SPACE. The course covered study skills but also interestingly raised the matter of religion, something which the pupils themselves asked to discuss. While the school refused to teach religion per se, it was clear that the discussion of religion and values was very much in line with the manner in which it had been handled in the past. The programme also aimed to strengthen links with the community raising both ideological matters, such as whether charity work should be given a higher profile in a caring school such as KAS, and practical issues such as the forms which community involvement should take, including a Christmas show for old people's homes. Alongside the SPACE programme was another on responsibility in relationships run by Sheila King-Lassman.

Two areas of the curriculum which at times in the past had proved problematic were modern languages, especially the desirability of a second modern language and which it should be, and music. The former was a hardy perennial whereas the latter tended to resurface at irregular intervals in council discussions. In the case of modern languages, French was as strongly entrenched at KAS as it was in more traditional independent and state schools, without its priority ever being challenged since Russell's era. In fact as Françoise Burford, head of languages, pointed out to council in 1988,[46] the advent of GCSE had strengthened its position in throwing a greater emphasis on the spoken word. The debate focused upon whether the second modern language should be German or Spanish. Council had favoured the former although take-up had been small. Pressure from some parents led to a reconsideration of the importance of the latter. The head of languages favoured a compromise with the retention of German, and Spanish being introduced as an optional subject in the choice programme, or as an afterschool subject or as a sixth-form option. The pressure group within council which favoured Spanish found these suggestions un-acceptable and the matter was referred back to the headteacher to investigate various possibilities, including offering Spanish as an addi-tional subject to German, or as a replacement for German and/or as a sixth-form option. The perennial problem which thus had limited pupil choice for several generations remained unresolved for the moment. Its introduction as a sixth-form option in 1989 could have paved the way for its expansion throughout the upper school but the three sixth-formers who took it up abandoned it, leaving the matter in an even more unsatisfactory position. The Gabbitas Thring report of 1986 had indicated that only five respondents wished to add Spanish to the curriculum, so perhaps the general lack of support was not surprising. The addition of Latin had the backing of eleven respondents (but not necessarily their children) and while it would not have solved the second modern language problem, it would nevertheless have been a more useful direction of the school's energies. The wish, however, to keep KAS distinct from the usual run of independent schools may have militated against its reintroduction, especially as its presence in a school usually increases the competitive spirit, selection for the Latin class being seen as one of the hallmarks of academic excellence. Such a move would have increased parental pressure on pupils, driving KAS further from its ideological roots.

The second area of spasmodic difficulty was music, pushed to the periphery of the national curriculum by the government's thirst for the basics but a subject which should have occupied a more secure and central position in a progressive curriculum dedicated to fostering individual talents. Neither council nor the head were in doubt about its ideological merits nor about its value in projecting a positive image of the school in the neighbourhood. The problem was that in the past it had not always appeared to deliver what was expected of it. In November 1989 the head of the music department, Anne Elliott, pointed to some of the constraining factors, including the lack of a third music specialist, of suitable music rooms for class lessons and for practice, and the need for more private teaching rooms. The recent timetable changes were also seen to disadvantage the subject. However, with ten peripatetic teachers enabling tuition in extra-curricular brass, wind, baroque string and rock, the subject was in her view thriving, especially as the number of such teachers was greater than that possessed by any other independent North London school. The problem for KAS as for other schools was that music was often seen by many pupils as an extra, non-examination subject. Nevertheless, there were eight GCSE music candidates, the result largely of a shortened course for high fliers. This number, in her view, led to a greater examination take-up at KAS than in most independent or state schools with larger intakes. Her exposition to council of 'Music in the Curriculum' did not, however, dispel all concerns. In particular, the problems of the lack of enthusiasm for the subject by some age groups and the embarrassment experienced by some middle school pupils about being interested in classical music were raised in council.

Such difficulties were not unique to KAS, but in a school where the creative and expressive arts had a firm place in ideology and where several members of the parent body were musicians, the subject area was expected to have a more positive image and a much larger following, particularly in the middle and upper schools. The absence of choirs in these areas of the school was seen to be indicative of a poor response. In the view of the chairman of council in 1990, Ari Zaphiriou-Zarifi, 'The general standard of music both in teaching and performance has a generally mixed reputation.'[47] However, if the subject was perceived by many pupils to be of secondary importance then the music teachers' task in firing pupil enthusiasm and in maintaining an appropriate classroom and rehearsal-room atmosphere was probably much greater than that of many of their colleagues in core subject areas where the dynamics of the classroom and the examination status of the subject facilitated easier classroom control. Much also depended on the attitude of parents, whose far from

149. Computers under David Reynolds played an important part in the curriculum of the 1990s: L to R Antonia Rosati, Jenny Grant, David Reynolds, Eliza Karakitsos

150. A lower school brass group in the early 1990s: L to R (back row) George Gretton (parent), Thomas Frazer, Heydon Prowse, Matthew Gretton, Duncan Smith, Robert Hersey (staff); (front row) Jonathon Stone, Martin Lawley, Jack Gore, Rachel Frazer, Simon Kirk, Jean Mercer (staff)

enthusiastic support for concerts[48] gave the wrong messages to the children. The fact that the school had invested some £7,000, twice the budgeted figure, in the years 1988 to 1990 in 'band method' for first years and in paying for instrumental teachers for small groups, led the chairman of council to feel a little disappointed. A change in attitude could not be achieved overnight, particularly if this meant raising the status of a largely, non-examination subject in the eyes not just of pupils, but of parents, whose expectations were being formed by a constant

151. 'Catherine's Lodgers', a KAS jazz quartet, winners in the 1995 Youth Jazz Competition: L to R Liam Fletcher, Dominic Green, Joe Leader, Oliver Rockberger

barrage of political propaganda from all parties about 'back to basics'. As was mentioned in a council discussion in June 1991, the answer partly lay beyond the classroom. What was needed was 'the vetting of parents and not just their children – a balance needed to be kept between recruiting only those who were devoted to KAS ideals and keeping the school viable'. In 1994, the head of music, Andy Hampton, reported to council that the tide had turned in class music. Creative and stimulating courses, a new middle school teacher, well-organized concerts and close links between music and drama were among the factors which he believed had led to its strengthened position, with subsequent moves afoot to build a middle school choir and to extend the number of

152. One aspect of musical education, the Jazz revival under Andy Hampton: L to R (back row) Tom Frazer, Charlie Walker Wise, Oliver Anderson, Luke Burton, Jack Abraham, Sam Hodges, Joe Leader, Heydon Prowse, Matthew Gretton, Samuel Potter, Alexis Karlin; (middle row) Liam Fletcher, Genna Lucas, Bruno Cavell, Nik Engineer, Naomi Hampton, Antonia Rosati; (front row) Joe Frazer, Oliver Rockberger, Teddy Leifer, Catherine Gill, Tom Sabbadini

evenings for popular concerts. Music had thus left the doldrums, at least for the time being.

To the government's call of 'back to basics', like many schools, KAS could always reply, 'We never left them.' However, following Baker's announcement of his GERBIL, the school considered more closely the kinds of provision which it made for its pupils, particularly in English, mathematics, science and technology. A year after she had listened to the Education Secretary outlining his plans to the Governing Bodies Association, Areta Hautman asked council to request a report on 'the teaching of English at KAS, particularly the teaching of grammar – much in the news of late'. The head, with his experience of English teaching, saw the issue as vital, especially as the Kingman Committee set up by Baker, was about to report. The spotlight tended to fall more upon mathematics than English in the next two years, partly because of the extension from the junior to the middle school of the School Maths Project 11–16, which related 'mathematics ideas to situations the children can understand thus giving them the opportunity to grasp the meaning of the ideas'. In the first two years, the course focused on number, algebra, graphs, space and statistics, using individualized schemes and extension work to stretch high achievers. The success of the scheme depended in part upon homework, an hour a week minimum in its early stages, but much more intensive in the GCSE years when the course also became much more teacher-led.

KAS could not ignore government reforms. It was not simply that they helped to mould parental expectations. The decreasing of the percentage of the overall assessment for GCSE coursework, demanded by Kenneth Clarke and other education secretaries, was likely to have an adverse effect on the school's examination results in the view of the head, although subsequent results did not support his pessimism. Also the undue emphasis given by the media to levels 8–10 of the national curriculum's key stage 4, equivalent to GCSE A and B grades, made it difficult to keep children motivated if they and their parents perceived these grades to

153. A second aspect of musical education: Robert Hersey conducting a performance of Purcell's music on St Cecilia's Day, 1995

be the only ones that mattered. In a non-selective school there was the danger that these and other pressures would lead pupils to specialize earlier and to unwelcome changes in the learning experience. For example, changes in the English coursework requirement, hitherto 100 per cent of the assessment and now reduced to 20 per cent with 20 per cent for speaking and listening and 60 per cent for two two-hour examination papers, could have an inhibiting effect on KAS styles of learning and internal assessment.

The head and the chair of council, Kara Conti, felt that it was time to make a stand and penned a letter to *The Times* and other newspapers in January 1992 attacking plans to reduce the element of assessment through coursework and the absurd timetable for the change. In addition, Nicholas Hai, a member of council wrote to Hampstead's Member of Parliament, John Marshall, about the changes. Although Marshall sent the letter on to the Education Secretary, Kenneth Clarke, the reply came from Tim Eggar, in whose area of respons-

154. Useful projects: play house built in 1981 as a Choice CDT project, taken in 1990; L to R Olivia Weale, (on the roof) Sam Reynolds, John Dunn, Ryan Saban, (on the bar) Lydia Samuels, Nina Stenham

ibility the matter lay. Declining Hai's request for a meeting, Eggar reaffirmed his belief in the advantages of coursework but pointed to its shortcomings, especially its 'lack of objective standardised markings, distorting external influences and the inadequacy of some moderating procedures'.[49] These points, together with the government's insistence on the priority 'of the academic rigour that comes from the ability to express knowledge and understanding under the controlled conditions of a terminal examination', expressed a philosophy at odds with the KAS view of the learning and assessment process. Perhaps not surprisingly, Areta Hautman raised the matter in council of the time being 'pertinent to look at what we stood for and how it was under threat'. With the government's close control of the public examination system and its insistence that GCSE be integrated with the national curriculum, the school had less room for manœuvre to escape examination pressure than at any time in the past.

KAS continued to gain very creditable examination results. Prior experience at teaching pupils for the joint 16+ examinations, the forerunner of GCSE, gave teachers expertise and confidence in teaching the new examination. Equally important was the increased confidence which many pupils had gained through dedicated teaching and through contact with 'special needs' teachers. Expectations were raised, with teachers less tolerant of underachievement and with pupils more concerned than ever before to acquire the necessary qualifications to enter the difficult employment market, or to go on to further or higher education. Certainly the headmaster detected a change in upper school culture. This was a matter for immense satisfaction but not for complacency, for the cost of the achievement might well be a decline in the KAS ethos. Kara Conti saw the matter as a damage-limitation exercise 'by developing those areas of school life that are between and around classes where the real spirit of the school has chance to flourish, The Spaces in Between'.[50] The head in his strategy paper for council in 1994 did not believe that national educational policy threatened KAS, 'except in the short term – even there it is more a nuisance than a threat'.[51] Yet he realized that the moves to limit GCSE coursework could hit the school's examination results and as a consequence could affect recruitment. Schools were, he believed, increasingly being judged by hard-edged aims, those that could be easily identified and defined, including examination results, uniform, and formal discipline.

In his strategy document he was quite willing to consider adopting such clear aims to safeguard the school's future. In many ways this is what John Russell had done in coming to terms with examinations and was a strategy which Nikki Archer and Alan Humphries had adopted in dealing with the problems of the 1960s. Francis Moran, however, realized that the possible changes required in the 1990s could be more than some parents and many on council would be willing to accept, including making the school more academically selective, making progression within the school less automatic and dependent upon standards of work and behaviour, and turning the sixth form into a good tutorial college. In his view such a shift in goals would not necessarily alter much of its day-to-day working. It would make KAS more like other schools, and yet actually leave staff freer to experiment. Clearer and more definable aims could also assist 'realistic negotiation between staff and students about work and behaviour requirements'.[52]

Exactly how much scope there would be for experimentation in teaching was a matter which Stephen Webster of the school's science department addressed in an article in the *Journal of Biological Education* in 1995[53] after Dearing's review of the national curriculum. In many ways he reflected the concerns of the history, geography and other departments when he argued that education was perceived in terms of the rote learning of facts, ready to be tested and used as fodder for league tables. Dearing's reformulation, in Webster's view, had some merits in permitting a wider range of investigation and eliminating the statements of attainment but it gave little encouragement to talking about and around science. The factual content remained massive, the earlier ideas on discussion, drama and role play in science teaching having fallen by the wayside since the first science working group published its recommendations in 1989. That report was in his view 'the swan-song of the liberal science education establishment'.[54] Certainly the curriculum technocrats were unlikely to leave the more progressive elements of GCSE undisturbed. The dictates of assessment still dominated the new Dearing curriculum, making no less of a mockery of the old adage that assessment ought to be the servant rather than the master of the curriculum than those that preceded it.

This review of the way in which some of the principal areas of the KAS curriculum were affected by the advent of the national curriculum (or more appropriately a series of national curricula) is important to an understanding of how carefully council and staff considered the matter. It is unlikely that many other independent schools, progressive or otherwise, devoted so much of their time and energies to considering

155. One of the 'spaces in between': the camp tradition continued

156. The tree house of the 1990s, designed and built during the Choice period: L to R Amie Berman, Portia Mishcon, Liberty Mosse

government policy. For state schools just keeping up with its implementation absorbed all their energies. This overview is also important to an understanding of some of the major influences on pupil experience. To describe the kinds of experience which pupils at KAS enjoyed without considering the debates and discussions which helped to define them would scarcely do justice to the immense efforts which were made to retain those aspects of a KAS education which previous generations had valued.

Squaring the ideological circle: school life in the 1980s and 1990s

The grasp which Alan Humphries had of curriculum theory and innovation and Nikki Archer's philosophical understanding of the possible deleterious effects of a liberated society upon KAS ideology served the school well in the 1960s and 1970s. The challenge of the next two decades was altogether different. Government-initiated, curricular retrenchment was likely to have marked, if generally indirect, repercussions upon the quality of school life, unless the threat was mitigated by careful counteraction by council, the head and the school staff. Fortunately KAS was well positioned to undertake such measures. It had a headmaster who had squared the ideological circle at Eton and a council and parent body which recognized that the school could not entirely opt out of the world of examinations and the national curriculum. Francis Moran had pioneered progressive teaching methods in what many perceived to be the most formal of academic environments, Eton, and one which government itself would take as a bench mark. The main body of parents, though drawn largely from the professions of the founders or their modern counterparts, the law, teaching, architecture, and the arts, together with a more liberal sprinkling of company directors and people drawn from the media and entertainment,[55] were less radical than their forebears, and more ready to come to terms with the educational world of the 1990s. As the head pointed out in his strategy paper for council in 1994, neither the school nor parents could ignore the policies of the New Right. Redesigning schools in the 1990s to make them as radical and progressive as they were in the 1890s was to redesign them into oblivion. He quoted Dartington Hall as an example, although the *Guardian*[56] attributed its closure more to the headmaster's wife posing for pornographic pictures (which in fact they were not), a girl drowning and the headmaster calling in the police to deal with the school's drug and drink problem.

Besides generally avoiding these excesses, KAS made other advances which enabled it not only to survive but to flourish and to preserve much of its original character. Not least of these was the peculiar combination of radical and conservative elements in the school's constitution, which, although placing ultimate control in the hands of parents, left a series of hierarchies intact which gave a sense of security to pupils without the heavy hand of authority. Some pupils thought that their own council gave them 'a large say in the running of the school',[57] but it never had sufficient power to subject the school to the whims of the pupil body. Successive chairs of council made great efforts to soften hierarchical arrangements but at the end of the day KAS was no Summerhill.

The minutes of the pupils' council, a body which experienced both extreme lethargy and vigorous action, depending on the make-up of the moment, show that when active it discussed matters such as raising money for charities, the litter problem, school dinners, protective clothing, school camps, the common room, the feeding of school animals and skate boarding, but that it rarely dealt with issues central to the curriculum or school organization. As one member of the parent-elected council put it when discussing the expulsion of a boy for drug-taking: 'How the children felt on the matter was beside the point as they were not running the school.'[58] This was in keeping with the views of the founders, who intended that the school should be an experiment in rational education run for and not by children. The inevitable consequence of such a view was that some members of the pupils' council saw it as 'empty of purpose and power' but KAS pupils had the best of several worlds, the security of an unobtrusive but nevertheless clearly defined framework of authority which could remove pupils, staff and heads for what was believed to be the greater good of the school, and an environment, both physical and spiritual, which enabled each individual to develop with a fairly minimal number of constraints. Thus interestingly while outside observers commented first of all on the trappings of freedom in the 1980s and 1990s, 'no uniform – jeans, holey jumpers, trilbies and leather jackets',[59] pupils were more immediately impressed by the quality of relationships which such freedom encouraged. It was not simply that pupils and teachers were on first-name terms. It was what this meant that counted. As Mischa Brearley aged twelve commented to a *Guardian* interviewer after five years at the school, 'We're all respected by the teachers.'[60] Thus it was the practitioners, not the politicians, who dominated their world of education, John Peisley not John Major, Tony Grounds not Tony Blair.

Not that pupils, at times, were unable to distinguish sound teachers from those who were only able to establish good informal relationships. The latter was seen as a prerequisite for, not synonymous with, the former. One ex-Alfredian, with a rather exceptional view of the staff, concluded that in the early years of the new headship there were 'very few good teachers' but 'a lot of nice enough people amongst them'.[61] Most were happier with their teaching. Mike 'really ace' Young and Guy Christiansen were generally regarded as friendly and approachable, diligently registering camps and checking that structures were safe. Mark 'total-heart throb' Owen was seen as an excellent teacher, as was Laszlo Horvath who, as head of mathematics, possibly had one of the most difficult tasks in the school. As one former student confessed, 'I have always hated maths and was always very bad at it (but) Laszlo the maths teacher was excellent.' These were but a few of the tributes to staff, but what perhaps is of particular interest is the way in which people such as Roy Greenfield and Denise Gibbs were identified with the spirit of KAS and its ideals – approachable, well-loved, gentle and well-respected. In the case of the latter, one ex-pupil who was at the school for a decade commented that she was 'one of the old school, of KAS attitude, of a generation under whom the school's atmosphere evolved and without whom I feel it will become much less like the school I started at'.

The idea that KAS had a distinctive ethos that ought to be preserved was widespread among pupils. They guarded it jealously, believing those who were its chief defenders, the staff, could also be its principal threat. One ex-Alfredian recalled how a new teacher decided to instigate detention, a punishment which raised not only practical difficulties for parents wishing to collect their offspring but which was 'seen as a total affront on our freedom and on the school ethos . . . totally un-Alfredian'.[62] As a consequence, the pupils' council in one of its few major decisions affecting matters of principle 'voted it out and that was an end to detention'. In the view of this particular former pupil, this episode indicated a difference in outlook between the staff who remained after Nikki Archer's retirement and the new group of teachers of the Moran era who 'were more formal and disciplinarian in their teaching and approach to students'. Whether such a division existed, or if it did whether it was so marked is open to discussion, but what is not is the general condemnation by the student body of teachers who overstepped the mark. KAS did its best to select teachers carefully and monitor their teaching discreetly. The enemy from within was seen to be a far greater threat than the occasional journalistic attacks from without.

The less hurried manner in which the school went about its teaching and the emphasis it gave to allowing pupil–teacher relationships to develop rather than to be established through a stiff disciplinary code were always likely to be misunderstood. As one parent, who later became a champion of the KAS style of education, confessed in 1994, 'I must come clean that King Alfred School was at the bottom of my list of potentials 14 years ago, as I heard very dubious things about it.'[63] Yet the emphasis which the school placed on friendly relations between staff and pupils, upon respect for children as individuals so that they were able to learn to respect others and upon self-esteem where they were 'encouraged rather than pressured to learn' won many, but not all, parents over. The worries of some waiting in the playground to collect their offspring, that others elsewhere 'could read perfectly by now', 'had much more homework' or 'were much more advanced in maths', led some to withdraw their children from KAS. For those parents for whom academic achievement was not the sole driving force but for whom the right guidance and environment were rated equally highly KAS was a good choice. Their children could probably have a happier school life at KAS and in the more relaxed coeducational surroundings achieve 'positive and well adjusted' relationships.

In the 1980s and 1990s, KAS worked hard at its relaxed style of discipline, probably harder than at any other time in its history, for its size, the complexity of its curricular arrangements and the social problems which inevitably affected the school seemed to push it in the direction of more regulation. As the headmaster made clear in a confidential letter to a parent in 1991, what he prized particularly in the school was its gentleness, which he saw 'as being an easily lost quality in the school which I try to underpin, illustrate, expand'.[64] If he were to be more dynamic, to behave more 'confrontationally and urgently . . . some of the things you would like to see would happen very quickly (and incidentally, some of the things I would like to see)' but 'certain aspects of the school regarded as traditional and highly-prized would disappear'. This approach, however, was open to misinterpretation, especially by those students who failed to understand the reason behind his style of headship. Some of his students saw him simply as a 'quiet, friendly man with a terrible dress sense'[65] in his early years, as someone who preferred to 'operate from his office' who had 'less of the Alfredian spirit epitomised by Nikki, Roy Greenfield and John Peisley'.

Others perhaps a little more perceptive did not mistake his style for his goals. Certainly less extrovert than Nikki Archer, he nevertheless shared her concern to preserve the essential qualities of a KAS education. In the era of the New Right and New Labour he 'wanted to run a tight ship with capable staff, hardworking pupils, with a good atmosphere and relationships throughout the school',[66] according to one of his former pupils. The goals, not really different from those of Nikki Archer, could best be achieved by a more carefully regulated community but at the expense, as one ex-Alfredian pointed out, of KAS becoming more 'similar to other schools but less intense'.[67] How similar KAS was to other schools depended a great deal on a pupil's previous experience. One who moved from St Christopher's in Hampstead found her former school 'too pressured' and KAS 'comfortable' as she was an anxious child. The fact that some pupils found it difficult to settle in easily if they transferred to KAS in the second year of the middle school suggests that there was a difference, especially in terms of the more informal, less directed and less pressured environment which small classes facilitated. These characteristics generally helped pupils who came from abroad to adjust to their new life. However, as one pupil from Holland commented, 'KAS is not for everyone', certainly not for those who might thrive in a hothouse, academic atmosphere. In the view of an Alfredian who went on to a career as an art illustrator, 'Maybe the relaxed atmosphere didn't encourage academic dedication; you really had to push yourself if you wanted to make good grades. Some people blame the school for letting them down but it works both ways.' However, the difference between KAS and other schools was one of degree rather than of kind.

What attracted some pupils to KAS during this period was its distinctive environment. Children were able to roam the grounds, establish camps, move through the woods, play by the amphitheatre (which was often derelict or on one occasion filled with water to test some newly built boats), to establish their first romance, possibly as the result of spinning the bottle, or to smoke, despite the head's strong disapproval of the practice. The environment was deliberately kept 'soft' with piles of logs, for example, to encourage wild life. To some the grounds lacked the organized appearance of the traditional public school but then again, as one ex-Alfredian noted, the rather basic charm and ramshackle nature of the site made others who were the 'children of socialist parents . . . feel less uncomfortable about being at a private school'.[68] The school had a deliberate policy of continuing the tradition of Manor Wood being more an adventure playground rather than an ordered environment. Hence the introduction of the flying fox slide, aerial cableway, and climbing apparatus, the latter meeting with the opposition of some of the residents from nearby houses but which in fact was but an extension of tree-house living which characterized the school in its earlier years. Squirrel Hall also provided pupils with opportunities for climbing among its many beams before the ground underneath was paved, but, as might be expected, camp building and tree climbing took their toll on the environment.

One of the most publicized aspects and distinctive uses of the grounds was Village Week, which became a feature of the school programme. In 1989 the idea of a village project was launched by Stephen de Brett of the craft, design and technology department and quickly gained the support of other members of staff. Pupils would design and live in their own huts for a week, with the aims of developing design and practical building skills, and of fostering social skills, team-work and negotiation and the discovering of resources for entertain-ment. The village camp held in the May of the following year was reported in the local press and more fully in the *Guardian*: 'For four days last week, 45 second-years ate, lived and slept in the huts which they had made after studying the structures of primitive villages.'[69] The emphasis, however, was on self-sufficiency not survival techniques. Life in 'thatcher's Britain' was not intended to be entirely without the benefits of modern living. The 1994 village week was reported in the *Times Educational Supplement*,[70] when the interviewer emphasized the extensive preparations, the joys and responsibilities which communal living entailed and the culture shock. Perhaps to those who did not understand the aims of the project, the exercise tended to reinforce the image of the 'zoo on the hill'.

Yet another distinctive aspect of life in the early 1990s, particularly for a school drawn from many nationalities, was the involvement of some of the pupils in the Paris-based international project in myths, legends and folk tales. KAS was one of five British schools participating in the venture. In all eighty-two schools from eight countries were involved, with the broad aims of bringing together children of all nationalities to explore the arts, using national myths and legends to bridge and to extend relationships between cultures. Such projects, though important, involved only a minority of pupils. As in most schools far more were involved in less spectacular but other equally important 'extra-curricular activities'. Throughout its history KAS had integrated camps and excursions into its curricular aims, something which had evolved only recently in some state schools, because of the demands of GCSE. The excursion in the age of the grammar school was often seen as a treat or reward by many teachers, an occasional disruption of the timetable tolerated to provide a welcome relief from the daily tedium. This view was one which KAS had never held. Thus in the 1980s and 1990s as in earlier decades there were strictly no extra-curricular activities but only activities which aimed to foster the school's social and academic aims in another environment. The popular destinations, a former teacher's cottage in Wales, the Devil's Punch Bowl in Surrey, or nearer home, Swaylands, Barnet's environmental studies centre, were all deliberately designed to foster interpersonal and more formal academic skills. As one ex-Alfredian commented: 'These were invaluable in terms

157. Opposite page: Village week, 1990

of learning skills you would not learn at school and in forming relationships, seeing the other side of life and people.'[71] With the advent of coursework, particularly at GCSE, these kinds of aim and experience became common to many secondary schools, though perhaps KAS could have gone further than many schools in exploiting the cultural capital on its London doorstep.

The village project, that on myths and legends and the wealth of extra-curricular projects brought valuable publicity to the school in the local and national press. However, not all publicity was so positive or helpful. On entering the school in the early 1990s a visitor would probably be met not by a member of staff but by one of the inquisitive school goats whose breeding habits had provided a practical dimension to biology lessons. In December 1993 the head decided, on the advice of the Goat Society, that a three-month-old, male non-pedigree goat should be humanely destroyed. The headline in a local newspaper that 'Billy's First Noel is his last'[72] helped to bring protesters to the school gates and the resulting photographs of demonstrators led by Vivien Clifford, who had helped to persuade Margaret Thatcher to ban seal imports, gave a short burst of negative publicity. In the 1980s and 1990s the school became more publicity-conscious than at any other time in its history. It had little choice, for if the school was to increase or even to maintain its numbers in difficult economic times and improve its building stock, which defined so much of pupil experience, then it had to engage in high-profile fund-raising activities in which all could share.

In September 1983 the school population was 380, a figure which increased to 484 by October 1989, and remained around that total in the 1990s. The fund-raising activities which had been so regular a feature of school life at Manor Wood since 1920 became even more intensive and more inventive in an era of escalating costs, greater parental expectations and increased curricular demands. In the interwar years Wicksteed and council could trade on the romanticized image of the open-air, rural idyll, to disguise, in part, the shortcomings of the ex-army huts cum classrooms. In the last decades of the twentieth century the school had to embrace fully the age of the computer and bespoke sports facilities with the heavy building costs involved. Parents expected these to be available as a matter of course, as Areta Hautman pointed out to council in 1991: 'Naturally the type of education on offer is the primary interest of parents thinking about a school. The infrastructure, the buildings, tend to be taken for granted.'[73] Yet, with a curriculum which was generally more classroom-based than at any other time in the school's history, the buildings played a more important part in the life of pupils. Their recollections do not always reflect the great efforts which the school, including themselves, made to improve the infrastructure. 'Always messy,' concluded two former students, 'Always cold and constantly dirty. But it was our second home and to be honest it didn't matter.'[74]

By the time that Francis Moran arrived at King Alfred, the new gymnasium had been in use for a year. Pupils benefited immediately and considerably from the new building in terms of their own individual skills and in easing their transitions between the different sections of the school through having a common facility. However, it stood in stark contrast to the main classroom block, the Green building, which was described by a visiting inspector as a disaster area. The pupils saw things differently. The temporary, timber-framed two-storey building with a single-storey brick appendage resonated and vibrated at change-over time when children thronged the one internal staircase and packed the lobbies. It provided a kind of excitement which the adult world of staff and inspectors found nerve-wracking. In its last week of life, pupils and building came together in one final duel (leading to the suspensions mentioned later in this section). Cramped, worn and outgrown, it suffered the indignity of one last assault at the hands and feet of some of the pupils before being finally demolished to make way for a more solid building. 'About time! a good move',[75], concluded two pupils in retrospect, perhaps forgetting that sounds and smells are as much a part of how pupils react to their surroundings as is the more overworked visual sense. The demolition of a building which had been much adapted in its life, kept in use much longer than was planned and housing more children than originally envisaged, was not without loss, despite the obvious advantages of its successor.

Raising the money to provide the block of classrooms alongside Squirrel Hall was more of a community task than in the past and involved novel methods. The appeal was launched in a spectacular manner in November 1985 when three parents famous in the world of arts and entertainment, Pauline Collins, John Alderton and Tom Conti, began a firework display watched by about 1,000 pupils, teachers, parents and friends. Food of different nationalities was served while entertainment was provided by the school orchestra, drama department and school groups playing popular music. Dr Conor Cruise O'Brien

158. Victorian Day, 1988: (left side, front to back) Annabel Behar, Sarah Kovar, Sarah Jones; L to R Reg Corbett (s), Ruth Katz (s), Steven Vischer, Christian Panayiotou, ?, Silvia Beevers (s), Eva Goodliff (s), Nick Barbachano Hickmott, Denise Gibbs (s) (s – staff)

agreed to act as the appeal's president. One of the most novel of the fund-raising activities was an auction of promises, held in May 1987. Among the 222 lots were a week's holiday in Florida, half an hour in the nets bowling at Mike Brearley, a former England cricket captain, the chauffeur services for a day of Tom Conti, a place in Paco Pena's summer school in Spain, tea for two in the House of Lords and five lessons from a world-famous rock guitarist. Certainly the contacts of what John Welsh called a 'left-wing meritocracy of actors, writers and journalists'[76]

159. The flying fox in action: L to R Olivia Weale, Julia Brownlow, Nina Stenham, Lydia Samuels and Daisy the goat

proved very helpful. This imaginative approach led to additional income when Kara Conti, then chair of the parent–staff committee, wrote a pamphlet *How to Run an Auction of Promises*, which was published by the Institute of Social Inventions and reviewed in the *Guardian* by Nicholas Albery. The profit from these ventures of £16,000, augmented by the proceeds from fashion shows, guitar concerts, the buy-a-brick scheme and a grand ball celebrating the school's ninetieth birthday, helped to swell the amount raised through the less spectacular but more substantial method of covenants. The whole school community had thus contributed to the new Green building, named after the much respected teacher Roy Greenfield, who retired in 1987 and the energetic Ted Greenway, who retired from council the following year after twelve years of service, including that of having been a very able chairman of the grounds and buildings committee and of council. The building completed in October 1988 was officially opened in July 1989, ensuring that the pupils of the 1990s would enjoy a better quality environment, if perhaps one which lacked something of the improvised character of its predecessor. To this generation it was 'a civilised facility to have',[77] a vast improvement, except for 'the lighting in the library which in typical KAS style was inadequate'.[78]

Such shortcomings were negligible compared with those of the lower school whose pupils had suffered a rapidly deteriorating building in which the teachers were hard-pressed to deliver the best of a KAS education. The pupils were less concerned about the fact that in the 1930s when it was built by E. C. Kaufmann (later known as E. C. Kent) the lower school's flat roofs, white rendered walls and large steel and glass foldaway shutters had marked the arrival of the Modern Movement in school architecture than they were by the problems which

160. Brearley's successors? The cricket team, 1997: L to R (back row) Luke Burton, Oliver Morris, Frankie Frears, Nik Engineer, William Merricks, Adam Lorenz; (front row) Tom Boltman, Nick Guthrie, Teddy Leifer, Sam Hodges, Samuel Potter

fifty years of weathering and settlement had brought. The solid foundations had not allowed for settlement and the landfill site encouraged movement, all of which was not helped by the presence below of the Northern Line underground railway. Whatever the causes, the pupils were well aware of the results during their daily school lives: rising and falling damp, rainwater coming through the roof, dilapidated bay windows close to collapse, cracks in the building, and loose cladding. In terms of its aspect and layout, however – single-storey buildings facing the sun for much of the day, easy access to the open air and the organic relationship of its buildings – the lower school still had much to offer. These assets, which played such an important part in the lives of the young pupils, were retained by the architects in the new plan, Van Heyningen and Haward. Classrooms were arranged in pairs either side of a common cloakroom and toilets with easy access to the school grounds up a small slope. The new classrooms and library were to be accommodated under a single pitched roof with an extensive eaves overhang to protect the patios and entrance slope from the rain. For the new generations of children in the lower school the building was made to appear light and airy by the introduction of sky-lights running the length of the building. The interior design greatly assisted the display of pupils' work. Thin batons covered the panel joints, providing natural subdivided areas for display. The contrast between the clearly organized displays of work and the healthy anarchy of materials being worked at

161. Architect's sketch of the new lower school

table height, provided a pleasing experience for pupils so different from the constant retreat from mud and rain in the old buildings. The phased replacement of these buildings, with the most decrepit 'pavilions' on the eastern perimeter first, followed in later phases by the small corner hall and northern strip, was intended to cause least disruption and to expand gradually the benefits of a building better able to deliver a KAS education to successive generations of pupils. As a result of an anonymous donation by a wealthy benefactor and with the official opening ceremony performed by another parent, Bob Hoskins, the first phase was completed in 1993 and the second by March 1995 when the third and fourth phases began to be considered.

162. Part of the new lower school built between 1990 and 1996

Pupils at KAS in the 1990s were also better accommodated and provided for than their 1980s counterparts in other ways. A memorial drinking fountain provided by the actor Alan Bates was a constant daily reminder for many pupils of his son, Tristan, who died in tragic circumstances in Tokyo. The Blue building opened in May 1995 by Anthony Gormley, winner of that year's Turner Prize, provided much-needed accommodation for the special needs department and bursary. Designed by Sue Bollas, it fitted in with the KAS tradition of innovative architecture which dated back to Unwin's school hall of 1926. The Blue building was raised on steel stilts as a second storey over an existing classroom, a 1950s prefabricated building which can be replaced separately at the end of its useful life. This adventurously designed structure freed accommodation in the old special needs building for use by the craft design and technology department.

163. The new lower school hall in use: L to R Philip Elstob, Theo Sion, Alexander Smilansky, Daniel Spackman

These improvements compensated in part for the school curriculum which became less distinctive because of the need to accommodate New Right reforms, although through the Wednesday afternoon choice period and the 'spaces in between' concept, the headteacher attempted to reduce academic pressure and to offer opportunities for individual development in other directions. The 'spaces in between' idea was a deliberate attempt in the words of the chair of council in 1993, to foster

164. The DIY tradition: digging the new pond for lower school: L to R Annie-Jo Leslie, Ilya Kovar, Douglas D'Arcy, Phoebe D'Arcy, Sarah Kovar, Anthony Gormley, John Leslie, Robert D'Arcy, David Kovar, Vicken Gormley

165. Environmental education: the pond in use

'those areas of school life that are between and around classes where the real spirit of the school has a chance to flourish'.[79] The pressure to accommodate a full range of academic subjects and to allow adequate time for the practical skills inherent in coursework had been met in part by the reorganization of the timetable soon after Francis Moran arrived. In responding to these pressures and demands the school became more like other secondary schools in its timetable. Contrary to popular myth 'the day was organised around lessons and not free time',[80] as one student recalled. In March 1985, John Peisley, with the headmaster's support, outlined to council a pilot project to increase the number of double periods, claiming that more staff preferred double to single periods. Although some of the advantages of the scheme were recognized its application to the lower school would not, in the view of Mike Young, the head of the junior section, be entirely beneficial as many pupils had a limited concentration span.

The new timetable was put in place for a week and the staff and pupils were then asked for their views, an extensive process of consultation not normally found in schools. The greater ease with which pupils were able to understand the new timetable, the greater number of shorter breaks and the value of double lessons were counterbalanced in the views of several staff and students by the lack of longer breaks, the loss of callover and the feeling that there was too much rigorous academic work before lunch. The overall impression, was that if the four double-period arrangement was to go ahead as a pilot project from September 1985, then a longer morning break was necessary. The double-period format did not fit the KAS ethos entirely, particularly in the lower and middle schools where the day was seen by some as overlong and thus more stressful. Yet if the savings on the time taken to move between classes could be translated into a shorter day this tendency could be counter-acted and KAS ideology strengthened by reducing the number of 35-minute periods, which tended to be teacher-centred, in favour of longer periods which encouraged a variety of pupil-centred activities. In December 1986 it was decided to broaden the school's core curriculum of subjects and reduce options, a move which brought the school's formal curriculum even more in line with that of other schools. However, none of these issues was finally resolved, although the head was still in favour of longer periods to deliver the broader curriculum, in the belief that few changes meant better work output, a view, he argued, which was sup-ported by timetable experiments elsewhere. Though concentration spans could be of small duration initially, he believed they could be lengthened to the full seventy minutes and where this was not possible, activities could be varied.[81] These and other timetabling matters, including the length of the school day, continued to occupy the attention of the senior management of the school for some time.

There was one other major organ-izational change in the Moran era which

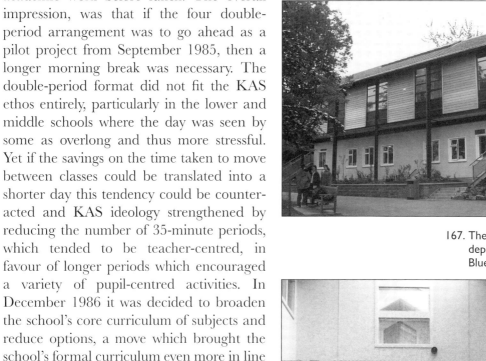

166. The exterior of the Blue building

167. The special studies department in the Blue building

tended to mark something of a departure from past progressive practices and that concerned the family-grouping system which had been introduced in the wake of the Plowden Report of 1967. The formal reappraisal of combining two age groups in one class was initiated after the Gabbitas Thring parental survey of 1986. Moran concluded that 'the most useful thing thrown up by the survey was a certain disquiet about the two year family grouping in the lower school'.[82] Yet there was no clear and outright condemnation of the practice either at the time of the survey or later. Only a minority of parents expressed concern and ex-Alfredians since have pointed to its positive aspects, especially in mixing age groups and extending friendships, part of a child's healthy development, including the inevitable sadness when such friendships were disrupted when the older children and mentors went 'over the field'. They also recognized that such groups were less homogeneous, especially in terms of ability, and that older children might forfeit time to develop their own academic skills while helping the younger ones. In 1986, the matter was considered so important that, in keeping with the founders' ideal of independent evaluation, the headteacher, with the support of council, invited a retired HMI who had undertaken her teaching practice at King Alfred, Miss Renata Feldmeier, to report on the effectiveness of the system, which was, in essence, for KAS a long-established method of organization as a natural extension of the family. Her conclusions were much in line with those of the staff, in supporting 'the family grouping system especially at the lower and middle parts of the Lower School'.[83] Although it made considerable demands on teachers, the staff were nevertheless successful in encouraging children to work at their own pace, and in finding their own levels of attainment in the lower and middle family groups. She concluded, however, that it was least successful with the upper family groups, where a larger chronological peer group would facilitate greater academic stretching and a larger balanced gender peer group would be of social benefit. Most staff generally agreed that, even if the younger section of the family group gained from the organization, the older section lost by working too slowly or by being held back. It also hindered curriculum experimentation, particularly with the introduction of the Scottish Mathematics Project for ten year olds.

As a consequence, the upper family groups were degrouped first, leaving the middle groups in families for a year to avoid overstraining the system and to assess the effects of degrouping. By January 1989 council was asked to consider degrouping the middle section of the lower school, seven and eight year olds, the following September. The process of degrouping continued apace for the seven year olds and upwards, as space became available with the construction of the new Green building. By 1992 the teachers of the five and six year olds favoured degrouping but keeping a two-year teacher cycle so that lengthy contact with one teacher, so favoured by parents, would be maintained. The reception class would stay as a unit. By October 1993 the process was complete with the head of the lower school, Mike Young, reporting to council that 'teaching was easier and classes more cohesive'. The greater emphasis on academic attainment in the basics which the national curriculum had encouraged had thus had an effect on the school's organization with some loss of the social benefits which had accrued from mixing age groups. KAS had made a deliberate decision in the light of the needs of pupils in the 1980s and 1990s to reject one of the principles of the founders to whom family grouping was both a guiding principle as an extension of the family, and in the era of the small school, a necessity. The underlying principle, however, was that KAS was still a rational school, an experimental school, which tested various ideas in the light of knowledge about child development, not an institution like Summerhill wedded to a set of unchanging principles which could be termed 'progressive'.

Certainly in its attitude to discipline KAS was very different from Summerhill. Guidelines given to staff indicated how behavioural matters were to be dealt with by the use of blue forms. The blue forms were given to disruptive pupils who were sent to the upper and middle school heads or the headteacher who would deal with the problem and discuss appropriate action with the teacher concerned. The forms were then placed in the student's file, three such forms resulting in parents

168. Alexis McCue and Anna Tuckett in a lower-school production of *Achilles' Heel* in the open-air theatre, 1995

being asked to come to school to discuss the matter. With high expectations of pupils' attitudes and behaviour, the school thus had a clear system for dealing with transgressions which, though rather formalized, was well in keeping with KAS traditions. These measures affected only a small number of students, and more serious forms of punishment even less. In 1986, three boys were suspended from school for being involved in the disappearance of a bottle of mercury from the science laboratory. Such action by the head sent clear messages to students about the way in which KAS would deal with serious deviations from acceptable behaviour. These included drug abuse.

169. The new Green building, 1988

170. The library in the new Green building: L to R Ana Karic, Catherine Gill, Tom Keverne, Lara Brearley, Kate Greensted, Alison Berman

Moran's approach to the problem of drugs at KAS is best summarized in his policy statement to council in May 1992. 'Any child bringing drugs to the school risks expulsion. Drug-taking is considered a very serious matter. No blanket punishment is enforced, however. Each case would be considered on its own individual merit.'[84] Students were very much aware of the seriousness with which the head and council viewed drug-taking and drug distribution. One who attended KAS for the first decade of the Moran era recalled, 'Francis . . . was very against drugs and took heavy action against offenders.'[85] However, his was not an unthinking, automatic response. For example, he was willing to accept the inevitable outcry in council when he offered to give a boy a fresh start at KAS who was said to have been involved in a drugs problem in another school, even though he had recently expelled a boy from KAS for what his parents believed to be a slight exposure to drugs. The school also offered professional guidance to pupils exposed to the risk of drug abuse. Drug incidents were always likely to arouse controversy because of the head's natural desire to deal with each case individually and, if possible, without involving outside parties which could result in harmful and exaggerated rumour. He thus met parents and took action, backing up his view of the seriousness of such incidents by addressing sections of the school if necessary. However, no routine testing for drugs was introduced as was said to have been the case at Rugby in 1996.

He was ever aware of the possible distortions which could arise if such matters reached the press, distortions which, on the one hand, could be used by some Hampstead residents to misrepresent the school as a hotbed of indiscipline, or on the other, could be used by some parents to demand a tightening of discipline and a more authoritarian response by the head, which could undermine the KAS ethos. One such matter recalled by most students of the late 1980s was the premature demolition of sections of the Green building. In 1987, in a local newspaper,[86] a former teacher criticized the 'soft treatment' of pupils who started to kick down the plasterboard walls of the ageing Green building, having been given permission, at the end of term, to write on them, a few days before contractors were due to demolish them. The suspension of some of the culprits for one or two days until the end of term was said to be 'barely anything at all' and indicative of the fact that 'Children at King Alfred's can get away with almost anything.' The newspaper's editor allowed the head the right of reply. In exercising the right he effectively underlined the school's unusual response to indiscipline. It was regarded first and foremost as a breach of trust. In expressing their anger about and detestation of such vandalism the staff had conveyed to pupils their view that such actions were a violation of the civilized ground rules upon which the trust and respect between staff and pupils were founded. Automatic, retributive punishment was not in keeping with KAS ideology, and as the following recollection of the event emphasizes, the shock at being suspended for being involved in the incident was profound:

> An emergency meeting was called and Francis said anyone not responsible could leave but if they were later found to be lying he would suspend them for a term. You must recall that very few of us had ever been punished before as there were so few rules to be broken . . . I stayed, as did most people, out of fear more than guilt and we were suspended for this last day of term. This meant missing 'Sing-Song' and saying goodbye to some staff I liked who were leaving so I was upset at my punishment.[87]

Others were upset because they believed that if they owned up no action would be taken against them. What is clear is that within the confines of the school the whole matter, in one way or another, revolved around the idea of a breach of trust, a view which each of the previous headteachers of the school took.

The taking of illegal drugs and vandalism were matters upon which the school could make a firm and clear stand. Legal drugs, particularly the smoking of cigarettes by pupils of legal age, were another matter in that they raised the issue of pupil choice and freedom. Not surprisingly therefore they appeared to take up an inordinate amount of the head's time and, impinging on KAS ideology, were matters for discussion in council. As Sir William Wood, the society's president, reminded council in 1986, 'When smoking was allowed in 1974 it was considered to be a liberalising move to give the Sixth Form more freedom',[88] a position which he continued to favour unless staff were also banned from smoking. Subsequent discussion resulted in the decision that pupils should be forbidden to smoke in school and staff should also consider desisting. There were several issues at stake. One person's freedom to smoke was a denial of another person's freedom to breathe smoke-free air. Furthermore, at a time when the school was doing its best to encourage healthy living, aspects of which were a healthy diet promoted in the school canteen, good-quality drinking water and measures to reduce the harmful effects of the screens of visual display units, it was incongruous that it allowed pupils to engage in a proven health risk and to risk the health of others. It did not take pupils long to recognize that 'Francis was very against smoking.' When the school six reported to council in l990 that a vote among pupils showed forty-two out of forty-six in favour of dividing their common room into two to allow smoking, the chairman reminded them that, though the views of pupils 'might be taken into account, the authority to ban or allow smoking rested with council'.[89] Up to the sixth form infringement of the ban resulted in 'automatic suspension', a position which seemed to contradict the denial of the use of blanket punishments by the head for other misdemeanours. The sixth form were treated more 'delicately' from 1988, with a first offence resulting in a warning, a second in suspension and expulsion if the offender remained unrepentant. This did not, of course, resolve the matter of staff smoking, which set a bad example to children. However, the emphasis was placed upon reason not retribution in an effort to dissuade pupils from taking up the habit and to persuade partakers to give it up. To this extent, KAS did not differ from most schools in its handling of the matter but it differed considerably from many sixth-form colleges where the matter of influencing young pupils was not a consideration.

The matter continued to be a concern for council. By 1992 there was still a minority of sixth-formers smoking, despite the growing feeling against the practice. A variety of views on the problem at the March meeting of council in that year covered much of the old ground, especially that of smokers going to the park to smoke, possibly in front of young children, if it were banned altogether. Yet it was left to the chair of council to point to a principle which had guided KAS intermittently since its creation, that one of the aims of its education was to encourage pupils to make their own decisions even if they were the wrong ones. The school's task was to ensure that choices and decisions were made in the light of the latest information. This applied as much to staff and parents as it did to sixth-formers. Staff had in-service training days to help guide their teaching, especially of GCSE. For parents evening discussions were provided on such topics as Aids, drug awareness, coeducation (which in the 1980s and 1990s was coming increasingly under fire) and helping children to succeed, as well as on broader curricular areas of progressive education. Whether having noted expert and other opinion, students, staff and parents chose to heed it in making decisions was their own concern. For pupils, making wrong decisions was as much a part of maturation as being guided into making what many school staff believed to be the right ones.

The context of curriculum delivery was thus very different from that of many schools, even if the curriculum itself was not too dissimilar. Choice (the afternoon when non-examinable activities were on offer, including games, fifth-year current affairs and fourth-year computing skills and personal and social education) helped to broaden the curriculum, but there was a core of compulsory subjects, including English language, mathematics, science and French, together with a series of options from the arts, sciences, technology and languages to allow for a moderate measure of choice. The resulting curriculum was not greatly different from that of many state schools with a non-selective academic intake, although subjects such as drama and photography were probably more popular than elsewhere. Perhaps something of a departure from the usual options lists were the notes for guidance which accompanied them. Students and parents were informed of the work commitment outside school hours, an important factor in a school which had in the past minimized the amount of homework, and how parents could assist their offspring, again an important matter in a school where the ultimate authority lay with parents and which prided itself in being an extension of the family. The notes also took a long-term view of subject choices, giving advice of relevance to later choices, including advanced level and possible future careers.

Such close guidance was essential if pupils were to gain the maximum benefit from their years at KAS. It was also of significance for the school's examination results, for poor choice could lead to poor results and KAS was keen to show that its relaxed style of learning was not just compatible with but for many children a prerequisite for sound achievement in public examinations. Without such visible and easily measurable evidence, the school could spiral to closure. League tables ignored the nature of the candidature and to this extent KAS had to work much harder to achieve good results, paradoxically at the same time as maintaining a relatively unpressured approach. In 1991 the chairman of council, Ari Zaphiriou-Zarifi, summed up the task bluntly when he said 'The school had to be seen to be successful at A level',[90] and he could have added at GCSE. Thus much of the experience of KAS adolescents centred upon preparation for examinations, to an extent which Russell and his successors to 1945 would not have thought possible while still remaining faithful to the school's ideals. The advent of GCSE (with its coursework) in 1988 made the task easier than it had been in the days of

Montgomery, Humphries and Nikki Archer, but the downward adjustments in the value of coursework as a percentage of the total assessment in the 1990s took away some of its peculiar benefits. Tables 10 and 11 show how successful the school was in the decade 1985 to 1994 in its examination results.

One increasingly prominent feature of school life was careers education, something which KAS a century earlier had not thought necessary. By 1990 under the careful guidance, first of Liz Yates and then of the head's wife, Norma Moran, it had been extended down the school. Rather than leaving the matter until the fifth or sixth years when students could find possible avenues closed to them because of their choice of subjects, the careers programme began in the third year to clarify the implications of subject choice, to provide interest guides and information and possibly personality tests. What was provided in the form hour in the third year was extended in the fourth year in the personal education programme to include talks about employment opportunities by various people from many walks of life. The intention of these developments was to place pupils in a better position to consider their employment and education options based on their interests and subject choices and to discuss their aspirations with the careers teacher individually. Careers evenings and fairs provided additional and complementary information and guidance to sixth- as well as fifth-formers. In the case of the former, university open days and the completion of application forms played a major part in their preparation for the future. The kinds of career which fifth- and sixth-formers leaving between 1983 and 1994 pursued are shown in Tables 12 and 13.

It must be remembered, however, that an education at KAS was not primarily or directly concerned with vocational preparation. If the latter were the case then the relaxed style of learning in which respect was earned and not an automatic entitlement of a higher hierarchical position was singularly inappropriate. The words of a person who was a recent member of the school provide an interesting comment on the subject:

> I got the job on the back of responsibilities at school. Most of the qualities have to be brought out on the job. Staff (in my firm) are treated like rubbish, which I suppose shows me what a lucky school life I have had and that I have not been prepared for real life. When I leave this job, go to university and then become a teacher, I know the qualities such as communication, respect and listening that I learnt at KAS will come in use.[91]

While the dichotomy between 'real life' in the commercial world and the qualities which an Alfredian education encouraged is presented in

Table 10 **Fifth-form examination results 1985–1994**

Year	No. in year	5A–C passes	Entries per student	Entry	A/A*	B	C	D	E	F	G	U/X	A*–C passes
1985	30	18	6.8	205	26	59	59	32	17	1	0	11	144
%	100	60	–	100	12.7	28.8	28.8	15.6	8.3	0.5	0	5.4	70.2
1986	43	22	6.9	296	43	59	87	56	31	7	3	10	189
%	100	51	–	100	14.5	19.9	29.4	18.9	10.5	2.4	1.0	3.3	63.9
1987	38	24	7.6	287	29	71	88	51	37	6	0	5	188
%	100	63	–	100	10.1	24.7	30.7	17.8	12.9	2.1	0	1.7	65.5
1988	40	14	7.7	308	61	62	79	58	33	10	5	0	202
%	100	60	–	100	19.8	20.1	25.6	18.8	10.7	3.2	1.6	0	65.6
1989	49	37	7.6	370	87	111	99	36	19	8	6	4	29
%	100	76	–	100	23.5	30.0	26.8	9.7	5.1	2.2	1.6	1.1	80.3
1990	37	29	7.5	276	99	66	67	29	10	3	2	0	232
%	100	78	–	100	35.0	23.9	24.3	10.5	3.6	1.1	0.7	0	84.1
1991	47	34	7.6	358	84	92	92	58	21	10	1	0	268
%	100	72	–	100	23.5	25.7	25.7	16.2	5.8	2.8	0.3	0	74.9
1992	45	39	8.2	363	115	120	81	36	9	5	1	1	316
%	100	87	–	100	31.3	32.6	22.0	9.8	2.4	1.4	0.3	0.3	85.9
1993	41	38	7.9	322	106	107	75	18	10	4	0	2	288
%	100	93	–	100	32.9	33.2	23.3	5.6	3.1	1.2	0	0.6	89.4
1994	43	38	7.6	325	123	110	60	19	8	3	0	2	293
%	100	88	–	100	37.8	33.8	18.5	5.8	2.5	0.9	0	0.6	90.2
Total	413	293	7.54	3115	773	857	787	393	195	57	18	35	2417
%	100	70.9	–	100	24.8	27.5	25.3	12.6	6.3	1.8	0.6	1.1	77.6

Note: To make a fair comparison over this period, the following grades at O-level GCE, CSE and GCSE are taken as equivalent. GSCE replaced the other exams in 1988. The A* grade was introduced in 1994.

GCSE Grades	A/A*	B	C	D	E	F	G	U/X
O-Level	A	B	C	D	E	U	U	U
CSE Grades		1	2	3	4	5		

Table 11 **Upper sixth A-level results 1985–1994**

Year	No. in year	A	B	C	D	E	N	U	A–E Pass	Average per taker	% pass
1985	17	8	10	5	4	6	11	4	33/48	1.9	69
1986	19	6	15	8	7	8	7	1	44/52	2.3	85
1987	11	8	7	7	5	3	1	1	30/32	2.7	94
1988	16	9	11	3	7	5	4	5	35/55	2.2	80
1989	21	5	8	12	3	9	12	6	37/55	1.8	6
1990	23	9	13	13	11	4	4	6	50/60	2.2	83
1991	22	6	14	22	9	6	4	3	57/64	2.6	89
1992	23	23	16	14	4	7	3	3	64/70	2.8	91
1993	14	7	8	7	$8\frac{1}{2}$*	7	2	1	$37\frac{1}{2}/40\frac{1}{2}$	2.9	93
1994	13	15	11	5	4	3	3	1	38/42	2.9	90
Total	179	96	113	96	$62\frac{1}{2}$	58	51	31	$425\frac{1}{2}/507\frac{1}{2}$	2.4	84

starker terms than many former pupils experienced, nevertheless these words provide a fitting tribute to the quality of school life in the 1980s and 1990s.

In their own way these decades were a second golden age in the history of KAS, not as a mirror image of the first which spanned the interwar years but as a period when the school settled back into its more traditional role of maintaining a progressive outlook when the pressures upon the school in the era of the national curriculum were towards conformity and uniformity. Preserving the essential principles of the founders was much more difficult in the 1980s and 1990s than in the 1920s and 1930s. The government controlled the public examinations system more closely and was intent that its ideology should be reflected not just at eighteen or sixteen-plus but throughout the school years. In the mid-1920s it had relinquished its control over much of the curriculum, thus freeing KAS even from indirect pressures. By the 1990s it had reasserted its control with a national curriculum, league tables of examination results and the weakening of rival areas of authority, especially the local education authorities, all of which were to have an impact upon KAS to a greater or lesser degree. Its formal curriculum was thus much more in line with that of state schools and many other independent schools. Yet in the broader values which the school fostered in terms of human relationships and of individual development (through such means as choice and spaces-in-between) it succeeded in retaining its distinctiveness, and this at a time when the school had a larger population than at any time in its history. It had adapted to rapidly changing times and yet preserved ideals which past

Table 12 **Fifth-form leavers**

	1983	1984	1985	1986	1987	1988	1989	1990	1991	1992	1993	1994
Left country	1	2[1]	1[2]	1[2]	2				8[3]	1[4]	3[5]	
A-levels elsewhere	2	7	10	12[6]	10	11	17	9	17	25	10	22
FE nursing					1		1[7]		1[8]	1[9]	1[10]	1[11]
FE leisure							2[12]		1[13]	1[14]	1[15]	1[16]
FE accounts							1[17]		1[18]			
FE photography							2[19]					
FE fashion		1			2							
FE business		1				1[20]			1	1		
FE YTS		1										
FE secretarial		1					2		1	1		
FE drama						1	2	1				
FE construction												
FE caring NNEB									1[21]	1[21]	1	
FE cooking/catering			1	2			1		1			
FE horticulture												
FE dance			2									
FE sports	1											
University	2	2	6	4	3	8	11	5	15[22]	10		
Polytechnic	1		1		5	1[23]	4	1				
Art College		1	2	5	4	1	2	4	2	6		
Work	4	2	5	8	2	1	3	1	1	3	1	1
Own business	1	1							1			
Odd jobbing & travel		1		2	1	2	1	1				
Musicians/bands		2		3	2	1			1			
Army			1									
Unknown	3			2	1	3	2	2	4		1	
Year off 18+		2			1	2						
Retake 16+							4		6	4		
Total pupils	13/31	15/31	19/31	32/45	20/39	19/40	31/50	16/37	32/47	33/46	17/42	26/43
HE	3/13	4/1[24]	10/19[25]	15/32[25]	8/20	13/19	14/31	9/16	18/32	16/33	n/k	n/k
FE	1/13	4/15	3/19[26]	4/32	3/20	1/19	10/31	3/16	9/32	5/33	2/33	2/26

[1] 1 univ. Brazil; 1 univ. USA
[2] univ. Japan
[3] 1 Degree
[4] 1 Colorado College
[5] Israel, France, Switerland
[6] 2 dropped out
[7] Access
[8] Film
[9] Marine Design
[10] Engineering
[11] Film School
[12] Film
[13] Art
[14] Design 3D
[15] Royal Academy of Music (Dip)
[16] Beauty
[17] Media Studies
[18] Design
[19] Art and Design
[20] Sound Engineering
[21] Montessori
[22] Polytechnics become Universities
[23] Drama
[24] 1 Brazil, 1 USA
[25] Japan
[26] Plus 1 Diploma in Surveying

generation of KAS students would have recognized instantly. This surely was the principal achievement of the Moran era. Perhaps none but an Etonian progressive could have succeeded in squaring the KAS circle.

Managing change: council in the 1980s and 1990s

John Pemberthy, a marketing consultant, presented an interesting pen sketch in the *Daily Telegraph* in November 1995 of what he saw as the principal characteristics of many governing bodies of independent schools.[92] Cumbersome and overlarge, with usually twenty to twenty-five members, they consisted of out-of-touch amateurs, the great, the good and certainly the elderly, usually retired service or public figures,

Table 13 **Analysis of sixth-form leavers**

	1983	1984	1985	1986	1987	1988	1989	1990	1991	1992	1993	1994
University	5[1]	8[1]	13	12	9	7	5	11	12	15	10	10
Polytechnic	4	1	4		3	5	2					
Art College	2	3	2[1]		2	4	6	3[1]	5	5	4	2
Other training		1[2]		1	1[3]	1[4]	2		1[5]			1[6]
Drama							1	2	1			
Year Off*			3	6	3	6	11	12	11	16	7	5
Left Country		1[7]	1	2		1[7]	1[8]	2[9]		2[10]		
Not known		1	1	2				1				
Retaking									1			
Work	2	2	4			1		2	1	1		
Odd Jobs/travel/ bands				1		1						
Died							1					
TOTAL PUPILS	9	19	23	22	12	18	21	23	21	23	14	13
HE %	77.7	84.2	73.9	7.2	91.6	83.3	95.2	82.6	85.7	95.6	100	92.3

*Overlaps with HE group

[1] dropped out
[2] Montessori
[3] Banking
[4] Nursing

[5] Legal
[6] Hotel Management (Lausanne)
[7] American University
[8] Canadian University

[9] 1 (Israel), 1 (Boston, USA)
[10] USA, VASA & NY

together with some professional people, a token member of the opposite sex to the school body, one or two businessmen, the headteacher, bursar and a member of staff. Such groups, he believed, were incapable of responding to changes in educational policy and the market-place and ought to be replaced by smaller, more efficient and informed bodies of about ten people who met more regularly and about half of whom should be drawn from the school staff, whose professional lives they controlled. Presumably the transition from the antediluvian to the modern would be accomplished through the employment of consultants such as Pemberthy and his like. As a professional marketing consultant he appeared to rule out the idea that modernization could be accomplished through self-improvement. The governing bodies were too steeped in tradition and self-importance to instigate reform. Change could not come from within.

Few would identify the council of KAS with this stereotype, except in terms of size. As an annually elected body of a coeducational school it respected neither tokenism, title nor tradition. If anything its problem was, according to the new head, that of a surfeit of new blood. How unlike Pemberthy's antediluvian model KAS was, was underlined by Francis Moran when, in his annual address to council in 1991, he commented that 'he knew of no governing body whose members changed so often as they did at KAS'.[93] Pemberthy's chronic stability was not the problem. For Moran, it was council's 'inherent instability', though Ari Zaphiriou-Zarifi, the out-going chairman in 1991, preferred the term 'delicate balance'. With half of council having served one year or less and only a third five years or more, the head's assessment was probably the more accurate. Rapid turnover in a body of twenty-one members had the obvious advantage of new blood, new ideas and an infusion of new forms of expertise but it also had potential drawbacks in terms of role definition, communication and the steep learning curve which faced each newly elected member and indeed some of the older members. Problems in these areas in the past had led to the accusation that council had been run by a clique, contrary to the broad democratic spirit of the society. The only way forward after the crisis of the early 1980s, which ruled out any major reduction in the size of council, was to tackle the problem areas which made for Moran's 'inherent instability'. The old battle over size might well have to be refought in the future but its success was not a prerequisite for modernization. The post-crisis chairs, Ted Greenway, Ari Zaphiriou-Zarifi and Kara Conti, recognized the need to improve communications and to define more closely powers and responsibilities within council and between council and the other constituent elements of the school and society. While the expertise of outside agencies could be drawn upon in these tasks, council believed that the management of change in the 1980s and 1990s was primarily its own direct, non-delegated responsibility. The Pemberthies of the world of consultancy would have made a thin living at KAS where decision-makers had largely chosen the path of self-improvement. Yet with the reshaping of the governing bodies of state schools demanded by the Baker Act of 1988, council could also draw on the professional expertise of the consultancy industry which sprang up rapidly in response.

Self-improvement was never likely to be painless, particularly in the fraught atmosphere which remained after Nikki Archer's retirement. General goodwill was in short supply throughout the summer and autumn of 1983. Deep divisions and suspicions remained which suggested that the crisis was much more than a simple disagreement about her headship; hence Ted Greenway's reprimand to council six months after she retired 'to stop fighting the battles of the past'.[94] It took more than the chairman's exhortations to defuse tension. One of the main factors which helped to de-escalate the crisis was the firmness of the new head in his demand for a standard Governing Bodies Association–Headmasters' Conference (GBA–HMC) contract. In essence this meant the restoration of the powers of headship whittled away in the last years of his predecessor. He was supported in his stand by the president of the society, Sir William Wood, and a Gabbitas Thring adviser who helped to prepare the way for such a contract. The only full extant account of the crucial meeting of the appointment panel in which the matter was thrashed out is that by the president. Five years later he recalled how a majority initially wanted specific limitations on the power of the head concerning appointments, promotions, the dismissal of staff and the expulsion of pupils.[95] He and the consultant's adviser spoke in favour of the contract model agreed between the GBA and the HMC. The outcome of the discussion was to leave the form of contract open for negotiation with the successful candidate. Francis Moran was in no doubt what he wanted. He prefaced the 'letter of intent' requested by the appointment panel in July 1983 with the statement: 'on my insistence that the contract offered me as Head should follow closely the HMC–GBA model (a simple, basic and tried compromise between the respective parties)'. This was, in his view, merely a confirmation of the position which the chairman of the panel, Lewis Keeble, had expressed before his fellow selectors on Moran's appointment. Yet what was 'pushed' at him was 'a contract which was so altered that' he felt 'it was unrecognisable'.[96] It took most disciplinary powers away from the head; the head was not responsible for the appointment of heads of department. These and other restrictions led Moran to block all attempts at reducing the powers in the standard GBA contract. It took six months to gain general acceptance for what the head believed had been settled the previous July. In the December meeting of council, Areta Hautman argued that council 'went along with the head's explanation that at the outset council had not made clear its intention to offer any contract other than the standard-GBA contract'.[97] As a consequence it accepted the contract with some changes proposed by the new head. An amicable compromise was reached in which the head informally invited council members to discuss staffing and other matters, thereby establishing a positive atmosphere of trust and 'an air of partnership' at the beginning of the new headship.

Behind the issue of the head's contract lay the key matter of the exact extent of the head's powers over the formal and informal curriculum. In December 1984 Sir William Wood, in offering some advice on the role of council, argued that the

> traditional role of council was to look after the business side of the school . . . and to leave matters of the curriculum to the head . . . Council should always support the Head in the academic administration of the School and would always be interested in educational matters.[98]

This echoed Storr's view in 1901 that council should reign but not rule. At the following meeting Areta Hautman questioned whether the term 'interest' adequately reflected the fact that ultimate responsibility for general educational policy lay with council, while its day-to-day interpretation lay with the head. Such a dualism left immense grey areas where council could charge the head with changing policy by stealth or unwitting decision and the head could charge council with using its powers to interfere in daily routines and decision-making. At the end of the day the whole system rested on mutual trust and confidence.

Apart from the head's firmness, the de-escalation of the crisis was assisted by a second factor, the election results of the society's annual general meeting in November 1983 attended by an unprecedented turn-out of 243 members, partly the result of parents wishing to see and hear the new head. According to Sir William Wood's view of the result, they 'voted by a majority of two to one for the loyalist candidates. The losing side were stunned by this decisive verdict on their year of office.'[99] In reply to this view A. Hautman, a member of council from 1979 to the present, argues that 'It is true that the two candidates who had been part of the "new majority" were not re-elected and that two loyalists were re-elected but the other five additional members elected to fill the seven vacancies were all new . . .'[100] As Felicity Taylor, member of council 1980–3, has pointed out it might also have been the case that there was 'a feeling that new blood was needed to support the new Head'.[101] Council, she adds, was still led by 'one of the reforming group'.

However one interprets the results in terms of the past divisions, in terms of their future significance they paved the way for a return to the traditional relationship between head and council and the dismantling of the education policy committee, which was seen by Sir William as a consequence of council's approval of the head's contract confirming his responsibility for the teaching and the curriculum within the general policy approved by council. To Lewis Keeble and some other members its abolition could herald a return to decision-making by a small cabal; to Sir William, dismantling the education policy committee would enable the head to become part of a real partnership in decision-making and educational policy, allowing him to criticize and make changes without being accused of interfering in the business of a council committee. A decisive vote of twelve to three in favour of its abolition 'in its present form' resolved the issue. A proposal to replace it with a more general 'think-tank' or 'educational forum' was deferred at the head's request, a mark of the trust which was developing between council and the new head. The return of the headship to a more traditional relationship with council was not accompanied by immediate normalcy in the relationship with staff who believed they were overburdened with meetings and thus could not spare the time to attend those of council. Nevertheless, the door was left open for their return and they resumed their representation in October 1984. It remained firmly shut to pupil representation, although pupils had six of the thirty-seven places on the parent–staff committee, only two less than the staff and far outweighed by the twenty-three parent representatives.

Moran's determination to stand firm, what he termed the 'loyalty to the head vote', the election result of November 1983 and the developing trust between council and the new head were three of the four factors which led to a de-escalation of the crisis and a reduction in political tension. The fourth was the clarification of council's committee structure to assist its smoother running. The process of role and procedural definition and review which began in the last stages of the council crisis with the negotiation of the new head's terms and conditions of service continued apace during the more peaceful chairmanships of Ted Greenway (1983–8), Ari Zaphiriou-Zarifi (1988–91) and Kara Conti (1991 to the present). Council had the advantage of membership of the GBA and ISIS (the Independent Schools Information Service), especially their general advice on administrative and financial matters and their *Guidelines for Governors* and *Guide to Good Communications*. However, their assistance was not always deemed necessary, as in the case of the obvious and logical starting-point of the updating process, the articles of association. It is perhaps a measure of the speed with which most of the heat left the crisis that the review suggested by the president in October 1984 was undertaken by an uncontested *ad hoc* working party under Jack Black, set up in December of that year, with their recommendations being discussed but not challenged in council and passed unanimously in May 1986. Two of the three areas of revision, the subscription structure and borrowing powers, were non-controversial, except for the special terms for staff in relation to the former. The third, the unusual powers of the president, particularly to take the chair in council when the chairman was present could have raised dissent but did not. The anomaly remained 'because it worked well in practice'.[102] What perhaps was surprising was that in its definition of members of council in May 1986 there was no mention of the school staff, and in the powers and duties of the council no reference was made to education policy. The draft of the revised articles was submitted to the Charity Commissioners before being put before and accepted by the annual general meeting of the society in November 1986 with one member dissenting.

There was no provision in the revised articles of association for student representation on council. However, in 1989 Ari Zaphiriou-

Zarifi began the first of the annual visits to council by the school six. Inevitably their address to council was used to vent their feelings about increased restrictions and pressures which were, in their view, leading KAS to drag its progressive anchor. This helped to convince some, especially the head, that the student body should remain outside the decision-making process. The 'views of the sixth form should be borne in mind when making decisions and . . . the Head's encouragement of Pupils' Council should be reinforced wherever possible by other means of communication', but essentially the pupils were to be left in the cold. A school whose very ethos was concerned with developing a questioning outlook and which stood against unthinking deference to authority could hardly expect its products to be polite conformists. The decision of the chairman of council to allow the school six to speak on any subject was brave, if not provocative, given their political inexperience, their forthright manner of expression and the likelihood of their dealing with matters which could well be 'irritating for the Head and members of staff'.[103]

It was not long before the head was complaining about a 'gladiatorial scene in Council', when in a defence of sixth-form smoking in the common room and in an attack on the sixth-form general course, the school six went well beyond what was deemed to be their main task of reporting on the year. Only after considerable discussion and the threat of one council member to resign if they were banned was it agreed to invite the school six to address council the following year, 1991, but only if they kept to topics agreed in advance with the head and chair of council. The school six were thus in a weak position, without any real part in the decision-making process and attending only one meeting of council each year to report on agreed matters, after which they were obliged to withdraw. Even this small privilege was under constant review. The chairman favoured a less restrictive position. In his view, 'We either permit the School Six to speak to us or not at all.'[104] This approach and that of another council member, who asked that staff remember the age and inexperience of the school six who were being expected to behave as council behaved, was more in tune with the school's ideological position on student behaviour. However it was a position with which many heads of KAS would have disagreed, maintaining a clear distinction between pupil behaviour in the classroom and behaviour in the council chamber. The way forward was to allow the school six their annual visit but with vetted topics and advice on how to conduct themselves at council meetings, all part of their political education and a preparation for the world beyond the school gates. It is not surprising that the school six were not always as willing to accept the restrictions of committee procedure and debate for they had no regular place on council and were thus likely, on occasions, under the guise of the impetuousness of youth, to make the most of their one visit. If, as was declared, the school six 'would observe the workings of council at first hand' by attending council, then more regular attendance rather than an annual report and immediate exit would have assisted their education in the workings of committees, and perhaps have led to more temperate conduct on their part and indeed that of some other council members. The usual method of reserving items for discussion only by full council members would have helped to regularize their position. In addition their presence would have helped to dispel the view that council was 'a mysterious and secretive body which . . . emerges from purdah once a year at the AGM'.[105]

Some limited but regular form of student representation, based upon but not identical with the model for staff representation, was perhaps one of the areas of school government which KAS could have pioneered in the years following Baker's 1988 Act. It was not necessarily an idea which the National Association of Governors and Managers (NAGM) would have supported, and pupil power was certainly not one of Baker's priorities, but it would have helped to realize the ideals which John Dennis of the NAGM put before council in April 1989 of 'challenging entrenched practice' and stimulating 'thought of what was going on inside the School'.[106] However, KAS was not even united on the role of the teacher representatives on council. While charitable status precluded the equality which the NAGM's charter for governors demanded for teacher-governors, there were some, including the bursar and secretary, P. A. Allan, who wanted a very circumscribed role for teachers in council discussion, limited 'to assisting council when their special knowledge and experience as teachers is relevant to the subject'.[107] Such thinking certainly did not place KAS in the forefront as constitutional pioneers, in that it did not give an adequate voice to those who could have contributed greatly to discussion, the consumers (the pupils) and the purveyors (the staff).

Tim Siney, a member new to council, asked whether, in fact, the school 'as now governed might be behind the times'.[108] He suggested the creation of a small group to review the role of council members in the light of NAGM and GBA recommendations, clarify their responsibilities and make recommendations concerning the latter, a position supported by another member of council, who, as a governor of two maintained schools, pondered on the question of why she was more involved with the work of those schools than she was with that of KAS, a rather surprising state of affairs. The spotlight which Baker's Act was indirectly throwing on council was having the beneficial effect of causing it to step up its continuing examination of its own nature, purpose and workings. The first measure taken was that of organizing a 'teach-in' for those council members who wished to clarify their task, with the secretary, P. A. Allan, preparing a briefing document on the powers, duties and responsibilities of council as directors of the company. Council did not see itself as the sole training agency and encouraged its members to attend the training sessions of the NAGM. These helped in providing an additional yardstick by which council could measure its powers, responsibilities, procedures and productiveness. The nine members who attended them, including Sue Bollas, Xenia Bowlby, Kara Conti and Tim Siney, concluded that KAS meetings were good in many respects but that they fell short in five ways: in not providing all papers and reports with agendas; in not clarifying fully what the objective of each item was (mainly matters of information, or for discussion or for decision); in not always allowing sufficient time for discussion of issues requiring a decision; in not giving sufficient detail of discussion in the minutes; and in not giving adequate time for the systematic consideration of the previous minutes.

Perhaps the more important lessons to be learned from the sessions concerned the role of council members, particularly the clarification of the role of staff members and encouraging their greater involvement, the briefing of new members, the closer definition of the issues with which council should be involved, the review of the AGM and the consideration of ways of improving communication. GBA document 208 was used as an additional source of guidance on the role of governors, though it was recognized that their method of election distinguished KAS not only from state schools but also from many independent schools, where vacancies were filled either by the votes of remaining governors or by a separate body of trustees. KAS was thus one of the few schools whose council was elected by a society consisting mainly of parents, and as such, areas including teacher representation, communications and elections were more problematic.

The working party, which had reached thirteen after the 'teach-in', found earlier documents on council's responsibilities to be imprecise, with the exception of the Articles of Association. This was perhaps an advantage to those members who had been involved in the controversies of the late 1970s and early 1980s for it enabled them to underline the importance of the size of council, fixed at a maximum of twenty-one, to lay the emphasis upon open discussion 'without fear of embarrassment or upset, where the school's work can be honestly assessed, successes recognised, differences reconciled and weaknesses identified and corrected'[109] and to indicate that it was each member's duty to preserve the full exercise of council's powers and duties against any attempt to subvert them, including any committee seeking to decide policy. It was clearly a centralist definition of powers, with council deciding policy and the means of achieving it, but with the leavening of avoiding constant scrutiny of the head's actions and decisions or interfering in the day-to-day administration of the school. The head's power to select and appoint staff remained in accordance with his contract, though council's input into the process was defined. The emphasis in the final paragraph upon dialogue and co-operation between and within the various groups left the impression of a constructive document, which, though without legal standing, was long overdue, a view which was echoed in council's discussion of it. Though the involvement of council in staff recruitment and assessment remained a sticking point, there was a general feeling that the working party had performed a valuable service. The outstanding issue was resolved in March 1991 by a form of words agreed by Tim Siney and the president and backed by the chairman. The 'Guidelines on the Powers and Responsibilities of Council' was a fitting tribute to Tim Siney and the working party and to Ari Zaphiriou-Zarifi's chairmanship of council.

His successor, Kara Conti, tended to work in those areas of reform in which her particular talents as a teacher and actress with a first-class degree in psychology were most readily needed, in the broader skills of communication. Paper definitions, such as those which had emerged under her immediate predecessors, were valuable, particularly as a source of reference, but that what enabled them to work in practice was the creation and maintenance of harmonious relationships between and among the constituent elements. This included a group to which little or no reference was made in the council guidelines, the staff. Though the most numerous of the groups comprising KAS (apart from parents) they felt the constitutional chill of a marginalized position on council and were unhappy at their role and weak numerical representation on the parent–staff committee. At the beginning of the autumn term in 1990 a staff association was founded 'whereby staff in all areas of the school could meet to discuss various matters of concern'.[110] Lest there was any doubt about the political position of the association, the chairman of council in October 1990 reminded the staff representative that 'the Head held the sole responsibility'. Kara Conti, who took over the chair of council in December 1991, aimed to promote constructive links with the association, particularly when she, as a temporary member of the teaching staff, gained insights into the problems facing teachers. One of the main problems was that of Outer and Inner London allowances. With the school being close to the Inner London boundary, the staff argued for all teachers, and not only those already in receipt of such allowances, to receive the additional salary. Behind this, and other matters such as the association's grave concern over the dismissal of a member of the administrative staff in 1992, lay the broader issue of communication between staff ('not from the management team') and council. The chair and bursar attended many of the association's meetings so the lines of communication were open. However, staff representation on the finance committee, a means of broader communication requested by the association, was resisted by the committee itself,[111] though the idea of staff attending other council committees from time to time was not ruled out.

The new chair of council made clear her intention in February 1992 'to ensure that council loses its anonymity'.[112] Individually this meant placing the photographs of members on the council notice-board; collectively, it was facilitated by the publishing of *Council News*, whose first issue appeared a month later. It provided short paragraphs on the main discussions in council as well as announcing forthcoming events. Other innovations such as the use of first names in council minutes and the availability in school once a week of the chair of council to discuss matters of concern with parents and staff, helped to break down the perceived barriers between council and the other constituent groups in the school and society. *Council News* was part of another venture, the newly formed communications committee whose task was to co-ordinate the various efforts being made to help communications within the school and to promote a positive image of the school to the community at large. In the case of the latter, for example, the committee was concerned that KAS should not be perceived in the locality primarily as a 'special needs' school, a view which the new version of the school magazine, *The Alfredian*, helped to dispel. The attempt to improve communications and to expel stuffiness from council was also apparent in the chair's annual reports from 1993 when, after two years in office, Kara Conti adopted a less formal, but no less effective, mode of address. Councillors' traits were commented upon lightheartedly but meaning-fully: for example, Jean Lockett's 'unflinching application to a filthy job' (1993) and a personal awards ceremony (1995) when Tom Bloch, the new bursar, took two awards, for the most promising newcomer and the best overall performer. A further council-led initiative in 1995 which brought council not only out into the open but to ground level was its donation of spades to the school to enable the turning of celebratory sods to mark the fiftieth anniversary of the school's return to Manor Wood. By then the planning for the much more important anniversary, the centenary of the founding of the school in 1898, was well under way.

Yet even in the closing years of Moran's headship, after over a decade of conciliar reform and initiative and a good working relationship with the head, division and acrimony developed. An earlier disagreement between the head and some members of council over his expulsion of some children for alleged involvement with drugs had been patched up by the president but in 1995 and 1996 in a series of closed sessions a much more serious conflict occurred. It focused on matters relating to members of staff to whom many council members took exception and against whom they passionately demanded swift action. The headmaster's more cautious and practical approach and his un-willingness to divulge to council the content of confidential conversa-tions was, in the heat of debate, wrongly interpreted as inaction. However, despite genuine differences on how the matter should be handled, there was a satisfactory resolution and good relations were soon restored with council committed to finding ways to resolve similar conflicts in the future.

Spring in winter

By the early 1990s a chill had descended upon state education. The promise held out by the New Right's introduction of the GCSE was soon dashed by a return to a national curriculum more prescriptive than its predecessors with its accompanying myriad of tests and tables. Although some of its worst excesses had been removed by the mid-1990s, nevertheless it remained firmly in place, backed up by the cry that it was the only means of raising the educational standards which had been undermined by progressive teaching methods since the 1960s. Labour and Liberal Democrats vied with the Conservatives to score political points in their denunciation of progressivism. The educational winter thus looked set to continue into the new century with little difference between the political parties in their support for a state curriculum and their belief that it was the main bastion against

171. Most members of Council, 1996/7: L to R (front row) Xenia Bowlby, Leslie Kirk, Kara Conti, Areta Hautman, Peter Luck-Hille, Jo Cleary, Susan Himmelweit, Ralph Harris; (back row) Tony D'Arcy, David Weale, Simon Carson, Christopher Simpson, Walter Merricks, Kate Engineer, Stephen Brandes

172. Most of the school staff who faced the inspectors in 1996:
L to R (back row) John Peisley, Stephen de Brett, Brian Rance, Dermot Allen, Carol Davidson, Heather Bussell, Shirley Gamsu, Keith Moore, Rita Murray, Mark Owen, Jennie Ingram, Melanie Leigh, Edo Skender, Ray Walker, Liz Croker, Pam Oliver; (4th row) Françoise Burford, Laszlo Horvath, Bill Hall, Tony Murray, Thelma Thomas, Dee Tailor, Beatrice Osei, Brenda Chaloner, Sheelagh Stanley, Jeff Robinson, Dave Reynolds, Joe Keating, Andy Hampton, Chris Potter, Nora Evans, Catherine Bazell; (3rd row) Dan Robinson, Cathy Williams, Lucy Bailey, Sarah Fraser, Dennis Cook, Chris Balyuzi, Karen Watson, Carole Hamilton, Bob Rowland, Jan Bradley, Androulla Nicholas, Dianne Sharp, Cathy Brown, Ilona Ullmann, Sue Harrison, Angela Ratner; (2nd row) Tricia Still, Graham Hale, Joan Bradshaw, Silvia Beevers, Joan Morris, Mandy Rowland, Alison Mackessack-Leitch, Charlotte Langham, Larisse Green, Claire Eason, Sue Keverne, Fiona Wyndham, Shukra Bountra, Feven Ghebremdhin, Peter Andrews; (front row) Francis Moran, Norma Moran, Mike Young, Jane Stevens, Jane Townsend, Andrea Hegde, Araxi Djian, Denise Gibbs, Sue Boulton, Tom Bloch

progressive ideas and practices. The simplistic, polarized model served politicians well.

It does not, however, accord with educational realities, and certainly not those at KAS. An inspection of the school was undertaken by the Accreditation Review and Consultancy Service in 1996. The summary report of May 1996 showed that the inspectors were generally impressed with the teaching and levels of achievement in all areas of the school, lower, middle and upper. As the team leader succinctly put it in the debriefing session:[113] 'You've got a great school.' 'Your head looks worried,' another inspector commented, 'but he has no reason to be worried.' The teaching was generally rated as impressive with no lesson being given the lowest rating. Teachers were said to be 'enthusiastic, well-qualified and committed'. As with all inspections, areas for improvement were noted, but generally speaking the KAS ethos and good academic standards were seen as by no means incompatible.

Creativity and close teamwork in the lower school, teaching matching enlightened aims in the middle school and rich and varied work in the upper school at key stages 3 and 4 and in the sixth form – all left a clear impression upon the inspectors. However, the KAS traditions

173. Denise Gibbs and Mike Young, deputy heads: two key members of the curriculum review team

174. Chris Potter, deputy to Mike Young in the lower school from 1988

of down-playing competition, of open and frank classroom discussion, of relaxed discipline and of avoiding overpressure through generous play times and a short day, especially in the infant school, were not always fully appreciated. When asked in the year preceding inspection if KAS still offered a child-centred education, the head replied: 'Well . . . yes, just. In the Lower School very much; Middle School, pretty much; but inroads have been made at GCSE and A level as the exam system has been tampered with for the sake of factors other than the examinees themselves.'[114] The positive and indeed the critical aspects of the inspectors' report of 1996 suggest that Francis Moran was being unduly modest. The school thus headed towards its centenary celebrations with an agenda for improvement suggested by the inspectorate, including the broader use of information technology across the curriculum, improved record-keeping and a close examination of the most effective uses of time throughout the school, but essentially with the KAS ethos intact. In essence, the inspection report was part of an ongoing evaluation of the KAS curriculum in which the headmaster, Sue Boulton, Denise Gibbs, Mike Young and Laszlo Horvath played a leading part. The educational spring still flourished at KAS, alongside the winter that pervaded the state sector.

Notes and references

1. Reply 2 to Moran questionnaire (RMQ2), 1996.
2. For Moran's appreciation of Britton's work, see his report to council, 24 May 1994.
3. Annual Report (AR), 1993.
4. Statements made by his referees.
5. Quoted by B. Simon, *Education and the Social Order, 1940–1990* (London, Lawrence & Wishart, 1991), 522.
6. AR 1991, 11.
7. AR 1986, 11.
8. Council revised its view in February 1996. When the government reopened the assisted place lists, it agreed in principle to join the scheme.
9. It only offered around three CSE courses.
10. AR 1984, 5.
11. Council minutes (CM), 15 October 1985.
12. AR 1988, 8.

13. AR 1990, 20.
14. AR 1991, 8.
15. F. Moran, 'A Strategy for KAS' (1994), 9.
16. CM, 28 February 1984.
17. RMQ4, 1996.
18. RMQ7, 1996.
19. AR 1987, 10.
20. AR 1987, 6.
21. RMQ8, 1996.
22. AR 1987, 14–15.
23. 'The trend that has gone into reverse', *Financial Times*, 24 September 1983, 21.
24. 'Progressive schools ruffians and education', letter to the *Financial Times*, 5 October 1983.
25. RMQ6, 1996.
26. AR 1987, 6.
27. AR 1986, 8.
28. 'What is KAS?' Report of a working party which met from September 1988 to July l991.
29. Ibid., 3.
30. In an interview for the *Guardian* (pp.22–3), 11 June 1991. Croall, the reporter, is author of *Neill of Summerhill: The Permanent Rebel* (London, Routledge, 1983).
31. Letter to F. Moran, 20 July 1987.
32. RMQ10, 1996.
33. RMQ7, 1996.
34. Letter to F. Moran, 20 July 1987.
35. CM, 24 March 1987.
36. AR 1989, 4.
37. Ibid., 5.
38.

1904 Regulations for Secondary Schools	*1988 National Curriculum*
English	English
Mathematics	Mathematics
Science	Science
History	History
Geography	Geography
Foreign language	A modern foreign language
Drawing	Art
Physical Exercise	Physical Exercise
Manual work/housewifery	Technology
	Music

39. Reported to council. CM, 22 March 1988.
40. CM, 13 May 1986.
41. Ibid., 2.
42. Ibid.
43. CM, 22 January 1985.
44. RMQ13, 1996.
45. *Which School*, 1989/90, 65th edition, xvi.
46. CM, 17 May 1988.
47. Letter to the head, 2 January 1990.
48. AR 1984, 6.
49. Letter to John Marshall from Tim Eggar, 28 January 1992.
50. AR 1994, 14.
51. Strategy Paper, 8 February 1994, 9.
52. Ibid., 19.
53. *Journal of Biological Education*, 29/2 (1995), 83–5.
54. Ibid., 84.
55. CM record of the occupations of those applying for membership of KASS.
56. *Guardian*, 4 May 1988.
57. RMQ8, 1996.
58. CM, 5 May 1992.
59. Joanna Briscoe, *Guardian*, May 1988.
60. Ibid.
61. RMQ3.
62. RMQ8.
63. Letter by Claudia Nielson published in *The Alfredian*.
64. Letter to a parent, 23 April 1991.
65. RMQ9.
66. RMQ6.
67. RMQ9.
68. RMQ10.
69. *Guardian*, 30 May 1990, 16.
70. *TES*, 1 July 1994.
71. RMQ10.
72. *Hampstead and Highgate Express*, 10 December 1993.
73. AR 1991, 27.
74. RMQ5.
75. Ibid.
76. *RIBA Journal* (July 1993), 17.
77. RMQ4.
78. RMQ12.
79. AR 1993, 5.

80. RMQ12.

81. CM, 21 January 1987.

82. Letter to the Appointments Group, Bedales, 20 October 1991.

83. CM, 24 March 1987.

84. CM, 5 May 1992.

85. RMQ10.

86. *Hampstead and Highgate Express*, 31 July 1987.

87. RMQ8.

88. CM, 13 May 1986.

89. Appendix 1, CM, 20 April 1990.

90. CM, 15 October 1991.

91. RMQ10.

92. *Daily Telegraph*, 1 November 1995, 25.

93. AR 1991, 19.

94. CM, 13 December 1983.

95. Sir William Wood, 'The King Alfred School Society: A Time of Trouble, 1982–1983', November 1988. This view has been challenged recently by A. Hautman in 'A Response to A Time of Trouble', August 1996 (unpublished, KASS Archives).

96. Letter to council by F. Moran, 4 July 1983.

97. CM, 13 December 1983.

98. CM, 4 December 1984.

99. Wood, 'Time of Trouble', 3.

100. Hautman, 'Response', 2–3.

101. F. Taylor, 'The Argument for Change: King Alfred School Society 1980–1983', August 1996, 2.

102. CM, 13 May 1991.

103. CM, 15 May 1990.

104. Ibid.

105. CM, 16 December 1991.

106. CM, 25 April 1989.

107. Ibid.

108. CM, 16 May 1989.

109. 'Note for Guidance of Council Members on the Powers and Responsibilities of Council', 15 May 1991, 2.

110. CM, 16 October 1990.

111. CM, 19 May 1993.

112. CM, 4 February 1992.

113. Notes made by the chair of council and others at the debriefing meeting with the inspectorate.

114. AR 1995, 5–6.

Chapter 8

A Welshman at the Court of King Alfred

In 1901 the first generation of KAS pupils trooped off to Winchester with John Russell to see Hamo Thornycroft's statue of King Alfred, recently unveiled with much pageantry, oratory, song and thanksgiving as part of the millenary celebrations of Alfred's death.[1] Such a visit seemed entirely appropriate as a triple tribute, to the creative skills of Thornycroft, one of the society's founders, to the legendary monarch who gave the society and school its name and to Queen Victoria, who had died earlier in the year and who represented the very fulfilment of the Alfredian vision of a strong, imperial kingdom. Thornycroft's bronze of the Christian warrior with scabbarded sword held aloft in the sign of the cross seemed to fit the mood of a grieving nation but this view of

175. The original school sign in Squirrel Hall in the 1990s

Alfred, derived largely from the *Anglo-Saxon Chronicle*, scarcely made him an appropriate symbol for a movement dedicated to a humane rationalist education. Muscular Christianity fitted the ethos of the traditional public school but what the society was seeking to do in 1901, amid the tremendous controversy surrounding Balfour's Education Bill, was to pioneer a progressive model based upon humane, secular values which could serve as a paradigm for the new secondary schools which the prime minister was proposing. A more inappropriate patron seemed scarcely imaginable.

How then could the Hampstead Fabians have claimed Alfred as their own? Wherein lay his iconic appeal? The answer lies largely in the writings of a Welsh cleric, Asser,[2] who was summoned to Alfred's court around 885 'from the remote, westernmost parts of Wales . . . to the Saxon land'[3] to assist in the cultural revival of both court and kingdom. Asser's biography provided

349

the founders of KAS with the details of his educational accomplishments which made it almost imperative that they adopt his name for the society and school rather than the more bland alternative of the New Century School. Furthermore, Asser's account of Alfred translating Latin texts into the vernacular had a particular appear to the founders, who wished to replace Latin in their rationalist schools with English and modern languages. How supportive they would have been of the appointment of Francis Moran, the head who led the school into its centenary celebrations, for in true Alfredian tradition he had rescued the teaching of English at Eton from the hands of classicists. 'The vernacular triumphant' could well have been his as well as the school's motto, but it was not the most obvious message emanating from Thornycroft's statue.

Asser joined Alfred's court for several months each year to write a propagandist biography of his tutee, designed in fact to show his fellow Welsh clerics the wisdom of choosing Alfred as their overlord 'to check the mischief inflicted on St David's by Hemeid, king of Dyfed'[4] (as a biographer around the time of the founding of KAS succinctly put it). The present writer, also a Welshman, but from a more northerly part of Wales than Asser, was invited to 'King Alfred's Manor Wood court' not to write a propagandist account of its achievements but to assess its work during its first century. Yet what is striking about both accounts, separated by some 1100 years, is their underlying common theme, the political realism which enabled man and movement to survive, Alfred for fifty years to lay the foundations of a nation-state and a cultural revival, and KAS for at least double that, to help establish progressivism in education, not in the form of protected, progressive,

176. Hamo Thornycroft's statue of King Alfred

Winchester, King Alfred's Statue.

350

rural hermitages such as Abbotsholme, Bedales and Summerhill, but as a coeducational, day-school movement based in the capital. It had constantly to prove its worth in direct competition, in a much more open market-place, without the endowments to subsidize its fees and building programmes which many other independent schools enjoyed and without state finance which gave maintained schools their security and stability. Furthermore its heads were not in its predecessor's tradition of legislators. There were the inherent instabilities of power residing ultimately in the hands of a society, consisting largely of a constantly changing body of parents, and immediately in their elected council, another frequently changing group with powers to hire and fire and to influence the curriculum. Yet despite occasional internal crises and constant external challenges, although not quite on the Viking scale facing Alfred, the society and its first and only school reached its first century in a healthy condition, as the official inspection of May 1996 revealed.

Like Alfred, the school learnt when to sally forth when times were propitious for pressing its missionary cause, but like its patron it knew when to consolidate and pay tribute to the forces of the age, no matter how alien they were to its traditions. It, too, paid its danegeld.[5] By and large its gilded age was its first half-century, when it was able to put the principles of its founders into practice in a relatively undiluted manner. Its danegeld years followed the school's return to Manor Wood from Flint Farm, in 1945, when the pressures of public examinations weighed more heavily after the advent of the general certificate of education in 1951, when youth in the 1960s and 1970s were urged 'to tune in, turn on and drop out' and when the school in the 1980s and 1990s was subjected to the intense pressures of the national curriculum which caused KAS to redefine its role and make concessions without jettisoning the principles of its founders.

For convenience this concluding chapter will thus utilize the subheadings of the gilded age (1898–1948) and the danegeld years (1948–98), though the former was not without tarnish and the latter not without their educational splendour.

The gilded age, 1898–1948

When Isobel White Wallis wrote in 1898 of 'the great juggernaut of modern education, the examination craze' she was using the metaphor in a more precise way than the reader in 1998 might recognize, in terms of the ceremonial sacrifice of devotees and others under the religious vehicle's huge wheels. In one statement she condemned the examination-driven and religion-based contemporary educational model, in favour of one based upon the extension of the family, that is one which was child-centred, coeducational, and took into account the ideas of leading educational reformers, such as Pestalozzi, and their views on the realization of individuality. It was, of course, one thing for a small like-minded group of parents to offer such an educational experience to a small group of children in a couple of houses in Ellerdale Road; it was very much another to expect that their ideas would set Victorian and Edwardian Britain alight, even if the society which they founded succeeded in creating other 'experimental' or 'demonstration' schools. The chances were that once the dust had settled after the intense controversy surrounding Balfour's Education Bill, the new secondary schools which the Conservatives intended to establish would be patterned upon the traditional public school model. The schools which Wales had pioneered had already gone down that path, partly under the direction of Joseph John Findlay, the first headteacher of Cardiff's Intermediate School for Boys. The founders of KAS employed him as their curriculum consultant but the progressive curriculum he devised for their Hampstead school, based on an areas-of-experience model, stood at the opposite pole to that which he introduced at Cardiff. Sir Philip Magnus criticized severely his intensely subject-based, examination-led curriculum but it was to this kind of model rather than his ambitious Hampstead curriculum that the new secondary schools would look after 1902. Morant's Regulations for Secondary Schools in 1904 ensured that this would be so. There were to be no instant conversions to the rationalist cause.

The King Alfred School Society had thus to demonstrate the value of a rationalist education and to publicize its cause over a long period of time. Its first step after founding its Hampstead school was to choose its headteacher. Charles Rice was an excellent choice. He seemed to be just the right person to launch KAS into its golden age. As a science graduate of Caius College, Cambridge, who had earlier aspirations for a career in medicine, he appeared to have all of the necessary qualifications to evaluate the latest research on child development and to pioneer a radical yet effective role for KAS in science teaching. Morant's Regulations for Secondary Schools gave science a high priority, yet King Alfred's predecessors, Abbotsholme and Bedales, could only offer a liberal arts model. Furthermore, having spent two years on the office staff of the London School Board and five years at Bedales, the school of Badley (his brother-in-law), he had that peculiar combination of a close knowledge of school-based science and progressive thinking which few reformers possessed. His premature departure in 1901 robbed the school of the opportunity of pioneering a radical experiment in education in which science played a major part. Instead under his successor,

John Russell, the school drifted into the predominantly liberal arts tradition, which it took over half a century to shake off.

Rice was also a realist, and it was this that proved to be his most lasting legacy. He quickly modified Findlay's ambitious curriculum to make it a workable scheme, retaining its conceptual framework of areas of experience but basing it upon a series of subjects which would have been recognizable to the Board's inspectors. He also saw the restricting influence of public examinations on the school curriculum but was willing to offer 'a year's special preparation which can be given at the school'[6] for anyone wanting to enter them. His clash with council in 1901 showed him to be both a realist and man of principle. He opposed the idea of turning KAS immediately into an all-age school both on the grounds that providing schooling for fourteen to eighteen year olds would be financially crippling in view of the great costs needed to provide for a small number, and on the grounds that education after the age of fourteen would not be coeducational as most boys would have gone elsewhere. To Mrs White Wallis the society's mission took priority over the individual pupil's needs, for if KAS were to prove itself to be a working model for the new secondary schools then it had to retain as many pupils as possible to the age of eighteen. Furthermore if the school imposed a transfer age of fourteen then many parents would, in her view, not send their children to KAS in the first place and so the whole future of the venture would be imperilled. The clash over the issue led to Rice's resignation and that of many within council.

The golden age had got off to a slow start but the arrival of John Russell in 1901 signalled a period of stability and expansion. 'J.R.', as he was known to parents and pupils alike, set much of the pattern for the next century. His appointment broke with the idea that only those of pure progressive pedigree were suited for the headship. The appointment of a series of headteachers, beginning with Russell, all but one of whom were without links with Abbotsholme or Bedales but with broader educational backgrounds and experience, probably enabled the school to reach its first century. It was, after all, a day, not a boarding school, coeducational not single-sex and situated in the capital, all of which called for a rather different brand of radicalism than that of its single-sex, boarding predecessors. A broad progressive outlook, coupled with an understanding of the adjustments that had to be made to ensure survival within the highly competitive London market, were more important than a purist, progressive background. Hence the revisionist, integrated curriculum proposed by Isobel White Wallis did not feed through into Russell's classroom which remained largely subject-based. This was a necessary requirement if KAS was to prepare pupils for examinations. The subject-centred, examination-driven curriculum of the upper school introduced by Russell, always carried with it the possibility of a clash with the purists on council yet none occurred, due largely to his diplomatic skills and the memory of the recent upheaval. To Russell, progressive teaching lay more in its delivery and aims than in its framework. Hence the inspectors in 1913 found it difficult to understand first-name terms, the great amount of time given to questioning, the shortness of the thirty minute lessons (due to Russell's anxiety not to overpressure his students), and his opposition to home-work. Russell's creation of a school parliament also perplexed them but in fact this, like much of the framework within which the school oper-ated, was far less radical than it appeared for any decision-making rested with the head and council. If we are seeking innovation in the curricular infrastructure it is to his successor, Wicksteed, that we must turn.

Buildings impose their own constraints. At Ellerdale Road, Russell found it difficult to adopt adventurous ideas about classroom usage and planning, the two houses being cramped and not susceptible to major alteration. Wicksteed was more fortunate. The school's move to Manor Wood with its spacious grounds in 1921 enabled him to develop a largely unoccupied site at the very time when ideas about open-air education and new forms of classroom arrangement and use were being discussed in progressive educational circles. Furthermore, initially, he was a lot more radical in his curricular thinking than Russell and questioned the latter's increasing resort to tests and homework. Wicksteed's adoption and implementation of a modified version of Helen Parkhurst's Dalton plan was probably his greatest achievement. It provided the school's curricular framework for forty years, enabling pupils through a system of stagework and open rooms to learn at their own pace whilst still providing preparation for external examinations. It was accompanied by improvements to the school's material fabric with the beginning of the replacement of the school's ex-army huts with more permanent buildings, especially the dining hall, new accommodation for arts, crafts and science, and the sports field.

The appointment of two members of staff, Violet Hyett and Birkett, to the headship on Wicksteed's retirement in 1933 ensured stab-ility and continuity. These were vital in view of the swingeing effects of the Depression and the unsettled state of Europe in the 1930s. In some ways these developments gave an added strength to the voice of those who advocated the extension of a KAS education to the state sector, for it helped to develop the flexibility of mind necessary in young people if Britain were to avoid future recession and the critical awareness vital in the upholding of the principles of democracy. Violet Hyett lost little time in demonstrating these benefits of a KAS education and even the Board of Education's inspectors warmed to KAS principles in their inspection in 1938 more than in previous years. Certainly, Kaufmann's new junior block impressed upon them the importance of modern, well-designed buildings in pursuing the kind of educational ideals which stood between Britain and the dark forces of dictatorship. When the battle became one not just of ideologies but of armed forces in 1939 any plans for new buildings were shelved and KAS, like other schools in the capital and other areas vulnerable to aerial bombardment, was evacuated. The high point of the school's golden age had been reached. Survival, rather than expansion, was the priority after 1939.

Council had given its support to the idea of an outpost in Royston long before war broke out. Miss Hyett and Miss Hibburd had already bought Flint Hall Farm, which was to be the home of KAS in exile until 1945. As early as 1942 KAS had begun to re-establish its presence in North London when Miss Robey opened a nursery school in the Beloff's house in Holford Road. Montgomery opened a middle and senior school nearby in Oakhurst in 1944, so the move back to Manor Wood in September 1945 was a natural process of consolidation. Miss Hyett and Birkett remained at the Royston school until its close in July 1946, when the local children were forced to reintegrate into the local schools. They had thus led the school through its golden years as well as its most troubled period.

The danegeld years, 1948–1998

King Alfred, the scholar monarch, survived to establish the basis of a nation-state, partly because he was willing to come to terms with the principal force of the age, the Vikings. He negotiated with them, and paid them off with danegeld when occasion demanded it. KAS, too, even in its most prosperous times, paid its form of danegeld, making concessions particularly to parental demands for preparations for public examinations. However, during its first half-century, the alien, political forces were fairly easily contained, especially within the Dalton-style curricular framework which Wicksteed introduced after the First World War and which Violet Hyett and Birkett maintained until the end of the Second. For a short while after the school's return to Manor Wood in 1945 under Montgomery it seemed that Dalton could also serve the needs of the new age, that KAS using its tried and tested curricular arrangement could meet most of the demands of parents in postwar Hampstead without having to make too many concessions to the world outside. However, the brave new educational world which Butler's Education Act promised might have left the independent sector largely unscathed but the developing forces of the age were soon to have a great impact on KAS. There could be no return to the 1930s.

Montgomery was not a new-blood appointment, having been a teacher at KAS since 1932 with a short break for some of the war years. While his achievements included rebuilding the school in the postwar years and maintaining the informal relationship which had characterized pupil–teacher relationships since the school's inception, he did not possess the intellectual prowess nor provide the dynamic leadership necessary to develop and implement new curricular strategies to meet the challenges of the new age. In the age of the grammar school and the new general certificate of education, Dalton was not replaced by a new progressive curricular theory but subjected to a slow and painful death by a thousand modifications. The introduction of a co-headship first with Hettie Barber and then with Audrey (Nikki) Paul Jones did not immediately produce a new progressive synthesis. In the end Dalton was overwhelmed by the increasing number of pupils and by the traditional forces of the age. At a time when some local authorities were experimenting with comprehensive schools, KAS had lost an opportunity to pioneer mixed-ability teaching methods of a whole-class kind and involving some of the principles of negotiated learning which could have served their needs. The problem was that many of the school's curricular goals were being imposed from outside by the demands of examination boards. Danegeld was being paid in large sums, although with the same political realism with which King Alfred had paid it, in order to preserve some of the more progressive elements against barbarian values. The school had thus to wait for a new regime before it could hope to advance the frontiers of progressivism.

By that time, however, new social forces seemed to threaten the venture. It was the great achievement of the joint headship of Nikki Archer and Alan Humphries (1962–70) that the school successfully resisted the lure of the siren voices of permissiveness at both a practical and ideological level while at the same time yielding to the new educational forces of the age, especially in terms of Nuffield science and family grouping. That KAS continued to offer its distinctive kind of education in the less favourable 1970s was largely the achievement of Nikki Archer, the first unchaperoned female head, and her staff. The work of council in providing a new science and arts block and a new gymnasium was evidence of the support given to the school's longest serving head. The crises of the early 1980s which eventually led to her resignation masked two decades of fruitful co-operation by council and head. The crises were as unnecessary as they were protracted.

It was during the headship of Francis Moran that KAS was forced to pay most danegeld. Although the national curriculum was in essence a curriculum for state schools only, nevertheless King Alfred's was obliged to align its curriculum to it in some measure, particularly in the upper school where examination pressures and parental expectations were at their strongest. Nowhere in the ISAI accreditation report of 1996 is this crucial influence mentioned. To this extent the assessor's comment that the school was very successful in achieving its overall aims, especially in fostering an industrious approach in a relaxed and friendly environment, tends to underestimate the magnitude of the achievement. If pupils from the Rice era had been able to visit the school in the Moran era they would certainly have found a more industrious community but they would also have recognized a similar quality of pupil experience. Danegeld had to be paid in order to preserve the essentials of a distinctive KAS culture.

Notes and references

1. The millenary celebrations of his death took place in 1901, although now it is generally agreed that Alfred died in 899.
2. Asser's writings are the subject of much dispute, with some historians claiming that they are an eleventh-century forgery. A. P. Smyth's *King Alfred the Great* (Oxford, OUP, 1995) is the latest in the line of what appears to be a minority view.
3. Alfred the Great, *Asser's Life and Other Contemporary Sources* (London, Penguin, 1985), 95.
4. C. Plummer, *The Life and Times of Alfred the Great* (Oxford, Clarendon Press, 1902), 42.
5. The term 'danegeld' was not used, as such, until later.
6. The First School Prospectus, 5.

Appendix 1
Preliminary Circular, issued July 1897

Proposed rational school

A few Parents residing in this neighbourhood have been for some time casting about to find means for the better education of their boys and girls. They appreciate the well-meant efforts of High Schools and Private Schools, but they find that these institutions are (for many reasons which need not be detailed) out of touch with the broader and healthier views of the training of children that science and the scientific study of child-nature have of late roused. They feel the time has come when this rational spirit should find expression, not merely in theories and books, but in a permanent Institution.

They propose, therefore, if sufficient support is accorded the scheme, that a committee be formed, and a School started at Easter, of which the following are some of the special features which it is hoped will distinguish it.

Individual training and the development of character

The whole training of the school will be based on the laws of physiology, and the close study of the individual child. It is proposed to maintain physical culture in due relation to mental culture, and to carry out hygienic conditions of life in practice throughout the school life, both in buildings and occupation.

For the first three years, probably, a plan of teaching will be arranged adapted only to the needs of children between the ages of 8 and 12.

Classes will consist of not more than 12 to 15 children on an average.

The hours of school will be regulated by medical advice, and a medical officer with special experience of children, mentally and physically, will be engaged for the service of the school.

A permanent record of the life of each child, physical and mental, will be maintained.

Since the object of the teaching will be to develop faculty in all directions, and to draw out the self-activity of the child, all apparatus will be such as the child may be allowed to use himself, under direction, rather than to merely see exhibited by the teacher. Oral methods, especially for the younger children, will be chiefly used; and subjects, where possible, approached from the concrete rather than the abstract. When and where possible the education will be carried on out of doors, in garden, field, and hedgerow.

Co-ordination of studies

All studies and occupations will, as far as possible, be carefully co-ordinated, so that, instead of being treated as separate 'subjects', the various branches of instruction will be so interlinked that each will afford illustration to the others.

For this purpose the teacher will regularly confer upon their daily work in school, to ensure that all are animated by a common spirit.

Religious education

The whole work of the school will be carried on in a religious spirit, but as the school will be undenominational in character no special religious creed will be inculcated.

Co-education

In the belief that the family is the ideal to emulate in school life, it is proposed to educate boys and girls together, that they may reap the advantage, as in the family, of the influence for good which the diverse character naturally have on one another. This has long been the custom in Scotch schools, and the principle has been most successfully tried in England.

Home lessons

The curriculum will contain all subjects deemed necessary to the aims of the school for the all-round development of the child, and no subjects will be set by the school to occupy the children's leisure, either as independent studies, or in the form of preparation by home lessons, at least among the juniors.

Scholarships and prizes

No scholarships, prizes, or awards will be worked for, it being understood that all the children's energy and interest will be directed to learning for its own sake and for its value in training and development.

Holidays

With less strain on the child by a more rational system of learning, and shorter hours of mental work, and with the teachers' labour lightened by simpler and more scientific methods, the need for the present extravagantly long holidays will cease. Seven weeks may not be too long in summer when outdoor life, so important for the health and growth of the child, is possible, but a fortnight at Christmas and a week in the Spring, should serve all the needs of holiday making at other seasons of the year.

Control of the school

The school will be administered by a Governing body who will derive no pecuniary advantage from its success, and organised on the lines of a public school so as to secure for the pupil that feeling of *esprit de corps* so desirable to encourage in the young, and which is won by the sense of attachment to a continuous corporate body.

This Governing body for the first three years will consist of a small Committee appointed by the supporters of the school.

This Committee will appoint a Director or Principal empowered to arrange the school curriculum and choose his staff, subject to the approval of the Committee, in strict accordance with the aims of the school.

The school in its relation to parents

The ideal contemplated by such a school cannot be realized in the lives of its children by the teacher alone. The home must help the school. The school will fail to achieve its aim unless a common bond of sympathy between home and school is maintained.

Therefore, Parents will be invited to confer with the Principal and Teachers at regular intervals, or privately by arrangement, on subjects of general interest in regard to the aims and methods of the school, and to individual pupils. Every facility will be given to Parents to understand the educational lines upon which it is proposed to conduct the school, and to watch its progress.

Aims

While loyally pursuing these ends, the school will aim so to educate boys that at the age of 12 they will be able, in two terms, to prepare either for entrance examinations into any public school; or, at the age of 16, to fit themselves for any special career that is open to them.

So to educate girls that at the age of 16, they will be able, in two terms, to prepare for the entrance examinations into Women's Colleges for higher education; or, at the age of 18, to enter any department of work open to women not requiring special training.

St John's Wood,
July, 1897.

Should you be in sympathy with the proposal to form a School on the lines suggested by the above circular, would you sign the enclosed and return it, either to

Mr E. WHITE WALLIS, 76, Carlton Hill, N.W.,

or to

Mrs E. ROSCOE MULLINS, 24, Greville Road, N.W.

Appendix 2

Society and School Officers

Headteachers

1898	Mr C. E. Rice
1901	Mr J. Russell ('J.R.')
1920	Mr J. H. Wicksteed
1933	Mr H. de P. Birkett and Miss V.A. Hyett
1945	Mr B. H. Montgomery
1952–1958	Mr B. H. Montgomery and Mrs H. Barber
1959–1962	Mr B. H. Montgomery and Mrs A. Paul Jones
1962	Mrs N. Archer and Mr A. Humphries
1970	Mrs N. Archer
1983	Mr F. P. Moran

Treasurers

1899	Mr J. G. Hickson
1901	Mr T. H. Frood
1908	Mr H. Cohen
1910	Mr G. C. Maberly
1924	Mr C. D. Corbett Fisher
1950	Mrs G. A. Weiss
1963	Mr E. N. Epstein
1972	Mr B. M. Igra
1982	Mr J. J. Phillips
1983	Mr J. Richards
1987	Mr J. D. Burke
1990	Mr S. A. Berman
1991	Mr P. Twachtmann

Secretaries

1901	Ada Read
1906	Christina Smith
1913	Mrs N. Spiller
1920	Miss P. M. Beddall
1923	Miss E. Rocke
1927	Miss E. M. Hibburd
1962	Mrs B. M. Bassett
1971	Mr V. Shelley
1983	Mr P. A. Allan

1989	Mr J. J. Lenz
1992	Mr G. P. Cooper
1995	Mr T. Bloch

Presidents

1899	Professor L. C. Miall
1908	Professor P. Geddes
1921	Mr J. J. Findlay
1937	Miss A. Woods
1941	Dr J. C. Flugel
1950	Lady Thornycroft
1958	Mrs C. D. Corbett Fisher
1959	(vacant)
1977	Sir William Wood

Chairs of Council

1898	Mr C. Sharp
1899	Professor H. F. Heath
1900	Mr F. W. Miall
1901	Mr G. C. Maberly
1903	Mr E. Rose
1904	Mr G. C. Maberly
1908	Mr J. Russell
1909	Mr G. C. Maberly
1910	Mr H. B.Garrod
1912	Mrs E. M. Rea
1913	Dr C. Addison
1914	Mr G. C. Maberly
1915	Professor Foster Watson
1916	Mr G. C. Maberly
1917	Professor Foster Watson
1919	Professor Foster Watson
1922	(vacant)
1926	Mr E. M. Gray
1927	Mr W. McGregor Ross
1929	Mrs G. P. Hopkin Morris
1931	Mr A. E. Sewell
1933	Mrs C. D. Corbett Fisher
1936	Mr A. Horton
1938	Mr W. P. Revell
1946	Mrs C. D. Corbett Fisher
1949	Mr L. W. Picknett
1951	Mr E. N. Epstein
1953	Mrs R. Jobson
1958	Mr J. W. Strange
1960	Mr R. P. A. Garrett

1966	Sir William Wood
1978	Mr J. Black
1982	Professor L. B. Keeble
1983	Mr E. C. Greenway
1988	Mr A. C. Zaphiriou-Zarifi
1991	Mrs K. D. Conti

Council Minutes are missing for 1901–18 so elected chairmen cannot be identified. Listed are those persons who chaired successive AGMs.

Appendix 3
Members of Staff at the time of the School's Centenary, 1998

Year joined		Subject
1983	*Head:* Francis Moran, MA (Cantab.), PGCE (London)	English

Deputy Heads:

1985	Sue Boulton, MA (London), BA Hons., Cert.Ed.(Sussex) (Senior Deputy with responsibility for Upper School)	Mathematics
1975	Denise Gibbs, FETC (Deputy with responsibility for Middle School)	French
1982	Mike Young, BA (OU), Dept. of Ed. Cert. (London) (Deputy with responsibility for Lower School)	English

Upper and middle schools staff
Art:

1985	Jan Bradley, Dip.A., Ceramics (Glasgow), HDD, PGCE (Manchester Poly)	Head of Art, Pottery
1996	William Lewer, BA Fine Art (Bristol Poly), PGCE (Goldsmiths')	Fine Art
1997	Jeanette Sylvester, BA Hons. (West Surrey), MA (RCA), PGCE (London Inst.)	Art/Textile Design

Careers:

1983	Norma Moran, B.Sc. Hons. (Leicester), PGCE (Leicester), Cert. Counselling, PG. Dip.	Careers Guidance and Counselling

Computing:

1991	David Reynolds, B.Sc. Hons. (London), ARCS	Director
1996	Sarah Fraser, B.Ed. Hons. (Goldsmiths')	

Craft, Design and Technology:

1988	Stephen de Brett, Cert. Ed. (Exeter), Dip. Ed. (Bristol), MA (RCA)	Head of CDT
1995	Charlotte Langham, BA Hons. 3D Design (Sheffield Hallam), PGCE (Leeds Met.)	
1990	Bob Rowland	CDT Technician

Drama Department:

1996 Araxi Djian, BA Hons. Performing Arts (Middx),
        PGCE (Goldsmiths')   Head of Drama
1997 Andrea Manzi Davies, BA Hons. (Exeter), PGCE (Central)

English Department:

1996 Peter Andrews, MA (London), B.Ed. Hons. (Reading)   Head of English
1987 Nora Evans, BA Hons. (York), PGCE (London)
1981 Mark Owen, BA Hons. (Nottingham), PGCE (Nottingham)

Geography Department:

1976 Rita Murray, MA, B.Ed. Hons. (London), Cert. Ed. Head of Geography
1993 Joan Morris, B.Ed. Hons (London), Cert. Ed.

History Department:

1990 Dermot Allen, MA (London), BA Hons. (SSEES London),
        PGCE (Bristol)   Head of History
1983 Androulla Nicholas, B.Sc. Econ. Hons. (London), PGCE (London),
        Diploma in Counselling (WPF)
1992 Ludmila Vavrovicova, MA (London), BA Hons. (London), PGCE

Languages Department:

1965 Françoise Burford, Licence d'Anglais (Rennes), CAPES   Head of
                                            Languages/French
1975 Denise Gibbs, FETC (Middle School)   French
1985 Jennifer Hill, BA Hons. (London), Dip.Ed.   German
1997 Nicole Gelister, BA Hons. (London), PGCE (London Inst.)   French
1992 Dianne Sharp, BA (Cardiff), Dip. Ed.   French
1993 Montserratt Robinson, BA Hons. (London)   Spanish

Librarian:

1987 Catherine Bazell, BA Hons. (CNAA), ALA

Mathematics Department:

1979 Laszlo Horvath, B.Sc. Hons. (London), PGCE   Head of Maths
1993 Jeff Harlow, B.Sc. Hons. (Soton), PGCE (Greenwich)
1985 Sue Boulton, MA (London), BA Hons., Cert.Ed. (Sussex)
1996 Shukra Bountra, B.Ed. Hons. (Cantab.)
1997 Fiona Wyndham, BA Hons., Dip. Ed. (Sydney) (Exchange)

Music Department:

1987 Andy Hampton, B.A. Hons. (York), LTCL   Head of Music

1997   Anna Rufey, B. Mus. (Royal Northern), PGCE (London Inst.)

1996   Peter Hopkins, BA (Birmingham), Mmus. (Goldsmiths'),
         PGCE (Cantab.)

Photography:

1989   Dan Robinson, B.Sc. Engineering (USMA West Point),
         NSM, MBA (ICAF)   Head of Photography

Physical Education:

1985   Keith Moore, B.Ed. Hons. (SSPE Jordanhill)   Head of P.E.

1990   Edo Skender, Visoka Sprema (Zagreb)

1995   Claire Eason, B.Ed. Hons. (Edinburgh)

Science Department:

1974   John Peisley, B.Sc. (ANU), BA Hons. (OU), Dip.Ed.   Head of
                                                          Science/Physics

1980   Bill Hall, B.Sc. (London), M.Sc. (CNAA), M.I.Biol.,
         PGCE, DPA (London)   Chemistry

1989   Stephen Webster, B.Sc. Hons. (Bristol), M.Phil. (Cantab.),
         PGCE (London)   Biology

1973   Joe Keating, MA (Oxon), M.Sc. (London), M.Ed. (London),
         DIC, PGCE (Oxon.)   Chemistry/Examinations

1984   Catherine Williams, BA Hons. (Oxon.)   Lab Assistant

1997   Harald Molgaard, B.Sc. Hons. (Birmingham), D.Phil. (Sussex),
         PGCE (Goldsmiths')   Physics

1997   Kate Moss, B.Sc. Hons. (Toronto), M.Sc. (Dalhousie),
         PGCE (Oxon.)   Biology

Special Studies Department:

1988   Heather Bussell, BA Hons. (Keele),
         PGCE (Liverpool)   Head of Special Studies

1982   Michele Freind, BA (UCT), STD (UCT), Dip. of Rem. Ed. (London),
         Dip. Dyslexia Therapists (Barts)

1981   Shirley Gamsu, BA Hons. (Witwatersrand)

1995   Carole Hamilton, Cert. Ed., Adv. Dip. Ed. (OU Special Needs)

1984   Trish Kreling, BA Hons. (Durban), Dip. Ed. (Durban)   EFL Tutoring

Lower school staff

1983   Mike Young, BA (OU), Dept of Ed. Cert. (London)   Head

1988   Chris Potter, BA Hons. (Essex), PGCE (Goldsmiths'),
         Deputy to MikeYoung   10+

1983   Beth Levinsky, BA (OU), Cert. Ed. (Cantab.)   10+

1968	Andrea Hegde, BA Hons. (Bristol), Dip.Ed. (London)	9+
1996	Karen Watson, B.Ed. (North Queensland)	9+
1989	Lucy Bailey, B.Sc. Hons.(UEA), PGCE (Cantab.), Dip.Drama	8+
1995	Tony Murray, B.Ed. Hons., Cert. Ed. (NELP)	8+
1985	Chris Balyuzi, Dept. of Ed. Cert. (West Yorks),	
	Extramural Dip.Archaeology (London)	7+
1994	Ilona Ullman, B.Ed. Hons. (N. London Poly)	7+
1990	Lindy Dumas, Cert.Ed. (Goldsmiths'), BA (OU)	6+
1995	Alison Mackessack-Leitch, BA Hons. (Oxford Brookes),	
	PGCE (Kingston)	5+
1987	Jane Townsend, B.Ed. (London), Cert. Ed.	4+
1981	Jane Stevens, B.Ed. Hons. (Cantab.)	Librarian
1994	Melanie Leigh, Mont.Dip. AMBDA	Special Needs
1981	Jennie Ingram, BA Hons. (UEA), PGCE (Exeter)	Special Needs/ Maths/IT
1996	Liz Zahedieh, Dip. Sp.N. (Dyslexia)	Special Needs
1989	Miriam Umney, BA Hons., MA (Ed.Psych.),	
	PGCE, TEFL (London)	Special Needs
1994	Cathy Brown, BA Hons. (Sussex), PGCE (London)	Librarian
1987	Susan Keverne, Cert.Ed. (London), Art Dist.	Art
1988	Christine Prowse, BA (New South Wales), Dip.Ed.	
	(Alexander Mackay, Sydney)	French
1986	Reg Corbett, HNC + End. (Northampton Poly), C.Eng., MIEE	
		Woodwork
1996	Sarah Fraser, B.Ed. Hons. (Goldsmiths')	IT
1989	Dennis Cooke	L/S Assistant
1983	Carol Davidson, Cert. Ed.	Reception Assistant
1987	Lisa Gepheart, NNEB	Class Assistant
1985	Josie Steed, Cert. Ed., Dip. Ed.	Class Assistant
1994	Camilla Ovenden, B.Ed. Hons. (Cantab.)	Music

Instrumental teaching staff

1992	Dinah Beamish, LTCL, BA Hons., NCOS	Cello
1992	Phil Capone, GDLM, LGSM	Guitar
1976	Jaffa Galbinski, GRAM (Tel Aviv)	Piano
1993	Hannah Lang, FTCL, LTCL	Flute
1990	Claire Philpot, ARCM	Oboe
1994	Matt Skelton, LRAM	Drums
1995	Neil Thompson, GLCM, LLCM, ALCM, PGCTL	Brass
1996	Jon Halton, MA (Cantab.), M.Phil. (Cantab.)	Clarinet, Sax, Jazz, Piano
1996	Angela Knapp, BA Hons. (Cantab.), PGCE	Voice
1996	Richard Wade, MA (Bristol), B.Mus. Hons. (Sheffield), ARCM	Violin

Administrative staff

1984	Pam Oliver	Head's PA
1980	Liz Croker	Receptionist
1986	Silvia Beevers, NNEB	Nurse
1991	Pam Corbett	Lower School Secretary
1993	Sue Harrison	Secretary/PR
1993	Angela Ratner	Admissions Secretary
1997	Katy Oliver	Lower School Secretary

Bursary

1995	Tom Bloch, FCMA, ACIS	Bursar
1989	Joan Bradshaw	Assistant Bursar
1994	Tricia Still, ONC Business Studies	Accountant
1994	Graham Hale	Accountant
1997	David Gladwin	Estate Manager

Caretaking Staff

1983	Brian Rance, B.Sc. Hons. (Newcastle), PGCE	Caretaker/Archivist
1989	Jeffrey Robinson, Nat. Cert. in Horticulture	Assistant Caretaker
1995	Dave McGee	Groundsman

Catering

1985	Sheelagh Stanley	Head of Catering
1985	Brenda Chaloner	
1995	Teresa Gurrin	
1990	Beatrice Osei	
1991	Dee Tailor	
1994	Thelma Thomas	

Advisers

1988	Suzanne Bollas, BA, Dip. AA	Architectural Adviser
1990	Ruth Green, RSA Cert. in Counselling Skills, Member of British Association of Counsellors	Counsellor
1984	Dr Michael Jolles, MB, BS, MRCGP	Medical Consultant

Appendix 4

The King Alfred School Society

Bibliography

This bibliography covers the main books and other sources used in this study.

Books and pamphlets

Alfred the Great, *Asser's Life and Other Contemporary Sources* (London, Penguin, 1985).

R. Brooks, *Contemporary Issues in Education: An Historical Perspective* (London, Longman, 1991).

R. A. Butler, *The Art of the Possible* (London, Hamish Hamilton, 1971).

H. A. T. Child, *The Independent Progressive School* (London, Hutchinson, 1962).

F. Clarke, *Education and Social Change* (London, Sheldon, 1940).

C. B. Cox and A. E. Dyson (eds), *Black Paper 1. Fight for Education* (London, Dent, 1969); *Black Paper 2. The Crisis in Education*, (London, Critical Quarterly, 1969); *Black Paper 3, Goodbye Mr Short* (London, Critical Quarterly, 1970).

C. B. Cox and R. Boyson (eds), *Black Paper 4. The Fight for Education* (London, Dent, 1975); *Black Paper 5. Black Paper 1977* (London, Temple Smith, 1977).

J. Croall (ed.), *Letter from Summerhill* (London, Routledge, 1968).

J. Croall, *Neill of Summerhill: The Permanent Rebel* (London, Routledge, 1983).

C. A. R. Crosland, *The Future of Socialism* (London, Cape, 1956).

S. J. Curtis, *Education in Britain since 1900* (London, U.T.P., 1948).

J. C. Dancy, *The Public Schools and the Future* (London, Faber, 1963).

I. G. K. Fenwick, *The Comprehensive School 1944–1970* (London, Methuen, 1976).

A. G. Good and J. D. Teller, *A History of American Education* (New York, Macmillan, 1956).

G. Greene, *The Old School* (London, Cape, 1934).

E. M. Hibburd and B. Montgomery, 'A Short History of KAS' (1962, unpublished).

C. W. Kimmins and B. Rennie, *The Triumph of the Dalton Plan* (London, Nicholson and Watson, 1932).

J. Lewis, *Women and Social Action in Victorian and Edwardian England* (London, Elgar, 1991).

Ministry of Education, *The Organisation of Secondary Education* (London, HMSO, 1945).

C. L. Mowat, *Britain Between the Wars* (London, Methuen, 1955).

P. Nunn, *Education: Its Data and First Principles* (London, Arnold, 1920).

H. Parkhurst, *Education on the Dalton Plan* (London, Bell, 1922).

C. Plummer, *The Life and Times of Alfred the Great* (Oxford University Press, 1902).

H. Rée, *The Essential Grammar School* (London, Longman, 1958).

B. Simon, *Education and the Labour Movement 1870–1920* (London, Lawrence & Wishart, 1965).

B. Simon, *The Politics of Educational Reform 1920–1940* (London, Lawrence & Wishart, 1974).

B. Simon, *Education and the Social Order 1940–1990* (London, Lawrence & Wishart, 1991).

W. A. C. Stewart, *The Educational Innovators*, vol. II: *Progressive Schools, 1881–1967* (London, Macmillan, 1968).

R. H. Tawney, *Secondary Education for All* (London, Labour Party, 1922).

R. Wake and P. Denton, *Bedales School* (London, Haggerson Press, 1993).

Which School? (London, ISIS, 1989/90).

J. H. Wicksteed, *The Challenge of Childhood* (London, Chapman and Hall, 1936).

A. Williams Ellis, *The Modern Schools Handbook* (London, Bell, 1933).

Articles

J. R. Brooks, 'Lord Eustace Percy and the abolition of the compulsory education curriculum in 1926', *Contemporary Record*, 7/1 (1993).

R. Brooks, 'Dr J. J. Findlay, first headmaster of Cardiff Intermediate School for Boys, 1898–1903: instinctive traditionalist or enterprising empiricist?', in G. E. Jones, *Education, Culture and Society* (Cardiff, University of Wales Press, 1991).

R. Brooks, 'Professor J. J. Findlay, the King Alfred School Society, Hampstead and Letchworth Garden City Education, 1897–1915', *History of Education*, 21/2 (1992).

'Daring to be different', *Times Educational Supplement*, 1 July 1983.

Official publications

Board of Education, *Report of the Consultative Committee on the Primary School* (London, HMSO, 1931); *Report of the Committee on Public Schools* (The Fleming Report) (London, HMSO, 1944); *Report of the Central Advisory Council* (England), *Children and their Primary Schools*, vols. i and ii (Plowden Report) (London, HMSO, 1967).

First Report of the Public Schools Commission, vol. i (The Newsom Report) (London, HMSO, 1968).

Second Report of the Public Schools Commission, vol. i: *Report on Independent Day Schools and Direct Grant Schools* (1970: Donnison Report) (London, HMSO, 1970).

Newspapers and journals

Daily Telegraph

Financial Times

Guardian

Hampstead and Highgate Express

Journal of Biological Studies

Journal of Education

KASS archives

Annual report
Bulletin
Minutes and memoranda of Council and its Committees
Preliminary circular
Prospectuses
School magazines

Index